GW01466559

Open Chemistry

Edited by
Mark Atlay Stuart Bennett Steve Dutch Ralph Levinson
Peter Taylor Dick West

Hodder & Stoughton
LONDON SYDNEY AUCKLAND TORONTO
in association with The Open University

This text forms part of the Open University Course PS547 *Chemistry for Science Teachers*. The Course was made possible with funding from the Department of Education and Science, British Petroleum Plc and Unilever Plc and with the active support of The Royal Society of Chemistry and The Association for Science Education.

Opinions expressed in this book are not necessarily those of the Course Team or the University.

For general information on Open University study packs and courses, write to the Central Enquiry Service, PO Box 200, The Open University, Walton Hall, Milton Keynes, MK7 6YZ.

British Library Cataloguing in Publication Data

A catalogue record for this book is available from the British Library.

ISBN 0 340 58487 4

First published 1992

Edited, designed and typeset by The Open University.

Printed in Great Britain by St Edmundsbury Press, Bury St Edmonds for the educational division of Hodder and Stoughton Ltd, Mill Road, Dunton Green, Sevenoaks, Kent TN13 2YA, in association with the Open University, Walton Hall, Milton Keynes, MK7 6AB.

I.I

CONTENTS

CONTRIBUTORS

Di Bentley	County Inspector for Monitoring and Evaluation, Buckinghamshire Local Education Authority
Frances Betts	Head of Chemistry, RNIB New College, Worcester
Judy Brophy	Chemistry and science teacher at an inner-city comprehensive school
Steve Dutch	Lecturer in Science Education, the Open University and member of the Chemistry for Science Teachers Project
Philip Evans	Headmaster, Bedford School
Sandra Evans	Educational Consultant
Bob Fairbrother	Senior Lecturer in Science Education, Centre for Educational Studies, King's College, London
Maggie Farrar	Language and Learning Coordinator, Haggerston School, Hackney, London
Chris Haines	Flexible Learning Regional Adviser, London
Bill Harrison	Director of the Centre for Science Education, Sheffield City Polytechnic
Terry Hudson	Senior Lecturer, Centre for Science Education, Sheffield City Polytechnic
Roland Jackson	Education Adviser, Imperial Chemical Industries plc
Edgar Jenkins	Reader in Science Education, and Chairman of the School of Education, The University of Leeds
Richard Kempa	Professor of Education, University of Keele
Ralph Levinson	Lecturer in Science Education, the Open University and member of the Chemistry for Science Teachers Project
Mary Linington	Senior Inspector (Secondary) for the London Borough of Islington
Christine McCormick	Chemistry and science teacher at an inner-city comprehensive school
Mick Nott	Lecturer in Physics and Education, Sheffield City Polytechnic
Phil Ramsden	Advisory Teacher for Secondary Science, Sheffield Local Education Authority
Neville Reed	Education Officer, The Royal Society of Chemistry
Richard Rose	Head Teacher, Wren Spinney School, Kettering, Northamptonshire Local Education Authority

Kabir Shaikh	Chief Inspector for the London Borough of Ealing
Clive Sutton	Senior Lecturer in Science Education, University of Leicester
Mike Watts	Reader in Science Education, Roehampton Institute of Higher Education
Dick West	Professor of Science Education, the Open University and member of the Chemistry for Science Teachers Project
Elizabeth Whitelegg	Academic Liaison Adviser, the Centre for Science Education, the Open University

ACKNOWLEDGEMENTS

Grateful acknowledgement is made to the following sources for permission to reproduce material in this book:

Chapter 2

Figures 3 and 4: 'Sugar challenge', *Experimenting with Industry Project*, (1985), Standing Conference on Schools Science and Technology/Association for Science Education. © SCSST 1985.

Chapter 9

Figures 1 and 2: © Crown Copyright 1989, produced by The Training Agency (Department of Employment), reproduced with the permission of the Controller of Her Majesty's Stationery Office.

LIST OF ABBREVIATIONS

ABPI	Association of British Pharmaceutical Industries
APU	Assessment of Performance Unit
ASE	Association for Science Education
ATs	National Curriculum Attainment Targets
CBI	Confederation of British Industry
CIA	Chemical Industries Association
CIEC	Chemical Industry Education Centre
CLEAPSS	Consortium of Local Education Authorities for the Provision of Science Services
CLIS	Children's Learning in Science project
COSHH	Control of Substances Hazardous to Health
CPVE	Certificate in Pre-Vocational Education
CSE	Certificate of Secondary Education
DARTs	Directed Activities Related to Text
DES	Department of Education and Science (now the Department for Education)
GASP	Graded Assessments in Science Project
GCE	General Certificate of Education
GCSE	General Certificate of Secondary Education
GIST	Girls into Science and Technology project
HMI	Her Majesty's Inspectorate
ILEA	Inner London Education Authority
ILPAC	Independent Learning Project for Advanced Chemistry
INSET	In-service Education and Training of teachers
LEAs	Local Education Authorities
LMS	Local Management of Schools
NCC	National Curriculum Council
NCET	National Council for Educational Technology
NERIS	National Education Resources Information Service
PSI	Problem Solving with Industry
RSC	Royal Society of Chemistry
SATs	Standard Assessment Tasks

SATIS	Science and Technology in Schools
SATRO	Science and Technology Regional Organisation
SCIP	School Curriculum Industry Partnership
SCISP	Schools Council Integrated Science Project
SCSST	Standing Conference on School Science and Technology
SEAC	School Examinations and Assessment Council
SICCI	Schools Information Centre on the Chemical Industry
SISCON	Science in a Social Context
SLIP	Science Lessons from Industrial Processes
SMT	Senior Management Team
SSCR	Secondary Science Curriculum Review
TECs	Training and Enterprise Councils
TVEI	Technical and Vocational Education Initiative

INTRODUCTION

Until quite recently school chemistry was a well defined academic subject taught by chemistry specialists in school chemistry laboratories. It was either introduced as a specialist subject at age 11 or included as an option at age 13 following a two-year introductory course of general science. Little, if any, chemistry was taught in primary schools. As a specialism the story of school chemistry from the Bunsen burner to organic functional groups was largely determined by examination syllabuses for the Ordinary and Advanced levels of the GCE, which were themselves determined by the content of degree level studies. Chemistry, like physics and biology, was taught to a selected, or self-selecting, minority of young people largely drawn from the upper range of scholastic ability. The rest of the ability range only met those aspects of descriptive chemistry that were commonly included in general science courses.

All this is now history and the aim of this book is to provide an up-to-date review of the present role of chemistry in the general education of all young people up to the age of 16 years. The movement away from the teaching of chemistry, biology and physics as separate subjects to GCSE level is well documented and culminated in the inclusion of science as a core subject in the National Curriculum. The key texts outlining the case for balanced science are *Alternatives for Science Education: a discussion document* (Association for Science Education, 1979) and *Education through Science: a Policy Statement* (Association for Science Education, 1981). The inclusion of science as a compulsory subject for all young people and its definition within four attainment targets forces one to rethink the contribution chemistry can make to the teaching of balanced science, and to reconsider the wider implications for chemistry teaching.

Perhaps the most profound change brought about by the National Curriculum is that important chemical concepts once the preserve of specialists are now part of a common curriculum, or common language, that has to be open to all. This has major implications for both teachers and learners in terms of course design, teaching strategies, and techniques for assessment. These issues are addressed in this book but it is important to underline at this point the basic assumptions underpinning its structure and organization. From the outset we have accepted that it is important that the contribution of chemical education to general education should not be over-constrained by the formal documentation of the attainment targets and programmes of study set out in the National Curriculum. Whilst there are prescriptive parameters imposed by legislation, especially with respect to assessment and reporting (see Chapter 6), it is vital that these should not dominate teaching and learning. One of the great dangers of a centrally defined curriculum is that it might degenerate into a series of routine tasks that are summarized through checklists and pen and paper tests. It is essential to the well being of school science, and school chemistry, that this is not allowed to happen. We, therefore, have taken the National Curriculum as a starting point and a significant opportunity for opening up the study of chemistry to a wider audience. Hence our title *Open Chemistry*.

To make chemistry 'open' requires us to consider the nature of the subject, where we should start from in terms of story telling, how we relate chemistry to other aspects of science, and in conceptual and practical terms the particular problems the subject generates. Finally, a whole host of issues that relate 'openness' to equal educational opportunities have to be considered. This is a tall order and every effort has been made to commission articles from experienced practitioners in the teaching, research, industrial and professional fields in order to present an authoritative and up-to-date overview. The book is addressed to a multifaceted audience which will include:

(i)   experienced teachers of chemistry seeking to redefine their subject within a framework of balanced science for all;

(ii)   experienced teachers of biology and physics keen to integrate chemistry into their science teaching;

(iii)   Heads of science departments/faculties planning and resourcing the teaching of balanced science;

(iv)   students training to become teachers of science;

(v)   qualified science teachers wanting to return to teaching after the introduction of the National Curriculum;

(vi)   primary science co-ordinators keen to see how their work relates to the next stage of formal education.

It is our hope that the following pages will satisfy, in whole or in part, this diverse audience and we thank all the contributors who have made this book a reality.

PART I
STARTING POINTS

As indicated in the introduction, one of the key questions when planning lessons and schemes of work is 'From where do I start?'. The stock answer these days is to start from the attainment targets and programmes of study of the National Curriculum. However, this presupposes that the National Curriculum is correctly structured and that the chemistry content of Science: Double Award; Science: Single Award; or even GCSE chemistry studied alongside GCSE biology and physics as separate subjects, makes conceptual sense. In this Part of *Open Chemistry* we ask readers to consider a number of related starting points when planning schemes of work that will deliver the statutory and non-statutory requirements of the National Curriculum as already indicated. One of the great dangers of a centrally imposed curriculum is the emergence of a checklist orthodoxy that relegates teaching and learning to a series of can/can't do statements. In Part 1 of *Open Chemistry* we seek to provide other starting points which arise from a broader and more rounded view of the place of chemistry in the curriculum up to GCSE level.

Attainment Target 1 in the revised National Curriculum provides teachers and pupils with the opportunity to explore science as a process of thought and investigation. This raises the question of the nature of scientific method—summarized in school science under the traditional laboratory notebook headings—aim, apparatus, method, result and conclusion—or in the world of formal science by the scientific paper. An alternative view is that science is a social activity governed by as wide a range of factors as intuition, serendipity, happenchance, opportunity, funding and hard work. Nott, in Chapter 1 presents a historical case analysis of the nature of science through his study of Brown and Brownian motion. One starting point for the teaching of chemistry is to look back into the history of the subject to explore the way in which sensible and logical explanations in their time were displaced in due course by more sophisticated explanations. This approach to the teaching of chemistry has many attractions and warrants our attention.

In Chapter 2 Harrison and Ramsden explore the tension between starting from theory and starting from applications. The academic tradition has always been theory led, where the paramount interest has been to tell a theoretical story and then see how it is applied in practice. The alternative has been to start with everyday and socio/economic applications of chemistry and then ask 'What do I need to know and understand in order to see why chemistry is applied in this way?' The first approach places a strong emphasis on the epistemology of the subject—its logic, organization and structure, the second is somewhat more cavalier and focuses on the issues in chemical education—the need to know and understand.

In Chapter 3 we explore an alternative starting point which may be encapsulated in one word—relevance. Jackson, from an academic and industrial perspective, sets out to underline the importance of chemistry to the economy and asks the question 'Is this not why we should encourage young people to engage with chemistry?' It is significant that few secondary science textbooks include discussion or presentation of the practical and vocational uses to which the subject young people are studying might be put. Hence, regrettably, secondary science can appear somewhat irrelevant in the context of the 'real' world.

Chapter 4 presents a totally different starting point which is reflected in a number of other Chapters in the book. Kempa, in a review of the findings of educational research in the teaching and learning of school chemistry, analyses the contribution this research has made to changing patterns of teaching and learning. The Chapter, which should be read in conjunction with Chapter 15, explores the gap between research and practice and ends with an injunction to reduce this gap by translating research findings into practicable instructional strategies via the development of teaching and learning materials that reflect research findings; and finding the ways and means of implementing these strategies in the classroom/school laboratory.

CHAPTER 1

THE NATURE OF SCIENCE OR WHY TEACH BROWNIAN MOTION?

Mick Nott

INTRODUCTION

The aim of this Chapter is to make you think about the nature of science not to concentrate on how to teach it. It is hoped that the ideas in the Chapter will make you think and reflect on your own understanding in preparation for working with children on theirs!

The nature of science is concerned with trying to answer such questions as:

'How do scientists know a theory is reasonable or reliable?'

'What are the assumptions and methods of science?'

'What are the beliefs and values implicit in the scientific enterprise?'

'How is science related to the culture in which it takes place?'

In other words, in what ways is scientific knowledge created.

THE NATIONAL CURRICULUM AND THE NATURE OF SCIENCE

The programmes of study of the National Curriculum specify that children should be introduced to the history of scientific ideas. This is the first point to make about the nature of science: it is not possible to discuss it without discussing some science and, in the end, discussing particular cases of scientific ideas. So I would like to start with a story about a particular scientific idea that is relevant to chemistry and school science teaching. It appears essential that school children should understand the basic ideas of kinetic theory as applied to chemical and physical changes—this is the story of one part of the development and institutionalization of that theory: the story of Brownian motion.

ROBERT BROWN: EDUCATION AND TRAINING

When Robert Brown decided to investigate the motion of pollen grains in water in the summer of 1827 he had good reason for doing so although the school textbooks do not tell you what it was. It wasn't a chance discovery; one doesn't assemble a good expensive microscope, pollen, water and slides together by chance. He was no mean botanist and he had a research question in mind. To understand what he was looking for and why we need to provide some of the background to his life and scientific culture up to these experiments.

Robert Brown was born in Montrose in 1773. He grew up and was educated in Scotland. He embarked on the study of medicine at Edinburgh University in the early 1790s and then became a doctor in the army. In 1798 he met Sir Joseph Banks, the naturalist who had sailed with Captain Cook and was the doyen of London scientific society and with Banks' support and encouragement Brown changed careers by serving his scientific apprenticeship. He did this in the same way as Banks had done before him; in 1801 he set sail on *HMS Investigator* to undertake the duties of ship's naturalist on a voyage to Australia and New Zealand. He returned in 1805 and by 1806 was librarian to the Linnaean Society. Brown's skill as a botanist was appreciated by Banks and Brown helped in the classification of Banks' collection as well as his own. By 1810 Brown took up the position of Banks' librarian. Brown was particularly interested in the sexual characteristics of plants and in the decade from 1810 to 1820 he found and described the sex difference between flowering and non-flowering plants. This work required and developed good competence with a microscope.

In 1820 Banks died and Brown was left in charge of his house, library and herbarium. By 1827 Brown had left the lot to the British Museum provided they start a Botany Department and he promptly took up post as the curator. So that was Brown's position in 1827. Now think about the pattern of his life so far. Brown had changed career in his early twenties and started to serve his 'scientific' apprenticeship in 1801. He worked under and then alongside the most eminent naturalist of his day for 20 years in the analagous position to today's doctoral and post-doctoral students. His work in the 1810s showed a high degree of technical skill and theoretical importance. The lesson is the same now as it was then—to become a scientist who is recognized as a significant contributor to any field requires dedication, time, and particular technical and/or theoretical competences recognized by your peer group. It also helps to have a powerful and influential mentor and colleague (this is not necessarily to imply corruption or nepotism—it means your work is recognized as coming with a creditable pedigree).

But why was Brown looking at pollen during the months of June, July and August in 1827?

Brown had sex on his mind. In fact a few scientists had sex on their minds. A deep question that concerned some of them was the origin of life. Where did life's vital forces reside and how did they transfer and manifest themselves in living things? Brown's hypothesis was that the vital forces of life in plants were transferred by the 'active' male parts.

Brown's research question was framed by the culture in which he lived—the activity was hypothesized to reside in the male parts as it was (is?) a 'natural' characteristic of the male parts to be active with respect to the 'natural' characteristic of the female parts to be passive. The cultural perspective on gender was determining the scientific questions asked.

The experimental prediction was that this vitality would be manifested as movement in these parts. Hence Brown was looking at the granules from plant pollen through his microscope. This research programme was helped by a technical advance in instrumentation. In 1824 the successful invention of the achromatic doublet objective lens allowed microscopists to see smaller objects more clearly. Brown's research methods were greatly enhanced by the facility of the new lenses with less aberration—developments in instrumentation were allowing new experiments to be planned and executed.

REPLICABILITY

Brown realized that he should do experiments that others felt they could replicate if they so wished so he couldn't rely solely on the new lenses. Brown noted that most of his experiments were done with the more common single lens in order to ensure that others could repeat the work. This also meant that his results couldn't be solely attributed to unknown aberrations produced by the new lenses.

Then, as now, development of and verification of new ideas may depend on new instrumentation. However, scientists have to do experiments that other scientists recognize that they themselves could replicate if they wished—the experiments have to be judged to be replicable and the instrumentation has to be judged as reliable by the peer group. If these conditions aren't fulfilled then nobody would know what is supposed to happen in an experiment—in other words the actual results would be not just uncertain but indeterminate as well!

GOOD NEWS, BAD NEWS;
VERIFICATION AND FALSIFICATION

Brown started with particles from pollen and did indeed find motion which he could not attribute to thermal currents or evaporation. (Brown was not the first to record this motion but he was the first to study and analyse it as far as he was able.) Next, Brown asked himself if this motion was intrinsic to the particles as part of a living plant. So he investigated pollen from plants which had been dead a few days, then decades and finally samples which were at least a 100 years old. In all cases the pollen particles showed this motion. From this Brown inferred, at first, that his hypothesis that activity would be demonstrated by male parts of plants was reasonable. To infer means to go from the particular to the general—the process of induction. However, induction as a method of producing reliable knowledge is neither logically nor empirically valid. To illustrate this point think of the following example: Brown's hypothesis could have been that the male parts of plants move not because they have the active molecules of vitality but because they will need to actively seek the female parts for reproductive purposes. Therefore they will display an intrinsic movement.

Which hypothesis would the observations support? Logically the experimental observation supports neither, in that whilst a cause may imply an effect, an effect cannot logically imply a cause. But psychologically the evidence supports both hypotheses as verification of predictions! The second example is to consider the range of pollens which Brown investigated. He wasn't exhaustive, in fact it would be impossible to test every known pollen for this movement, and yet it is still conceivable that an unknown pollen may exist which at some other place and/or time which will not exhibit motion. At some point a scientist has to stop and say that by some criteria enough examples have been found. These criteria are not objective in that they do not originate outside the experts in the field. They will be determined by the members of the peer group and are therefore intersubjective.

Two of the basic assumptions in this case would be that the motion observed is considered to happen to all pollens wherever they are and whenever they are— in other words these observations apply everywhere and at all times. These two assumptions, that the underlying mechanisms of the Universe are eternal and universal, are very deep in the cognitive values of modern science.

Values apart, hypotheses and theories generate predictions. Verification of a prediction is psychologically very powerful and provides faith in the hypotheses and theories. However, the knowledge generated is tentative as it is possible to conceive of counter examples which may arise or alternative explanations—as Brown was to find out!

Having initially satisfied himself as to the veracity of his original hypothesis Brown wanted to see if the activity of male parts could be used to distinguish between parts of plants to determine their sexuality. The chosen specimens were some problematic mosses. At first he chose the parts thought to be male and again his hypothesis was confirmed—the particles moved. Then he went on to look at granules from supposed female parts and he found that the motion was also intrinsic to these particles. This is where an accident had some part in the story, Brown managed to bruise some particles from the leaves onto the slides and again he found the movement. Small particles from all parts of plants showed the motion. At this point Brown lost faith in his original hypothesis but thought that his findings supported an alternative hypothesis also current in the botanical and vitalist schools of thought: this was that all parts of all organic bodies will contain small 'molecules' which are elementary and contain the life forces.

Brown had made observations which falsified his original predictions and so he abandoned his hypothesis. This is a logically valid procedure—if your hypothesis makes a testable prediction and the prediction is not found to hold then logically the hypothesis is false, logically a falsified effect also falsifies the cause. Whilst this may be logical you are asked to consider if this is necessarily rational in the sense of being an effective way of behaving? The falsification may be due to a fault in the apparatus, a lack of competence on the part of the experimenter, or perhaps to the optics of these new-fangled lenses being suspect. Abandoning a hypothesis because your experimental results don't support it is not necessarily a rational act. Sometimes scientists need to keep on trying at an experiment to get it to work—that is give the expected answers! The disconcerting and unsettling thing is that neither falsification nor verification provide us with logical or empirical grounds for accepting or rejecting theories or hypotheses. Verification is the psychologically more powerful event but falsification may be telling the scientists more about their competence and their apparatus than their hypotheses.

But the fact of the matter is that scientists do change their minds as a result of experiments or alternative explanations, so why did Brown change his? His original hypothesis was only one of the contemporary vitalist hypotheses.

There were other hypotheses which were part of his overall paradigm—vitalism—and were consonant with the observations that he had made, so perhaps he could change his mind on the precise location and manifestation of vital forces without abandoning his overarching belief in vitalism itself. In summary, Brown had confidence in his own experimental competence and the technical skill and knowledge of his instrument makers and he had another hypothesis handy which didn't conflict with his underlying beliefs. On balance falsification of his original hypothesis looked more probable in his considered, professional and personal judgement—and at this point Brown hadn't published any results. Publication is the point at which the scientist goes public and puts the results and conclusions up for public scrutiny. Changing his mind at this point carried no risk from adverse criticism.

So where had Brown got to? The movement couldn't be used to differentiate between the sexual parts of plants or whether the plants were alive or dead. Brown wondered as to whether the motion was due to the organic origin of the particles so he tried a variety of vegetable products 'particularly the gum resins' and found the movement in small particles from them. He also tried observing small particles from animal tissues and again he saw the motion whether the tissue was from dead or live animals. At this point it appears that Brown was now working on a practically led or heuristic programme where each result was leading to a consequent experiment. This procedure is built on confidence in experimental techniques.

His curiosity led him to look at fossilized remains of vegetable matter and again providing the particles were small enough he saw the motion. He noted that London soot seemed to be 'entirely composed of these molecules'. So bodies that had once been vegetable and were carboniferous exhibited moving 'molecules'. Brown's next step was to explore petrified wood, where all the carbon had been replaced by silicates. In this inorganic material, providing the particles were small enough, the motion was found. At this point Brown concluded that the moving molecules were 'not limited to organic bodies, nor even their products'.

Whilst his original hypothesis now lay falsified in his mind he was keen to verify the above inference. He tried window-glass, metals, igneous rocks, sedimentary rocks—he even tried a crushed piece of the Sphinx and bits from the eyes of haddocks! Anything he could reduce to a fine powder was found to have these particles. Part of Brown's conclusion was to state:

> '... nor shall I hazard any conjectures whatever respecting these molecules
> which appear to be of such general existence in inorganic as well as in organic
> bodies ...'

Brown had not verified his original or secondary hypothesis. In the end his experimental work led him to believe that he could find no explanation at the moment for what he observed, but he had every faith that he had shown the motion was a property of all matter. But note, Brown was not claiming that he had falsified vitalism; just that he could offer no explanation for what he observed.

GOING PUBLIC

Brown wrote his results up in a paper which at first was privately circulated. It is not written in a third person impersonal style which even for a scientific paper of that time is unusual. The style makes it a good read because Brown doesn't reconstruct or re-present his experimental work or methods—he tells the story as he uncovered it. The paper was originally published in 1828 [1] and circulated privately and then subsequently published in journals in Scotland, Germany and France. Brown had ensured that the results he had obtained had been circulated to other eminent scientists he knew prior to publication.

This ensures that priority is established. This has been common practice for scientists since at least the time of the formation of the Royal Society when experiments were often performed in front of 'virtuosi'. Priority is an important currency in science; as a research scientist you are only as good as your last discovery. There is no fame or recognition in being the second person to find something. Brown was not the first to see this motion but he was certainly the first to study it in so much detail and to identify that the motion was present in all particles of the right size independent of their origin.

Brown's paper was widely read at the time and its conclusions were resisted for the implied self-animation of inorganic bodies. It was suggested that the motion Brown had seen could be attributed to surface effects, convection currents, electrical attraction and repulsion between the particles or perhaps he was missing something and the active particles were animated. So other scientists doubted his inferences or his experimental skill. Many of the readers thought that Brown had asserted that the particles were animated. In his next paper Brown acknowledged that this particular misreading of his work was due to the idiosyncratic style of the original paper.

In fact if you read the first few pages of Brown's original paper on 'active molecules' you would believe that he thought the particles to be alive. This teaches us that communicating through text is a risky business—maybe not all the text is read, readers maybe are lazy or busy. For whatever reason you have to state the main points in the text clearly and early otherwise the salient points may not get communicated. This erroneous reading of Brown has persisted to the present day in some textbooks.

Hence an important feature of the structure of scientific papers is the abstract at the front—in fact people are now so busy that the collected abstracts become journals in themselves and most scientists turn to them first. In fact, very few people read any one scientific paper—on average the readership is a handful or less!

A scientist's peers and rivals in the field, however, will read it and evaluate it against their work and ideas. Brown's critics raised serious objections to his findings and offered alternative explanations. Brown noted all these objections and explanations for the motion he was willing to leave as an unexplained phenomenon.

Brown had a number of options, he could have left it at that, simply ignored the criticism; decided it was an unprofitable research area and done something else. This would have left the critics unanswered and also implied that his work was indeed trivial or misguided. This action would have undermined his considerable professional reputation.

He could have challenged his critics to prove or verify their ideas and try experiments to substantiate their own theories. This action would not necessarily have diminished his reputation but it would not have enhanced it either.

He could have reviewed the criticisms and tried further experiments to test the other ideas proposed for the motion. The consequences of this course of action would depend on the experimental results. The results could verify, falsify or leave indeterminate the proposed reasons or hypotheses for the motion.

If the results of the experiments verified the other hypotheses then Brown's original conclusions would be shaken but he would still collect recognition for being the first experimentalist to verify new ideas. If the experimental results falsified the other hypotheses then Brown's hesitancy to offer any explanation for the motion would be supported and he would again collect recognition for his experimental abilities. If any further experiments left the hypotheses indeterminate then Brown may at least have indicated further directions for a research programme.

On balance the last option looks the one with the least risk and the possibility of the most reward. It is the option that Brown chose to take.

RESPONSE TO CRITICISM

In 1829, a year after his original paper, Brown published a further paper called 'Additional remarks on active molecules' [2]. In this paper, as has already been stated, he first noted that the style of his original paper led many to believe that he, himself, had thought the particles to be animated. He repeated that he did discuss the hypotheses that stimulated his original inquiry but reasserted that in the end he could offer no explanation for the motion. Brown was not dismissing vitalism but he was implying that vitalism would need other phenomena to support it. Vitalism was a theory held by many, and probably Brown himself. This one experiment would not be enough evidence to dismiss it.

He went on to state that he had repeated the experiments and found the motion in all particles of small enough size. He was also clear that these experiments could be done with the old and the new (achromatic) microscopes. He stated the hypotheses that other scientists had proposed to explain the motion and then he said:

> 'Some of the alleged causes here stated, with others which I have considered it unnecessary to mention, are not likely to be overlooked or to deceive observers of any experience in microscopical researches: and the insufficiency of the most important enumerated, may, I think, be satisfactorily shown by means of a very simple experiment.'

What was Brown doing here? The tone is plain: some of the ideas proposed are either too foolish to be considered or too dismissive of his skill as a microscopist. They were rejected outright because they were beneath consideration for the above reasons.

Two of the proposed norms of science as an activity are that all knowledge claims should be treated equally, independent of their source—the norms of universalism and impartiality. However, Brown wasn't working like this. He was following norms of particularism and partiality. Only certain counter claims were worth entertaining and they were dependant on who had made them and Brown's judgement of their scientific competence compared to his evaluation of himself. So not all ideas are of equal worth and not all proposals can or should go forward for experimental testing—it depends who you are and what your pedigree is considered to be!

Two hypotheses were recognized by Brown as worth consideration. The first was that the particles moved because of forces of attraction and repulsion between them; the second was that the particles moved due to evaporation from the water drop that contained them.

CRUCIAL EXPERIMENTS

Brown devised two experiments to test these ideas. First, he took some water with the particles in and shook it up in almond oil which has approximately the same relative density as water. In this way he made a suspension in the oil of minute drops of water. In turn, the drops of water had the 'active molecules' suspended in them (see Figure 1). In fact some of the water drops were so minute that they only contained one 'active molecule'.

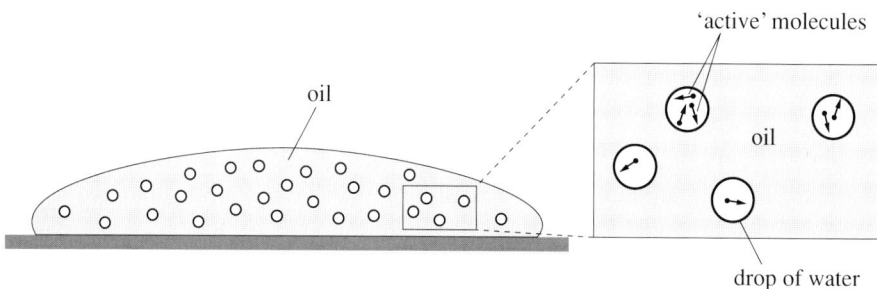

Figure 1 A drop for the first experiment.

Brown noted two things. First, the water drops were unable to evaporate in the oil yet the motion of the particles persisted. Second, in the water drops which contained only one particle then these solitary particles were still seen to be moving.

Brown considered that the first observation implied that the motion had nothing to do with evaporation and the second observation indicated that the motion wasn't due to a mutual interaction between the particles.

For the second experiment Brown went on to see if surface effects could account for the motion. This time he added almond oil to water with a suspension of the particles. He shook this up so that the water contained a suspension of both the particles and minute drops of the oil (see Figure 2).

minute drops of oil on
the surface not moving

'active' molecules found in the body of the drop

'active' oil drops found as well

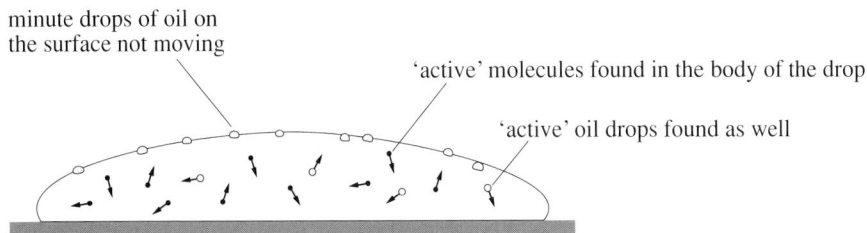

Figure 2   A drop from the second experiment.

He noted that oil drops on the water surface didn't move and yet those in the bulk of the water exhibited movements similar to the neighbouring 'active molecules'.

Brown inferred that the motion wasn't due to any surface effects. So Brown had done two simple, yet ingenious, experiments which falsified the main contenders for explaining the motion.

Lastly, Brown finished this second paper by reviewing the literature on the motion that he had described. He noted that early microscopists like Leeuwenhoek may have seen it and described it and that some of his own contemporaries and immediate predecessors had seen it and attributed it to the vital forces residing in the 'active molecules'. Brown notes that previous scientists may have confused animalcular motion with molecular motion—in other words the motion of small beasts for that of small bits of matter but we need to be careful here.

The meaning that Brown assigned to the word molecule is not the same as our contemporary meaning. One of the vitalists proposals was that organic matter contained organic molecules as the unit of life so Brown had perhaps found these but had anomalously found them in inorganic matter as well!

This intellectual struggle to find a coherence to Brown's observations is reflected in the response of two contemporaries. Faraday, in a lecture given in 1829, supported Brown's work in that he thought it experimentally convincing but he concluded that whilst it may tell people something about 'molecules' he wasn't able to extend the inferences to anything about the nature of 'atoms'. The Scottish scientist David Brewster supported Brown's work from another viewpoint. So what if Brown had found movement with his active molecules; this should not surprise people as sciences from geology to astronomy were telling people that a lot of physical explanations were predicated on physical motions. Indeed, the movement of Brown's active molecules may have provided a way forward in explaining the motions necessary to explain geological formations.

Two points can be drawn from these observations. From Faraday we can see that our definitions of atoms and molecules were not the ones that he shared. Scientific concepts are not fixed entities nor are they singular things. The meaning of concepts is a process of social negotiation involving imagination and experiment.

From Brewster we can see a positive attitude to the results that is not saying that these results are problematic in that they need explanation, but is saying that if these results are accepted as facts then they may help us in explaining phenomena from other fields; indeed, these results may be worthy of a whole new research programme! Transferring ideas, results or techniques from one field to another is a way that scientific research can develop or radically change direction.

DEAD ENDS

What was the reaction to this apparently invincible work? Brown had successfully refuted his critics but had provided no underlying explanation for the observed motions. As has already been noted not all scientific papers are read. This certainly happened to Brown's second paper, it wasn't as widely published as the first and it is to this day relatively obscure. As far as is known the research question of the active molecules wasn't a major question in botany. Brown didn't pursue it. He had plenty of work to do classifying the flora of the world. He went on to reinforce his botanical reputation in 1831 by describing clearly the structure of plant cells—Brown was the first person to give the name to the cell nucleus.

This name and idea of 'nucleus' was one appropriated by the physicists in the early 20th century to help them describe their growing conceptions of atomic structure. Perhaps we ought to recognize Brown's deeper contribution to scientific ideas by supplying a metaphor—the root of the word nucleus is the latin for 'little nut'—that turned out to be so fruitful! Words like nucleus and fission demonstrate how images from one field help another field form ideas even if the final concepts are dissimilar. Similes, analogies and metaphors are constantly used in science to explain and innovate, e.g. 'It is as if ...' or 'I wonder what if it was like ...'.

Anyway, collectively, botanists weren't interested in pursuing Brown's work. Scientists could try and look for support for vitalism in other phenomena, e.g. spontaneous generation, and although the original paper was read by a diverse range of scientists it didn't initiate any sustained research in other fields.

Brownian motion only started to become a phenomenon to which scientist's referred from the late 1850s. Brown died in 1858 by which time the motion he had described was well known but considered an anomaly that could await explanation.

PHYSICAL SCIENCE BECOMES AGITATED

So what happened next to Brownian motion? By 1856 the cause had been attributed to heat and in 1858 it was suggested that the heat from the particle somehow heated the surrounding water and caused thermal currents which made the particles move. This suggestion was countered in 1863 by attributing the motion to internal motions in the fluid. This resonates with our own explanations until we realize that the German scientist concerned, Wiener, was discussing the wave like oscillations of the 'aetherial atoms' in the fluid! By 1868 the Italian, Cantoni, was identifying Brownian motion with the thermal motions of the liquid particles. Brown's papers had been 'lost' in the sense that many repeated his work or seemed unaware of his second paper on the topic.

By the beginning of the 1880s the consensus, but not unanimity, on Brownian motion was that the motion was associated with some thermal explanation but there was no clear way of testing any theoretical ideas.

The next major development came with the physical scientists who cited it as evidence for their theories. In the 1860s the physicist James Clerk Maxwell had synthesized Clausius's work, on a simplified kinetic model, with the growing field of statistics. Others like Boltzmann and Gibb developed this work into statistical mechanics. This branch of mathematics had been developed to help build and find scientific laws about society and the behaviour of people in it. The creation of scientific theories and ideas is stimulated by cross-fertilization of concepts and techniques that are part of the culture in which the scientist lives.

By 1888 a French scientist, Gouy, had established, by reviewing the literature and devising new experiments, the following information:

- Brownian motion was independent of electric and magnetic fields, light intensities and vibrations;
- the rapidity of the motion depended on the temperature and viscosity of the fluid (which could be any fluid, not just water) and the size of the Brownian particles.

Gouy also pointed out that it was probably inappropriate to measure the velocity of a Brownian particle, as some scientists had allegedly done, because he imagined it as discontinuous and changing too frequently.

CLOSURE OF THE DEBATE

At the end of the 19th and beginning of the 20th century the reality of atoms was a matter of considerable debate. The French scientist Jean Perrin was involved in these debates. Perrin by training would be classified as a physical chemist. He was a scientist convinced of the social good of science and its methods. Politically progressive and scientifically innovative he was a keen supporter of the atomic hypothesis and its concomitant kinetic theory. A major part of his life's work was dedicated to the proof of the reality of atoms.

His work brought him into close contact with Brownian motion and the supervision of a doctoral thesis (completed in 1904) on diffusion in colloids gave him the idea for a new research programme pertinent to the question of the reality of atoms.

As a physical chemist Perrin was familiar with Van't Hoff's work on osmosis which had shown that dilute solutions of undissociated particles could be shown to obey the gas laws. Perrin speculated that if the gas laws worked for hypothesized solute particles then an emulsion of Brownian particles may, if his belief in kinetic theory was right, also obey some of the predicted consequences of kinetic theory. In particular they should distribute themselves in an isothermal solution according to the exponential law for a gas atmosphere. If they did this then he reasoned that Brownian particles obeyed kinetic theory. The next stage in the argument is to state that if this is so for particles we can barely see, then particles which are just invisible should surely obey the same rules and if this is conceded then surely any particle of whatever size will be governed by kinetic theory. In other words by observing visible particles obeying kinetic theory we can infer that hypothesized invisible particles will do the same and this will provide not just a real explanation for Van't Hoff's work but also support the entire atomic hypothesis as a view of reality.

Perrin knew the work of Gouy and therefore had a clear idea of which variables were relevant and which were irrelevant to the study of the phenomena of Brownian motion.

Perrin devised experiments to determine a value for Avogadro's number. From his observations this was found to be between 6.5×10^{23} and 7.2×10^{23} which he felt close enough to that predicted by kinetic theory (6.2×10^{23}) to accept as proof that Brownian motion was of kinetic theory origin.

Perrin published this work in 1908; he must have started it from about 1905. This was the year that one of the other personalities enters the story. In 1905 Albert Einstein had three papers published. One was on special relativity, one was on the quantization of light waves and the third was called, 'On the movement of small particles suspended in a stationary liquid demanded by the molecular kinetic theory of heat'.

In later recollections Einstein said that the main aim had been to provide a theory that would lead to experimental predictions that would justify the existence of atoms—one of the current scientific debates. He also professed that he was unaware of Brownian motion although when the title of the paper is read that seems scarcely credible which indicates that the writings of scientists about science should be treated as critically as any others!

Perrin seized on this other theoretical work which became known to him immediately his work was published. He also immediately recognized the significance that here was a theoretical prediction of something that could be measured, the displacement, against time rather than what other scientists had tried to measure up till then which had been the velocity. He had the apparatus to test these ideas and he had the skill plus some willing doctoral students. He and his students steadily published their findings through 1909, 1910 and 1911 and he undertook many speaking engagements both in France and elsewhere in Europe on Brownian motion and molecular reality. The speed at which this work was completed and published suggests that Perrin was very well prepared to undertake it. It may be true to suggest Brownian motion was a phenomenon awaiting a theory but it would be unfair to Perrin to suggest that he simply verified the theoretical work of Einstein. The detailed theory of this random Brownian motion provided experimental additions and corroboration to Perrin's earlier work.

Perrin's copious and thorough research papers, in addition to his textbook *Atoms*, were rapidly disseminated [3]. The reality of atoms was hot news on the science front! The simultaneous experimental and theoretical work on radioactivity, cathode rays, black body radiation and the scattering of light by colloid solutions were all part of the atomists' evidence against their opponents.

In 1926, 99 years after Brown's original experiments, Perrin, the physical chemist was awarded the Nobel prize for physics for his experimental work on Brownian motion. The award of a Nobel prize, the highest accolade in science, can be viewed as recognition of Perrin's contribution to the closure of the debate on the reality of the atomic hypothesis.

SUMMARY

I have stressed the view that science is a social activity and that the creation of scientific theories and the acceptance of procedures and results is also a matter of social negotiation. Scientists operate to social norms and those norms can be prescriptions, as well as justifications, for behaviour. It may be that science education should concentrate more on the explicit development of a range of attitudes and norms as well as knowledge and skills.

The story should have also stressed that no scientist works in a professional or cultural vacuum. The results of their work are professionally shared and their research programmes have a professional and public accountability.

This story, by focusing on a single phenomenon, probably goes against modern historiography. However, the 99 years between Brown's original research and Perrin's Nobel prize should indicate that scientific concepts take time to develop and for meanings to be negotiated to a shared clarity. Brownian motion has not ossified—the topic of fractals has a whole part dedicated to paths randomly generated called 'brownians'. This illustrates that 'old' phenomena and ideas can still remain plastic and fruitful.

One conclusion is that the notion of revolution in scientific thought may be an inappropriate one to analyse changes in science. Revolution may be a useful pedagogic device to learn science. How can it be anything else when we ask children to absorb in the 11 years of a school science education what it took some of the best minds centuries and millenia to develop? This is not to say that scientists don't change their minds or science's aims, methods and facts but it is to say that changes may not be cataclysmic events where everything changes at once.

Lastly, I would argue that learning about scientists and science may help us understand scientific ideas through studying their development. The evidence that does seem to exist is that students who study the nature of science when studying science have a much more positive attitude to science with no discernible detriment to their cognitive achievement.

REFERENCES

1   Brown, R., 'A Brief account of microscopical observations made in the months of June, July and August 1827 on the particles contained in the pollen of plants: and on the general existence of active molecules', privately published, Science Museum (1828). An abridged version is in Magie, W. F., *Source Book in Physics*. (Harvard, 1965).

2   Brown, R., 'Additional remarks on active molecules', privately published, Science Museum (1829). An unabridged version is in Cohen, I. B. and Jones, H. M. (eds), *Science before Darwin*. (Deutsch, 1963).

3   Perrin, J., *Atoms*. (Constable, 1916).

FURTHER READING

Barnes, B., *About Science*. (Blackwell, 1985).

Brush, S. G., 'A History of random processes: Brownian movement from Brown to Perrin', *Archives for the Exact Sciences*, 1968, **5**, pp. 1–36.

Bynum, W. F., Browne, E. J. and Porter, R., *The Macmillan Dictionary to the History of Science*. (Macmillan, 1983).

Collins, H., *Changing Order, Replication and Induction in Scientific Practice*. (Sage, 1985).

Gillespie, C. (ed.), *Dictionary of Scientific Biography*. (Scribners, 1974).

Grinnell, F., *The Scientific Attitude*. (Westview Press, 1987).

Latour, B., *Science in Action*. (Open University Press, 1987).

Laudan, L., *Science and Values*. (University of California Press, 1984).

Mulkay, M., *Sociology of Science*. (Open University Press, 1991).

Nye, M. J., *Molecular Reality: A Perspective on the Scientific Works of Jean Perrin*. (Macdonald, 1972).

Perrin, J., 'Mouvement Brownien et Grandeurs Moleculaires', (1911), in L. Bragg and G. Porter (eds), *Royal Institution Library of Science*. (Applied Science Publishers, 1970). Vol. 7, pp. 164–183.

Richard, S., *Philosophy and Sociology of Science: an Introduction*. (Blackwell, 1987).

Ziman, J., *Reliable Knowledge*. (Cambridge University Press, 1979).

CHAPTER 2

WHERE DO WE START FROM, THEORY OR PRACTICE?

Bill Harrison and Phil Ramsden

THE WAY CHEMISTRY IS PRESENTED IN TEXTBOOKS

An analysis of 20 chemistry textbooks from 1925 to 1960 by Bassey [1–3] led him to conclude that:

> 'It is as though the 400 pages of a common ancestor, perhaps it was Holmyard, have been shuffled and reprinted with the addition of a handful of pages to mark the individuality of the 'new' book.'

A more superficial analysis of the 'contents' pages of 15 GCE/GCSE textbooks spanning the time between 1893 and 1987, broadly supports this conclusion although there are of course some significant omissions from the very early books. The more recent texts also have additional content, particularly physical and organic chemistry, but it is nevertheless the similarities rather than the differences which are striking. If one looks at the extent to which the applications of chemistry are dealt with, Bassey's estimate of up to 10% of the content is probably not exceeded by most modern texts. Although there are several modern exceptions, a notable early exception was Bailey's *The New Matriculation Chemistry* [4], with no less than six chapters out of 30 dealing in some detail with topics such as 'Rocks and Soils in the Earth's Crust', 'Pigments, Vegetable and Animal Substances' as well as the more familiar 'Metals and Alloys'.

Although most textbooks contain the disclaimer that their order of contents is not necessarily a suitable teaching order, there is also the admission that the author nevertheless sees the chosen order of presentation as a logical and coherent one. Given that this is the case the clear preference of textbook authors from the turn of the century to the present day has been to deal with the theory of chemistry first, e.g. states of matter and laws of combination, bonding, before going on to exemplify these in the chemistry of the common elements. Although applications may to some extent be dealt with as they arise they are often left to separate chapters at the end of the book. A moments reflection on the way you were taught chemistry at school will no doubt confirm that this has been the method of most chemistry teachers.

At first thought such an approach seems to be eminently sensible and even to be the only possible one. How can a pupil understand the application of a theory if they have not first understood the theory itself? Such a question begs others about the ways in which pupils might develop their understanding of a theory or concept on its own and the answers which are emerging to such questions can challenge the apparently intellectually tidy 'theory-first' approach. Current theories on the development of understanding are often based on a model of the human brain as an information processor. For a concept to be well understood it needs to be 'processed' in as wide a variety of contexts as possible thus enabling many links to be made with the pupils' previous understanding. It is possible to speculate that our natural inclination to a 'theory first', 'application later' model has its origins outside chemistry itself and in 19th century ideas, where the purity of abstract knowledge was valued far above its applications. Such bias by the intellectual establishment had disastrous consequences for industries such as the chemical industry in the latter part of the 19th century, which were only fully exposed by the First World War shortage of chemicals and munitions. The links between mathematics and science and in particular the idea of derivation from first principles, which mathematics held in such high esteem, had an inevitable effect on the way science was taught.

It is also true to say that mathematics and science have an appeal for pupils intellectually able to cope with abstract theory. This is the implicit promise, not always fulfilled, of them becoming independent of the drudge of factual learning by being able to work everything out from a few simple principles. Such an appeal, whether valid or not, should not ignore the important contribution to conceptual understanding which an applications-first approach can make.

As Bassey's analysis implied, textbook authors are heavily influenced by existing texts. Since textbooks are still a major influence on the way chemistry is taught, this makes the introduction of applications-led teaching much more difficult. However, it is encouraging to see some shift in the way chemistry is presented in some recent texts and the influences which have brought about this change will be addressed later in the Chapter.

THE IMPACT OF HIGHER EDUCATION AND A-LEVEL DEMANDS ON PRE-16 CHEMISTRY

Traditionally, the O- and A-level examination boards were administered and largely controlled by the universities and it was not until the establishment of the GCSE examining authorities in the mid-'80s that their influence on the pre-16 sector was diminished. Therefore, the view was generally held by examination board subject committees, that any study pre-degree level in chemistry for example, was primarily for the purposes of ensuring that the pupil was adequately prepared for entrance to university! In other words, they must have studied a basic core of pure chemistry at A-level which to a large extent mirrored the main areas of chemistry covered at degree level. In turn, a similar argument was applied to O-level in relation to A-level. This resulted in O-level syllabuses being largely designed or tailored to prepare the small minority of pupils who would continue through to study the subject at degree level—a good example of 'the tail wagging the dog'.

This situation clearly resulted in what can be termed 'a top-down, decontextualized curriculum' in which the needs of the higher education sector dictated the content of O- and A-level courses and it did not really matter if the chemistry was not presented in terms of its everyday life and industrial applications and implications, relevant to the pupils' own lives. The important thing was that they should know and understand the foundation chemistry necessary for degree studies. (The irony here being that many university courses in the first year simply repeated or reinforced A-level work.)

Such a course of study *may* have been acceptable for the relatively small number of pupils, highly motivated by the subject itself and who wanted to study chemistry beyond school—but it was certainly not so for the majority. In fact it is undoubtedly the case, that this diet of 'pure' chemistry, taught out of context, demotivated many able young people from further study after the age of 16.

It is not difficult to see how this approach to chemistry teaching continued, and indeed in some cases may still continue, when one considers that the vast majority of chemistry teachers have been through the same academic cycle, i.e. 'school/university/back to school to teach chemistry'. Without the opportunity of experiencing chemistry in the world of work themselves it is not surprising if school chemistry is often presented as an academic study in pursuit of knowledge and understanding of the subject only for its own sake.

Fortunately, this situation is changing and it is not too difficult to identify the influences. These will be discussed later in this Chapter and elsewhere in this book. However one can simply mention in passing some of the major influences such as the *Nuffield projects* [5], *Schools Council Integrated Science Project* (SCISP) [6], *Science and Technology in Society* (SATIS) *Project* [7], *Salters' Chemistry* [8], the Secondary Science Curriculum Review (see for example [9]), the Technical and Vocational Education Initiative (TVEI), GCSE, National Curriculum and a growing number of schools–industry projects. GCSE, and more recently, the National Curriculum, have begun to reverse the trend and established the crucial importance of 'bottom-up' curriculum development, influencing not only content and process but also context, and teaching and learning methodology. Changes pre-16 are beginning to influence the post-16 curriculum. The greater emphasis on flexible/active learning, modular course structures and 'applications-led' A-levels (e.g. *Salters'* and *Wessex* A-level Chemistry [10]), alongside the growing interest in combined academic/ vocational courses post-16 will greatly influence the type of chemistry offered and the way it is taught and learned in schools.

Higher education is also responding to the pressures for change. There is greater interest in the quality of the student learning experience; personal and professional skills and qualities; industrial experience; employer involvement; problem solving; new methods of assessment, etc. The Enterprise in Higher Education initiative, developments in open learning and distance learning will all influence the way chemistry is taught and learned in higher education.

It would be satisfying to think after so many years of the 'top-down' model that the curriculum change which has taken place in schools has indeed made an impact on higher education and that we now have the beginnings of a truly bottom-up, contextualized science curriculum.

THE PROCESS/CONTENT DEBATE

There are interesting parallels between the debate about the influence of higher education on what is taught in schools and the so-called 'process/content debate'. If the former is basically a debate about what is taught the latter is more concerned with how it is taught.

The influence of higher education on school chemistry was largely on the content of what was to be taught. Although there has always been fierce discussion about content, it was the emergence of the process/content debate in the '60s which made it even more important to questions higher education's influence as well as providing the means to do so.

The phrase 'process/content debate', whilst a convenient term does not really do justice to the issues involved, and also has the unfortunate effect of suggesting that one must come down in the end in favour of one or the other. There is no point introducing 'content' to pupils unless they understand it and understanding itself is a learning process. It may therefore be strictly more appropriate to use the phrase 'process/process debate'. However, it is not too difficult to see why this has not been readily adopted! Chemistry teachers have long been aware of the importance of scientific process as the introduction to *The New Matriculation Chemistry* (Bailey [4]) shows:

> 'Let us then follow the course of investigation by experiment which will enable us to see how the information we require is to be obtained and what deductions might be made from the observations.'

Bailey [4]

Equally there has always been concern about the amount of content that needs to be covered in a given course. It was often assumed that teaching which provided good opportunities to develop science processes would also be a good way to develop an understanding of science content and to some extent this remains true today. The debates which led to *Nuffield Chemistry* [5] forced teachers to look critically at such assumptions and led to a recognition that scientific processes had their own intrinsic value. Such recognition still might not have led to the great changes which occurred had not *Nuffield Chemistry* also relied on the ideas in Bloom's *Taxonomy of Educational Objectives* [11] as shown in Table 1.

Table 1   The main categories in Bloom's taxonomy of educational objectives [11].

Category	Example
1 Knowledge	of facts, terms, conventions, theories
2 Comprehension	interpreting and extrapolating
3 Application	of theories in concrete situations
4 Analysis	of relationships
5 Synthesis	producing a unique communication
6 Evaluation	judgements in terms of criteria

This gave teachers a common language with which to conduct the process/content debate and in particular it gave them a precise tool for analysing chemistry examination questions [12].

It was on the question of what percentages of marks should be devoted to understanding content rather than, for example, designing experiments or interpreting their results, that the process/content debate was at its fiercest. This was not unexpected since, where teaching time is at a premium a teacher will 'not want to spend time on things which will not earn marks in the exam'. Indeed, during the time when *Nuffield Chemistry* was gaining ground such concerns were frequently bourne out. Newly-qualified teachers who were committed to developing a wide range of process skills were appointed to teach in schools following 'old' syllabuses which did not examine and reward these skills. Their pupils who had developed a good range of science processes could not gain credit for these in an examination which only tested knowledge and understanding of chemistry content. Such debates have largely been overtaken now by National Criteria for GCSE which specify a significant percentage of marks for a wide range of science processes.

Although courses such as *Nuffield Chemistry* required pupils to carry out scientific investigations these were largely based around 'pure' chemistry topics. The *Nuffield Sample Scheme* contained some 140 investigations and although 24 of these had titles which linked them to their industrial applications the emphasis was still very much on the pure concept. Even the promising sounding investigation based on 'the importance of the structure of metals to engineers' contains no information about the real engineering problems caused by the defects which pupils modelled using bubble rafts. In other words, even though the *Nuffield Courses* allowed science processes to be assessed and 'given credit', they did not really take the extra step of doing this in the context of real industrial applications.

The mid-'70s saw the beginning of several initiatives which were designed to enable chemistry and other science teachers to work closely with colleagues in industry. The most successful of these SLIP (*Science Lessons from Industrial Processes*) courses enabled teachers to produce lesson materials which were based on real industrial processes and their problems. Here for the first time the recently legitimized science processes were being used to study real applications in such a way as to make clear the relevance of the 'pure' science concepts involved.

SCIENCE FIRST OR APPLICATIONS FIRST?

There has been a growing recognition that a wider understanding and appreciation of chemistry which addresses the impact that chemistry makes on society, industry, the economy and the environment is important. This has been reflected in GCSE National Criteria for science, National Curriculum Orders and in the increasing number of relatively recent industry/applications focused curriculum projects such as *Salters' Chemistry* [8], SATIS [7], *Problem Solving with Industry* [13], *Exciting Science and Engineering* [14], *Chemistry in Action* [15] and *Chemistry Plus* [16].

Apart from the *Salters' Projects*, which offer the entire course in the form of an applications-first approach, the others provide industry/applications enriching resources to support a science-first approach. The difference between the two approaches can best be summarized in Figure 1.

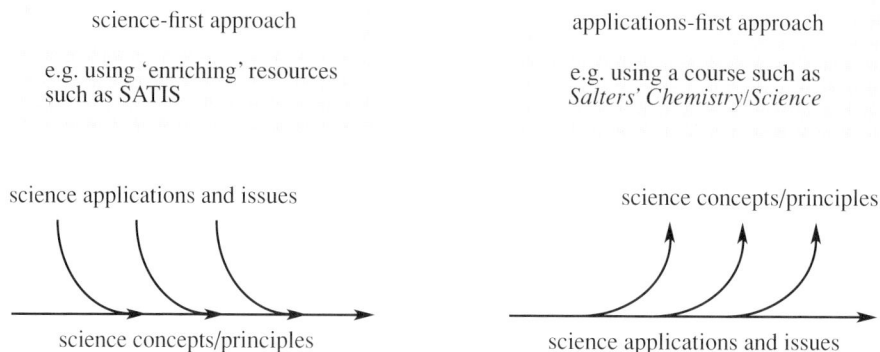

Figure 1   Contrasting the 'science-first' and 'applications-first' approaches (adapted from Holman [17]).

It is easy to see from Figure 1 the difference in the two approaches. For example, when teaching about acids, bases and salts use of any of the SATIS units *Making Fertilisers*, *Which Anti-Acid?*, *Acid Rain*, or *Chemicals from Salt* could be made to highlight the everyday or industrial applications and issues surrounding acids, bases and salts. Also, when teaching about rates of reaction, by using the *Problem Solving with Industry* [13] unit *Hot Cans*, pupils could see how a knowledge of reaction rates was important in the design of a commercial canned food product in which the inner can containing the food is heated by allowing water and lime in the outer can to react.

However, with the applications-first approach as in *Salters' Science* [18] each unit is designed around a particular application of chemistry. For example, a unit entitled *Drinks* deals with:

*   atoms and molecules;
*   states of matter;
*   changes of state;
*   solubility and its explanation in terms of the kinetic theory;
*   simple distillation;
*   monitoring water quality;
*   the social implications of alcohol use and abuse.

Although it would be possible to use *Salters'* units or sections of a unit as a resource for a science-first approach, chemistry teachers have generally adopted the whole course. In this way it is much easier to ensure that there is full coverage of the key chemistry concepts and in the most appropriate order. One of the major educational issues in adopting an applications-first approach without using a course like *Salters'* is the problem of introducing several concepts at the same time, when the pupils may not be ready or able to deal with them. Unfortunately topics based on applications of science do not normally fall neatly under one syllabus heading. As with many *Salters'* units, this is also typified in the *Experimenting with Industry Project* [19] unit 8, *Extracting Metals from Scrap*, in which the following concepts/principles are introduced:

- action of acids on: metals, metal oxides and carbonates;
- neutralization;
- precipitation of salts;
- thermal decomposition of hydrates and carbonates;
- calculations involving the mole;
- general electrolysis including purification of copper, selective deposition, choice of electrodes;
- crystallization;
- volumetric analysis.

This may give rise to a number of disadvantages and possible barriers:

- each of the above topics is unlikely to be given adequate coverage in the unit, so unless sufficient time is given to introduce the topic, if new, and then to give it full treatment, it would have to be returned to at another time;
- it may impose an order of teaching which is considered inappropriate;
- it is often difficult and very time consuming to design practical work which simulates or mirrors the industrial application;
- time and effort are required to assemble resources, in some cases to liaise with industry and, possibly to update the teacher's own knowledge and understanding of the industrial application or issue.

However, there are several clear advantages in using this approach:

- a real life and relevant context is provided for the teaching and learning of chemistry which is likely to be more motivating;
- pupils gain a much wider understanding of chemistry and its role in their lives;
- chemistry facts and principles are not divorced from the social, economic, environmental and technological aspects;
- it provides excellent opportunities for introducing aspects of the cross-curricular themes, e.g. economic and industrial understanding, environmental education, careers education;
- it provides opportunities for teachers, pupils and industrialists to work in partnership, often to the advantage of the school.

Despite the increasing volume of industrially-related resource material becoming available and the greater involvement and support of industry in curriculum development there has been limited take up of the applications-first approach in school chemistry. It seems that although many teachers recognize the need to provide pupils with a more holistic view and understanding of chemistry the difficulties of developing applications-first resources are just too demanding particularly at a time of major curriculum change in science. It may also be that the majority of chemistry teachers are not ready or even willing to make a change which is radically different to the generally accepted pedagogy of chemistry teaching.

Clearly the applications-first approach has a great deal to recommend it and it is one to which we should be making greater efforts to develop. However, the science-first approach has also many benefits:

• teachers are starting from a position of experience, expertise and confidence, i.e. their subject knowledge and teaching methodology;

• applications and issues can be introduced at appropriate points within the scheme of work without affecting the order of teaching and learning;

• less time and effort is required to prepare materials since there are many suitable enriching resources available;

• it is much easier to design or locate resources than it is to design a unit or module of work or even a whole course based around applications;

• it still enables close links with industry to be developed.

If time is taken to ensure that the applications and issues of chemistry are addressed by carefully integrating resources and activities into the scheme of work then pupils can still be guided towards as fuller appreciation and understanding of the relevance and impact of chemistry.

Both strategies, although very different in approach, nevertheless have the same intention.

SCIENCE AND TECHNOLOGY IN SOCIETY ISSUES

Science and technology in society issues are now firmly established as an integral component of the science National Curriculum. That this is so is clearly demonstrated within the GCSE National Criteria for science and in the National Curriculum Orders. Although this has only been achieved during the last five years the debate has taken place over the last 20 years.

Probably the first major attempt to bring science and technology in society issues into the science curriculum began with the *Schools Council Integrated Science Project* (SCISP) [6] developed in the early '70s and was examined as a double GCE by the Associated Examining Board.

The SCISP course involved teachers in considering topics such as fossil fuels, alternative energy sources, diet and disease, supersonic air travel, earthquakes and volcanoes, in such a way that the basic science involved was set firmly in the context of the social, environmental and economic issues involved. What gave SCISP teachers a greater incentive to fully develop such issues and not simply to deal briefly with them after the 'real science' had been taught was the fact that they were examined in the GCE examinations. Indeed a substantial portion of the marks was allocated to them. Not until the advent of GCSE, was such a significant allocation in other science syllabuses made.

A range of resources appeared during the late '70s and early '80s which addressed industrial, technological and social issues in science, notably: the *Interactive Chemistry Teaching Packages* [20], *Studies in Industrial Chemistry* [21], *Experimenting with Industry Project* [19] and *The Physics Plus Project* [22]. Interest was growing in biotechnology and a range of resources began to appear in the mid-'80s. Policy statements from the Department of Education and Science and the Association for Science Education (ASE) along with encouragement from the Secondary Science Curriculum Review (SSCR) and TVEI created a groundswell for change. There had previously been some developments in the 16–19 phase, e.g. *Science in Society, Science in a Social Context*, Joint Matriculation Board A-level Chemistry Case Studies but these seem to have had little influence pre-16. It was not until the appearance of SATIS resources [7] in 1986 that there was any significant take-up of industrial, technological and social issues in science lessons other than on SCISP courses. There is little doubt then that SATIS, established by the ASE and supported by considerable funding, mobilized many science teachers, advisers, scientists, industrialists and many other contributors. Such a major, high-profile project had a very significant influence on science education curriculum development. The timing of SATIS and the increasing recognition of science and technology in society issues coincided with the production of GCSE National Criteria. It was therefore not surprising to find that the Criteria required all GCSE science courses to have no less than 15% of the syllabus content devoted to industrial technological, social and economic issues.

It is interesting to note that GCSE chemistry was most influenced by this requirement with up to 30% of the syllabus content devoted to industrial, technological, social and economic issues.

Now that science teachers were required to teach about social and technological issues they turned to SATIS materials as one of the few, readily available resources. The project materials offered good coverage of GCSE topics and were presented as photocopy masters. They were extremely well disseminated and very reasonably priced. The project was highly successful with excellent take-up of the materials. It was subsequently extended to cover the 16–19 age phase and more recently the 9–14 age phase.

There is no doubt that SATIS has had considerable influence on the National Curriculum for science. Furthermore, it has also influenced teaching methodology through its emphasis on active learning. It was recognized that to deal effectively with social and technological issues, at times sensitive and controversial, required pupil-centred, active learning strategies such as small group discussion, role-play and simulation, problem solving, etc.

As was stated at the beginning of this section the National Curriculum has firmly established science and technology in society issues as an integral part of the science curriculum. The programmes of study, which are statutory, clearly endorse the teaching of science within the context of its everyday life and industrial applications. Furthermore the introduction of National Curriculum cross-curricular themes also encourages an applications approach. Science can undoubtedly make a major contribution to these and is particularly able to offer relevant content and contexts for teaching the cross-curricular themes of health education, economic and industrial understanding and environmental education.

Running alongside these developments has been the increasing involvement of industry in curriculum development. This has resulted in a much wider choice of applications-based resource material for science teachers and further support for teaching about social and technological aspects of science.

SCHOOL–INDUSTRY COLLABORATION IN CURRICULUM DEVELOPMENT

Despite the very high level of school–industry collaboration in recent years it is certainly not a new development. Indeed, it has been going on for many years, ranging from small scale school–industry links at a local level to high profile national initiatives with multinational organizations. Major companies such as BP, Unilever, ICI, British Gas, British Telecom and British Steel have a long-standing commitment to school–industry partnerships and each have education liaison sections within the company.

The chemical industry in particular has an excellent record of education liaison and has its own Chemical Industries Association (CIA) which helps to promote school–industry links. In 1988 the CIA, in collaboration with the University of York, established the Chemical Industry Education Centre based at the university. This was a development of earlier work established at North London Polytechnic by the Schools Information Centre on the Chemical Industry (SICCI). It provides a central reference point for school teachers needing information about the chemical industry. The Centre also develops teaching materials and publications and helps to create opportunities for school–industry links.

There have been several significant changes in the nature of school–industry links from the '60s to the '90s. Early links were often between an individual chemistry teacher and a local chemical plant and involved little more than an annual visit to the plant often without any structure, preparation or follow-up.

This progressed to the level of a structured visit [23] where a teacher might visit a plant and identify key features which they would prepare their class for in advance and would follow-up afterwards. This was time consuming and involved much duplication when several teachers visited the same plant. To overcome this problem and also to try to help schools who could not visit chemical plants, an approach which came to be know as SLIP (*Science Lessons from Industrial Processes*) was developed. SLIP started in Sunderland LEA and then the idea spread to Leeds and many other LEAs in the mid-'70s. It involved a team of science teachers being seconded for typically one day a week for a term in order to spend time working with a contact in a particular industry. They would develop a series of lesson resources based on a particular process, or even part of a process which illustrated some scientific principle. These resources may be a preparation for a visit but often could be used by schools who could not visit the plant, as videos and slides were often included. ASE also took up this idea when it produced the *Application of Science and Maths in Industry and Technology* (ASMIT) cards which each had an industrial application of some scientific principle or idea.

The SLIP resources were often considered as a pack or kit which covered several industries and attempted to include physics and biology as well as chemistry. Some went further and dealt with economic issues and careers information.

It is interesting to note that many current school–industry links, whilst they revert to the 'one school one industry model' are now driven by careers and economic awareness concerns and tend to be whole-school initiatives. Whilst this is undoubtedly a good thing it does carry with it the danger that the 'science potential' of such links may not be fully exploited.

Although school–industry initiatives have been going on for many years the relatively recent growth of activity was fuelled during Industry Year (1986). This initiative evolved following:

'a period of growing frustration that Britain's poor economic performance was in part due to a lack of understanding of Industry's purpose and contribution, indeed to an anti-industry culture. This culture, if not caused by, was certainly felt to be being fostered by education, which became the chief target for Industry Year activities.'

Marsden [24]

As a result of the huge level of activity during Industry Year, followed by the CBI's Taskforce report on school–industry links and the government's marketing campaign aimed at increasing the level of involvement of business with schools, business appeared to be mobilized into activity. At about the same time as this was happening in business, as we saw earlier, there were considerable pressures for change in science education to include industrial, technological, social and economic issues in science courses. Both parties had clear incentives to work together.

Whilst during the '70s the level of collaborative activity was fairly limited, we have moved in the late '80s, early '90s to a very high level indeed, encouraged and supported by TVEI projects, SATRO (Science and Technology Regional Organisation), SCIP (School Curriculum Industry Partnership) and many other organizations, business and curriculum projects. It is interesting to trace the development of some of these initiatives.

In the late '70s the Chemistry Department at Glasgow University in collaboration with the Scottish Education Department produced a series of 16 interactive chemistry packages [20]. These covered a wide range of topics highlighting the social, industrial, economic and technological aspects of chemistry and involved O-grade or O-level pupils in small group discussion, simulation, problem solving/decision making strategies. This was very good material probably well ahead of its time.

Studies in Industrial Chemistry (Harrison and Wright [21]; first published in 1982), a book of eight case studies for O/CSE pupils, was one of the first attempts to produce a text which highlighted the major industrial chemistry processes covered by most syllabuses. Social and technological issues were covered and pupils were encouraged to engage in small group discussion and to tackle controversial issues, role-play and decision making.

In 1985 an innovative project *Experimenting with Industry* was established by the Standing Conference on School Science and Technology with the ASE [19]. This involved 13 experienced science teachers being linked with industrial companies to devise experimental work. The work was drawn from industrial applications, which illustrate scientific concepts and show how they are applied in industry. Thirteen units were produced which covered a wide range of school practical work based on industrial applications. (One of these, *Extracting Metals from Scrap* was referred to in an earlier section.)

The first 70 SATIS units were published in 1986 and reference has already been made to the importance of this project and its influence on science education curriculum development. There are now over 100 units aimed at the 14–16 age group many of which have been developed in collaboration with industry and which highlight industrial applications of science.

During the late '80s and early '90s many collaborative projects were initiated, and as mentioned earlier, industry became much more pro-active in curriculum development during this period. Whilst it is not possible to refer to all of these developments it is worth highlighting a number of key initiatives with a significant chemistry content involving close collaboration between teachers and industrialists.

Problem Solving with Industry Project (PSI) [13] based in the Centre for Science Education, Sheffield City Polytechnic involves some 20 science teachers and advisory teachers, each working with a company to produce problem solving investigations, either based on a real industrial problem or an application of science. Eighteen problem solving units are being developed in four packs aimed at Key Stages 3 and 4. The first pack of three units, together with a teacher support manual on the teaching of problem solving, was given free of charge to all secondary schools in England and Wales in March 1991. Packs 2, 3 and 4 are also now available.

Chemistry Plus Project [16] is coordinated by SCSST (Standing Conference on School Science and Technology) and together with previous projects *Physics Plus* and *Biology Plus* forms the *Science Plus* series. As with the PSI project, chemistry teachers were linked with chemical companies and experts in the field in order to develop resources which present chemistry principles and understanding within the context of its everyday and industrial applications. Twenty units were published in January 1992.

Chemistry in Action [15] was developed in 1987 by the University of York Science Education Group in collaboration with Granada Television and several chemical companies. Ten units were developed with the aim of illustrating the social, industrial and economic aspects of chemistry highlighted in GCSE, TVEI and CPVE schemes.

Exciting Science and Engineering Project [14] is one of several projects being developed at the Chemical Industry Education Centre (CIEC) at the University of York. This major project developed in collaboration with BP is producing teaching materials for the 7–14 age range which illustrate through a problem-solving approach the importance of science, technology and engineering. (CIEC also plans to produce a guide which will simplify the process of developing profitable links with the chemical industry. Many other collaborative projects are being developed at CIEC and for further information readers should write to Miranda Mapletoft, Manager CIEC, Chemistry Department, University of York.)

Collaborative projects with industry have been undertaken involving major companies such as ICI, BP, Shell, Unilever, British Steel, British Gas and many others.

There is little doubt that the Technical and Vocational Education Initiative (TVEI) which was launched in 1982 brought industry into closer contact with schools at classroom level. However, it is worth noting that this initiative, significant though it was, only involved some LEAs. Even within an LEA only some schools would be involved and within a school only some portion of a year group. Nevertheless the increased staffing and funding of the pilot scheme did make possible many substantial links with industry. The majority of these involved an emphasis on economic awareness and careers, and the direct involvement of science teachers and LEA science advisory staff was not common.

The TVEI Extension scheme launched in 1986 and now operating in almost all LEAs with all secondary schools and all Year 10 and Year 11 pupils, has had much more of a whole-curriculum focus. There has also been a greater emphasis on the learning experiences of pupils and of ways of enriching these. Industrial links are seen as one very valid way of achieving this.

It is worth mentioning the role of professional associations in bringing schools and industry into closer contact in order to promote a better understanding of one another and to assist curriculum development.

For several years, the Royal Society of Chemistry has been organizing Industry Study Tours which enable groups of chemistry teachers to spend up to 3 days visiting the chemical industry. These provide opportunities for teachers to find out more about the work of the company and to get ideas and materials for classroom use.

The ASE is involved as a clearing house as well as an initiator in several schemes which involve science teachers spending some time in industry in order to produce curriculum resources. These began with a British Gas project in 1981 which led to the publication of the *Gas Application in School Science* (GASS) booklet [25] which contained pages of resources based on a wide range of British Gas activities, from automatic burner ignition to pipe descaling.

British Telecom (since 1985) has offered, via ASE, several teacher fellowships each summer at all of their major sites in the UK. ICI and British Gas also now offer similar short fellowships.

The Chemical Industries Association (CIA) and the Association of British Pharmaceutical Industries (ABPI) are also pro-active and supportive of curriculum development. There are a very wide range of collaborative activities which fall under the heading of curriculum development other than simply the production of teaching resources. It may be helpful to conclude this section with a summary of what the range of activities might be as given in *Why Business should Work with Education* [24].

'For teachers

- attachments to industry—short term/long term
- attending company training courses
- attending education based courses with industrial contribution
- researching external learning resources
- developing new learning opportunities involving external resources
- developing and maintaining personal contacts
- providing services for industry
- receiving industrial visitors into the classroom
- advice/help with technical information

For industrialists

- provide industrial contribution to the student and teacher activities
- consultant—school management/curriculum development/assessment, e.g. records of achievement
- industrialist 'in residence'
- helping with students' project work
- acting as personal adviser to students
- development of industry-related learning materials
- education committee work
- school governors and members of school boards

For students

- work experience/work shadowing
- work simulation
- school enterprises
- industrial site visits
- using industrial resources—on site—in school
- using industrialist as personal adviser
- special events, e.g. 'insight into ...', courses, competitions, business games
- joint education industry curriculum development projects, e.g. problem solving, GCSE, etc.
- joint education industry training exercises, e.g. mock interviews, communication skills, etc.'

Marsden [24]

COMPARING 'PURE' AND 'APPLIED' TEACHING APPROACHES

It is interesting to explore the dynamic between the notion of 'pure' and 'applied' approaches to teaching chemistry/science. Figure 2 shows the two approaches at the opposite ends of a continuum.

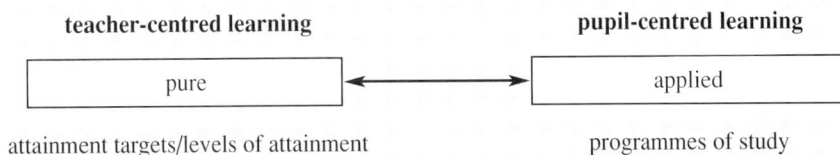

teacher-centred learning   **pupil-centred learning**

| pure | ←———————→ | applied |

attainment targets/levels of attainment   programmes of study

Figure 2   Comparison of 'pure' and 'applied' teaching approaches.

If one looks at the National Curriculum it seems clear that the way in which the attainment targets and the levels of attainment are presented fits comfortably with a more academic or pure approach to teaching a topic—they simply outline what the pupil should know, understand and be able to do. Teaching science from the attainment targets would largely encourage the teaching of knowledge and understanding outside of any everyday life context. In other words a very 'pure' approach. However, the programmes of study contain many references to everyday life applications, and starting from these as recommended, would surely encourage an 'applied' approach to teaching science. One might also go further and suggest that an applied approach favours a pupil-centred approach to learning. First it relates the science to the pupils' own experiences and tries to make it relevant, and second, in addressing real-life applications and issues of science it encourages the use of more pupil-centred strategies such as small group discussion, role-play, problem solving and decision making.

On the other hand, does a more academic or pure approach to teaching science favour a more teacher-centred model of learning? Clearly it is not inevitable, yet there is considerable evidence to show that such an approach is characterized by teacher exposition, teacher-directed, passive learning.

It is helpful at this point to show how an applied approach can be used to introduce a range of chemistry concepts or principles yet at the same time raise pupils' awareness of the applications of chemistry within an industrial context. The unit *Sugar Challenge* from the *Experimenting with Industry Project* [19] illustrates this well. This particular unit was developed in collaboration with chemists and engineers from British Sugar plc. The unit, suitable for 12–14-year-olds, uses a problem solving approach and requires about 8 hours lesson time.

Pupils are set the problem of designing and undertaking an investigation to extract sugar from sugar beet. In solving the problem, they will in fact be carrying out some of the tasks that chemists and chemical engineers undertake at British Sugar and therefore finding out about the applications of chemistry in industry.

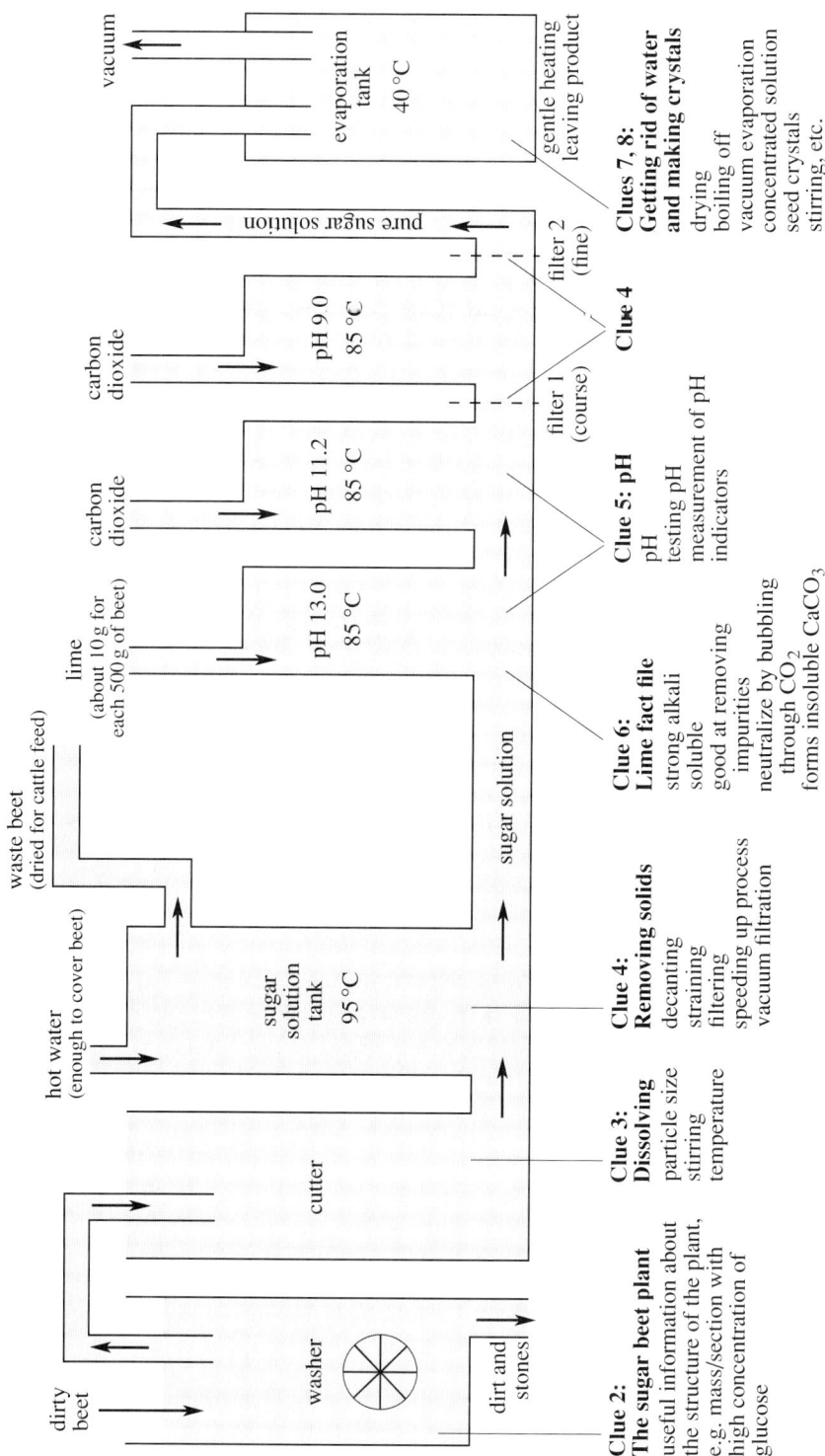

Figure 3   Clue 1: The sugar factory plan (adapted from the *Sugar Challenge* unit of *Experimenting with Industry Project* [19]).

Having been set the problem the pupils are then given helpful information and advice about the problem solving process, followed by a series of eight clue sheets to help them analyse the problem and draw up action plans. The clue sheets are carefully designed to provide details about the factory process and information relating to the chemistry concepts and processes used at the different stages of the process. Figure 3 illustrates clue sheet 1 of the *Sugar Challenge*. Figure 4 illustrates the clue sheet for Clue 3: Dissolving, that is mentioned in clue sheet 1.

Clue 3: Dissolving

When you put salt into hot water, the salt disappears. We say that it has dissolved. Solids that dissolve are described as *soluble*. Although salt will dissolve well in water, it does not dissolve at all in methylated spirits. We say that salt is *insoluble* in methylated spirits. Liquids that allow things to dissolve in them are called *solvents*. The solids that do the dissolving are called *solutes*.

How can we get things to dissolve more quickly?

Clue 3a: Making jelly

Jelly comes in a large oblong shape in a box. When you take it out of the box you will see that it is marked into squares ready to cut up into smaller cube shapes. When you pour the water onto the jelly, you can see it dissolving from the surface of the cubes.

Here are pictures of two identical amounts of jelly.

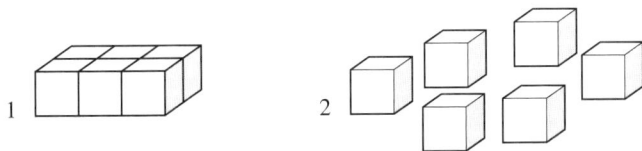

Which one has the largest surface?

Which one is going to dissolve the quickest?

Clue 3b: Making tea

Tea is a solution of some of the chemicals from the tea leaf. When you make tea, you need boiling water, to pour over the leaves. You also need a spoon to stir the tea just before you pour it out.

Does hot water help?

What do you think stirring does?

Figure 4   The clue sheet for Clue 3: Dissolving (adapted from the *Sugar Challenge* unit of *Experimenting with Industry Project* [19]).

A look at the clue sheet in Figure 4 shows a fairly typical pure approach to the concept of dissolving, even allowing for the fact that it uses everyday examples to illustrate the point. The other seven clue sheets use perhaps a more academic approach than that in used Figure 4. However, one can see that the author has skilfully combined the need to provide the pupil with the pure chemical understanding necessary in order to even begin to effectively tackle the problem, along with the highly motivating and relevant applied context in which to set the problem and the learning situation. This unit has been thoroughly trialled and younger secondary school pupils, of average ability and above, coped well and were well motivated.

CONCLUSION

The *Sugar Challenge* unit demonstrates that a good range of chemistry concepts and practical skills can be learned and reinforced by this approach, as well as developing problem solving and investigative skills. This seems to have been achieved by providing a balance of pure and applied approaches.

The applications-first approach has the obvious advantage of providing an everyday context which can both stimulate the learner and provide a relevant framework in which to present the chemical ideas. However a science-first approach which seeks every opportunity to inject everyday applications and issues into the course could perhaps be as effective.

Unless there are more courses developed like *Salters' Chemistry/Science* then clearly this latter approach will be the most common and pragmatic one to encourage. However, with the development of more materials like *Experimenting with Industry, Exciting Science and Engineering* and even closer collaboration with industrialists and others outside of the profession, then surely the two approaches can successfully be combined. As with all good teaching isn't 'variety the spice of life?'.

REFERENCES

1   Bassey, M., *Technical Education*, 1960, **2**(12), pp. 13–17.

2   Bassey, M., *Technical Education*, 1961, **3**(1), pp. 18–19, 21.

3   Bassey, M., *Technical Education*, 1961, **3**(2), pp. 15–17.

4   Bailey, G. H., *The New Matriculation Chemistry*. (University Tutorial Press, 1905).

5   *Nuffield Chemistry*. (Longman, 1987).

6   *Schools Council Integrated Science Project* (SCISP), The Schools Council. (Longman, 1975).

7   *Science and Technology in Society* (SATIS) *Project*. (Association for Science Education/Heinemann, 1986).

8   *Salters' Chemistry Course*. (Science Education Group, University of York, 1987).

9   *Better Science: Making it relevant to young people*, Curriculum Guide 3, compiled by D. Stewart, Secondary Science Curriculum Review. fff(Heinemann Educational Books/Association for Science Education, 1987).

10 Gadd, K. F. (ed.), *The Wessex Project.* School of Science, Yeovil College, Somerset. (1989).

11 Bloom, B. S., *Taxonomy of Educational Objectives*, Book 1, *The Cognitive Domain*. (David McKay, 1956).

12 Jenkins, E. W., 'Public examinations and science teaching methods in grammar schools since 1918', *Durham Research Review*, 1971, **1**(26), pp. 548–556.

13 *Problem Solving with Industry Project* (PSI). (Centre for Science Education, Sheffield City Polytechnic, 1991).

14 *Exciting Science and Engineering Project.* (Chemical Industry Education Centre, University of York, 1991).

15 *Chemistry in Action.* (Science Education Group, University of York/Granada Television, 1987).

16 *The Chemistry Plus Project*, Standing Conference on School Science and Technology (SCSST). (Hobsons Publishing, 1992).

17 Holman, J., 'Resources or Courses? Contrasting approaches to the introduction of industry and technology to the secondary curriculum', *School Science Review*, 1987, **68**(March), pp. 432–438.

18 *Salters' Science Course.* (Science Education Group, University of York, 1987).

19 *Experimenting with Industry Project*, SCSST/ASE. (Standing Conference on School Science and Technology/Association for Science Education, 1985).

20 *Interactive Chemistry Teaching Packages.* (Scottish Education Department/Glasgow University, 1977).

21 Harrison, B. and Wright, D. J., *Studies in Industrial Chemistry for GCSE.* (Edward Arnold, 1988).

22 *The Physics Plus Project*, Standing Conference on School Science and Technology (SCSST). (Hobsons Publishing, 1992).

23 Harrison, B. (ed.), *Active Teaching and Learning Approaches in Science.* (Collins Educational, 1992).

24 Marsden, C., *Why Business Should Work with Education.* (BP/Education Service, 1988).

25 *Gas Application in School Science.* (British Gas, 1981).

CHAPTER 3

WHY STUDY CHEMISTRY?

Roland Jackson

There are two simple answers to the question posed in the title—because it's essential and because it's fascinating. The first answer leads to the social, environmental and economic importance of chemistry, discussed in the initial parts of this Chapter. The second develops logically to the possibilities open to people who wish to make chemistry a part of their subsequent working lives, and the careers that are open to those with qualifications in chemistry.

WHY IS CHEMISTRY ESSENTIAL?

It is barely necessary to list the areas of human need addressed by the applications of chemistry. To quote Lord Porter, recent President of the Royal Society: 'One might as well try to do without chemistry as attempt to stop the world'. Nevertheless, just so the record is clear, it should be said that chemistry makes vital contributions to the provision of food, health care, shelter, clothing, transport and communication. The applications of chemistry are shown in Figure 1, which illustrates the relative importance of the various sectors of the chemical (including pharmaceutical) industry in terms of output. I challenge anyone to identify a single area of human activity untouched or not enhanced by chemistry.

Yet, not everything in the garden is rosy. There is genuine concern and fear about the potential damage that some chemicals can do, and have done, to humans and to the environment. Some of this concern may be misplaced, based on beliefs which see natural substances as necessarily preferable to synthetic chemicals, but it is no less real for that. However, on the positive side this concern has contributed to the increasingly stringent examination of the operations of the chemical industry which is now taking place, both in terms of the management of individual plants and the environmental impact of products, considering the implications of the operation right through from raw material to disposal of the product after use.

CHEMISTRY: SOLVING PROBLEMS

Chemically-related disasters are only too well-known, e.g. Bhopal, Flixborough and the Columbia space shuttle. Unforeseen consequences of using particular chemicals can also result in major problems—the use of DDT and of CFCs. Two points follow from these concerns. The first is the need for a clear recognition by all—both the general public and scientists—that knowledge and understanding are never complete, that there will always be risk and uncertainty attached to any new development. That is not to deny the seriousness of some potential or actual problems, but to say that science permanently poses questions and that any uncertainty needs to be identified as

Sectors of the industry 1988 (gross value added)

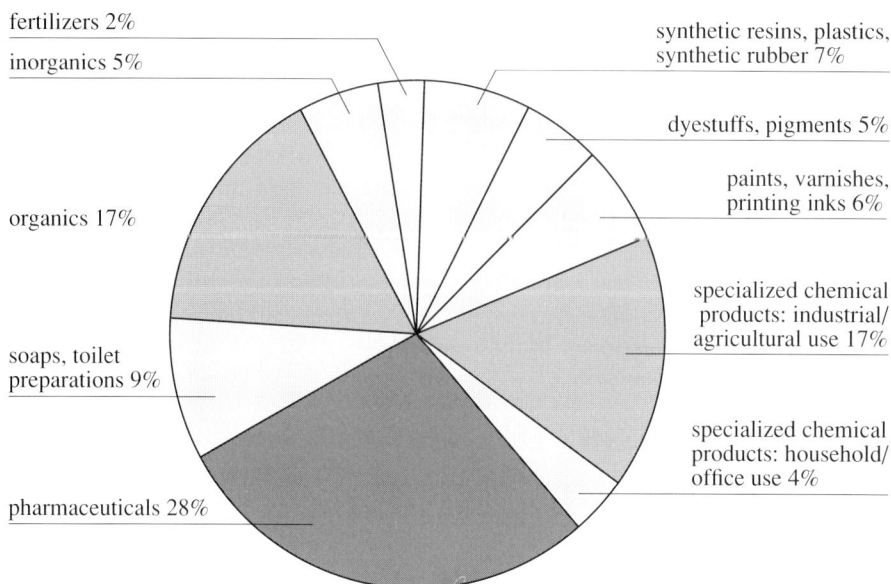

fertilizers 2%

inorganics 5%

organics 17%

soaps, toilet
preparations 9%

pharmaceuticals 28%

synthetic resins, plastics,
synthetic rubber 7%

dyestuffs, pigments 5%

paints, varnishes,
printing inks 6%

specialized chemical
products: industrial/
agricultural use 17%

specialized chemical
products: household/
office use 4%

Sales of principal products/£ million (1990 prices)

1970	1980	1988	1989*	1990*
3 448	13 661	24 740	27 300	28 500

*Estimate by the Chemical Industries Association.

Figure 1   Output of the UK chemical industry.

such and any anticipated risk judged as acceptable or not when balanced against
the possible advantages. The second point is that it is the creative application of
science and technology, frequently involving chemistry, that will alleviate or
solve known problems and provide solutions to new ones. Doing nothing is not
an option. The positive message for young people is that it is their actions and
the application of their ideas which have the potential to make the world a
better place.

The public perception of science is a key area within which teachers and
scientists, both inside and outside the chemical industry, have an important role
to play. The message is that communication and debate about scientific and
technological issues has to be open, honest and a two-way process, and reflect
the ways in which people understand and make use of science in their lives.
Scientific research and the applications of science are not value-free. Choices
about areas of research and the means of application depend on social and
cultural views and beliefs. Teachers should recognize this major human
dimension in their approaches to teaching.

THE UK CHEMICAL INDUSTRY

The chemical industry in the UK is a success story. It is a prime wealth-creating sector of the economy, with an outstanding export record. It has succeeded in maintaining excellent employee relations in times of substantial political, technological, economic and social change. It sustains an extensive research and development programme together with a high level of capital investment; both necessary to ensure its future.

The chemical industry is the UK manufacturing sector's major export earner (Figure 2). Exports were valued at £13.2 thousand million in 1990 with a net export surplus of £2.3 thousand million—a substantial contribution to the UK balance of payments. This is both important and fortunate for the UK, but it should not be taken for granted. The world's major chemical companies (Table 1 overleaf) operate on a global scale and compete internationally. National performance is a part of a whole and not an end in itself. ICI, as a major UK-based company, is a prime example. ICI employed 50 000 people in the UK in 1990, out of a total work force of 130 000, and generated 75% of its income outside the UK, contributing at least £1 thousand million to the UK balance of payments in the process. The company also pays taxes in the UK, through corporation tax and tax on employees' earnings, of several hundred million pounds per annum, financing substantial public expenditure.

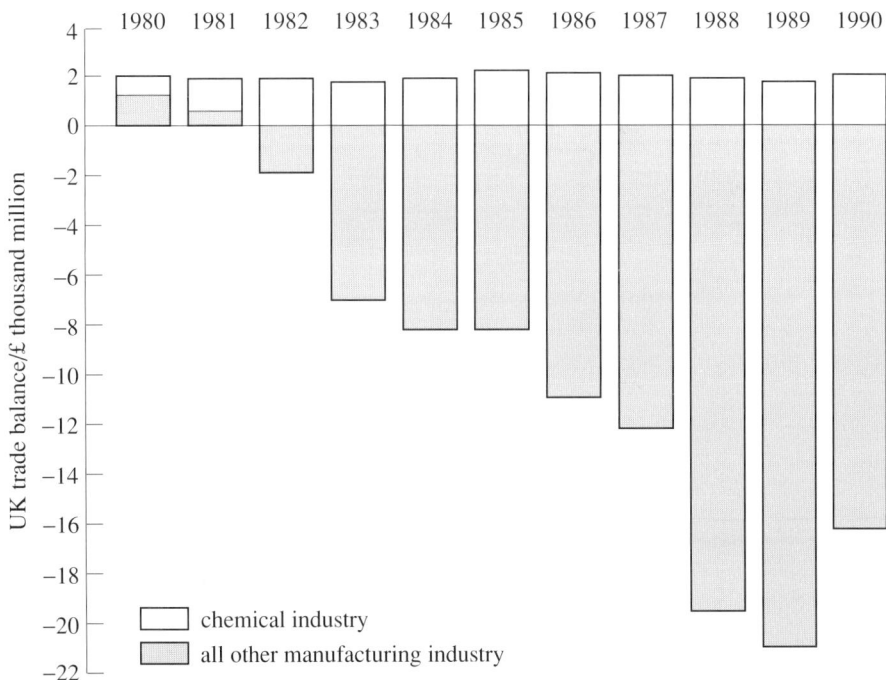

Figure 2   Comparison of the contribution of the chemical industry and all other manufacturing industry to the UK trade balance 1980–1990.

Table 1   The world's major chemical companies.

	Market capitalization 2 May 1991 ($bn)	Pre-tax profits* 1989 ($bn)	Sales (world-wide) 1989 ($bn)
Du Pont	28.2	4.4	35.5
Dow	13.6	3.9	17.6
ICI	13.4	2.5	21.6
Bayer	10.5	2.2	23.1
Hoechst	8.9	2.2	24.4
BASF	8.4	2.3	25.4
Monsanto	7.8	1.0	8.7

* published figure adjusted to be comparable to ICI accounting treatment.

The chemical industry in the UK employs over 300 000 people, supporting several hundred thousand additional jobs throughout the economy. This level of employment is lower than 10 years ago, yet over a 10-year period from 1978 to 1988 output rose substantially (Figure 3). Perhaps surprisingly, energy consumption actually fell over the same period. This fall in energy consumption has lead to a fall in the emissions of carbon dioxide and other waste products related to energy consumption. These improvements in energy efficiency along with other improvements in pollution control, which continue to be made by the chemical industry, do not support the common assumption of greater production being linked to ever-increasing pollution.

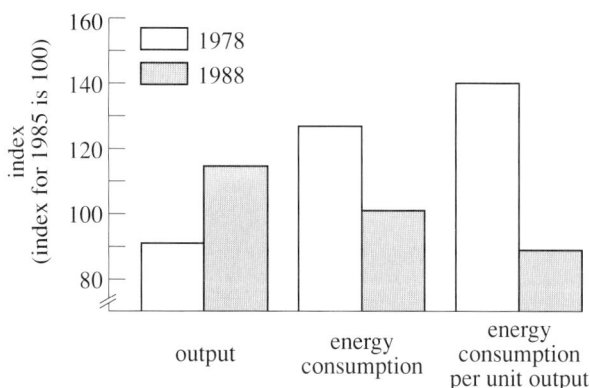

Figure 3   UK chemical industry output and energy consumption indices for 1978 and 1988.

Part of the challenge for those joining the industry in the future is helping to ensure that it operates in harmony with the environment. This is a task which should not be underestimated, given a global population increasing both in numbers and in sophistication. Environmental performance, quite rightly, has become a crucial consideration for chemical companies. Legislation has set the minimum standards which companies have to reach. In addition to this the Chemical Industries Association, the main trade association in the industry with around 200 member companies, launched (in 1989) a Responsible Care programme backed by its member companies. This provides a framework within which companies should manage their activities to provide an acceptably high level of protection for their employees, customers, the public and the environment. In addition to this individual companies are taking their own initiatives. As an example, ICI announced four new objectives in 1990 designed to provide substantial environmental improvements:

- all new plants will be built to standards capable of meeting all regulations that might reasonably be expected in the most environmentally demanding country in which ICI will operate that process;

- waste from operations will be reduced by 50% by 1995, paying special attention to that which is hazardous;

- an even more rigorous programme for conserving energy and resources will be established, paying special attention to actions to safeguard the environment;

- waste-recycling programmes will be set up in-house and in collaboration with customers.

These issues will not be addressed without the creative and innovative application of technology by those currently within the industry and those who will join in the future.

CAREERS

There is an enormous amount of information about chemistry-related careers and qualifications available both from the reference publications used by career services and from literature produced by individual organizations. This section is a brief summary of major employment possibilities and is followed by a section on qualification and career progression routes. More detailed information can be obtained from the resources given at the end of this Chapter.

Chemists in industry and industrial associations

The most obvious area open to chemists is research and development, often requiring particular skills of analysis and synthesis. In addition to this, chemical expertise is relevant for those working as chemical analysts, information scientists and chemical engineers, and for those working in patent departments and production. Sales and marketing roles are also open to those with chemistry qualifications, and many chemists proceed to senior management positions within companies via any of the above career routes.

Chemists in the public service

The scientific civil service, including areas such as defence, food safety and forensic work, is a major employer of chemists. Hospitals require chemists and biochemists in pathology and clinical biochemistry departments to aid medical diagnosis. Chemical analysis is vital to the work of environmental health and trading standards offices. The Research Councils undertake substantial amounts of work requiring chemists, often linked to research in universities and polytechnics.

Chemists in education

Science teaching is the key to the future and there is a need for science teachers at all levels, from primary schools to higher education institutions, with an understanding of chemistry.

CAREER PROGRESSION ROUTES

It is only possible to make the most general statements about career progression routes, given the variety of different qualifications, careers available and differences between the requirements and indeed flexibility of individual organizations. For detailed information consult the reference books listed in the next section.

The most common routes into scientific careers are at graduate level, with a degree in an appropriate science subject, or at technician level with four GCSEs at grades A–C (or Scottish equivalent) or one A-level and three GCSEs at grades A–C. Entry at technician level with the above qualifications could lead to study for BTEC/SCOTVEC Higher National Awards, which in turn could lead to various advanced qualifications of the professional scientific institutes and societies resulting in recognized professional status. An example of the latter is the Graduateship of the Royal Society of Chemistry (GRSC), which is often taken on a part-time basis by people already in employment in the chemical industry.

The wide variety of possibilities open to graduate chemists is illustrated in Tables 2 and 3, which show the first destinations of chemistry graduates and

Table 2   First destinations of chemistry graduates (%).

	1985		1986		1987		1988	
	P	U	P	U	P	U	P	U
permanent employment in the UK	52.0	46.0	45.8	44.7	54.5	45.6	58.5	48.7
short-term employment in the UK, expected to cease after three months	2.7	1.5	3.2	2.4	4.8	2.2	2.4	2.1
further academic study	21.5	32.3	25.0	34.5	17.8	34.5	22.0	33.4
teacher training	3.8	5.5	5.3	5.3	4.5	4.9	2.8	3.8
other training	1.3	2.1	0.8	1.6	1.4	2.7	1.8	1.8
overseas (including students returning overseas)	3.2	2.4	4.0	2.0	4.8	2.0	2.1	1.9
unemployed	14.7	8.8	13.4	7.4	10.3	6.0	8.0	5.1
not available for employment	0.8	1.4	2.5	2.1	1.9	2.1	2.4	3.2

P = polytechnic graduates; U = university graduates.

Source: *What do Graduates do?* Hobsons Publishing, Bateman Street, Cambridge CB2 1LZ.

the types of work carried out in first employment. A substantial proportion of chemistry graduates pursue careers outside the field of chemistry, particularly in financial work. The analytical and numerical skills developed during chemistry degree courses are highly marketable outside science and it is indeed important for the country as a whole that people in positions of influence outside the immediate world of science have a good understanding of science and of scientific issues.

Table 3   Type of work carried out by chemists in first employment (%).

Type of work	1985		1986		1987		1988	
	P	U	P	U	P	U	P	U
administration and operational management	10.0	10.5	10.2	9.4	13.3	9.5	8.9	10.9
research, design and development	45.6	36.9	40.7	34.8	34.1	34.5	46.5	34.1
scientific support service	16.2	6.6	14.4	6.4	22.0	4.9	16.7	5.0
sales, marketing, buying	11.5	11.2	6.0	9.8	11.7	9.6	11.5	9.2
financial work	4.2	16.4	9.7	20.1	6.8	23.6	6.0	24.3
other	12.5	18.4	19.0	19.5	12.1	17.9	10.4	16.5

P = polytechnic graduates; U = university graduates.

Source: *What do Graduates do?* Hobsons Publishing, Bateman Street, Cambridge CB2 1LZ.

RESOURCES

The standard reference books (updated annually) on employment possibilities used by the careers services, which should be available in school and public libraries, are:

> *Occupations 92*, COIC (Careers and Occupational Information Centre), Room N1105, Moorfoot, Sheffield SP1 4PQ
>
> *Jobfile 92*, JIIC–CAL (Job Ideas and Information Centre – Computer Assisted Learning), Hodder and Stoughton.

Much specific information is available from industrial organizations and professional institutions.

The Chemical Industries Association (CIA) publishes a range of booklets on careers for school-leavers and tertiary education students, as well as the *Teachers' Handbook – The Chemical Industry* which is part of a larger CIA careers package. The handbook contains many further references to useful publications on careers, courses and resources. These are available from: Employment Affairs Directorate, The Training and Education Department, Chemical Industries Association Ltd, King's Buildings, Smith Square, London SW1P 3JJ. Tel: 071 834 3399.

The Royal Society of Chemistry produces a range of leaflets on careers open to those with chemistry qualifications, again detailing further sources of information. These are available from: Royal Society of Chemistry, Burlington House, Piccadilly, London W1V 0BN. Tel: 071 437 8656.

The number of resources produced by industrial and professional organizations to support teachers of chemistry and of science in general is quite bewildering. The most comprehensive national database of such resources is NERIS (National Educational Resources Information Service), which operates a subscription service for schools. The information is available electronically on-line or via a CD-ROM. Over 40 000 records are listed. The *NERIS Curriculum Thesaurus* has been produced which gives key words for teachers to use to search the database. Further information is available from: NERIS, Maryland College, Leighton Street, Woburn, Milton Keynes MK17 9JD. Tel: 0525 290364.

In addition, information may be obtained from the catalogues of individual organizations, many of which mail regularly to schools.

The Chemical Industry Education Centre, based at the University of York, holds substantial information on teaching resources related to the chemical industry and acts as a centre for curriculum development. Their publications include *The Good Resource Guide*, a summary of resources recommended by teachers for secondary school science. Further information is available from: Chemical Industry Education Centre, Department of Chemistry, University of York, Heslington, York YO1 5DD. Tel: 0904 432523.

CHAPTER 4

RESEARCH IN CHEMICAL EDUCATION: ITS ROLE AND POTENTIAL

Richard Kempa

INTRODUCTION

Research in chemical education is now a firmly established activity of chemical educators. The main thrust towards this area of research came in the wake of the major science curriculum development movement in the late '60s and early '70s, although some research activities in science education in general, and chemical education in particular, had been conducted before then. However, it was largely after the early curriculum developments in science (including chemistry) had been completed that science education (including chemical education) began to be recognized as an academic discipline in universities. The first development in this direction was the establishment, in 1967, of the first chair of Chemical Education at a British university: this was at the University of East Anglia, with the late Professor H. Frank Halliwell (who had been the coordinator of the *Nuffield O-level Chemistry Project*) as the first incumbent of this chair.

The development at the University of East Anglia was followed by similar developments at other universities, although most of these related to science education, rather than to chemical education in the specific sense. The new science education units or departments thus formed, rapidly began to provide Masters and/or doctoral programmes in science education/chemical education. As a result of this, research in these areas intensified and began to evolve as a major activity on the part of those concerned with science education and/or chemical education.

The growth in science education (including chemical education) research over the past 20 or so years can readily be gauged from the appearance, during that time, of a number of new journals that are devoted either completely or primarily to the publication of science education researches. Here are some of the best known, together with the year of their first appearance:

Journal of Research in Science Teaching (USA): 1963
Research in Science Education (Australia): 1971
Studies in Science Education (for review articles) (UK): 1974
International Journal of Science Education (UK): 1979
Research in Science and Technology Education (UK): 1983.

In addition to these journals, others regularly feature reports on research studies on chemical education, including the following:

The Journal of Chemical Education (USA)
Education in Chemistry (UK)
School Science Review (UK)
Science Education (USA).

Whilst journals such as the foregoing usually carry major research reports, not all science education/chemical education researches that are conducted result in formal publications. Many studies, especially those undertaken for higher academic degrees in universities and polytechnics, are reported in dissertations or theses which are usually found in university/polytechnic libraries only. Two publications provide a useful insight into the range of these studies: (i) the annual publication *Studies in Science Education* which regularly includes a list of doctoral and Masters studies in science education and mathematics education, and (ii) a volume on *Science Education Research and Development Abstracts* [1] published recently by the Royal Society of Chemistry.

CHEMICAL EDUCATION RESEARCH: WHAT IS ITS SCOPE?

As its name implies, chemical education may be viewed as a 'hybrid' discipline in the sense that it has a chemistry dimension and an educational dimension. This is inevitably true for researches into chemical education also: some of these clearly relate to the scientific aspects of what is to be taught and learned, whilst others focus on the processes of learning and teaching. Figure 1 illustrates this by identifying some of the concerns in chemical education research that may be associated with these two dimensions. It should be noted that in the listing of topics in Figure 1 is by no means comprehensive.

Researches into chemistry-related issues of chemical education tend to be linked closely to curriculum development activities. For instance, the systematic reappraisal of curriculum content, the development of new approaches to experimental work (including the design of novel teaching equipment and experiments) and the generation of teaching and learning materials for 'new' topics to be covered in chemistry curricula (e.g. those relating to 'applied' chemistry and environmental issues) are all examples of research and/or development work that relates to the chemistry dimension shown in Figure 1.

Whilst in the early days of chemical education research, most research efforts were focused on chemistry-related matters, nowadays the majority of research appears to be concerned with issues of the learning and teaching of chemistry. Thus, the 'educational dimension' of chemical education research has gained in prominence. In part, this is due to the fact that curriculum development of the kind that took place during the '60s and '70s has gone into a relative decline and, with it, our interest in reappraising the content and concepts of chemistry that feature in school or college chemistry courses. (A noteworthy exception to this is the work done at the University of York: this includes the development of the *Salters' Chemistry/Science* programmes.) However, it is also due to the fact that interest in chemistry-related aspects of chemical education has been overtaken by a growing interest in, and concern with, matters relating to the learning of chemistry. In this sense, chemical education research has become indistinct from science education research generally.

Perhaps the most prolific area of research to have emerged during the past 15 or so years is that concerned with the exploration of pupils' learning difficulties in chemistry, especially those that arise from misconceptions and 'wrong ideas' held by pupils prior to being exposed to formal chemical education. Numerous

```
                        ┌─────────────────────────────┐
                        │     chemical education      │
                        └─────────────────────────────┘
              ┌──────────────────┴──────────────────┐
              ▼                                      ▼
┌──────────────────────────────┐    ┌──────────────────────────────────┐
│      chemistry component      │    │                                  │
│                               │    │       education component        │
│ • analysis and appraisal of   │    │                                  │
│   the 'content' of chemistry  │    │ • study of concept acquisition   │
│                               │    │   by learner                     │
│ • selection of concepts and   │    │                                  │
│   skills to be taught         │    │ • studies of learning behaviour  │
│                               │    │   and learning difficulties      │
│ • development of new          │    │                                  │
│   approaches to different     │    │ • exploration of factors         │
│   concepts                    │    │   affecting, e.g. learning,      │
│                               │    │      attitude formation,         │
│ • decisions about sequencing  │    │      effectiveness of            │
│   of concepts                 │    │      instruction                 │
│                               │    │                                  │
│ • development of novel        │    │                                  │
│   experiments, etc.           │    │                                  │
└──────────────────────────────┘    └──────────────────────────────────┘
              └──────────────────┬──────────────────┘
                                 ▼
                  ┌─────────────────────────────┐
                  │         application         │
                  │     of the foregoing in     │
                  │    curriculum development   │
                  │          and the            │
                  │    design of instruction    │
                  └─────────────────────────────┘
```

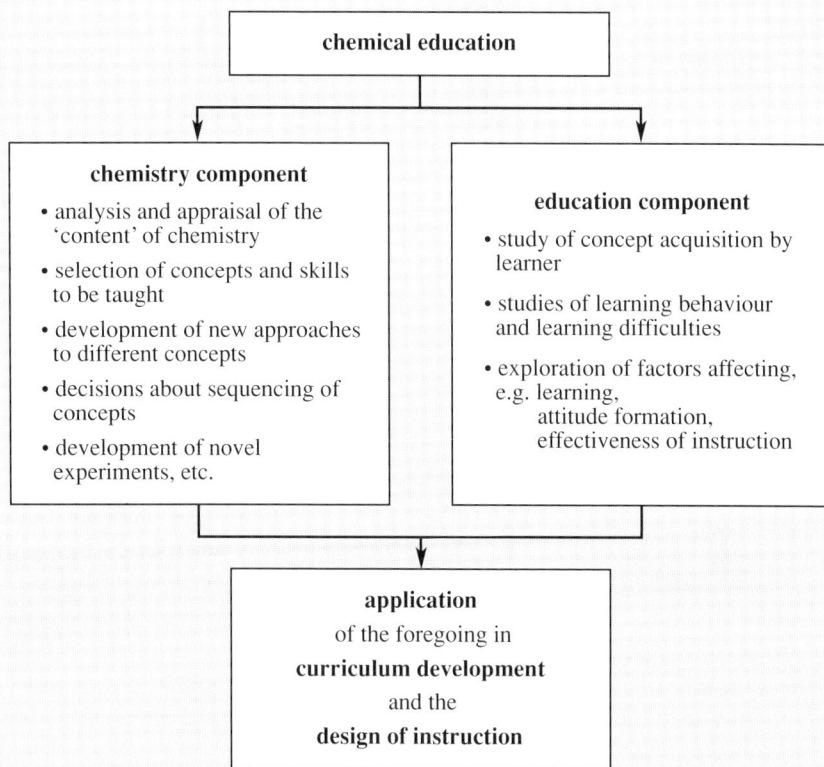

Figure 1   Components of chemical education research.

examples of such researches have appeared in the research literature, and new ones are being added almost daily. Other areas of research that have become well-established include studies of pupils' problem-solving and factors affecting it, and investigations into language and communication problems in chemical education.

FROM RESEARCH TO APPLICATION: HAVE WE SUCCEEDED?

Figure 1 suggests that the results derived from chemical education should, as far as possible, be applied in curriculum development and the design of instruction, i.e. all aspects of the teaching and learning process. When viewed in this sense, chemical education research is accorded a functional role: this is to generate insights and information on the basis of which informed decisions can be taken about major aspects of the teaching of chemistry. This view is not necessarily endorsed by those who wish to liken chemical education research to pure science research and see it as a quest for knowledge, regardless of whether such knowledge is 'usable' and useful, in a practical sense.

Unfortunately, the impact of chemical education research on the practice of chemical education has so far been relatively low. For example, the findings from studies into pupils' learning difficulties in chemistry are only gradually being taken on board by teachers and have yet to find their way into curriculum projects and textbooks. Likewise, the results of researches into chemical problem-solving have so far found only limited application in the practice of chemical education.

It is of interest to ask why it is that chemical education research has up till now not exerted much influence upon the teaching of chemistry in the classroom and laboratory. Why is it that, by and large, research and practice seem to co-exist as parallel pursuits, without interacting with each other? The answer(s) to this question may give us some clue as to how we may bring the two aspects closer together in the future and thereby ensure a greater cross-fertilization between them than has happened so far.

We may put forward and consider briefly two reasons which account substantially for the lack of interaction between research and practice in chemical education.

(i)   In reports of research findings, e.g. those found in articles and papers published in learned journals, the implications of such findings for the practice of chemical education are frequently not sufficiently elaborated for the teacher/practitioner to incorporate and apply them in his or her teaching.

(ii)   Research findings are often met by practitioners with considerable scepticism; this is particularly true if the research findings appear to be in conflict with the practitioner's personal convictions and opinions.

The first of these points is readily illustrated by reference to the considerable amount that has been done over the past 15 years to explore pupils' misconceptions in chemistry and their problem-solving behaviour. Such studies have provided us with valuable insights into the causes of pupils' learning difficulties in chemistry (and other branches of science), insights that ought to be translatable into improved classroom practices. Yet, by and large, this translation has not happened, chiefly because such studies have rarely been followed up by serious attempts to evolve instructional strategies for, e.g. overcoming pupils' learning difficulties or improving their problem-solving capabilities.

There exist, of course, welcome exceptions to this. For example, the Children's Learning in Science (CLIS) project has deliberately addressed itself to the task of exploring novel teaching strategies for overcoming learning difficulties that stem from pupils' misconceptions in science [2]. But such attempts to translate research findings into strategies for teaching are still relatively rare.

If genuine benefit is to be derived from chemical education research, it is essential that closer links are established between it and the practice of chemical education. This is a challenge that faces both researchers and practitioners and calls for a cooperative effort on their part. There are three lines of action that can be taken in order to close the existing gap between research and practice in chemical education:

(i)   evaluation of past researches to establish 'lessons to be learned' from them for classroom practice and curriculum design;

(ii)   setting of an 'agenda for research', in which particular attention is given to the identification of research topics that are both 'important' to and potentially 'beneficial' for, the practice of chemical education;

(iii) enhanced emphasis on 'classroom-related' research—with researchers and teachers working in partnership.

HOW GENERALLY APPLICABLE ARE RESEARCH FINDINGS?

Most empirical research in education (including chemical education) that concerns issues of learning and teaching, tends to be conducted in some instructional setting which has characteristics that are specific to that setting and not readily reproducible elsewhere. For example, we may conduct a study into problem-solving behaviour and would, for that purpose, select a particular range of problems to be tackled by a particular set of pupils who would previously have been exposed to particular curricular influences. Any findings obtained from this study would obviously apply to the particular situation investigated, but may not necessarily be applicable to other, apparently similar contexts. This raises the question of how 'generalizable' are the results derived from educational researches.

The issue of generalizability is of central concern not only to those who carry out research in chemical (and other branches of) education, but also to those who are interested in applying the results of research studies in, e.g. curriculum development and the design of instruction. Without some reasonable guarantee that research findings derived from one context are, in fact, transferable to another context (provided that the latter is fairly similar to the original one), the scope for making research 'applicable' would considerably diminish.

Some clue about the generalizability of educational research findings may be obtained from the comparison of results derived from different studies that apparently addressed themselves to the same basic research question, but investigated this for different contexts. A simple, yet instructive example of this was provided by Hermann who, in 1969, reviewed some 48 different research studies into the relative merits of discovery learning and expository teaching, respectively [3]. Recognizing that different researchers had used different research settings for their investigations (using, for example, different age groups of pupils and different subject matter to be learned, as well as somewhat different criteria of effectiveness and superiority of teaching approach), Hermann confined himself to counting the number of studies that had indicated a superiority of the one method over the other. Hermann's findings are summarized in Table 1. It should be noted that two measures of effectiveness were considered by him:

(i)   acquisition and retention of information/knowledge by the learner;

(ii)   acquisition of 'discovery skills' by the learner, i.e. his or her ability to derive knowledge and information through a process of (usually guided) discovery learning.

Table 1 Summary analysis of research findings about the relative effectiveness of discovery learning and expository teaching (adapted from [3]).

Criterion used	Result	
	Discovery superior to expository	Expository superior to discovery
retention of information		
early (after 1 week)	4 (1)	8 (2)
late (after 3 months)	5 (1)	5 (2)
discovery skills		
early (after 1 week)	10 (6)	3 (–)
late (after 3 months)	7 (4)	4 (1)

In each cell, the first figure represents the total number of studies for which the particular result was obtained. The figure in parentheses indicates how many of the studies yielded statistically significant results.

The results in Table 1 indicate clearly that the question of whether discovery learning is superior, as an instructional strategy, to expository teaching is still largely unresolved, at least in the sense that it cannot be answered in a generally valid way. If the issue is judged on a probabilistic basis, the case for discovery learning approaches appears to be somewhat stronger than that for the expository strategy: the overall ratio of the numbers of studies favouring the discovery approach to the number of investigations showing the expository method to be superior, is 26 : 20, if no distinction is made between the various criteria. However, when the late retention criterion is considered, the two methods appear equivalent, although initially the expository method produces better retention. For the discovery skills criterion, a distinct initial superiority of the discovery technique is noted, although this advantage apparently reduces in the course of three months. We need to view verdicts like these with appropriate caution, of course: they are summary verdicts which, even if they were accepted as a basis for instructional decision-making, would not necessarily apply to each and every situation for which the decision is made.

The qualitative 'head-counting' approach to the evaluation of educational research results that was used by Hermann, is relatively unsophisticated and has in recent years been superseded by an approach called meta-analysis (see Glass *et al.* [4]). The essence of meta-analysis is that it produces quantitative information about a relationship between two variables, e.g. a particular instructional intervention and learning outcomes, by estimating effect sizes.

The simplest, and most informative, measure of effect size Δ is the mean difference between experimental and control groups divided by the within-group standard deviation:

$$\Delta = (X_E - X_C)/S_X,$$

where X denotes mean scores and S represents the standard deviation. The subscripts E and C refer to the experimental and the control groups, respectively.

Table 2   Selected meta-analysis results concerning the effect of different instructional strategies on pupil learning and achievement (adapted from Fraser *et al.* [5]).

Instructional procedure (with brief descriptions)	Number of studies	Effect size /SD units
Use of 'advance organizer' techniques (deliberate orientation of learners, at the beginning of the instructional intervention, to the knowledge and skills to be acquired)		
• clear link established to knowledge previously acquired by learner		0.70
• non-specific bridging, making references to other, related subject matter and/or applications		0.00
Mode of presentation of 'advance organizers'		
• spoken		0.68
• written		0.34
Overall effect of 'advance organizers' in science (used under various conditions)	16	0.24
Questioning in science (systematic inclusion of pre-prepared questions into a structured teaching programme; this is not to be taken as 'casual questioning'; questions relate directly to the subject matter taught, and lead to pupil activities)	11	0.56
Wait-time in science (allowing adequate thinking time before answers to questions are expected or accepted, something like 8–10 seconds wait-time is recommended)	2	0.53
Provision of detailed feedback (on homework and assignments, with emphasis on explaining/correcting errors and/or suggesting ways of improving performance)	28	0.54
Expression of praise	14	0.16
Individualization of instruction (with emphasis on self-pacing)	131	0.17

The advantage of this effect size measure is that it is independent of the actual experimental results obtained during a particular research study: instead of focusing on absolute experimental mean scores, it describes the relative difference between them and does so in terms of units of a standard deviation. The larger the value of Δ calculated, the greater is the effect of the intervention to which it relates. In the evaluation of a multitude of different researches into the same basic relationship, an average effect size is normally determined.

Table 2 presents a range of meta-analysis results concerning the effect of different instructional strategies on pupil learning and achievement. The data have been selected from a comprehensive report by Fraser *et al.* [5]; in this selection, preference has been given to data that relate directly or predominantly to science education. Wherever possible, the number of studies considered in the meta-analyses is indicated.

The descriptions given in the first column of Table 2 should provide an adequate characterization of the various instructional procedures to render their further discussion unnecessary. However, it is noted that there are considerable variations in the effect size determined for these procedures. Among the procedures that appear to produce particularly strong enhancement in pupil learning are the use of 'advance organizers' (provided these establish clear links to the knowledge previously acquired by the learner), the use of systematic structured questioning, the provision of adequate 'wait-time' and the provision of detailed feedback to pupils on their learning. By comparison, certain other procedures appear to be relatively ineffective as means of enhancing pupil learning, among them the individualization of instruction and the expression of praise for achievement.

Effect size data, like those listed in Table 2, enable the science educator to make informed judgements about the likely benefit that can be derived from the adoption of a particular instructional feature, compared with a situation where it is absent: it is self-evident that the larger the Δ-value for a particular instructional feature, the greater is the potential benefit, in terms of pupil learning, that it produces. (There is no agreed threshold value for Δ below which the adoption of an instructional feature would be regarded as 'not worthwhile'. However, instructional procedures for which Δ is less than, say, 0.25, might be regarded as not holding out the promise of a significant enhancement of learning.) However, it is important to recognize that the adoption of a particular instructional feature does not, in itself, guarantee a significant enhancement in the quality of learning. Whether such enhancement actually takes place, needs to be examined by a special research study.

SOME EXAMPLES OF RECENT AND CONTEMPORARY RESEARCHES

Having discussed some general issues concerning chemical education research and its relationship to the practice of chemistry teaching, we turn our attention to some contemporary research areas. Inevitably, the selection of research studies for consideration here is somewhat arbitrary, but it is intended to illustrate some of the issues that currently engage our interest. All the examples chosen relate to the educational dimension of chemical (science) education, because it is here that most of the research efforts are nowadays made.

The overwhelming majority of recent and contemporary researches in chemical education is concerned with the exploration of causes of pupils' learning difficulties as they relate to, and affect, the acquisition of chemical/scientific concepts and problem-solving skills. The term learning difficulty, in this context, may refer to any situation where a pupil fails to grasp a concept or idea, or solve a problem, as the result of one or more of the following factors:

(i)   the nature of the ideas/knowledge already possessed by the pupil, or the inadequacy of such knowledge, in relation to the concept to be acquired or the problem to be solved;

(ii)   the demand and complexity of a learning task in terms of information processing, compared with the pupil's information-handling capacity;

(iii) communication problems arising from language use, e.g. in relation to technical terms or to general terms with context-specific specialized meanings, or the complexity of sentence structure and syntax used by the teacher (or in a textbook) compared with the pupil's own language capacity;

(iv) a mismatch between instructional approaches used by the teacher and the pupil's preferred learning mode (learning style).

The first of these factors has been the subject of considerable research in recent years and is closely linked to notions such as 'misconceptions', 'alternative frameworks', 'children's science', 'common sense science', etc., which are now well established in science education research. Aspects relating to this factor are described in Chapter 15. Likewise, language issues in the teaching of science (cf. factor (iii) above) are discussed in Chapter 16. Consequently, no further reference is made here to these factors.

In the following sections, some recent research work is presented and discussed that relates to factors (ii) and (iv) above. In the first, an account is given of some studies in which the effect of (learning) task variables on pupils' learning is explored; in the second, we report briefly on attempts to identify the effect of individual differences among pupils on their preference for different teaching and learning modes.

Task variables and learning outcomes

We shall examine two particular features under this heading:

(i)   the effect of different instructional conditions upon observational attainment in chemistry;

(ii) the effect of the complexity of problem-solving tasks upon pupils' problem-solving behaviour.

The examples quoted will illustrate how pupils' success in learning and problem solving is significantly affected by the way in which learning/problem-solving tasks are designed and presented.

Observational attainment in chemistry

Observation is a key skill in chemistry and lies at the heart of practical work. Success in observational tasks is often a prerequisite for success in practical work as a whole: erroneous observations will cause invalid or incomplete conclusions to be drawn. For this reason, it is desirable to maximize, if at all possible, pupils' observational attainment.

A survey of laboratory guides and worksheets produced by a variety of curriculum projects leads to the conclusion that three main modes of task orientation tend to be employed. These are, when expressed in a somewhat idealized form:

(i)   observational tasks have to be accomplished in an open-ended way, i.e. without any form of cueing to the nature of the observations to be made;

(ii) observational tasks are so formulated that the pupil receives cueing to some, but not all, observations to be made (partial-direction);

(iii) observational tasks are carried out with full cueing to all possible observations being provided through a checklist.

These three modes obviously provide different instructional conditions for the conduct of observational tasks. Therefore, the question is of interest whether the modes are equally effective or whether they lead to different levels of observational attainment.

In an attempt to shed light on this question, pupils aged 15 to 16 years following GCE O-level courses were exposed to a series of simple test-tube reactions and asked to record their observations on these reactions. The reactions involved changes in colour, the formation or disappearance of solids (from solutions), the formation of gases and thermal (temperature) changes. The observational situations chosen varied in their complexity (expressed in terms of the actual number of possible observations) from 0 to 9.

The detailed findings from these studies have been published elsewhere [6, 7], therefore, attention is drawn here only to the key results. The most important of these concern the influence task orientation made on observational attainment. The relevant data are as follows:

open-ended mode: mean score 58%

partial-direction mode: mean score 50%

checklist mode: mean score 64%.

It is evident from these figures that observational attainment is affected by the conditions under which observational tasks are carried out. The order of effectiveness is seen to be:

checklist > open-ended > partial-direction.

The superiority of the checklist mode can readily be ascribed to the fact that it provides the pupil with extensive cueing to the full range of possible observations. However, if the effect of cueing is to enhance observational attainment, why should this effect appear reversed in the case of the partial-direction mode?

To explore this aspect, attention was given to an examination of the nature of observational errors. This led to the recognition that two types of error were made by pupils: *errors of omission* where a pupil had failed to perceive changes that had actually occurred, and *illusory errors* which involved a pupil reporting changes that, in reality, had not occurred. The two types of error are, of course, independent of each other. Errors of omission effectively represent the difference between the maximum score on an observation test and the actual score obtained (in the present case, these have been expressed in percentages). Illusory errors, as such, do not relate to omission errors or observational attainment, except for those 'correct' observations that may have resulted from the pupil's illusion, rather than his or her actual observation.

A useful indication of the effect of the three task definition modes on the illusory error rate can be gained from the ratio of illusory errors to total errors:

illusory errors / (illusory errors + omission errors).

The relevant percentage values of this are given in Figure 2 which also shows the omission error rates. It is seen that the mode of task definition affects both types of error, but that the effect of the checklist mode is particularly pronounced for the illusory errors. As is seen, the use of a checklist induces

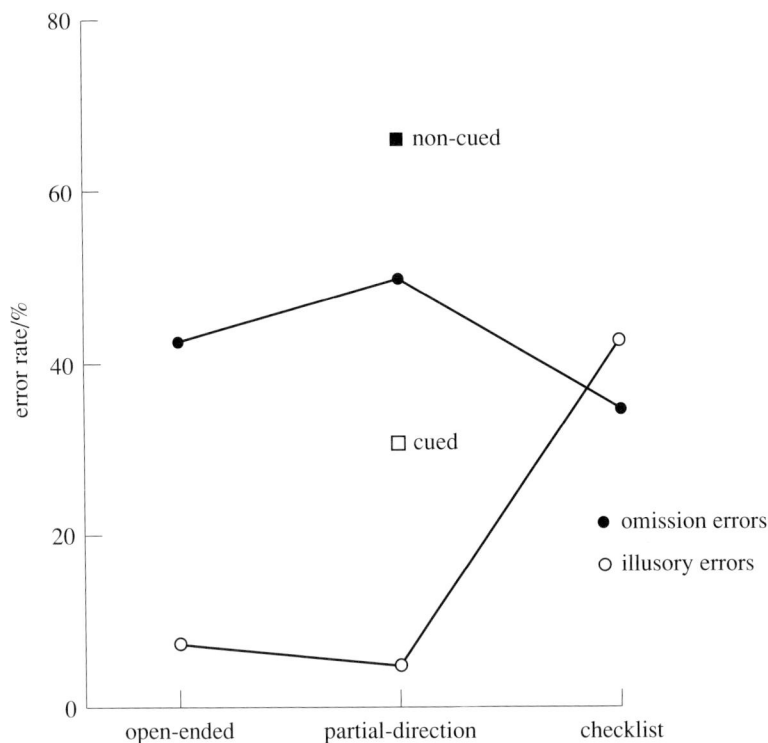

Figure 2   Observational error rates as a function of the three modes of
task definition: open-ended, partial-direction and checklist.

pupils to report observations which, in reality, could not have been made: it has
a strong 'suggestive' effect, something that is absent from the other two modes
of task definition.

For the partial-direction mode, the analysis of errors of omission can be taken
further, by relating it to cued and non-cued observations, respectively. When
this was done, a major difference appeared in that the omission error rates for
the cued observations amounted to 31%, whilst that for the non-cued
observations was 66% (see Figure 2).

The conclusion to be drawn from this is an interesting one. It appears that
observational attainment relating to those changes to which the pupils are
alerted, is actually enhanced as the result of specific cueing, even in comparison
with the general cueing provided through the checklist mode. However, in
relation to non-cued observation the partial-direction mode leads to a distinct
short-fall in observational attainment, compared with the open-ended mode: it
appears as though the provision of cueing to some observations introduces a
'blind-folding' effect on the non-cued observations.

This example demonstrates that instructional conditions and modes of task
definition can, and do, have a significant influence on pupil performance, even in
seemingly simple situations, such as observations made in the context of
qualitative test-tube reactions. Teachers need to be aware of these effects and

take them into account in the planning of their lessons and practical sessions. In this way, it may be possible to enhance the attainment of their pupils.

Question demand and problem-solving ability

An interesting and potentially useful line of research in chemical education has recently been developed by Johnstone and El-Banna [8]. The basis of their work is a set of psychological research findings concerning people's 'working memory capacity' which represents the number of pieces of information individuals can operate on simultaneously.

According to Miller [9], most people can hold only about 7±2 information units in their short-term or working memory, although this figure has been claimed by some researchers to be too high [10]. Regardless of what the actual figure is or might be, it appears that people's capacity to handle information units simultaneously is very limited. Some further important pronouncements about this aspect stem from the Canadian psychologist Pascual-Leone [11] whose work suggests that:

- the working memory capacity is different from person to person;
- for a particular person, the working memory capacity appears fairly constant, certainly over an age span of several years;
- the number of information units with which a person can work simultaneously, tends to fall within the range $Y = 4$ to $Y = 7$.

The immediate consequence of the foregoing points must be that, if a learning task makes excessive demands on a student's working memory, learning difficulties will ensue. We may postulate the following:

> 'If the number of information units required for a learning (or problem-solving) task is in excess of the learner's working memory capacity, the task cannot be solved.'

Johnstone and El-Banna, in a series of investigations, have provided considerable evidence in support of this postulate. In one of their investigations [8], they set out to investigate the relationship between the following quantities:

(i)   students' working memory capacity;

(ii)   the theoretical complexity of a range of chemical problems, measured in terms of the number of information units required for their solution;

(iii) the proportion of students who successfully solved the various problems.

The results of the study, which was carried out on 471 upper secondary and university students, are summarized in Figure 3. It is seen that the success rate in problem-solving situations decreases strongly as soon as the number of thought steps (Z) needed to solve a particular problem exceeds the working memory capacity of the learner.

Johnstone and El-Banna's findings furnish a further example of how the complexity or demand of a chemical problem influences the extent to which it can be solved by a pupil. However, it adds one additional facet to the relationship between task characteristic and achievement: this is a quality (working memory capacity, in this case) which resides within the pupil and thus functions as a mediating characteristic.

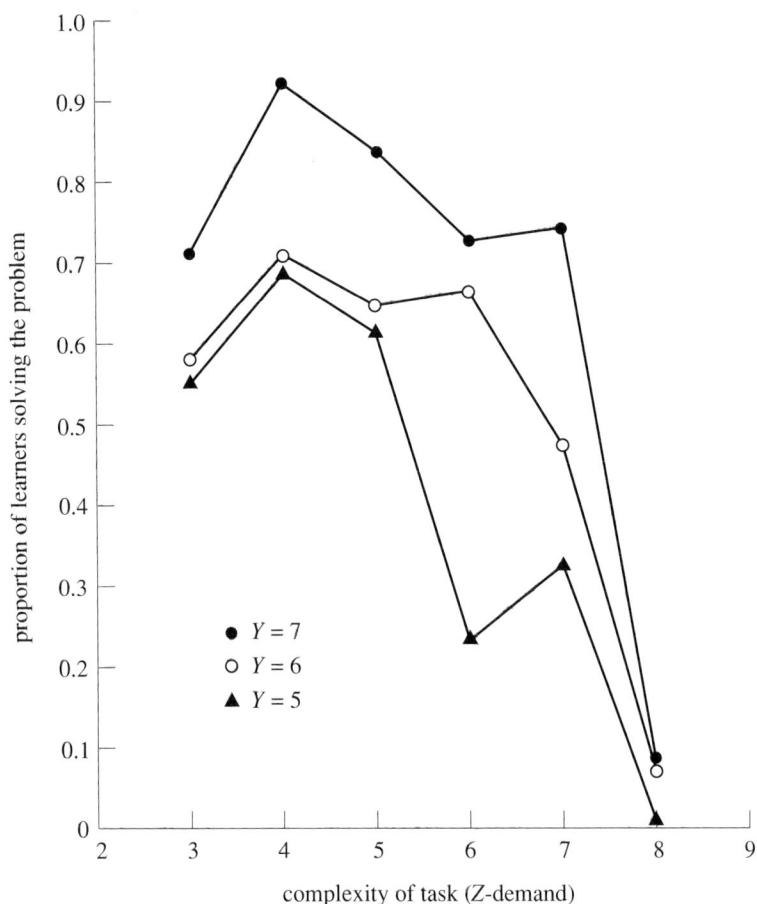

Figure 3   The relationship between question facility and question demand, for student groups with different working memory capacities. Y is the short-term (working memory) capacity of learner and Z is the number of thought steps needed to solve the problem. (Adapted from [8]).

The fact that pupils' working memory is limited needs to be borne in mind in the design and formulation of learning tasks: if a task is so formulated that it makes an undue demand upon a learner's working memory, it will not be tackled successfully by him or her. White [12] gives a simple, but instructive example of this with reference to the statement: 'Concentrated sulphuric acid is a powerful dehydrating agent'. He suggests that a relatively inexperienced student would probably perceive this statement as comprising a large number of information units, e.g.:

(Concentrated) (sulphuric) (acid) (is a) (powerful) (de)(hydrating) (agent).

Here, each information unit is enclosed in parentheses. An experienced chemist, by comparison, may perceive the same statement in a far less fragmented way, e.g.:

(Concentrated sulphuric acid) (is a) (powerful) (dehydrating agent).

Thus, what to the inexperienced learner appears as a conglomerate of seven or eight separate information units, is seen by the expert as a set of only four such units.

The process of bringing together elements of information into groups or parcels is generally referred to as 'chunking'. It is through the process of chunking that we reduce for ourselves the complexity of the information that reaches us. As White [12] aptly observes, when interpreting Johnstone's findings:

> 'Size and therefore number of chunks perceived in a situation is one of the big differences between the knowledgeable person (expert, teacher, adult) and the ignorant (beginner, student, child). Almost paradoxically, an expert inhabits a simpler world than a beginner because the expert breaks it into a smaller number of meaningful units.'

The last point in this statement is generally not sufficiently appreciated by us in relation to our teaching and our pupils' learning.

Individual differences and science teaching

The notion that instructional procedures in science education (and other areas of education) should be matched to learner characteristics in order to maximize the effectiveness of the teaching/learning process, has been widely accepted for a considerable period [13]. Among the learner characteristics that have been considered in this context are certain intellectual characteristics, e.g. pupils' conceptual level [14] and diverse cognitive styles [15]; personality variables, e.g. pupils' warmth/enthusiasm [15]; and a range of affective characteristics, e.g. pupils' attitudes, interest and motivation [16, 17]. (Cognitive styles represent relatively stable and characteristic ways in which people select, perceive and process information with which they are confronted. Some well-known cognitive styles are field dependence/field independence (expressing the extent to which a learner tends to extract information from an otherwise distracting background), convergent/divergent thinking, and impulsivity/reflectivity in thinking.)

It has to be said that the pronouncements found in the literature about the matching of instructional procedures with pupil characteristics are not always the result of empirical research: often they are based on epistemological analysis and then have the quality of hypotheses, rather than established research findings. Thus, the general question of how learner characteristics affect and influence pupils' response to different instructional approaches and features still offers much scope for deliberate and purposeful investigations and development work. It is one area of research that has considerable potential for bringing about a strong link with the practice of science education.

Cognitive styles and science learning

In the following, a brief account is given of some studies which sought to explore the effect of pupils' cognitive styles leanings on their learning of science/chemistry.

In one such study, carried out by Lourdusamy [18] in collaboration with the present author, an attempt was made to explore how pupils with different cognitive styles responded to discovery-based and expository instructional approaches in chemistry. In particular, the study focused on the way in which learning outcomes from the two instructional modes, and pupils' reactions to the modes were affected by different cognitive styles. Among the cognitive styles considered during the investigation were field independence/field dependence, convergency/divergency, and impulsivity/reflectivity.

The results obtained demonstrated that cognitive styles have fairly predictable influences on pupils' learning and attainment. For example, field-independent pupils tended to learn relatively better from discovery-based learning tasks than their field-dependent counterparts, even after allowances had been made for differences in pupils' pre-knowledge and IQ. For other cognitive styles, similar differentiations in achievement were found. Full details of these findings have been given by Lourdusamy [18].

No less interesting, and perhaps even more important in its potential implication for teaching, was the personal (attitudinal) response of pupils of different cognitive styles towards the two instructions strategies. Two particular aspects were examined:

(i)   pupils' perception of the ease or difficulty of learning from the two approaches;

(ii)   their enjoyment of learning from the two methods.

Table 3 summarizes the findings for just two of the cognitive styles examined and does so in a qualitative way. It is seen that field-independent and field-dependent pupils have similar perceptions about the ease or difficulty of learning by discovery; in contrast, as far as 'enjoyment' is concerned, a clear differentiation in perception occurs, with field-independent pupils reacting distinctly more favourably towards discovery learning. The pattern for the convergence/divergence style of thinking is evidently different from that observed for the field-independence/dependence style.

Table 3   The effect of pupils' cognitive styles on their reaction to discovery learning compared with expository teaching (adapted from [18]).

Cognitive style	Difficulty	Enjoyment
field independence / dependence	n.s.	field independent > field dependent
convergence / divergence	divergent > convergent	n.s.

n.s. = statistically not significant.

The results referred to in this section so far are given for illustrative purposes only. They are meant to demonstrate that the kinds of general pronouncements about what is 'good' in education and what is not, usually involve gross oversimplification, with the result that only limited credence can be given to them.

It should be mentioned here that several other studies have also looked at cognitive styles as potential determinants of—or, at least, as factors affecting—pupils' learning behaviour. In this context, the focus has been mainly on the field-dependence/field-independence variable. For example, Ward [7], in his examination of the effect of modes of task definition on observational attainment in practical chemistry, also found field dependence/independence to have a significant effect on attainment: field-independent pupils tended to outperform the field-dependent ones.

Another study suggesting that a significant relationship exists between pupils' attainment (in chemical problem solving) and their level of field independence, is that by Johnstone and El-Banna [19]. As already stated above, the main purpose of this study was the exploration of pupils' ability to solve chemical problems as a function of (i) the complexity of the problem to be solved, and (ii) pupils' working memory.

The main finding reported by Johnstone and El-Banna was that, when the number of pieces of information that had to be manipulated for the purpose of solving a problem, exceeded the pupil's working memory capacity, then the problem could not be solved. However, they also made the additional finding that students' success in problem-solving tasks could be affected by their level of field independence: when students solved problems with memory demands close to the limit of the students' working memory capacity, a fairly strong correlation was noticed between their attainment score and the degree of their field independence. The highest such correlation was $r = 0.5$, significant at the $p = 0.001$ level.

Johnstone and El-Banna offered an interesting explanation for this observation. Recognizing that field independence is a measure of the capacity to separate 'signal' from 'noise', they argued that field-independent pupils are better able to extract the signals from the problem-related information (and, therefore, to reject the noise associated with it) than their field-dependent counterparts, even if both groups show identical working memory capacities. Consequently, the field-independent pupils turn out to be the better problem solvers.

What the studies outlined here show, is that our students and pupils differ from one another in their dispositions and that these have, or can have, a marked effect on the way in which they (the students and pupils) respond to, and succeed in, the various learning situations in which we engage them. Unfortunately, relatively little has been done so far to identify the exact nature of the interactions between pupil characteristics and learning behaviour, let alone translate these into effective strategies for teaching.

Motivational traits and instructional preferences

Recently, the author and his colleagues have turned their attention away from cognitive styles to pupils' motivational characteristics. Of particular interest in this context has been the question of how such characteristics influence pupils' preferences for, or dislikes of, the various pedagogical (instructional) strategies that are used in science education or whose use is advocated.

This change in direction was made in the recognition that few previous researchers had focused on the exploration of possible matching between curricular features and affective variables, especially those relating to learner motivation and interest, despite the fact that the literature contains numerous suggestions about how pupils' motivation to learn science can be enhanced. On the whole, these suggestions fall into two broad categories:

(i)   suggestions relating to the nature, structuring and presentation of subject matter;

(ii) suggestions concerning the nature of the pedagogical procedures and intentions to be adopted by teachers, as well as the climate of the learning environment to be established by the teacher.

Numerous attempts that have been made to influence pupils' disposition to the learning of science (including chemistry) in the context of curriculum development projects, have focused on the first of these categories: a frequent approach has been, and still is, to build curriculum content around real-life problems or to establish the 'relevance' of a science by stressing its uses and applications. Essentially, these and similar strategies aim at bringing about an increase in pupils' interest in science.

By contrast, teachers' pedagogical procedures and activities which arise from the use of particular teaching strategies, may be claimed to have a direct bearing on pupils' motivation. It is logical to assume that instructional procedures and learning environments which the pupil perceives as agreeable will enhance his or her willingness to engage in learning activities; those that are found to be disagreeable will have the opposite effect [17].

Already in 1969, Adar had suggested that pupils differ in their motivational characteristics and that these differences may well influence their (the pupils') responses to different modes of instruction [20]. On the basis of her own investigations, she postulated the existence of four different 'motivational types' of pupil, based on the predominance in a pupil of the following 'needs':

•   the need to achieve;

•   the need to satisfy one's curiosity;

•   the need to discharge a duty;

•   the need to affiliate with other people.

The four motivational types of pupil were referred to by Adar as 'achiever pupils', 'curious pupils', 'conscientious pupils' and 'sociable pupils', respectively. A preliminary analysis [17] of the implications of this particular view of motivation and the existence of pupils with different motivational traits for the instructional scene, led to the conclusion that any interactions that might exist between motivational traits and learning behaviour would relate to the pedagogical features prevalent in a teaching situation, rather than the actual (subject matter) content of the instruction. As far as the nature of such interactions is concerned, the two authors made a number of predictions, for example:

(i)   achiever pupils have a definite preference for competitive learning environments, whilst sociable pupils prefer to learn in non-competitive settings;

(ii) curious pupils have a distinct preference for discovery-type learning and problem-solving tasks, whereas conscientious pupils prefer learning situations with clearly defined goals and structure.

Recently, Kempa and Martin Diaz [21, 22] have been able to probe empirically into the relationship between pupils' motivational traits and their preferences for different instructional procedures. The following is a brief summary of the main findings obtained from this work (for further details see [21, 22]).

Two main instruments were developed and used for the study. The first was a 60-item self-rating questionnaire, designed to determine pupils' motivational characteristics in terms of the four Adar traits. Each item presented a statement or some 'argument' concerning a motivational characteristic and called for a response on a five-point 'applicability-to-me' scale. The items were written to correspond to the four motivational patterns proposed by Adar [20].

The second instrument was developed for the purpose of probing into pupils' preferences for different instructional procedures and features. It comprised 80 rating items, covering the various dimensions and subdimensions of instructional procedures shown in Table 4. Both instruments were administered to 390 secondary-school pupils, aged 15 years, drawn from five different schools (in Spain).

In the evaluation of the results from the study, each motivational pattern was examined separately. In order to establish any trends with respect to the various instructional features, four levels of motivation were used in each case, based on quartiles, ranging from 'bottom' (denoting the lowest motivational level) to 'top' (denoting the highest motivational level).

Table 4   Dimensions and subdimensions of instructional procedures.

A	Modes of knowledge acquisition
	A1 Formal teaching with emphasis on input from teacher
	A2 Use of books and other materials as a source for obtaining information
	A3 Note-taking as a means of obtaining an accurate record of information
	A4 Discovery learning procedures
B	Working arrangements
	Bl Pursuit of study through individual work
	B2 Involvement in group learning activities
C	Practical work in science
	C1 Carrying out practical work (as opposed to 'non-experimental' learning)
	C2 Experimental work based on precise instructions given by teacher
D	Organization of teaching
	Dl Provision of opportunity to pursue one's own enquiry
E	Evaluation of progress
	El Regular assessment by teacher
	E2 General dislike of being tested

During the analysis of the data obtained from the study, a further subdimension could be identified. This was termed 'risk-taking' (RT) and denotes the willingness on the pupil's part to contribute ideas to discussions, even if they should prove 'wrong' (cf. Table 5).

Table 5   Summary of the relationships between pupils' motivational traits and preferences for instructional procedures.

Instructional procedure	Motivational trait			
	Achiever	Curious	Conscientious	Sociable
Mode of knowledge acquisition				
A1 Formal teaching	−	−	+	− −
A2 Learning from reference texts, etc.		++	− −	
A4 Use of discovery learning	+	++		(+)
Working arrangements				
B1 Individual work				− −
B2 Involvement in group learning			(+)	++
Practical work				
C1 Carrying out practical work		++		(+)
C2 Experimental work with instructions		− −	++	
Organization of teaching				
D1 Pursuit of one's own enquiry	+	+		++
Evaluation of progress				
E1 Assessment by teacher			++	
E2 General dislike of being tested				++
RT Risk-taking		+		

Strong preference trends are indicated by '++'; '− −' denotes the opposite. Moderate preference trends are indicated by '+', with '−' denoting moderate dislike; '(+)' indicates a moderate preference trend due to an indirect, rather than a direct relationship between preference and motivational trait.

A summary of the key findings of the study is given in Table 5. Only those relationships are shown for which a significant trend of preference for, or dislike of, an instructional procedure with level of motivation was observed.

As is seen, a number of strong relationships between motivational traits and instructional preference variables exist. Let us highlight just a few of them:

- formal teaching methods seem to appeal only to conscientious pupils;
- independent learning techniques (exemplified in the present case by 'use of reference books') is strongly liked by curious pupils, but equally strongly rejected by the conscientious ones;
- 'doing practical work' is an activity that appeals to the curious pupils, but not when it is highly prescribed. Conscientious pupils, in contrast, express a clear preference for rigorous instructions;
- sociable pupils display a distinct preference for group learning activities, which is coupled with an opposition to individualized work;
- conscientious pupils, unlike pupils in the other categories, show a distinct preference for having their performance and progress monitored by their teachers, which supports the idea that they are strongly teacher-dependent.

FROM RESEARCH TO PRACTICE: CHALLENGES FOR THE FUTURE

The foregoing examples will have demonstrated that learning behaviour (including achievement) and preferences for instructional procedures are significantly influenced by a variety of factors, ranging from task-variables (i.e. the way in which learning tasks are formulated and contextualized) to variables, such as cognitive styles and motivational traits, which reside within the learner. No doubt, as research into this area continues, we shall identify further factors that affect learning and, in this way, increasingly gain insights into determinants of learning and attainment in chemistry.

The development of such insights is, of course, one of the central tasks of chemical education research. However, unless we also attend to the task of translating research findings into practicable teaching strategies, the current gap between research and practice of chemical education will continue to exist, and little benefit will accrue from our research efforts.

The practicability issue merits particular attention in this context. The various examples of research that have been given here, lead to a growing realization that many factors that affect learning and attainment operate at the learner's personal level. For example, misconceptions about particular scientific phenomena are not necessarily common to all our pupils; likewise, studies involving cognitive styles and motivational trait variables demonstrate that different pupils respond differently to different instructional procedures and in what way(s) they do so.

A key question for us to ask is whether it is possible for us to respond to the diversity in styles and traits that we find among our pupils. Can we actually develop instructional strategies and processes that allow for differences among learners and optimize their learning? There is no ready-made answer to this question, but we may attempt to explore this issue briefly.

The task of translating research findings into practicable instructional strategies may be broken down into two subtasks:

(i)   the development of instructional strategies and teaching/learning materials that reflect the research finding;

(ii) the implementation of these strategies in actual teaching situations.

To illustrate how the first of these subtasks might be accomplished, let me draw upon our recent work into motivational traits [21, 22]. This revealed that pupils with different motivational traits differ in their preferences for, or dislike of, particular instructional procedures. If now the assumption is made that, for a particular motivational group, the best instructional approach is the one that matches the learners' preferences, it follows that curious pupils should be treated differently from, e.g. conscientious pupils*. Thus, it is in

---

* This, of course, raises the question whether pupils could satisfactorily be 'categorized' into different motivational types. In the study referred to here, it was possible to associate over 80% of the pupils with one motivational trait or another on the basis of which particular trait appeared strongest, compared with the others.

principle possible to deal satisfactorily with the first of the above subtasks. What about the second, though? How feasible is it to implement multiple teaching procedures in actual teaching situations?

It is in this respect that the greatest difficulties are likely to arise. Two problems, in particular, stand out. The first is that it would seem to be impossible, in conventional teaching settings, to cater simultaneously for a variety of different learning styles and/or instructional preferences. The second is that, even if the first problem could be solved, an actual matching of learner characteristics and instructional strategy might almost be impossible to achieve: for example, the determination of learner characteristics itself may prove too difficult and/or too unreliable. Also, some teachers may see such a process as labelling and object to it on ideological grounds.

In view of these difficulties, it is perhaps appropriate not to look towards conventional teaching settings when thinking of the implementation subtask, but to consider the potential of new approaches to teaching. In this context, current attempts to introduce 'flexible learning systems' come to mind; these can include features such as 'individualized learning', 'resource-based learning', 'open-learning' and 'distance learning'. All these strategies depart significantly from the conventional 'teacher-directed' approach to teaching and learning.

If a learning system is genuinely flexible, it ought to be able to respond to pupils' preferences and inclinations. It also ought to enable pupils to decide, or at least contribute to decisions about, what teaching/learning strategies they will be exposed to. Thus, a kind of self-selection of instructional procedure should become possible in which pupils themselves are the arbiters of what approach to learning suits them best. A possible sequence for achieving this might involve the following steps:

- translate information about learning styles and instructional preferences into teaching approaches;

- develop teaching materials in accordance with learning styles and preferences;

- offer pupils alternative learning routes, e.g. in the form of resource-based learning and flexible learning packages;

- allow pupils to choose their learning route in accordance with their personal preferences. (The assumption here is that pupils will choose so as to minimize the conflict between teaching approach and learning style/preference.)

CONCLUSION

In this Chapter, we have examined the way in which chemical education research has developed over the last 25 years. We have also looked at some areas of research that are of current interest. In doing so, the focus has been on the education component of chemical education research, rather than its chemical one.

There can be little doubt that the quality of chemical education research that is now undertaken, is as sound as the quality of research in chemistry or in other branches of education. Research publications on chemical education issues that now appear in learned journals are no less rigorous and scholarly than are the research papers in the various branches of chemistry or in the other educational sciences. Thus, we may claim that chemical education research has come of age.

However, one major challenge still remains. This is for us all, teachers and researchers alike, to forge closer links between research and the practice of chemical education. This requires practitioners and researchers to work together, with teachers acting as researchers and vice versa. To bring this about is a major task for the future.

REFERENCES

1   Dawson, B. E. and Letton, K. M. (eds), *Science Education Research and Development Abstracts*. (The Royal Society of Chemistry, 1989).

2   Needham, R. and Hill, P., *Teaching strategies for developing understanding in science*. (Centre for Studies in Science and Mathematics Education, University of Leeds, 1987).

3   Hermann, G., 'Learning by Discovery: a critical review of studies', *Journal of Experimental Education*, 1969, **38**, pp. 59–72.

4   Glass, G. V., McGaw, N. and Smith, M. L., *Meta-analysis in Social Research*. (Sage Publications, 1981).

5   Fraser, B. J., Walberg, H. J., Welch, W. W. and Hattie, J. F., 'Synthesis of educational research productivity', *International Journal of Education Research*, 1987, **11**, pp. 145–252.

6   Kempa, R. F. and Ward, J. E., 'The effect of different modes of task orientation on observational attainment in practical chemistry', *Journal of Research in Science Teaching*, 1975, **12**, pp. 69–76.

7   Ward, J. E., 'A study of observational attainment in practical work in school chemistry', PhD thesis, University of Keele. (1981).

8   Johnstone, A. H. and El-Banna, H., 'Capacities, demands and processes—a predictive model for science education', *Education in Chemistry*, 1986, **23**, pp. 80–84.

9   Miller, G. A., 'The magical number seven plus or minus two: Some limits on our capacity for processing information', *Psychological Review*, 1956, **63**, pp. 81–97.

10   Broadbent, D. E., 'The magic number seven after fifteen years', in A. Kennedy and A. Wilkes (eds), *Studies in Longterm Memory*. (John Wiley, 1975).

11   Pascual-Leone, J., 'A Neo-Piagetian interpretation of conservation and the problem of horizontal decalages', Paper presented at the Canadian Psychological Association Meeting, Montreal, 1972.

12   White, R., *Learning Science*. (Basil Blackwell, 1988).

13 Cronbach, L. J., 'How can instruction be adapted to individual differences?', in R. M. Gagné (ed.), *Learning and Individual Differences*. (Merrill Books, 1967).

14 Hunt, D. E., *Matching Models in Education. The Co-ordination of Teaching Methods with Students' Characteristics* (Monograph series No. 10). (Ontario Institute for Studies in Education, 1971).

15 Brophy, J. C. and Good, T. L., *Teacher-Student Relationships: Causes and Consequences*. (Holt, Rinehart and Winston, 1974).

16 Good, T. L. and Power, C. N., 'Designing successful classroom environments for different types of student'. *Journal of Curriculum Studies*, 1974, **8**, pp. 45–60.

17 Hofstein, A. and Kempa, R. F., 'Motivating strategies in science education: attempt at an analysis', *European Journal of Science Education*, 1985, **7**, pp. 221–229.

18 Lourdusamy, A., 'The Influence of Selected Cognitive Styles on Learning Behaviour', PhD thesis, University of Keele. (1981).

19 Johnstone, A. and El-Banna, H., 'Understanding learning difficulties—a predictive research model', in R. Kempa, B. Ben-Zvi, A. Hofstein and I. Cohen (eds), *Learning Difficulties in Chemistry*. (Weizmann Institute, 1988).

20 Adar, L., *A Theoretical Framework for the Study of Motivation in Education*. (The Hebrew University, 1969) (in Hebrew).

21 Kempa, R.F. and Martin Diaz, M., 'Motivational traits and preferences for different instructional modes in science—Part 1: Students' motivational traits', *International Journal of Science Education*, 1990, **12**, pp. 194–203.

22 Kempa, R. F. and Martin Diaz, M., 'Students' motivational traits and preferences for different instructional modes in science education—Part 2', *International Journal of Science Education*, 1990, **12**, pp. 205–216.

PART 2
CHEMISTRY AND THE NATIONAL CURRICULUM

Part 2 of *Open Chemistry* addresses a number of key issues that arise from the introduction of the National Curriculum following the *Education Reform Act* of 1988. It is often forgotten that Prime Minister James Callaghan initiated the move towards a National Curriculum in his Ruskin College speech of October 1976. Some of the history of what followed has been presented in the Introduction to *Open Chemistry* but a key issue remains—How does chemistry fit into and relate to the rest of the science curriculum?

In Chapter 5 Reed sets out the formal contribution chemistry is expected to make to the implementation of the National Curriculum and broadens his analysis to include chemistry in the context of cross-curricular themes and the whole curriculum. In Chapter 6 Fairbrother presents a very detailed analysis of the assessment of learning outcomes and how these are required to be reported under the constraints of the 1988 *Education Reform Act* and subsequent Orders. The assessment of outcomes is a very complex issue involving time, resources, INSET and purpose and Fairbrother has taken pains to present, as simply as possible, the nature of the legal requirement. To question much of this would require a separate book!

Chapters 7 and 8 are concerned with the concepts of continuity, progression and coherence. Chapter 7 is an action-centred case study of planning for continuity and progression from Key Stage 2 to the end of Key Stage 4 in a typical secondary school. It raises many important issues such as continuity and progression between Key Stages 2 and 3, assessment, record keeping and curricular planning on limited, and often arbitrary, resource allocations. It sums up many of the problems of National Curriculum implementation. The style of this Chapter is very different from that of the rest of the book for here the key focus is the problems the National Curriculum presents to schools and, indirectly governors, the lay public and others.

Chapter 8 explores the complex issue of articulation between the National Curriculum and the earlier innovation—GCSE. By its very nature this is a Chapter held in a moment of time, where issues of continuity and progression appear to give way to a conflict between norm and criterion referenced assessment and reporting. The Chapter reviews the examination boards' response to the challenge of the National Curriculum long before the dust has settled and equivalencies have been spelt and worked out.

CHAPTER 5

CHEMISTRY AND THE NATIONAL CURRICULUM

Neville Reed

WHAT IS CHEMISTRY?

According to the *Concise Oxford Dictionary* chemistry is defined as 'the study of the (chemical) elements and the compounds they form and the reactions they undergo'. It is the function of dictionaries to give all encompassing definitions for a word or subject but generally it is not possible to make such clear cut decisions. For instance, does fermentation of sugars to yield ethanol lie in the study of biology or chemistry? Similarly does the use of a lead accumulator battery to provide an energy source use chemical or physical principles?

The truth is that it is often difficult to ascribe a scientific phenomenon to only one area of science by using strict discipline boundaries, as is illustrated in the above examples. An added complication is that some scientific phenomena use different terminology depending on the scientific discipline involved. For example, in biology the bonds which link amino acids in peptides are called peptide bonds, whilst in chemistry the same bonds are known as amide bonds.

Not surprisingly the National Curriculum in science also throws up areas of claims and counter claims of what is and what isn't chemistry. To pursue this line of thought too strongly is to ignore the desired coherent nature of the science curriculum, and to promote arguments mainly based on semantics. The role of chemistry within the National Curriculum in science is to relate how the study of the chemical elements and their compounds contribute to the technological society we live in, and how by understanding chemical principles, scientists are able to exercise control over and to modify today's environment. Chemistry is involved in nearly every aspect of our lives and it is important that pupils are aware of this.

THE NATIONAL CURRICULUM

The National Curriculum in science began its phased introduction into schools in 1989, for pupils aged 5, 7 and 11. The statutory requirements only apply to maintained schools and grant-maintained schools (state schools) but not to independent schools nor city technology colleges (the latter are also state schools) which are free to determine their own curricula. However, in reality the independent schools and city technology colleges will be influenced by the National Curriculum if they follow General Certificate of Secondary Education (GCSE) examination courses. The term National Curriculum is curious in its own right, for 'national' the science curriculum is not. In this article, consideration is only given to the science curriculum to be followed in England

and Wales. This is slightly different from the National Curriculum in science devised for Northern Ireland, although both have common roots. Scotland has its own education system and its own form of National Curriculum. However, unlike the rest of the UK it is not statutory.

The science curriculum introduced in 1989 comprised 17 attainment targets and associated programmes of study. By 1991, even before the first cohort of pupils had completed courses based on the statutory requirements, concerns over the manageability of the assessment process led to a major revision [1]. The structure of the new National Curriculum and implications for reporting are discussed in detail in Chapter 6.

The National Curriculum in science has two important components—the attainment targets and the associated programmes of study. The latter is concerned with the material to be used to construct teaching programmes whilst the former relates to assessment. Consequently the attainment targets help to provide an interpretation of the programmes of study, but they do not describe the curriculum to be taught. However, both the programmes of study and the statements of attainment need to be covered by a science department's scheme of work.

The programmes of study are not prescriptive, i.e. they do not specify the context, examples or order in which the concepts and strands* are to be taught. It is up to the teacher to devise the appropriate learning strategies for pupils which takes into account their previous experiences, available resources, the teacher's expertise and interests, and the educational philosophy of the school, e.g. level 5(a) of Attainment Target 3 (AT3 *Materials and their properties*) at Key Stage 3 states:

> 'Pupils should learn how to separate and purify the components of mixtures using physical processes.'

How the pupils learn this part of the curriculum is not prescribed. There are many possible approaches to this topic including:

- using historical contexts, e.g. early salt making;
- problem solving, e.g. which type of crisps contains the most salt?
- role play, e.g. decide which is the most efficient method to obtain fresh drinking water in a desert;
- the so-called 'traditional approach' of teaching the various techniques, e.g. separate salt from sand.

The National Curriculum relies on the expertise of the teacher to choose the appropriate context.

---

* Strands link and develop scientific ideas and statements of attainment through each key stage.

A coherent science course

At each key stage, the programme of study for AT1 *Scientific investigations* provides the framework for delivering the science curriculum. Attainment Target 1 is concerned with the intellectual and practical skills that allow pupils to explore the world of science, i.e. it is concerned with the process of science.

It is planned that ATs 2 to 4 should each have equal weighting (at all key stages) for assessment purposes. The relationship between the weightings for AT1 and ATs 2, 3 and 4 are discussed in Chapter 6. The implication of the weighting is that equal emphasis should be given to the programmes of study associated with ATs 2, 3 and 4. In practice this may prove difficult to monitor because many science departments will choose to devise their own schemes of work based on the whole programme of study for a part or whole of a key stage. Such schemes of work will probably involve rearranging the material found in the programmes of study into new 'units' for teaching purposes. Therefore it will be very difficult to relate one teaching 'unit' to a single attainment target. This approach is to be commended if it enables science departments to deliver a coherent science course.

Each programme of study sets out unifying experiences for pupils. At Key Stage 1 pupils are required to develop communication skills; and to begin to appreciate the role of science in everyday life. By Key Stage 4 these experiences should be developed to include, in addition, the applications and economic, social and technological aspects of science, and the nature of scientific ideas.

In developing a coherent science course at all key stages, teachers will have to take cognizance of the role of chemistry in everyday life. For example in Key Stage 1, pupils could be made aware that chemists make disinfectants which are used to kill 'all known germs'. This idea could be developed more generally in the later key stages when chemistry will have an important role to play when discussing the application and economic, social and technological implications of science and the history of scientific ideas.

ATTAINMENT TARGET 3: MATERIALS AND THEIR PROPERTIES

The programme of study associated with AT3 is part of the school curriculum for all pupils aged 5 to 16. This is the attainment target that can be most closely identified with the study of chemistry.

Thus for the first time, chemistry, albeit in various guises, will have a place in the primary curriculum. Before the introduction of the National Curriculum in 1989, many primary schools taught science, but in the main the emphasis tended to be on biological science (e.g. nature studies) with only a minority of schools covering physical science. In addition science was not well represented in terms of curriculum time in primary schools. Now science, including chemistry, has an important role to play in the primary school.

Four strands are developed in the programme of study throughout the key stages:

(i)   the properties, classification and structure of materials;

(ii)   explanations of the properties of materials;

(iii) chemical changes;

(iv) the Earth and its atmosphere.

A feature associated with the programme of study is that as pupils progress through each key stage, the level of sophistication of the scientific ideas increases. For example, in AT3 the development of chemical ideas on the role of heating, start with melting and solidifying in Key Stage 1 and are developed as shown below.

Key Stage 1

Pupils should develop an awareness of which materials they are using are naturally occurring and which are manufactured. They should explore the effects of heating some everyday substances, for example, *ice, water, wax and chocolate*, in order to understand how heating and cooling bring about melting and solidifying. They should observe materials such as dough, wood and clay which change permanently on heating.

Key Stage 2

Pupils should be given opportunities to compare a range of solids, liquids and gases and recognize the properties which enable classification of materials in this way. Experiments on dissolving and evaporation should lead to developing ideas about solution and solubility.

Key Stage 3

Pupils should investigate changes of state, diffusion, dissolving, and the behaviour of gases under different conditions of temperature and pressure. They should be encouraged to explain these phenomena in terms of their developing ideas of the particulate model of matter. Their study should extend to an investigation of the temperature changes that occur during changes of state and to other changes, such as expansion, that occur during heating and cooling.

Key Stage 4

Pupils should investigate the quantitative relationships between the volume, temperature, and pressure of a gas, and use the kinetic theory to explain changes of state and other phenomena.

All pupils study AT3 *Materials and their properties* in Key Stage 4, but depending on whether they have chosen Model A (leading to a GCSE Science: Double Award examination) or Model B (leading to a Science: Single Award examination), the content is different. Some pupils may even choose to take a course leading to a GCSE examination in chemistry whereupon in addition to the chemical topics found in the programmes of study for Science: Double Award, new chemical concepts and additional material will be studied. (In schools statutorily required to follow the National Curriculum, pupils studying for a GCSE in chemistry will have to study simultaneously for GCSEs in both biology and physics.)

An important feature of the National Curriculum in science is that, as mentioned earlier, it does not prescribe how the material should be taught nor in what order. This is important because it allows a range of courses to be devised, each with a different approach. Examination groups and boards are able to construct GCSE examination syllabuses which satisfy the statutory requirements but present the programmes of study in Key Stage 4 in a variety of ways, e.g. Integrated Science, Combined Science, Co-ordinated Science, Modular Science, and Separate Sciences courses; and with different philosophies, e.g. *Salters' Science*, *Suffolk Science* and *Nuffield Science*.

As a consequence of following the single award in science route at Key Stage 4 pupils continue to study Strands (i) and (ii), but omit Strands (iii) and the (iv). Hence pupils following the route will have little appreciation of the scientific role played by the chemical and pharmaceutical industries in the economic and social development of the society we live in. This is to be regretted and is a cause of concern to many.

For those teaching in secondary schools the academic requirements of the National Curriculum are not onerous because little new material in chemistry has been added. The National Curriculum builds on the 'best practice' that was found in many schools so there is little requirement for 'chemistry teachers' to retrain in basic chemistry, however there will be a need for staff development in some areas such as assessment.

One consequence of the National Curriculum is that more chemistry (and physics and biology) is being taught. This is a direct result of compelling all pupils to study science up to the age of 16 rather than the old practice of allowing them the option to drop science subjects at the age of 14. Obviously this creates a demand for more science teaching, more chemistry teaching and more teachers of chemistry. In some cases, science teachers with no, or very little, expertise in chemistry, (or in many cases a lack of confidence or familiarity in the subject) may find themselves having to deliver the chemical components of the curriculum. Teachers who find themselves in this position will need to draw on the expertise of other colleagues or in-service provision available in their schools. However, in some cases schools will not have a chemistry specialist, so science departments may need to look outside of the school for expert advice from those with the relevant experience. The local science adviser may be able to help directly or should be able to put the school in touch with a chemistry teacher. Alternatively local institutes of higher education may be useful as a source of expertise, and any industrialists involved in the school–industry partnerships may be of help. Distance learning courses such as *Chemistry for Science Teachers* produced by the Open University; and resources produced by industry, professional bodies (e.g. The Royal Society of Chemistry and Institute of Chemical Engineers); and other organizations (e.g. The Association for Science Education and Chemical Industry Education Centre) may also be helpful. So there are many avenues to explore in order to seek advice and guidance.

CHEMISTRY AND ATTAINMENT TARGETS 1, 2 AND 4

The programmes of study associated with attainment targets other than AT3 also feature the development of chemical ideas. In AT1 *Scientific investigation* pupils will learn about chemical techniques, including how to make measurements and observations, interpret chemical data and communicate ideas in an appropriate form. It will also offer pupils the opportunity to carry out an extended investigation into a chemical topic, e.g. the effect of electroplating on the rate of rusting of iron.

Chemical ideas permeate the programmes of study for the other attainment targets as well. As mentioned earlier the notion of whether an idea is classed as chemistry or another subject can be important. No chemist could claim reasonably that 'Pupils should... learn about factors that contribute to good health...' (from Key Stage 2, AT2) is a central chemical idea. However, 'they should find out how animals and plants... are influenced by environmental conditions... and measure these changes, using a variety of instruments' (also from Key Stage 2, AT2) will probably involve the use of fundamental chemical techniques. So to define the study of chemical ideas as those only related to AT3 is incorrect. Hence it will be important for those with responsibility for designing science courses to be aware that chemical ideas are to be found in AT2, and (to a lesser extent) AT4 as well as AT3 and their associated programmes of study. Similar comments can be made for the other scientific disciplines.

It would be improper to claim that chemistry dominates the other attainment targets but it is possible to suggest areas where chemical ideas will be able to contribute to the understanding of scientific phenomena (Table 1).

Table 1 Statements of attainment at various levels which could have associated material in the programme of study involving chemical ideas.

Attainment Targets	Levels
AT2 *Life and living processes*	2a, 2d, 3b, 3c, (5c), (6e), 7b, (8d), (8e), (9d), (9e), 10b, (10d)
AT4 *Physical processes*	3b, 9b

( ) = statement of attainments excluded in the single award in science programme of study at Key Stage 4.

Given that chemical ideas are not restricted to one particular attainment target's programme of study, science departments will have to plan their schemes of work with care. Most secondary schools have subject specialists who will be at hand to advise on particular ideas and concepts. Where no subject specialist is available, the possible sources of advice given in the previous section may be useful.

Whatever the advice, and no matter where it comes from, it will be important that those teaching the schemes of work continue to follow the agreed aims and objectives of the science departments. By doing so a coherent, broad and balanced science course will be delivered that pays due regard to pupils' progression and achievement.

BEYOND THE SCIENCE CURRICULUM

The National Curriculum, in itself, is a matrix of subjects blended together by the use of cross-curricular themes.

The Whole Curriculum [2] describes how, in addition to the National Curriculum subjects, breadth in the school curriculum is to be achieved. The National Curriculum subjects form the foundation of the curriculum and are augmented by religious education, additional subjects (e.g. economics), an accepted range of cross-curricular elements and extra-curricular activities. Chemistry, like physics and biology, has its role to play outside of science because chemistry can contribute to the cross-curricular elements and extra-curricular activities. For the latter, field trips as part of chemistry lessons are now well established in some schools; and many pupils have the opportunity of work experience or work shadowing in industries that involve chemistry as part of their everyday operations. Through the study of chemical ideas pupils will have the opportunity to develop their skills in communication, numeracy, study, problem solving and information technology (e.g. by the use of spread sheets)—but not necessarily all at the same time! By the judicious choice of activities, the study of chemical ideas can yield situations where these skills can be developed.

CROSS-CURRICULAR THEMES

Interestingly, whereas the attainment targets and programmes of study are statutory, the cross-curricular themes are not. In theory, cross-curricular themes could be ignored. In practice, however, schools will benefit from the coherence these themes will bring to the school curriculum. As such, those charged with school inspections will wish to see the cross-curricular themes being used in an appropriate way.

The five cross-curricular themes are designed to help the overall curriculum to attain coherence and the National Curriculum Council has published a series of guides to aid this process [3–7].

To ensure that the themes are developed, science teachers will not only have to liaise with fellow science teachers but also with other colleagues throughout the school. In the end a whole-school policy will probably prove to be the only logistically sensible method of ensuring that the cross-curricular themes knit the whole curriculum together.

The five National Curriculum themes are not discrete entities in themselves but overlap. For example, whilst 'developing attitudes on sensitivity to the effects of economic choices on the environment' is linked to the 'education for economic and industrial understanding' theme, it could equally well belong to the 'environmental education' theme.

Because the science of chemistry takes place all around us and the chemical (and pharmaceutical) industry plays such a significant role in the country's economy, the subject has an important role to play as a vehicle to deliver parts of all of the cross-curricular themes. The cross-curricular themes are in no way prescriptive in what material should be used, hence it is difficult to give a concise description of the role chemistry has to play. However, some suggested topics for cross-curricular themes are given in Figure 1.

Science departments will need to review their teaching programmes at each key stage and consider how the various components of the five cross-curricular themes can be developed. Some components may be particularly well suited to chemistry, whilst others may be so obscure that links will be intangible. Discussions with other departments will then be needed because what must be remembered is that chemistry, and science for that matter, does not have to deliver the cross-curricular themes by itself. There are numerous other subjects (including non-National Curriculum subjects) that have their part to play. Thus the choice of appropriate material must be seen in the light of a whole-school policy, the experiences of the pupils, and the professional judgement and expertise of the teacher.

SUMMARY

Chemical ideas pervade the National Curriculum in science, and are not just associated with one attainment target's programme of study. By working as a team and drawing on specialist expertise from both within and outside of a school coherent schemes of work can be devised that will contain appropriate examples of chemical phenomena.

The extensive nature of the chemical industry and the proximity of chemistry in everyday life makes the study of the subject an ideal vehicle to deliver aspects of the cross-curricular themes.

The study of chemistry, by the judicious choice of examples, chemical ideas and experiences, has an important role to play in the whole school curriculum.

Education for citizenship

- health and safety at work and the law

Health education

- safety in the chemical laboratory
- what chemical additives are put in food?
- are all natural food additives good for you?

Careers education and guidance

- career opportunities for chemists
- career opportunities in the chemical industry
- what NVQs are available in chemistry?
- is there a European chemist qualification?
- training, qualifications and career development
  in the chemical industry

Cross-curricular themes

Environmental education

- effects of chemical pollution on climate
- resource limitation, e.g. supply of copper ore
- impact of industrialization on the environment,
  e.g. the pros and cons of limestone quarrying
- water cycle: how is it managed?
- fossil fuels as a limited resource

Education for economic and industrial understanding

- where are the largest chemical companies based in the
  world?
- how are large chemical companies organized?
- what does a chemist do in a hospital?
- how much does the chemical industry contribute to
  the national economy?
- simulation on running a chemical plant

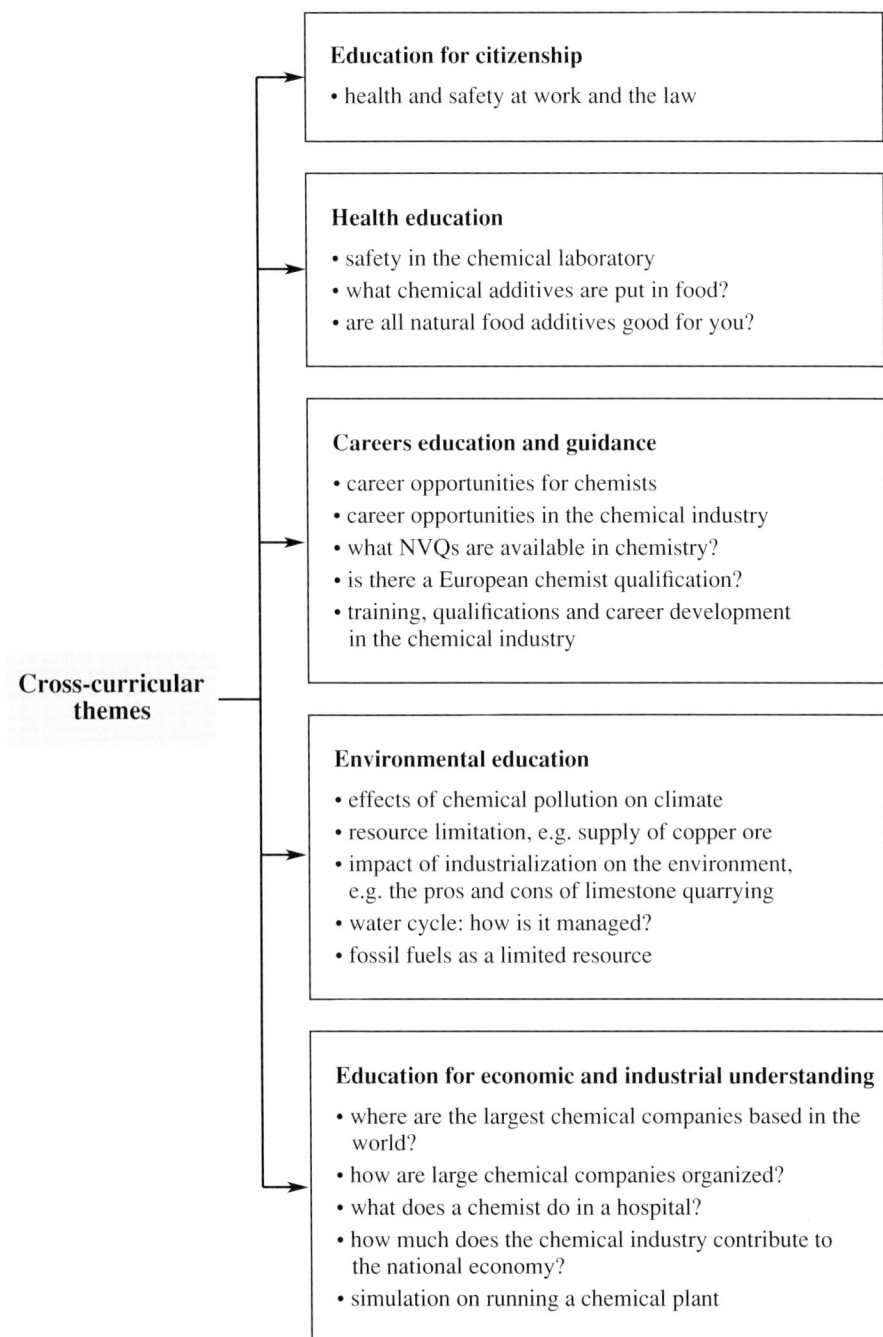

Figure 1   Some suggested topics to cover in cross-curricular themes.

REFERENCES

1 *Science in the National Curriculum (1991)*, Department of Education and Science. (HMSO, 1991).

2 *The Whole Curriculum*, Curriculum Guidance 3, National Curriculum Council, NCC. (HMSO, 1990).

3 *Education for Economic and Industrial Understanding*, Curriculum Guidance 4, National Curriculum Council, NCC. (HMSO, 1990).

4 *Health Education*, Curriculum Guidance 5, National Curriculum Council, NCC. (HMSO, 1990).

5 *Careers Education and Guidance*, Curriculum Guidance 6, National Curriculum Council, NCC. (HMSO, 1990).

6 *Environmental Education*, Curriculum Guidance 7, National Curriculum Council, NCC. (HMSO, 1990).

7 *Education for Citizenship*, Curriculum Guidance 8, National Curriculum Council, NCC. (HMSO, 1991).

CHAPTER 6

ASSESSMENT OF LEARNING OUTCOMES AND REPORTING IN THE CONTEXT OF THE NATIONAL CURRICULUM

Bob Fairbrother

INTRODUCTION

Before the arrival of the National Curriculum the closest the teaching profession came to a formal statement as to what pupils must do was the syllabuses from the various examining bodies. Over the years these have become more detailed and prescriptive, culminating in the National Criteria for GCSE. Attempts to incorporate into these criteria definitions of what a candidate must do in order to be awarded a particular grade foundered on the rock of complexity. When looking at past papers and scripts it was not possible to see what it was that a candidate who was awarded a grade B could do which a candidate who was awarded a grade C could *not* do. Differences between individual candidates could be identified but these did not apply to all candidates. The GCSE criteria only got as far as giving rather vague grade descriptions for two or three 'key' grades. Work to try to resolve the problems was cut short by the arrival of the National Curriculum. This replaced the letter grades (A–G) of the GCSE by ten numerical levels of attainment (1–10), and defined what pupils must do in order to achieve these levels.

THE NATIONAL CURRICULUM

Provision for the establishment of a National Curriculum is set out in *The Education Reform Act, 1988* [1] which became law in schools in September 1989. The detailed provisions of the National Curriculum are given in statutory instruments supported by non-statutory guidance and various circulars. The main source of information for teachers in schools is provided by subject documents which give much of the detail which has to be taught in each subject. This summary makes particular use of the subject documents in English [2, 3], mathematics [4, 5], and science [6– 8].

An additional and very important determinant of change is the work of the Task Group on Assessment and Testing [9]. This group set out the general framework for assessment in the National Curriculum. Central to its recommendations was the belief that assessment should be an integral part of the educational process, and that it should be the servant, not the master, of the curriculum.

Subjects and profile components

There are ten compulsory foundation subjects plus religious education. Three of the foundation subjects have special importance and are called core subjects.

> *core subjects*: English, mathematics, science
>
> *other foundation subjects*: art, foreign language (from age 11), geography, technology (including design), history, music, physical education

In Wales, Welsh is a foundation subject in all schools and a core subject in all Welsh medium schools. It is expected that in Key Stage 4 virtually all pupils will take the core subjects for the GCSE but a series of options and combinations will be available for other subjects.

In an attempt to give a more meaningful description of a subject, and to give more information about pupil performance, each subject was originally divided into profile components (PCs), and the profile components were divided into attainment targets (ATs). The first National Curriculum for science, for example, had two profile components, PC1 *Exploration of science*, which consisted of AT1, and PC2 *Knowledge and understanding of science*, which consisted of ATs 2–16. The new National Curriculum [7] has only four attainment targets (listed below) and these are not grouped into profile components.

> AT1 *Scientific investigation*
>
> AT2 *Life and living processes*
>
> AT3 *Materials and their properties*
>
> AT4 *Physical processes*

Each attainment target becomes in effect a separate profile component. The attainment of each pupil will be reported in each attainment target as well as in the subject as a whole. This structure for science is explained further below.

Attainment targets

Attainment targets are the knowledge, skills and understanding which pupils are expected to have.

As an indication of what is meant by these attainment targets, a description of them is given in Table 1.

The descriptions for all the attainment targets are quite broad. This breadth is necessary since the targets apply to all pupils and so have to cover a wide range of ages and ability. They must be broad enough to allow pupils to attain different levels within each target. A narrow, precisely defined target would not permit a range of performances.

Table 1   A description of the attainment targets in science.

AT1   *Scientific investigation*

Pupils should develop the intellectual and practical skills that allow them to explore the world of science and to develop a fuller understanding of scientific phenomena, the nature of the theories explaining these, and the procedures of scientific investigation. This work should take place through activities that require a progressively more systematic and quantified approach which develops and draws on an increasing knowledge and understanding of science. The activities should encourage the ability to plan and carry out investigations in which pupils:

   (i) ask questions, predict and hypothesize;

   (ii) observe, measure and manipulate variables;

   (iii) interpret their results and evaluate scientific evidence.

AT2   *Life and living processes*

Pupils should develop knowledge and understanding of:

   (i) life processes and the organization of living things;

   (ii) variation and the mechanisms of inheritance, selection and evolution;

   (iii) populations and human influences within ecosystems;

   (iv) energy flows and cycles of matter within ecosystems.

AT3   *Materials and their properties*

Pupils should develop knowledge and understanding of:

   (i) the properties, classification and structure of materials;

   (ii) explanations of the properties of materials;

   (iii) chemical changes;

   (iv) the Earth and its atmosphere.

AT4   *Physical processes*

Pupils should develop knowledge and understanding of:

   (i) electricity and magnetism;

   (ii) energy resources and energy transfer;

   (iii) forces and their effects;

   (iv) light and sound;

   (v) the Earth's place in the Universe.

Programmes of study

Statutory Orders prescribe attainment targets and also programmes of study, both of which are supposed to determine the *minimum* requirements for each subject. What is taught may go wider, but there is considerable doubt among the teaching profession about the amount of time available to do any more than the minimum.

Programmes of study set out the matters, skills and processes which must be taught to pupils during each key stage. They put more flesh on the bones of the attainment targets and spell out the context in which teaching should take place.

Programmes of study are essential to curriculum planning, and attainment targets are central to the process of assessment. One way to visualize the difference between them is to think of programmes of study as a syllabus and attainment targets as assessment objectives. More detailed information about the attainment targets is given by statements of attainment.

Key stages and progression

The 11 years of compulsory education are divided into four key stages as shown in Table 2.

Table 2   The key stages of compulsory education.

Key Stage	Minimum range of levels	Ages	Phase	
1	1–3	5–7	primary	
2	2–5	7–11	primary	} middle
3	3–7	11–14	secondary	
4	4–10	14–16	secondary	

Levels of attainment

Pupil progression through the subject from age 5 to age 16 is measured in ten levels of attainment. Each level provides a signpost for the next; a step which represents the average educational progress of children over about two years. Statutory reporting to parents of the level attained by their children has to be made at the end of each key stage. There will, of course, be a spread of attainment with some pupils at different levels from others. Typically pupils should be capable of achieving around levels 2, 4, 5–6, 6–7 at or near the reporting ages of 7, 11, 14 and 16 years, respectively.

Successive levels in an attainment target are defined by statements of attainment, and the main purpose of assessment is to help pupils to make progress. The statements of attainment for levels 1, 3 and 5 in AT3 are shown in Table 3. The even-numbered levels have been omitted in order to save space, however, looking at levels 1, 3 and 5 enables the intended progression to be seen more easily.

Table 3   The statements of attainment in levels 1, 3 and 5 of AT3.

Level	AT3 *Materials and their properties* pupils should:
Level 1 (a typical 5-year-old pupil)	(a) be able to describe the simple properties of familiar materials
Level 3 (a typical 9-year-old pupil)	(a) be able to link the use of common materials to their simple properties (b) know that some materials occur naturally while many are made from raw materials (c) understand some of the effects of weathering on buildings and on rocks
Level 5 (a typical 13-year- old pupil)	(a) know how to separate and purify the components of mixtures using physical processes (b) be able to classify aqueous solutions as acidic, alkaline or neutral using indicators (c) understand that rusting and burning involve a reaction with oxygen (d) understand the water cycle in terms of the physical processes involved

The statements of attainment are the main factors in deciding the level which a pupil has attained. Many people think of them as simple criteria which, on their own, enable reliable judgements to be made and common standards to be achieved. They can certainly help to do these things but decisions also have to take into account the age of the pupils being considered. For example, when interpreting the meaning of 'be able to classify aqueous solutions as acidic, alkaline or neutral using indicators' in level 5, it is necessary to make judgements as to what to expect of typical 13-year-old pupils. The criteria cannot be interpreted in isolation from the norms of what it is reasonable to expect of pupils. The need to use judgements in this way means that the assessment of pupils is not 100% reliable. This is no different from assessments which have been made in the past, say for the GCSE, and will be made in the future. All measurements are unreliable to some degree.

Programmes of study in key stages

In science there is a programme of study for each key stage. The programmes of study set out the matters, skills and processes in the attainment targets which must be taught to pupils during each key stage. There is a statutory requirement for the programmes of study to cover a *minimum* range of levels in each key stage. The ranges in science are shown in Table 2.

This means schools must have schemes of work for pupils in the different key stages which, as a minimum, cover the ranges of levels shown. So, for example, a school which has pupils in Key Stage 3 *must* have a scheme of work which covers the programmes of study and the statements of attainment for levels 3 to 7. It does *not* mean that all pupils in Key Stage 3 must lie within levels 3 to 7. There may be some low-achieving pupils in Key Stage 3 who are below level 3, or some high-achieving pupils who are above level 7. The school should try to cater for these pupils as best as it can by providing appropriate remedial or extension work.

The need to specify a range of levels for each key stage is a consequence of having a statutory National Curriculum which specifies what has to be taught in each subject. If it were not divided up in some way, then the whole of science would have to be provided in all schools, and schemes of work in infant and junior schools would have to go as far as level 10. Apart from the unlikely event of primary school pupils getting that far, it would be unrealistic to expect primary teachers to be able to plan to such high levels in all the subjects they teach, and for primary schools to be equipped to that standard.

Strands

Planning for progression in the attainment targets is helped by the identification of strands which describe a sequence of related statements of attainment. In AT3, *Materials and their properties*, there are four strands:

(i)   the properties, classification and structure of materials;

(ii)   explanations of the properties of materials;

(iii) chemical changes;

(iv) the Earth and its resources.

The second strand, explanations of the properties of materials, is set out in Table 4.

This strand starts at level 6 and then runs continuously to level 10. Most strands start earlier but not always at level 1. Some stop at level 8 or 9.

Table 4   The statements of attainment for Strand (ii) in AT3.

Level	Strand (ii) Explanations of the properties of materials
6	(b) understand the physical differences between solids, liquids and gases in simple particle terms
7	(c) understand changes of state, including the associated energy changes, mixing and diffusion in terms of the proximity and motion of particles
	(d) understand the relationships between the volume, pressure and temperature of a gas
	(e) understand the difference between elements, compounds and mixtures in terms of atoms, ions and molecules
8	(c) understand radioactivity and nuclear fission and the harmful and beneficial effects of ionizing radiations
	(d) be able to relate the properties of molecular and giant structures to the arrangement of atoms and ions
9	(b) understand the nature of radioactive decay, relating half-life to the use of radioactive materials
10	(b) understand chemical reactions in terms of the energy transfers associated with making and breaking chemical bonds
	(c) be able to relate the bulk properties of metals, ceramics, glass, plastics and fibres to simple models of their structure

ASSESSING

General

The National Curriculum is defined not only by attainment targets and profile components but also by regulations concerned with assessing. At the time of writing, statutory assessment Orders exist only for Key Stage 1, English, mathematics, science and technology. They came into force on 1 August 1991 for use in summer 1992. Those for English, mathematics and science replace the first assessment Orders made earlier for use in 1991. The dates for all the key stages and the core subjects are shown in Table 5.

The assessment Orders for Key Stage 1 do not apply to the other key stages but there will be strong pressure to have some uniformity across all key stages.

The level, from 1 to 10, achieved in an attainment target is determined by success in the statements of attainment which define that level. Information about performance in statements of attainment comes from teacher assessments which take place continually as a part of normal teaching, and from Standard Assessment Tasks (SATs) which are devised centrally but administered and marked by teachers in the school 'at or near the end of the key stage'. The SATs

Table 5   Timetable for the introduction of assessments at the end of each key stage.

Key Stage	Subject(s)	In force	First assessments
1	Eng., Maths., Sci., Tech.	summer 1990 summer 1991	summer 1991 summer 1992
2	Eng., Maths., Sci.	summer 1993	summer 1994
3	Maths., Sci., Eng.	summer 1992	summer 1993
4	Eng., Maths., Sci.	summer 1993	summer 1994 (GCSE)

are used in schools in the first half of the summer term at the end of the key stage.

The results of the SATs have to be combined with those from the teacher assessments. For the first statutory assessments [10] at the end of Key Stage 1 it was required that the teacher assessments be reported in about April, and that any discrepancies between teacher assessments and SATs be resolved by an appeal process. This procedure was changed for the following year and enabled the teacher assessments and the SAT results to be reported at the same time, when the SATs had been marked by the teachers. A report [11] about each pupil has to be made available by 31 July at the end of Key Stages 1, 2 and 3, and by 30 September at the end of Key Stage 4.

teacher assessments	+	SATs	=	final report
(continuous)		(sometime in June)		(end of July)

For the statutory assessments at the end of a key stage, rules* are applied to enable the attainment target levels to be determined from performance in the statements of attainment. The rules also state how the attainment target levels are to be aggregated to give profile component levels (where they exist), and to give subject levels. These requirements are summarized below for Key Stages 1–3.

statements of attainment	→	attainment target levels 1–10	→	profile component levels 1–10	→	subject levels 1–10

The detailed arrangements for Key Stage 4 are not yet known. The rules do not apply to the continuous teacher assessments which take place each year, nor to the reports which have to be made to parents in years other than at the end of a key stage.

SATs and teacher assessment

Standard Assessment Tasks and teacher assessments obtain information about pupils performance in different ways. SATs are constrained by problems of time and management which do not affect teacher assessments. Under current rules, which exist only for Key Stage 1, SAT and teacher assessment information is viewed side by side. If there is disagreement, it can be resolved

---

* The rules are set out in assessment Orders which are issued from time to time.

by an appeal process in which the teacher assessment information can replace that obtained from the SAT if the local education authority agrees. Furthermore, the SATs only occur at the end of a key stage. Information about pupil performance in intervening years comes entirely from teacher assessments. Understanding the differences between SATs and teacher assessments is vital if we are to obtain valid, overall information about pupil performance. We can start by looking at some of the principles which govern the SATs, most of which do not apply to teacher assessment.

The structure of SATs

It is the government's intention that SATs at the end of Key Stage 3 shall be timed, written tests taken simultaneously by all pupils under controlled conditions. At the time of writing it is envisaged that in science there will be three tests each of one hour covering ATs 2, 3 and 4. They will be set externally and marked by the teachers. None of these requirements apply to teacher assessments. Attainment Target 1 will be covered by a non-statutory 'SAT' using guidance produced centrally. The SATs have to provide a measure of each pupil's attainment, by level, within each attainment target. They must allow pupils to demonstrate their highest level of competence and must cater for pupils with special educational needs. In effect this means the SATs must cover all ten levels in the National Curriculum. The tests themselves will have to cover three or four levels in overlapping tiers, for example:

	three levels					four levels					
Tier 1	1	2	3			1	2	3	4		
Tier 2			3	4	5			3	4	5	6
				etc.						etc.	

A pupil is put in for the tier which best matches his or her level. This is determined by the teacher who can make the decision from information obtained by continuous teacher assessment. Such an arrangement reduces the amount which an individual pupil has to do in the SAT. These decisions do not have to influence the teacher assessments, any more than they do when making decisions about core and extension papers in the GCSE at the moment.

Assessing three attainment targets in three hours means giving one hour to each attainment target. This does not have to be done by allocating a separate attainment target to each one-hour test, although this would be the simplest way to get the information (one level per AT per pupil) which is needed. If there are three levels in a tier, 20 minutes will be available for each level; if there are four levels, 15 minutes will be available. In the National Curriculum for science there are eight statements of attainment in each of levels 6 and 7 in AT3. If only half of these are assessed, the most generous estimate is five minutes of assessment time per statement of attainment. These timings put constraints on the kinds of question which can be asked and the amount which can be covered in a level. It is particularly restrictive in the statements of attainment at the higher levels such as 9 and 10 shown in Table 4.

Differentiation

Questions will have to be written so that pupils who fail at one level can show what they can do at a lower level. Information about pupil performance in each attainment target needs to be obtained as smoothly and continuously as possible. One has to consider how best to arrange for there to be progression from one level to the next within a tier, and for judgements about the same level in different tiers to be the same. These are aspects of differentiation which enable pupils to show their best attainment. Questions will have to be written which enable pupils to produce evidence to show whether or not they are at a particular level in an attainment target, and so the decision about the level of performance comes at the stage of writing questions.

The decision about the attainment of a level does not depend on getting a certain percentage of marks, it depends on showing that the statements of attainment have been reached. A yes/no decision will have to be made about individual questions or groups of questions which are aimed at particular statements of attainment. If a range of marks is awarded, this will have to be converted into a yes/no decision. In traditional examinations candidates can get some credit (marks) for partially right answers which do not qualify for full marks. In the criterion-referenced National Curriculum this cannot happen unless the partial explanation gives information about the level below.

Differentiation by outcome requires the use of a single question in which an answer of one quality shows evidence of performance at level n, and an answer of a lower quality shows evidence of level $n-1$. However, experience of the SATs in the 1990 trial and the 1991 pilot has shown that this is very difficult, and often impossible, to achieve in a system in which the levels are criterion referenced. It depends on two factors:

(i)   the structure of the attainment target;

(ii)   the cues given to the pupils in the question.

Where the first of these is concerned there has to exist a strand where the statement of attainment at level $n-1$ refers to the same behaviour as that at level n but at a lower level of attainment. This can be illustrated by looking at levels 6 and 7 of Strand (ii), as shown in Table 4.

A question aimed at statement (c) in level 7 might also give information about statement (b) in level 6 provided it were suitably worded. However, it is *not* a case of marking the question out of 10 and then allocating a level to the mark, e.g. 7–10 marks (level 7); 4–6 marks (level 6); 1–3 marks (level 5).

It will be necessary to look at the answer and see that it satisfies agreed exemplars which show that the pupil 'understands changes of state, including the associated energy changes, mixing and diffusion in terms of the proximity and motion of particles'. If it does, the pupil is showing evidence of performance at level 7 and can be given a tick. If it doesn't, it would be necessary to look at other exemplars to see whether the pupil 'understands the physical differences between solids, liquids and gases in simple particle terms', if it does, the pupil is showing evidence of performance at level 6. Information about levels 5 and below cannot be obtained from this strand because it does not go below level 6.

This reveals one of the major problems of criterion referencing in the National Curriculum. A pupil may show some understanding but not enough for it to be said that a statement of attainment is satisfied at the right level. The pupil cannot, therefore, be credited with that attainment target. However, there seems to be no way that the limited understanding shown by the pupil can be carried downwards unless it relates specifically to a statement of attainment at a lower level.

The nature of evidence

The nature of evidence is a particular problem in written SATs. The information required for making a decision has to be written down by the pupil. If the pupil does not reveal the information, then a decision cannot be made. When making teacher assessments, however, there can be interaction between teacher and pupil which enables the teacher to explore pupil understanding. Some information may be written down by the pupil and form a permanent record. Other information will be revealed by the pupil saying or doing something; this is ephemeral evidence but it is just as valid. While SATs can only use permanent evidence, teacher assessment can use both permanent and ephemeral evidence when making decisions about pupil performance. The key point for both kinds of evidence is that they must arise from learning outcomes which have been planned into the teaching. The evidence will not be there if the pupil has not had an opportunity to produce it.

Key Stage 4 and the GCSE

Assessment of pupil performance at the end of Key Stage 4 is by way of the GCSE. The seven letter grades, A–G, will be replaced by the ten number grades of the National Curriculum. All ten levels will be covered by the examination, but only levels 4–10 will be reported on certificates. The lower grades will be reported in Records of Achievement.

Three options will be available in science:

(i)   Science: Double Award, which covers the full range of all the attainment targets;

(ii) Science: Single Award, which covers all of the attainment targets but omits some of the strands;

(iii) biology, chemistry and physics, which have to be taken as a group of three but will give three separate awards.

The main differences between traditional GCSE examinations and those which are for National Curriculum assessment in Key Stage 4 are:

• the National Curriculum is more clearly criterion referenced;

• the Key Stage 4 examinations will have to cover ten numerical levels;

• the meaning of a level is defined by statements of attainment;

• the Key Stage 4 examinations will have to cover four attainment targets including AT1;

- judging scripts will involve criterion-referenced decisions about evidence for a statement of attainment rather than the award of marks;
- levels 4–10 will be recorded on the certificate;
- the attainment target levels will be aggregated to give the subject level.

Current GCSE practice

Current GCSE procedures identify assessment objectives which help in the construction of valid examination questions and papers, but generally leave the decision about the level of performance until the end when all the marks have been added together. The traditional way of writing examination questions is to identify the content area (e.g. Ohm's law) and the process (e.g. explain), and then to write a question which asks pupils to explain something about Ohm's law. Marking is done by identifying the main points required in the answer and awarding marks accordingly. Candidates can get full marks, no marks or any number of marks in between. The marks are added to those obtained in other questions and a total mark obtained for the paper.

The marks from different papers are added together to give a total mark for the examination. Any contribution from internal teacher assessment can be incorporated simply by adding the contribution in the form of marks to the marks obtained from the external (written) examination. Different weighting of the contributions from different papers and from teacher assessment is arranged either by having different maximum marks available or by scaling marks.

A grade is awarded depending on the total percentage of marks obtained. Different cut-off points are decided for different grades. Despite a great deal of work over the years, there are no clearly defined criteria for the award of each grade. There are grade descriptors for some key grades but they serve only as general guides and come into use only after the procedures described above have taken place. The standard of the grades depends on the experience and expertise of the examiners who try to arrange for consistency from one year to the next.

GCSE practice and the National Curriculum

The above procedures are unlikely to take place when the GCSE has to comply with the National Curriculum (see Table 5). In particular, as discussed above in the section on SATs, a decision about the attainment of a level is unlikely to depend on getting a certain percentage of marks, but on showing that the statements of attainment have been reached. A yes/no decision will have to be made about individual questions or groups of questions which are aimed at particular statements of attainment. Some problems remain to be resolved about whether to ask questions on the programmes of study if the answer cannot be related to a statement of attainment and hence to a level.

A major point about the above is that percentage marks and percentage contributions from different components of the examination do not occur. It will be difficult, if not impossible, to identify a percentage contribution of teacher assessment *within* an attainment target if marks or percentages are not used to determine a level in an attainment target. Determining the performance of pupils in attainment targets at the end of Key Stage 1 has used a process of viewing SAT information alongside teacher assessment information and reconciling any disagreements. This was similar to the procedure explored in the trial and pilot phases of the Key Stage 3 SATs. The two sets of information were not added together using different weightings. Indeed, while the teacher assessments produced information about all the attainment targets, the SATs produced information about only a few of them. It would only have been possible to do a weighted addition with the attainment targets which were assessed in the SATs.

It will be possible to allocate a percentage contribution to teacher assessment if it is confined to just one attainment target and is used to determine the overall level for the subject. The most likely attainment target for this is AT1. The GCSE could have a teacher-assessed contribution from AT1 and an externally-examined contribution from AT2–AT4. (This seems to be the pattern which is likely to emerge for the end of Key Stage 3.) Each attainment target could contribute equally to the final level for the subject (add the four separate levels together and divide by four). Teacher assessment would then have a weighting of 25% in determining the subject level, 100% in determining the AT1 level and 0% in the AT2–AT4 levels. This would be consistent with an upper limit of 30% for coursework assessment in science, as recently imposed by the Secretary of State.

There are some anomalies in the above procedure when compared with what teachers and pupils will have been doing. Teachers will be assessing their pupils in all the attainment targets up to and including Year 10 in order that they can make reports to parents at the end of each year. (Parents have to be given information about the subject overall, and they can request attainment target information if they wish.) However, the GCSE approach suggested above would mean that all the information about AT2–AT4 which teachers have been gathering about the performance of their pupils up to and including Year 10 would be ignored in determining the final subject level in the GCSE.

In addition, many schools may use the teacher assessment information to report National Curriculum levels to parents at the end of Year 10. (They do not have to use levels, but the parents may start to insist upon it.) One year later the parents will get the GCSE levels which could show no change or even a drop. (Progress of one level in two years in the subject as a whole is the norm.) Indeed, for some pupils, there may be no change from the statutorily-determined levels at the end of Key Stage 3, two years earlier.

RECORDING AND REPORTING

Regulations concerned with school records have also been issued [12]. These affect all key stages, not just Key Stage 1. Briefly these state that from 1 September 1989 governing bodies have been required to make arrangements for the keeping and updating of a curricular record of each registered pupil. From 1 September 1990 arrangements must have been made to disclose and supply copies of the record on request to:

(i)   where the pupil is under 16, the pupil's parents;

(ii) where the pupil is 16 or 17, the pupil or the pupil's parents;

(iii) where the pupil is 18 or over, the pupil;

(iv) any school or institution of further or higher education to which the pupil may transfer.

A curricular record is a formal record of a pupil's academic achievements, skills and abilities, and progress in school. Other educational records which schools find useful relating to a pupil are also expected to form a part of the curricular record.

The regulations for reporting [11] state that at the end of each year brief particulars must be given to parents about performance in each subject of the National Curriculum. At the end of each key stage the levels reached in each profile component and subject must be given to parents who can also ask for information about the levels reached in each attainment target. If statutory attainment targets and profile components have not yet been decided for a subject, then brief particulars have to be given. More information is given below in the sections on reporting to pupils, parents and governors.

Reporting to pupils

Assessing and reporting to pupils has two main purposes, formative and summative.

Formative purposes

For formative purposes feedback is given to enable pupils to make progress. It is intended to enable them to build on strengths, and to identify and strengthen weakness. It is continuous, and is a part of the normal teaching and learning process of all schools.

The major difference brought about by the National Curriculum is the introduction of levels of attainment which are defined by statements of attainment as discussed earlier and illustrated in Tables 3 and 4. The existence of these statements means not only that teachers have a guide to what is meant by a level of attainment and what is needed for pupils to make progress, but also that pupils can have this kind of information and be helped to make decisions for themselves. The National Curriculum thus provides a framework to enable teachers and pupils to work towards common aims.

Information provided for formative purposes is often quite detailed and can be concerned with individual statements of attainment or even smaller attributes of the statements.

Summative purposes

For summative purposes this detailed information is summarized at various times (usually at the end of each year and at the end of each key stage) and is available for pupils to see as outlined above. At these times the main items of information are the levels achieved in each attainment target and profile component, and in the subject as a whole. This is the minimum amount of information that should be available and, since much of it arises from the continuous teacher assessments which have been made for formative purposes, should not come as a surprise to pupils.

Reporting to parents

Information about the attainment of individual pupils can be reported outside the school only to parents. If the pupils are 16 or over, the information can be given to the pupils themselves as described above. It will also be available to other teachers to help them to prepare suitable schemes of work. The report to parents at the end of each key stage must give the level attained in the subject as a whole and, if requested by the parents, in each attainment target.

A form, which will be standard for all schools in England and Wales for reporting pupil achievements to parents at the end of each key stage, may be issued by the Department of Education and Science, but no official form has been produced at the time of writing.

Parents will need help in interpreting what is said about their children. In general terms the onus for this will fall on everyone concerned. In more specific terms schools and individual teachers will have to develop clear explanations and ways of communicating them to parents. Perhaps the major factor is the need to put the information into a context which enables it to be interpreted sensibly. Generally speaking, strings of numbers on their own are not very helpful and will need to be augmented with more detailed information.

Reporting to governors

Governors have a responsibility to see that a record is kept of each pupil's academic achievements, skills, abilities and progress. The day-to-day responsibility for these arrangements may be delegated to the headteacher and other teachers in the school. However, it is reasonable to expect that the governors will wish to see the results of assessments particularly at the end of each year and key stage.

Figure 1 shows summary data for the levels achieved by a class of pupils in science at the end of Key Stage 2. This kind of detailed information is of particular use to the teachers of the pupils since large differences between performance in different subjects could serve a valuable diagnostic purpose.

Figure 2 shows these results, together with those for English, aggregated in a form which might be made available not only to the governors but also to a wider audience.

In Figures 1 and 2 the science data are presented using the four attainment targets. In Figure 2, the English data use three profile components, not the attainment targets.

CLARKE JUNIOR SCHOOL
Form: 6F   **School year**: 1993–94

Levels of attainment

PUPIL	SCIENCE				
	Scientific investigation	Life and living processes	Materials and their properties	Physical processes	Subject
Boyd Baker	5	4	4	3	4
Malcolm Bod	4	4	4	4	4
Lesley Book	3	4	3	3	3
Alan Buchan	5	6	4	5	5
Lew Clack	5	5	3	4	5
Daniel Clash	5	5	5	4	5
Tom Dainee	6	6	6	5	6
Ron Goss	4	5	4	4	4
Lanna Goy	3	3	3	2	3
Len Harrison	4	3	2	3	3
Colin Haswell	5	6	6	6	6
Helen James	5	5	5	5	5
Ron James	4	5	4	4	4
Vinny Key	6	4	2	3	4
Alan Ling	4	5	3	3	4
Frank Marsh	6	6	5	6	6
Steven Ord	2	3	2	2	2
Bill Oren	3	4	3	3	3
Agnes Orm	3	4	3	3	3
Janet Sinji	3	3	2	3	3
David Steave	3	3	4	2	3
Stuart Steel	3	4	3	3	3
Helen Walter	2	3	2	2	2
Weighting(%)	50	$16^2/_3$	$16^2/_3$	$16^2/_3$	

Figure 1   Data about the attainment of a class of pupils in science at the end of Key Stage 2. (The weightings are those which are used to determine the subject level from the attainment target levels.)

CLARKE JUNIOR SCHOOL
End of Key Stage 2

Number of pupils at different levels of attainment

ENGLISH	LEVELS									
	1	2	3	4	5	6	7	8	9	10
Speaking, listening	–	2	5	5	6	5	–	–	–	–
Reading	–	–	5	6	7	5	–	–	–	–
Writing, spelling	–	4	7	7	3	2	–	–	–	–
Subject	–	2	6	6	5	4	–	–	–	–

SCIENCE	LEVELS									
	1	2	3	4	5	6	7	8	9	10
Scientific investigation	–	2	7	5	6	3	–	–	–	–
Life and living processes	–	–	6	7	6	4	–	–	–	–
Materials and their properties	–	5	7	6	3	2	–	–	–	–
Physical processes	–	4	9	5	3	2	–	–	–	–
Subject	–	2	8	6	4	3	–	–	–	–

Figure 2   Aggregated results in science and English which might be made available to the governors and also published more widely.

Putting data into context

The information which is given in Figures 1 and 2 is the minimum which is likely to be required by law. There are several problems which emerge. One is that the minimum may become the maximum, and a set of numbers is all that a school will issue. The main reasons for this are a lack of time and lack of resources to put together more detailed and coherent information about the performance of an individual pupil and of the school. A portfolio giving more details of each pupil could go to the parents as well as to the teachers in the next school. Indeed, a portfolio could be kept by each pupil, updated regularly with additional contributions from teachers, and sent to parents at least once a year. More than this will be required, however. Some information has to be given which will enable parents to understand the meaning of levels in the National Curriculum. Common questions from parents will almost certainly include:

'What level *should* she be on?'

'How does he compare with the other pupils?'

'But she was on level 5 last year, why hasn't she made any progress?'

Answers can be given, but they may not be easy to understand, and it will be important for teachers to prepare good explanatory material which not only makes things clear but is also consistent throughout the school. It will be equally important for parents to take the trouble to read and understand what is said.

The detailed information which is given to parents may be inappropriate for governors, and should not be sent to the local newspapers. Another problem, then, is that only the numbers will be considered and published, and invidious and uninformed comparisons will be made between schools.

REFERENCES

1   *The Education Reform Act, 1988.* (HMSO, 1988).

2   *English in the National Curriculum*, Department of Education and Science. (HMSO, 1989).

3   *English in the National Curriculum*, Department of Education and Science. (HMSO, 1990).

4   *Mathematics in the National Curriculum*, Department of Education and Science. (HMSO, 1989).

5   *Mathematics for ages 5 to 16 (1991)*, Department of Education and Science. (HMSO, 1991).

6   *Science in the National Curriculum*, Department of Education and Science. (HMSO, 1989).

7   *Science for ages 5 to 16 (1991)*, Department of Education and Science. (HMSO, 1991).

8   *Science in the National Curriculum (1991)*, National Curriculum Council Consulation Report, National Curriculum Council. (HMSO, 1991).

9   *National Curriculum. Task Group on Assessment and Testing: A Report*, Department of Education and Science. (HMSO, 1988).

10   *The Education (National Curriculum) (Assessment Arrangements for English, Mathematics, and Science) Order, 1990.* (HMSO, 1990).

11   *The Education (Individual Pupils' Achievements) (Information) Regulations, 1990.* (HMSO, 1990).

12   *The Education (School Records) Regulations, 1989.* (HMSO, 1989).

CHAPTER 7

DIARY OF TWO CHEMISTRY TEACHERS AGED 92³/₄

Judy Brophy and Christine McCormick

INTRODUCTION

In this Chapter we describe how we set about writing a unit using chemistry for Key Stage 3 and Key Stage 4. This will highlight the problems we encountered in linking Key Stage 2 with Key Stage 3 because of the size of our school and the numerous primary schools that feed it, with whom in the past there had been no science links. The transition at the end of Key Stage 4 is much more defined and we describe our strategy for dealing with it.

We use the vehicle of a diary (*à la Adrian Mole*) to enable us to include anecdotes and criticisms and hopefully to convey the very real problems that our inner-city comprehensive school faces.

We explain how we achieved what we did in the time available, the resources we used, and include an evaluation of how they were received and how they could have been improved. (Details of the references cited in the diary are given at the end of the Chapter.)

THE DIARY

Friday 10 May 1991

Receive phone call from the Open University asking us to write an article for *Open Chemistry*. Never done anything like this before, but agree to have a go. After 20 years' chemistry teaching feel we are recognized at last!

Saturday 11 May 1991

Panic! Remembered how easy it was to learn to teach chemistry 20 years ago. All one had to do was begin at the beginning of the *Nuffield Chemistry Teacher's Guides* and work through to the end. Supplement this with excellent science centre courses where one could try out the experiments and receive help, and one could start with some confidence. Not so today!

Sunday 12 May 1991

Prayed for inspiration.

Monday 13 May 1991: break

Whilst still pondering the problems facing teachers having to learn to teach chemistry today ask our two depressed looking newly-qualified teachers why they look so depressed? They reply:

1   Balanced science—difficult when one is not accomplished in one's own discipline let alone someone else's. How good are the Russian teachers at teaching Spanish?

2   Mixed ability groups at all levels (often large)—lack of training in how to deal with these groups. Whilst every authority proclaims this to be the only way to teach, and the air is thick with 'accessing the curriculum to everyone', there is the worry (whispered) that many groups and teachers are not waving but drowning.

3   The staff room drinks machine is out of hot chocolate again.

Suggest they try the soup!

Tuesday 14 May 1991: break

Find diaries from 2 years ago to see how we organized Key Stage 3 work. Discovered that we wrote it assuming children arrive from primary school knowing no science at all. As pointed out in an article by Jarman this has been common practice for secondary schools for some time.

Just discussing what a mistake this is in the light of Year 7 pupils groaning with boredom as seeds come before them for a third year running, when joined by pompous colleague from history department. He is appalled to hear we have had no primary liaison in the past. Ask him what liaison the history department has—he looks sheepish and says he is not sure but will find out. Realize that all we know is that in the past we had no liaison because of rapid turnover of science staff, no post holder designated to work in this area, large number of feeder schools and only two days INSET (in-service training) to write the units. We had thought we had not done a bad job. Suddenly doubts creep in!

Tuesday 14 May 1991: lunchtime

Investigate what the science department is now doing about primary liaison. To our amazement discover it is doing a lot. We now have a bright and enthusiastic new post holder who is planning and implementing many new initiatives. She has set up a 'link lab' which is a fully equipped science lab and she has sent out details of this to all feeder primaries inviting them to book time in the lab. We will provide science staff to help the top juniors have a science lesson. This would involve all pupils since one of the problems in primaries is that only a small group of pupils are involved in a science activity at any one time, which is quite different from science lessons in secondary schools. They often are unable to use specialist equipment. This results in them not realizing that what they are involved in *is* science. Equipment is frequently put before them already assembled which leads to a lack of confidence in assembling. The post holder has gone, or intends to go, into local primaries and to teach a science lesson taking specialist equipment with her. Discussion with teachers and pupils after some of these visits has already brought out several areas needing further development. These include awareness of the use of language, limitations of apparatus and resources, assumed knowledge and different approaches to classroom learning. Primary teachers feel that language used in secondary science is too difficult. Secondary teachers moan about lack of commonsense about science in the primary pupils. Does this arise because what is so familiar to secondary teachers is actually totally unfamiliar to primary teachers and so to their pupils?

(Remember first science meeting as a new teacher—couldn't understand one word that was said!)

A science helpline is also to be set up for primary teachers to use to get help and ideas quickly. We have also run an explorations evening where teachers from a cluster of primary schools try experiments. This has shown up a great lack of confidence on their part in actually tackling experiments.

Armed with all these details of our primary/secondary liaison we look forward to tomorrow's break with colleague from history.

Wednesday 15 May 1991: break

History colleague avoiding eye contact.

Glowing with self-righteousness we sit him down and boast proudly of our department's initiatives towards continuity and progression at the primary/secondary interface. History colleague staggers away making mental note never to liaise with science department again.

Thursday 16 May 1991: break

Find all members of the history department avoiding eye contact.

Thursday 16 May 1991: 4 p.m.

Science departmental meeting.

Item 1 is primary/secondary links.

Post holder outlines to the department the initiatives she has already outlined to us. She also reports reluctance from some primary feeders who feel that their science has been set up and now requires no help from us. Younger members of department show apathy and eat biscuits. They express the view that if that is the primaries' attitude they can wire their own plugs! We are eager to quote Dawson and Shipstone (much to everyone's amazement) who found that liaison where it existed, was most commonly organized by heads of departments in the secondary schools. They found that it was the secondary schools that altered their emphasis to an increase in skills and processes, and a decrease in concepts. Both schools became much more aware of duplication. Our colleagues choke on the biscuits at all this but agree that as primary schools are teaching more and more science, we must amend our Year 7 work and certainly not assume that our pupils know nothing on entering the school. Colleagues stop eating biscuits and ask for photocopies of the article.

Promise to provide copies for next departmental meeting and make mental note to provide the biscuits.

Friday 17 May 1991: 8 p.m.

Over a bottle of wine and a pile of old diaries, we continue to muse about how we wrote Year 7 units and feel sad to realize how much better they might have been if we had had any liaison. However, remember how delighted we were to have management agree to increase Year 7 science time from 2×70 to 3×70 minutes a week. Remember also that after confiscating two computer games, one knife and two packets of cigarettes in the first lesson, that the delight soon faded. Was the extra time made possible by the headteacher being a science teacher and understanding our problems? Science department thought she was dead brave!

How were the LEA persuaded to provide extra staff? (Will LMS, Local Management of Schools, change this?) But like Scarlett we won't think about that now, we'll think about it tomorrow. Relieved that since we wrote the materials Year 8 and Year 9 groups have been reduced to 20, with Year 7 scheduled to be 20 next year. This makes a huge difference to teaching mixed-ability groups. Remember that the reason we came to write the chemistry-based units for Year 7 was that we found that no printed course ever matches what a group of teachers need. We were therefore given two INSET days to write our own units to match our needs. The diary entries for these days show them to be very hectic.

10 July 1989: INSET day 1*

Our first INSET day. Today we armed ourselves with a huge pile of books, masses of paper, glue, scissors, photocopying cards, tins of bully beef, bars of chocolate and bottles of ginger beer. We cut, pasted, chopped, wrote worksheets, designed investigations, designed work for individuals, pairs, groups, demonstrated, postered, videoed, taped, grouped for discussions, cross-referenced, explored, attainment targeted, and levelled ourselves into a frenzy.

We emerged with three units.

11 July 1989: INSET day 2

We analysed our work carefully and constructed a grid as shown below.

Content	Practical	Homework	Exploration	Attainment target

We filled these in for every lesson. These are to be used as a guide for teachers using the units. We have given the content in great detail to help new and inexperienced teachers. We firmly believe that to constantly have to look up masses of information when one is struggling on all fronts is not an efficient use of time and wastes the expertise of more experienced subject specialists. So at the risk of insulting those who already know it all, and to help those who know that they don't know but would die before admitting it, and finally to show those who don't know that they don't know, we have spelt it all out in words of one syllable. As our groups are of mixed ability we have used a variety of approaches. These include whole class practicals with teacher instructions (cooking), small group planning and designing experiments, with clue sheets available for the less able pupils. We included individual and group work on analysing, collecting and presenting information. As well as the more usual one child or one group/one poster approach, we have also included the approach of dividing up a story into several paragraphs with each group taking one part and producing a poster. The final display of all the posters then makes the whole story, with all the class involved. We also have videos with comprehensions. In line with our assessment policy and the requirements of the

<hr>

* A list of resources used during the INSET days is given at the end of the Chapter.

National Curriculum we have introduced open-ended investigations known as explorations. Some of these are to be used as homework, e.g. planning experiments, making models, testing household substances, doing Which *style surveys, etc.*
One of our INSET group has carefully analysed each lesson to make sure all the attainment targets have been included. We have taken care to see that these units progress in content, difficulty, concepts and process skills. In each unit we have gone from lower to higher levels but have made sure there were plenty of opportunities to revisit ideas in our later units so that children who had missed out the first time had second and third chances. Since taking up reading learned documents, we have discovered that this is something called 'a spiral curriculum'.
We emerged with three better units and feel more optimistic for the start of term in September.

Impressed to read in these diaries how optimistic we were after our two day's work. Open another bottle of wine to fortify us to read the diary entry for a year later.

June 1990

The units have been used for a year and have been well received. They are an introduction to science involving lots of practical work that fulfil the expectations of pupils transferring from Key Stage 2 to 3, whilst starting the process of drip feeding how scientists think and problem solve—at the same time covering a reasonable amount of content and teaching of laboratory skills. Proper evaluation and revision of the units needs to be done in the following ways.

1   *Remove and simplify experiments that are overlong and difficult.*

2   *Provide extension work for special needs, both for higher and lower level work.*

3   *Add homework from individual staff.*

4   *Demonstrate and teach those parts of the units found difficult by staff of other disciplines.*

Terrible things are happening! The Head of Science has got a new job, the person in charge of lower school science has got a new job and two others are leaving.
We know this is not uncommon in inner-city comprehensives, but it doesn't do much for continuity and progression.

July 1990

Emergency departmental meeting
In order to cope with the staff changes and with the demands of the National Curriculum, the department has decided that it would be expedient to purchase one of the more colourful sets of books currently flooding the market. These purport to be every science department's answer to the National Curriculum.
This relegates our units to the bottom of the dusty cupboard.

This course, based on the books purchased, has not proved to be the answer to all our prayers.

Thursday 6 June 1991

Working parties are now being set up to produce proper teachable units for Year 7 using the published books as resources. Open drawer, blow dust off old units and hand them to new Head of Science. Whilst looking through 1990's diary, amused to find entry for 1 April.

1 April 1990

All Fool's Day. INSET on Graded Assessment in Science Project (GASP)

At midday the Head of Science was thanked for such an entertaining session and hopes were expressed that we would have more such April Fool jokes in the future.

At 12.15 p.m. we realize that we have decided to trial GASP, no joke! We are going to continually assess the children.

9 April 1990

First training session on GASP

GASP trainer is to tell us about the philosophy of GASP. He has to ensure that he pervades us with the 'spirit' of GASP without which we can't implement it. Prepare to be pervaded. GASP is a complete assessment scheme for pupils aged 11 to 16 studying science in schools. It integrates with any existing science curriculum. The emphasis is on the integration of assessment procedures with the teaching and learning processes. It provides pupils with positive statements of achievement and assesses pupils when they are ready. This gives all the pupils a sense of achievement in science and helps with motivation throughout their schooling. Sounds great! Look forward to next session.

16 April 1990

Second training session on GASP

In this session we learn about the content and process skills. Content is knowledge of facts, scientific laws and concepts. These are assessed by written tests. Much to everyone's amazement these tests can be seen by the children before the topic is taught and the children mark their own tests. We would therefore expect everyone to get the required 75% to pass, but the trainer assured us this is not the case. We wish they'd done this with our O-level Latin. We also learn about process skills. We have to assess on two separate occasions whether pupils have manipulative skills and cognitive processes. This means we test to see if they can use pieces of apparatus and draw graphs and complete tables.

17 April 1990

Final training session on GASP

In this session we learn about explorations and record keeping. Explorations are to introduce pupils to open-ended imaginative and creative aspects of science. They plan, implement, evaluate and conclude. One of the outstanding features of explorations is that they provide continuity of methodology. The trainer says pupils like explorations because they bring together process skills and content along with their own knowledge, skills and creativity. Throughout the year very careful records of all pupils' achievements, along with their work, have to be kept. These will be externally moderated. We all feel motivated and willing to give it a go but our main area of concern is that there may be a lot more work involved in the record keeping than is immediately obvious.

Monday 1 July 1991

Departmental meeting to discuss year of GASP.

The department feels that GASP does indeed motivate the pupils, gives us a ready-made assessment scheme into which to fit the National Curriculum, will indeed provide continuity of teaching style throughout the five years, and will eventually replace the GCSE. To operate GASP successfully may have required us to be steeped in the philosophy of the scheme, but it has also required us to become steeped in mounds of models, heaps of explorations and sacks of paper. Eat your heart out Brazilian rain forests! Our new temporary Antipodean teacher who is uninitiated into the rites and rituals of everyday GASP thinks we are akin to a religious sect and calls us the GASPIES. He is practising the large *Guardian* crossword every day, so as to stand some chance of completing the pupil record cards. Agenda for next departmental meeting will be planning for transition from Key Stage 3 to 4.

Wednesday 10 July 1991

Departmental meeting

Item 1 is the past history of courses.

As the longest serving members of the department, we are called upon to recap on what we did in the past. Explain that we used to do separate science O-levels and we have always done double SCISP (*Schools Council Integrated Science Project*) integrated science O-level. We were involved in SCISP from early days as a trial school and it was always a very popular option into which we fed our most able children. It was highly regarded by both parents and pupils as being the 'trendy' thing to do. When GCSE arrived, we continued with an integrated course which grew out of SCISP but continued to offer separate sciences at GCSE including electronics. The LEA then reduced staffing which forced the school to be more economic and to rethink its use of teachers in the science department. It was decided to drop the individual sciences and to offer only integrated science. Different courses were needed to accommodate different ability groups and option choices. We continued with double integrated science for the more able pupils who wanted two sciences. We introduced single integrated science for academic pupils who didn't want to take up two options with science. We introduced a modular single science (grade limited to C) for the less able, less motivated children. A year later (in case we didn't have enough courses on the go!) we introduced a double modular grade-limited course for those pupils who wanted science to take up a larger part of their curriculum, but who found it difficult. Although this seems very complicated, we were trying to cater sensitively for all types of pupils. 'Thank you' said the new staff, reaching for their new brooms. 'We intend to make some major changes. These will be as follows:

1   Double science for all pupils. This is our interpretation of what the government requires.

2   We will teach a modular course. The benefits of this are that it follows the pattern of teaching and assessment in lower school courses in Year 7, 8 and 9. A module test every four weeks is advantageous to less able pupils and it is less demanding than a final exam.

3   Because of its modular nature the course allows flexibility to accommodate any future changes more easily, e.g. in the National Curriculum, TVEI, etc.

4   A modular course with its inherent maximum choice allows us to expand cross-curricular links.

5   As our ultimate intention is to make a final exam redundant and to use continuous assessment in the form of GASP, moving to a modular course now will give us valuable experience and help to facilitate the transition from GASP in the lower school to GASP in the upper school. This also overrides any considerations of staying with the course we already have on the grounds that there will be changes to any GCSE course to bring it in line with the National Curriculum. As we intend not to be doing a final exam in a few years we just need a course on which to 'hang' GASP.

6   Because we did it in our last school and we know it's the best!'

Meeting ends. Agenda for next meeting is mixed ability versus streaming.

Wednesday 17 July 1991

At the start of the meeting we are balloted on our views on mixed ability versus streaming. Mixed ability wins. Try to clarify our ideas on the philosophy of mixed-ability groupings. The outcome is hilarious with no two people agreeing. Ideas range from equal access to the curriculum through pupils choosing their own level, to allowance being made for different capabilities. As we failed to get a consensus, we decide to concentrate on strategies to teach mixed ability successfully, even if we don't know what it is. We try to think about appropriate teaching methods and modes of class management to meet the needs of the wide ability range within each group. We are aware that the schemes of work for different levels of ability should be adequately differentiated, but in practice this is very often difficult to fulfil. Schemes of work that we have written in the past often resort to whole-class teaching or great reliance on worksheets which results in individual but not individualized learning; that is, everybody working quietly on their own work but at the same level. We resolve to include as many approaches as possible in order to provide as many categories of pupils as possible with the quality and variety of work that they need. Indeed, one of the two criteria for good mixed-ability teaching laid down in *Improving Secondary Schools* by Hargreaves is that teachers should employ a range and variety of methods encompassing grouped, paired and individualized activities. The other criteria from Hargreaves is that lessons should be planned by teams or at least pairs of teachers wherever possible. We always fulfil this criteria because it is expedient to have teams of teachers working together to plan any new course. The only time ever made available for planning is INSET time and writing courses is hardly the best use of this time, and as it only amounts to two to four days a year, it is totally inadequate to plan courses properly. We split up into groups to write our course during the next INSET days.

18/19 July 1991: INSET days 1 and 2*

Our groups are made up of three or four members of staff chosen to match the nature of the unit and the expertise of the staff. After hours of the usual cutting, pasting, word–processing, etc., we produce teaching units which include plenty of resource material, practical details and homeworks. We select units which we have previously prepared for Key Stage 3 which give continuity with the National Curriculum. We realize

---

* A list of resources used during the INSET days is given at the end of the Chapter.

we have a big problem with continuity from Key Stage 3 to Key Stage 4. The final year of Key Stage 3 has not yet been written as we have only just received the book upon which we are basing the course. The earlier parts of the course for Key Stage 3 (Year 7 and 8) are still being trialled and need a great deal of revision and reorganization. Ideally this should happen before being integrated with the Year 9 course, but this is obviously impossible. This means that we are writing for Year 10 on weak foundations and this further exacerbates the problem of continuity. We try to choose Key Stage 4 units to match Key Stage 3 ones but invariably we find some units are too repetitive, whereas others have no preceding basic unit and consequently present great difficulties to the children. There has been so little time to prepare units for Key Stages 3 and 4, let alone coordinate the two stages, that many worksheets have been prepared from the same sources. We are sure that these problems arise in many science departments and will not be solved until the National Curriculum is well established in Key Stage 3 and the syllabuses for Key Stage 4 are finalized. This represents a major shift in emphasis. In previous years the GCE/GCSE prescribed the content of the lower-school courses. Now the reverse is true, with the National Curriculum in the lower school is determining the content of the GCSE. It will be up to the department to select a successful course in Key Stage 4 which will complement and provide continuity with our Key Stage 3 course.

Similar problems occur at the A-level/GCSE interface. We do the *Nuffield Chemistry A-level*, which has responded with impressive speed to the changes that have resulted from GCSE. However mixed-ability classes have often resulted in restrictions of content in programmes of work. Sometimes teachers avoid topics or activities deemed too difficult for pupils of average ability or below, or considered difficult to present to mixed-ability groups. This is a big problem for chemistry teachers as children leave Key Stage 4 and go on to A-level knowing very little chemistry or to be more honest, knowing no chemistry at all! The *Nuffield Chemistry A-level Course* that our Year 12 and 13 pupils follow is a very prescribed course, so that all we needed to do in the past was work through the student's guides. In the light of GCSE there has been a revision of this course material, with recommendations being made for suitable additions to plug the gaps left by the removal of hard topics from GCSE. This is inadequate for us, as all our children do balanced science. This leaves them as experts on the environment, pollution and recycling, but total novices as far as the basic skills and knowledge necessary for a confident start to A-level are concerned. Therefore we spend as much time as is necessary establishing the basic ideas such as the mole, Periodic Table, formulae and equations before the start of the A-level course. Later on when we meet such topics as rates and equilibrium, we always establish the simple ideas of the topic before proceeding with an in-depth study. This has led to a need for increased lesson time which often comes out of the lunch hour, or after school, which is far from ideal. Our able pupils themselves are often horrified when faced with A-level work, and start to realize how broad but shallow their mixed-ability balanced science course has been as a preparation for A-level. We find the *Independent Learning Project for Advanced Chemistry* (ILPAC) scheme is useful to supplement the A-level course. These problems may well be addressed by new initiatives such as the modular A-level science which is looming on the horizon. We realize that this is not just happening in our school, but is a nationwide problem as recognized by a report from the Council for National Academic Awards. This states that the replacement of O-level chemistry by GCSE had resulted in decreasing understanding of basic concepts and familiarity with calculations. 'A country not tops in chemistry is destined to be second-rate or worse' says the report.

Thursday 25 July 1991: last day of term

We are amazed at the changes revealed by looking back over our old diaries. Ten years ago the situation was relatively simple. Separate sciences taught by specialist teachers to banded groups. Three years ago everything started to change and in the space of three years, the changes gained momentum resulting in the present complex situation. This is due to five major initiatives that we have taken on board:

1   balanced science taught by non-specialists;
2   National Curriculum;
3   GASP;
4   mixed ability in Years 7–11;
5   liaison with primaries.

There are different reasons why these initiatives have been taken up. Balanced science is current thinking and most schools are being encouraged to move towards it. The National Curriculum is outside our control. The need to liaise with primaries has evolved from the introduction of the National Curriculum. GASP and mixed ability are personal preferences within the department.

The last few years have been characterized by many changes in the education system. The difficulties that these present are exacerbated in an inner-city comprehensive school by the constant turnover of staff. Let us hope that the department is moving towards a more stable situation where it can properly assimilate and then reflect upon these many changes. It may well be that some of these changes will be rejected. Our contribution to the debate is given in Table 1, which, in the event of our demise (being 92 3/4) can be used posthumously.

Table 1 *Advantages and disadvantages of the changes undertaken by our school.*

	Pros	Cons
Balanced science	Easy to staff	Content limited to three things:
	No specialist science	biogas
	No science teachers needed	acid rain
	No early specialization	food webs
	Three sciences for the time of two	
National Curriculum	Unknown	Watch this space
GASP	Motivates children	Kills teachers
	Purpose-built assessment programme	
	Assesses pupils when ready	
	Positive statement of achievement	
Mixed ability	Makes everyone equal	Shows them all to be different
Liaison with primaries	*Continuity*	
	Progression	

Saturday 27 July 1991

Post article for *Open Chemistry*.

REFERENCES

Dawson, R. M. and Shipstone, D. M., 'Liaison in science at the primary/secondary interface', *School Science Review*, 1991, **72**(261), pp. 17–25.

GASP Training Manual, Graded Assessment in Science Project. (Stanley Thornes, 1989).

Hargreaves, D., *Improving Secondary Schools*, Report of the Committee on the Curriculum and Organization of Secondary Schools. (Inner London Education Authority, 1984).

Independent Learning Project for Advanced Chemistry (ILPAC). (John Murray, 1983).

Jarman, R., 'Primary science–secondary science continuity: a new era?' *School Science Review*, 1990, **71**(257), pp. 19–29.

Review of Chemistry: Courses and Teaching. Report by Council for National Academic Awards. (1991).

Schools Council Itegrated Science Project (SCISP), The Schools Council. (Longman, 1975).

Resource books for preparing units

Coles, M., Gott, R. and Thornley, A., *Active Science*, Vol. 1. (Collins Educational, 1989).

Coles, M., Gott, R. and Thornley, A., *Active Science*, Vol. 2. (Collins Educational, 1989).

Gott, R., Thornley, A. and Price, G., *Active Science*, Vol. 3. (Collins Educational, 1991).

Hart, R., *Chemistry Matters*. (Oxford University Press, 1978).

Hill, G., *Chemistry Counts*. (Hodder and Stoughton, 1986).

Hunt, J. and Sykes, A., *Chemistry*. (Longman, 1984).

ILEA Modular Secondary Science Resources. (John Murray, 1986).

Insight to Science. (Inner London Education Authority).

Michel, M. (ed.), *Integrated Science. An Examination Course*, Vols 1 and 2. (Macmillan, 1986).

Modular Science for GCSE. (Heinemann, 1989).

Nuffield Chemistry. (Longman, 1967).

Suffolk Science, Co-ordinated Science, The Suffolk Development. (Collins Educational, 1987).

CHAPTER 8

CHEMISTRY FOR GCSE

Philip Evans and Sandra Evans

INTRODUCTION

All subject labels in science are essentially artificial divisions. When does surface chemistry become physics? When does biochemistry become biology? Is geology anything more than the physics and chemistry of the Earth? Yet despite the impossibility of watertight subject compartments, there is something familiar and reassuring about the ring of the major scientific disciplines. What makes chemistry the subject it is? What is it about this discipline that interests those who study it, and those who want to teach it? One of the nicest definitions of the subject, and one which captures the essentials in a way that few definitions do, runs 'Chemistry is about stuff'. When young pupils are given a definition of this sort, their immediate reaction is to question its scientific validity; after all, it's not even couched in 'scientific language'. (There are some good teaching points here alone—think about it!) Persist—chemistry is not only 'about stuff': it's about how to turn one sort of stuff into another, about knowing what rules the various kinds of stuff obey, about how living things use the raw stuff of the environment to make the 'stuff' they need. Here we have managed to define inorganic, physical and biochemistry, albeit in rather an unorthodox fashion. We therefore see that chemistry will emerge from a science course, whether it is explicitly recognized in the structure of the course, or whether it is integrated by syllabus or school organization into a package called 'science'. The dogma of titles should not prevent us recognizing that there is indeed a body of knowledge that is about 'stuff', and that it is intellectually satisfying, manipulatively taxing and really pretty good fun.

'Name a famous scientist.' Such a demand to a class usually elicits the name of a physicist—Einstein is a popular answer. 'Name a British scientist' produced Sir Clive Sinclair in a survey a few years ago. Despite this lack of general awareness (no-one ever mentions a chemist) and this lack of feeling that chemistry is at the forefront of scientific advance, the discipline is alive and well, and making a fair contribution to our well being and, incidentally, to our balance of payments. So despite the 'image problem'—and environmental issues haven't helped, since it appears that chemists are uniquely responsibly for all the world's problems—there is much of interest to teach, much of relevance to inculcate, and you need to be dextrous too!

Chemistry's evolution as a subject will help give an insight into present day ideas and concerns, so we turn for a moment to some recent history.

HOW HAS CHEMISTRY EVOLVED?

A comparison of an 'elementary' chemistry textbook from the early '50s with today's plethora of chemistry in textbooks reveals a staggering change in content, experimental work, presentation, language, use of colour and so on. The subject has changed more radically in the past few years than at any time since its introduction into the school curriculum in the 19th century.

The history of the subject itself is a colourful one, reaching back into the dubious motivation of the philosophers' stone and the elixir of life. The idea of turning base metals into gold and of achieving immortality through the subject are guaranteed to interest even the most recalcitrant pupil but are no longer in any syllabus validated by the School Examinations and Assessment Council (SEAC)! Nevertheless, it can be a useful exercise asking pupils to trace the origins of the subject and it also provides an opportunity to link with your history department for an interesting introductory lesson.

But it is the rapid changes themselves that give an insight into the altering perceptions that we have of our subject as we approach the end of the millenium. In those '50's textbooks, the subject was treated essentially descriptively, and the content was academically biased. Much of the thrust was for 'wet' inorganic chemistry, illustrated practically, if at all, by demonstrations given by the teacher. The philosophy is wonderfully emphasized by the classic *Lecture Experiments in Chemistry* by Fowles [1], and dipping into this book not only underlines the approach then used, but also—and perhaps more importantly—gives details of splendid experiments, which always work! Some penetrating comments are also present: 'It is almost impossible to melt sulphur to its mobile amber state whilst teaching a class at the same time'. True, and what a wonderful experiment to assess dexterity and the following of instructions. Pneumatic chemistry, now very under-played, was extensively studied perhaps not quite '100 ways of preparing and collecting hydrogen' but it probably did occasionally seem like that.

The changes, then, and we will return to these points in various guises in the Chapter, are a move away from content for its own sake—'But it's chemistry'—to content illustrative of the applications and relevance of the subject; to content supportive of the manipulative skills that run through modern day chemistry. Because of the increasing importance of skills in general, both at 16+ and at 18+, the practical side of the subject has become increasingly stressed in recent years. This is the predominant thrust of coursework and we shall look at the effect of this practical bias on presentation in the next section.

One central piece of advice at this stage. If you're nervous about practical work, then you must practise beforehand. Get it right! A well-executed demonstration of technique before the pupils begin their practical work will raise your status and credibility. Avoid being the science teacher 'whose experiments never work'. Ensure, too, that you are fully up to date with all accepted safety procedures—the COSHH regulations give the legal position regarding risk assessment and the safe handling, disposal and storage of hazardous chemicals [2]. You cannot run risks with your pupils' safety!

In a nutshell, the present day philosophy is that the subject is skills-led and applications-driven. 'Make the subject live, and make it live at the bench' is no bad motto, and syllabuses can be judged like this too.

PRESENTATION

The rapid change in chemistry outlined above shows that many, if not most, of today's chemistry teachers will have been taught, or had the subject presented to them, in a radically different fashion than that demanded by present day ideas. Unless a syllabus defines a course itself in a pretty prescriptive way, e.g. *Nuffield Co-ordinated Sciences* or *Suffolk Science*, there will always be considerable latitude given to the teacher in the approach adopted. It is difficult, and likely to be misleading, to imply that one presentation method is uniquely superior—in one sense, what is 'best' will depend on the type of class. 'Play your class like a violin' said one experienced science teacher, and it's quite good advice too.

What, then, are the extremes of presentation? Let's look from one extreme to the other, though anything of this sort will smack of parody. In experimental terms, they range from a lecturing style, with limited illustrative experimental work, (and that as demonstrations) to a totally practically-driven style, where even the content and theory is 'discovered' by the pupil. In application terms they range from a 'pure' style, where there is no compromise to the living nature of the subject—all is atomic structure, kinetics and abstract descriptive chemistry—to a completely application-driven approach (as originally introduced by the *Salters' Chemistry Course*). In practice, two useful discriminators can be applied: first, how is the practical work to be approached, and second, how are applications to be treated.

In terms of practical work one might begin with the 'Heuristic' approach of Armstrong a century ago (see for example [3, 4]). The pupil learns through the experimental approach and, although in many respects it was unrealistic in the purity of its philosophy, it did spawn the Nuffield revolution of the '60s. The Nuffield radicalism now seems tame, but the influence made its mark. Nowadays, even though the demonstration still has a place in teaching, the subject must be heavily experimental, focusing on the pupil's own work at the bench. The needs of the National Curriculum, with its skills emphasis, demand it, and the pupil seems to have intuitively come to expect it. Most lessons will ideally have a practical component, and this makes considerable resource demands on a school and equally daunting demands on a teacher's time, effort and ingenuity. An experienced colleague is invaluable here, as is a well-stocked filing cabinet of well-tested experimental sheets. If they are your own work, annotate them, revise them and file them as 'an ever-present help in times of trouble'.

From an applications point of view the debate is illustrated by Figure 1 in Chapter 2. Do you introduce the relevance as your theory advances or vice versa? In practice, the distinction is not always quite so clear-cut, and again the demands of the syllabus constricts freedom of action to some extent. These days there is no doubt that even if a purer approach is emotionally favoured by a teacher, GCSE general criteria and National Curriculum requirements demand a fair sprinkling of applications and 'relevance'. A more logical and enthusing approach is to avoid compromise and build in the chemistry as needed in an applications-driven style. In practice, the end result of such an approach appears reassuring, even to the traditionally-minded teacher, despite the complaints, for pupils emerge after the course chemically literate and, if it's done well, enthused.

These days, there is so much resource material available from industry or curriculum development groups that an applications-driven style need not demand extensive first-hand knowledge of the subject's applications (just as well, as few of us have such a polymath-like ability!) and time is all that is needed to bring reality into the classroom.

TYPES OF SYLLABUS

Any sort of analysis of the available syllabuses at GCSE with a complete or part chemistry content needs first of all to look at the various possible ways of constructing such a syllabus. There are to date, and will continue to be until the June 1993 examinations, five basic approaches to chemistry/science syllabuses, described as integrated, combined, co-ordinated, modular or single subject, offered in various guises by the individual examination boards. In one sense, of course, each syllabus is unique, but it will soon become obvious that, as Orwell might have said, 'some are more unique than others'. Syllabuses for the June 1994 examinations must however take account of the new National Curriculum science Orders (the four attainment targets model) and the requirements for Key Stage 4 assessment and reporting. A revised clutch of syllabuses are currently awaited from the boards. Although it is not yet known which syllabuses will gain SEAC approval, it is clear that at least one substantial collaboration has taken place between several boards to produce a more coherent suite of syllabuses. The five basic types of syllabus are still distinguishable and their salient features are outlined below.

Integrated

In an integrated science syllabus (the term is only applicable to science syllabuses) the material of the three major science disciplines is treated together, with no distinction being made. Indeed, there is no reason why the terms chemistry, physics or biology should ever be heard by the pupil in the context of the lesson! Thus, as a whimsical illustration, a lesson on 'cold weather' might include the chemical properties of ice, a coverage of rotational motion of skaters and the biological problem of keeping warm! Some educationalists see the non-division of subject matter and the efficiency of one teacher dealing with the course as strong advantages, whereas others see the loss of subject expertise as ensuring that, for example, bad physics will almost certainly be taught. The other curriculum advantage is that balanced science can clearly be delivered in this way, provided that the needs of the National Curriculum are covered by the course syllabus.

Combined

In the various combined science syllabuses, there may be some variation in what is presented, since the term itself is used in slightly differing ways. In general, though, it refers to a single course in which all three major disciplines are presented, but in which the three components retain some sort of individual identity. In this way, such a course could be taught either by one teacher or by a combination of subject specialists. The examination would usually make no distinction between the sciences and in this respect there would be little, if any, difference between integrated and combined syllabuses.

Co-ordinated

In co-ordinated syllabuses, the subject base is retained, so that chemistry, physics, and biology are visible as separately identifiable units. They would be taught (in general) by a team of teachers to help ensure subject expertise. The word co-ordinated also implies that care has been taken to avoid duplication of topics. It also means that opportunities are taken to link sections of the subject coverage together, for example, a study of fuels in chemistry coupled with energy changes in physics and respiration processes in biology. Generally the examination will contain science, rather than subject-specific, questions.

Modular

In a modular syllabus, the course would be presented within the syllabus as a series of watertight units, modules, and a selection would generally be required rather than all modules being tackled. A central core is usually studied by all pupils, so the course can be described as containing core and extensions. The essential and distinguishing feature of a strictly modular course, is that much of the assessment is done by an end-of-module test as each unit is completed, so that a terminal examination need not be extensive and only serves as a 'summing-up' of the course. Many pupils have responded well to the challenge of these short-term goals in their progression through the course. Recent changes in the allowed percentage of coursework for GCSE will however have serious implications for the modular approach.

Single subject

The single subject approach is of course self-defining. The main current interest here is the change in government thinking, if not that of educationalists, to allow National Curriculum requirements to be achieved by those studying the three separate sciences by a revised supplement to the science criteria. This will not be achieved before 1995 and pupils currently studying three separate sciences will be exempted from the National Curriculum requirements for 1994.

TYPES OF COURSE AND THEIR RESOURCING

There are two main ways of delivering the material contained in syllabuses—via a 'conventional' or a coursebook approach. In a conventional course, the syllabus would describe the factual, theoretical and practical content (including manipulative skills for example) and a teaching scheme would be constructed from this. This teaching scheme would not necessarily have any relationship with the order of the material in the syllabus, and may even include amplification if the departmental head saw this as useful to the coherence of the course within the classroom. Coverage of the National Curriculum programme of study and statements of attainment would obviously be built in. Choice of textbooks, worksheets and other resource material is then up to individual taste. A few single-subject syllabuses are still specifically referenced to the Nuffield approach, based on the experimental approach collected in *Revised Nuffield Chemistry* and the associated option books.

The other type of course is not just defined by a syllabus as such but also by published coursebooks and resource materials, e.g. *Salters' Science*, *Nuffield Co-ordinated Science* and *Suffolk Science*. Here the teaching order is already set out although alternatives are provided within the scheme. Syllabuses which rely on published courses are becoming less favoured by SEAC, but the resources themselves are very well-researched and can be an enormous boon to hard-pressed teachers as a source of lesson ideas. Many consider the purchase of a set of the course material as a useful acquisition even if the whole course is not to be taught.

There are other valuable curriculum resources which are not linked to any particular syllabus but cover or enhance topics that are to be taught. The *Science and Technology in Society* (SATIS) 14-16 has proved very popular for exploring real-life applications of science, and the new *Nuffield Modular Resource*, *Pathways through Science*, has been developed to provide different routes and strategies through science material to allow appropriate teaching and learning styles for pupils of differing ability.

COURSEWORK ASSESSMENT

Here is one area of GCSE work where even experienced teachers have had to learn on their feet over the past few years since the introduction of compulsory teacher assessment. Although it may not seem like it, the idea of assessing practical work and other skills is relatively new, although it has spawned huge quantities of rapidly produced literature over this short time. As is so often true, in-house material produced, and ideas and approaches thought through, within the department are an excellent means of achieving sound and successful coursework assessment.

For examination courses beginning in Autumn 1992, teacher assessment is concerned with Attainment Target 1 (AT1) of the National Curriculum. There is plenty of detail in the new science Orders, but syllabuses will presumably interpret these in order to give more guidance of what is required of the pupil and, by implication, of the teacher!

In designing an experiment to test certain skills, a checklist of good practice should be applied to ensure that all will work well, and that you achieve what you've set out to do, i.e. a successful and accurate assessment of candidates in a specific area. Discussion within the department with experienced teachers is the best way forward, but a typical set of guide-lines/reminders of good practice might run as follows:

(i)   Remember—assessing candidates individually is the best and fairest way—don't make the assessment too complex! With manipulative skills, and other skills observed and assessed 'at the bench', a checklist approach saves time. That is, have a list of (say) six points to look at, and a simple cross/tick system is then efficient. Division of the class into two, with writing for one half and practical for the other, followed by a reversal in the second half of the lesson can sometimes help.

(ii)   Design your experiment carefully. It is best to write it specifically for the task in hand rather than to use and slightly adapt an existing experiment. Remember the KISS approach used in industry: Keep It Simple, Stupid!

(iii) Try the experiment yourself!

(iv)   Make sure the chemicals, apparatus and prep. room demands are not excessive and that it can be done in the time available.

(v)   Have others look at it and read it through.

(vi)   Remember the ethos of GCSE and make it interesting, relevant and 'can-be-done' by the majority.

There are other aspects of assessment in some syllabuses, such as communication skills and working with others. In Nuffield single-subject courses, options may also have to be assessed. The extent to which they are required to be assessed in present syllabuses is small, and it is more a question of whether you feel happy with the philosophy of including them that matters here. It is certainly true, however, that their assessment is fully in line with the general aims of the GCSE ideal. It's also true that role play and other vehicles for pupil assessment are often great fun in the classroom.

Matters may well change with the new syllabuses; dealing with assessment issues sensitizes us all to the rate and extent of educational change in recent times.

DIFFERENTIATION TECHNIQUES

GCSE was designed from the outset to cover a large ability range—some 70% or so of the school population—and although observers differ in their assessment of how well this has been achieved, there is no doubt that it spans a greater range of ability than GCE and CSE taken together. All GCSE examinations are meant to be 'can-do' examinations; that is, candidates are to be given tasks that they are likely to be able to cope with. Present GCSE syllabuses address the problem of assessment via a range of methods, most usually a common set of examination papers giving access to a maximum of grade C, with optional papers giving access to higher grades. However, there are radical changes to the grading system from June 1994, and hence for courses starting in 1992, and it is sensible to consider the plans and issues in a little detail.

In June 1994, GCSE grading will change to a 4–10 scale which is intended to map onto what will become the 'old' A–G grading system. Given that the 4–10 scale is (at least partly) criterion-referenced via the National Curriculum statements of attainment, it is likely that some mismatch will occur between the 'new' and 'old' grades. It will be important to minimize these discrepancies by a variety of statistical techniques to retain public confidence in the new system. An additional complication is that level 10 is a form of 'super A' grade, and will mean that taxing questions capable of giving such high-level discrimination must be available.

It is likely that overlapping tiers of levels will be examined by different sets of papers, e.g. papers covering levels 4–7, 5–8 and 7–10. It is also likely that the syllabuses themselves will be set out in differentiated fashion, so that coverage of the material for lower levels will be less deep and detailed in syllabus terms as well as in final assessment terms. There will still be differences between syllabuses in this regard and it will be important to check that sanity and realism shines through the plans.

THE SYLLABUSES AVAILABLE

A detailed consideration of the current available syllabuses is rather a thankless task, since so much will change between 1993 and 1994. Nevertheless, a summary of the present syllabuses is given in Table 1. A few syllabuses have been omitted where it is already clear that they will not survive in any form for 1994. A brief outline is then given of some of the proposed syllabuses for 1994 examination, noting that at the time of writing these have not yet received SEAC approval. The left-hand column of Table 1 spans the range from separate subject chemistry (perhaps regarded as the 'purest' form) through to single-award science syllabuses at the bottom. The examination boards are set out across the top, and an asterisk in the grid represents the current availability of that particular type of syllabus on that board. Various explanatory comments are added to point out any further aspects of an individual syllabus. The term 'flexible' indicates that the syllabus is capable of being delivered by more than one teaching approach.

The first point that arises is the plethora of syllabuses available: how to choose? There are various ways of doing this of course, and the most obvious is to simply read through all the syllabuses, obtaining a 'feel' of ones that appeal. This is in fact quite unnecessary and a much better way is to use a checklist that asks pertinent questions, the answers to which should reduce the number of options to manageable proportions. The particular form of checklist used will depend on personal prejudice or perhaps, more acceptably, the various parameters such as those set by the policy of the school, the ability of the groups to be taught and so on. A personal checklist clearly needs to be tailor-made but the questions below set out one such list. It is worth pointing out

Table 1   A summary of the current syllabuses available (indicated by an asterisk) for June 1993 examination. (The numbers refer to the table footnotes.)

Syllabus	ULEAC	MEG	NEA	NISEAC	SEG	WJEC
Chemistry	*	*	*	*12	*	*
Chemistry (1 year)	*1					
Chemistry (*Nuffield*)	*2		*2		*12	
Chemistry (*Salters'*)		*4				
Science: Double Award						
co-ordinated		*5 and 6	*		*13	
combined	*3	*				*16
integrated			*		*14	
modular		*7	*10	*11	*15	*10
flexible route		*8 and 9				
Science: Single Award						
co-ordinated					*13	
combined						*16
integrated					*14	
modular		*7	*10		*15	*10
flexible route		*8				

ULEAC = University of London Examination and Assessment Council (formerly LEAG);
MEG = Midland Examining Group;   NEA = Northern Examining Group;
NISEAC = Northern Ireland Schools Examination and Assessment Council;
SEG = Southern Examining Group;   WJEC = Welsh Joint Education Committee.

1   ULEAC Chemistry (17) designed for candidates over 17 requiring a one-year course, can be taken over a longer period.

2   ULEAC and NEA courses both based on *Revised Nuffield Chemistry*. Coursework assessment includes one of the Nuffield options.

3   ULEAC Combined Science (Double Award) is examined by separate papers in biology, chemistry, physics and science topics.

4   MEG Chemistry (*Salters'*) Applications based course material in 16 units with teachers' guide from the University of York.

5   MEG Nuffield Co-ordinated Sciences: separate biology, chemistry and physics material in inter-related courses, with teachers' guide and pupil books.

6   MEG Co-ordinated Science (*Suffolk Science*): 100% school-based assessment over separate units with course materials available.

7   MEG Science Syllabus C (Single Award) and D (Double Award) are limited grade (C and CC) for pupils of average ability.

8   MEG Science Syllabus A (Single Award) and B (Double Award) are topic based, but permit flexible teaching approach, e.g. integrated, co-ordinated or alternative organization of material.

9   MEG Science (*Salters'*): Course units with teachers' guides (University of York), designed around familiar materials and issues and delivered by co-ordinated. integrated or combined approach.

10   NEA and WJEC Science (Modular) contains choice of core and option modules for Single or Double Award certification.

11   NISEAC The Science: Double Award (Modular) has a co-ordinated approach with core biology, chemistry and physics and options including earth sciences, biotechnology and electronics.

12   SEG Chemistry has four subject possibilities: chemistry and chemistry external, each in general (grades C–G) and extended (grades A–G) format. Nuffield approach can be used, but no option assessment is required.

13   SEG Science (Single Award and Double Award) Co-ordinated available in both general (grades C–G) and extended (grades A–G) format.

14   SEG The Sciences (Single and Double Award) Integrated are developed on a 'patterns' approach taking account of SCISP findings.

15   SEG Science (Single and Double Award) Modular has a choice of essentially integrated or co-ordinated routes.

16   WJEC Science (Combined) allows both Single and Double Award with content in distinct units of biology, chemistry and physics.

that the list has been drawn up with the availability of syllabuses in mind: there is little point seeking a modular, integrated, applications-driven dual award course if the grid indicates that no-one has designed it yet!

(i)   Does the school policy determine whether the syllabuses should be single award, dual award or full subject? The answer to this question reduces the choice substantially.

(ii) If your answer is 'yes' to single subject, is an option approach something you feel is worth considering?

Remember that some teachers feel that the options are arguably more difficult than the main bulk of the syllabus, and that, on this type of syllabus, the hard-working, competent pupil may find it difficult to gain a grade A. Incidentally, if you are going to use statistics to produce a 'best buy' in terms of likely results—beware—some syllabuses may have a larger than average entry from selective schools for example. Boards favoured by the independent sector fall into this category.

You may also feel that a subject with a small entry may be dangerous for a number of reasons: unreliability of cohort ability from year to year, a small group of schools with a high proportion of able pupils having a distorting effect and so on.

(iii) If a single or dual award approach is taken, do you prefer an integrated, combined or co-ordinated structure?

Various types of modular structure are also possible: do you see a modular approach as giving useful flexibility?

(iv) Do you want an applications-driven syllabus or one of a more conventional structure?

Many course-type syllabuses will be applications driven in the sense that the chapter headings will not have titles such as 'Acids and Bases' but, for example, 'Chemicals in our Food', 'Metals at our Service' or 'Keeping Warm'.

(v)   Are your own quirks as regards factual content catered for?

Even if you don't think in a factually orientated fashion, it is a good idea to look at syllabuses that appeal to you in a conventional content-minded way. In some syllabuses, you may feel that, when looked at in this fashion, there are certain illogical aspects. As a specific example, you may feel that the treatment of organic chemistry on an applications-driven syllabus contains so little organic fact as to make understanding difficult for the pupil. Don't forget, even if this is so, that a syllabus is *not* a teaching scheme and some degree of elaboration in some areas may be wise. Also, it is wise when planning a teaching order, to remember that the order in the syllabus is not necessarily— indeed probably *isn't*—the best order in which to teach the course. This does not apply to a syllabus based on a prescriptive course book.

(vi) Am I happy with the examinations involved in the course, and am I happy with the coursework assessment component? It is a good idea to send for past papers!

These issues have been dealt with earlier; don't forget them, they're important!

(vii) Has the course substantial new resource implications for your Department?

(viii) Is the course going to be fun to teach and fun for the pupils?

'Fun' has to be taken in context of course. Not many 15-year-olds would regard chemistry or science as preferable to many out-of-school activities, but in so far as is possible they should enjoy their course, and want to pursue the subject beyond GCSE. Given the figures for pupils studying science post-16, perhaps that must be our next crusade!

CHANGES FOR JUNE 1994 EXAMINATION

Two significant developments are the increased emphasis on syllabuses allowing flexible teaching styles and the collaboration between some examination boards in producing common syllabuses. NEA, ULEAC and WJEC have collaborated on a science framework syllabus consisting of 'content units' related to the strands of the National Curriculum programme of study. The units can be grouped for teaching in either a co-ordinated, integrated or modular approach, and differentiation is possible. The framework allows Single and Double Award certification and will later provide separate subject syllabuses.

ULEAC has also collaborated with SEG on a modular syllabus based on 'Science at Work'. Combined science syllabuses (revised) are proposed by several boards and MEG is intending to continue offering revised versions of the resource-based syllabuses; *Salters' Science*, *Nuffield Co-ordinated Sciences* and *Suffolk Science*.

REFERENCES

1   Fowles, G. *Lecture Experiments in Chemistry*. 3rd edn. (Bell, 1948).

2   *The Control of Substances Hazardous to Health Regulations, 1988*. (HMSO, 1988).

3   van Praagh, G. (ed.), *H. E. Armstrong and Science Education*. (John Murray, 1973).

4   Brock, W. H. (ed.), *H. E. Armstrong and the Teaching of Science 1880–1930*. (Cambridge University Press, 1973).

PART 3
TEACHING AND ASSESSING CHEMISTRY

This Part of *Open Chemistry* addresses important issues in the teaching and assessment of chemistry and avoids the quasi-legalistic aspects of the National Curriculum. Haines, in Chapter 9, considers the concept of a radical alternative pedagogy—supported self-study—which has always been a central component of Open University delivery processes and is rapidly gaining ground in post-16 science education. Haines first explores this methodology as a logistic response to a resource necessity—the shortage problem of qualified teachers and adequate resource backup. He then goes on to explore how the necessity can be seen as a virtue. Self-study, suitably supported, is a powerful pedagogy that empowers learners when linked to appropriate assessment strategies.

In Chapter 10 Hudson explores the role of chemistry in developing pupils' skills which are defined in terms of intellectual, motor and cognitive domains. The Chapter argues that much of current practice focuses on the development of memory skills at the expense of higher order skills, and that their development can only occur through the creation of active learning environments, a point also made by Haines. The Chapter also considers the links between active learning and assessment, an issue which is further explored by Dutch *et al.* in Chapter 11. They argue that assessment should arise naturally from the aims and objectives of teaching and learning strategies and not be a formula-based framework of testing and reporting that is imposed on the curriculum. They also argue that teachers should adopt a wider range of assessment strategies in the context of both the theoretical and practical elements of chemistry. Essentially Dutch *et al.* present the case for pupil-centred assessment strategies and the development of clear departmental assessment policies set within an overall school policy.

Finally, Bentley in Chapter 12, looks at the complex, and very important, relationship between teaching and learning in terms of the role of evaluation as a mechanism for providing vital feedback to teachers. Bentley argues strongly for the formulation of clear school policies with respect to the evaluation of the outcomes of teaching and learning and strongly supports the notion of keeping the curriculum under constant review. The last ten years has seen an increased interest in quality management in education and Bentley sets out some very practical scenarios whereby individuals and science departments can take this on board.

CHAPTER 9

THE ROLE OF PUPIL-CENTRED LEARNING IN THE TEACHING OF CHEMISTRY

Chris Haines

INTRODUCTION

Changes in the curriculum are having a profound effect on what is being taught, how it is being taught and how it is being assessed. The change in emphasis from content to process, shorter term learning goals, and the assessment of coursework in chemistry courses are forcing teachers to reconsider their teaching strategies. If teachers are to continue to dominate lessons with talk, as Bulman [1] and others suggest, it is going to be difficult for pupils to develop inquiring minds and to become autonomous learners.

Helping pupils of all ages to 'learn how to learn' should be the major goal of all teachers. As chemistry educators do we feel confident that we are helping our pupils to:

- achieve a measure of self-organization in their work?
- approach a variety of learning tasks independently?
- handle the resources available to them?
- develop skills and attitudes to assist inquiry?
- communicate effectively?

that is, learn how to learn?

Today there are an increasing number of *resources* and *systems* available to the teacher, which makes a pupil-centred approach to learning an interesting reality in the classroom.

What needs to be known is how to use these learning *systems*, and how to adapt these *resources* into a meaningful experience for the pupil. As Green [2] said when assessing the development of individualized learning:

'If science teachers are going to make some departure from their current practice then they need some good reasons and some know-how. Perhaps the most important thing is to show what is being done... to show what is possible... and to make it seem an exciting and realizable possibility.'

Green [2]

One such *resource* which has had an impact in the teaching of A-level chemistry is the *Independent Learning Project for Advanced Chemistry* (ILPAC) [3]. It can be used completely as an independent learning scheme or partially as a resource for other existing schemes of work.

One such *system* is supported self-study. The Council for Educational Technology (now called the National Council for Educational Technology,

NCET) first proposed the use of supported self-study during its investigations as to how educational technology might help to maintain breadth of curricula in the face of falling school rolls. It provides a framework for managing and organizing learning for pupils and teachers.

Supported self-study is a system that has been used successfully in the teaching of A-level chemistry, but has applications for GCSE and for science in the National Curriculum. Recent national developments have brought the features of different learning systems under the umbrella term *flexible learning*. A common feature in these systems is the pupil-centred philosophy. In 1989 the Training Agency gave formal recognition to the movement by establishing a Flexible Learning Development Programme within the Technical and Vocational Education Initiative (TVEI) which was designed to help implement pupil-centred approaches to learning. Two publications which provide an overview of flexible learning developments are, *Flexible Learning: A Framework for Education and Training in the Skills Decade* [4] and *Flexible Learning in Schools* [5].

This Chapter explores the principles of pupil-centred learning, describes the author's involvement with ILPAC at A-level and how ILPAC was used as a stimulus to develop a 'system for learning'. It documents how that system worked and suggests ways in which the features of the system meet the needs of new curriculum initiatives such as GCSE and the National Curriculum.

SYSTEMS FOR PUPIL-CENTRED LEARNING

The average person in the street has a clear picture of teaching, i.e. teachers stand in front of pupils in a classroom—the teacher talks and the pupils listen.

Classroom life is not that simple. The teacher is trying to achieve a number of goals at the same time:

- provide a variety of learning tasks and experiences;
- set tasks and provide resources to meet individual differences;
- provide opportunities for pupils to take responsibility and to reflect simply on their learning;
- provide a balanced style of management and control;
- keep records of the progress of pupils;
- ensure the learning programme is balanced and satisfies the National Curriculum.

This list is formidable, but it is not the full list as there are added complications. These arise, paradoxically, from valuable work which has taken place during the last two decades designed to improve the quality of teaching and learning. Much of the thinking and experimentation has led to the development of *systems* of teaching and learning. Most of these have been based on the pupil-centred philosophy with its concern for individual differences and pupil autonomy.

Secondary education in the '60s and '70s witnessed a number of developments in *resource-based learning*, and this was followed in the '80s by project development in *supported self-study*, which led to the Employment Department, through TVEI, launching *flexible learning*. Within adult education and further education the same period has been marked by developments in *open learning*.

Waterhouse [6] provides an extensive discussion on the range of systems for learning, documenting their characteristics. He concludes:

> 'the demands that all this makes on the teacher are considerable. It requires managerial skills of a high order. The teacher's work in the classroom is extraordinarily complex. *It is very different from the layman's image of teaching.*'

> *Waterhouse [6]*

However, many of the pupil-centred ideas have been taken up and incorporated into government plans and initiatives such as the Certificate in Pre-Vocational Education (CPVE), TVEI, GCSE, post-16 developments and the National Curriculum. The proliferation of systems and initiatives have led to some confusion, but teachers should not regard them as competing with each other.

Each system has its own emphasis and appeal, and each has made a valuable contribution to developments within the major government initiatives. They all use the same focus, i.e. they are pupil-centred and are therefore concerned with individual differences and needs. They are members of the same family and teachers are *well advised not to identify with any one system, but to use the insights gained from them all.*

It seems that teachers today have a better chance of really making a difference to the ways in which pupils learn and grow. There is increasing support among teachers for flexible approaches to teaching and learning which is reflected in government initiatives. Teachers have gained experience in implementing these approaches to teaching and learning. One such experience for chemistry teachers was the development of ILPAC.

ILPAC PROJECT

ILPAC is one of three A-level science projects sponsored by the now abolished Inner London Education Authority (ILEA) and was written for pupils studying for the A-level examinations of the GCE. The scheme was built upon a well prepared course consisting of learning resources, pupil guidance and teacher control materials, as well as a sound structure for the management of the classroom. It consists of twenty *Students' Guides* with an accompanying *Teachers' and Technicians' Notes*. Four starter units act as a bridge between GCSE and A-level as well as providing a foundation for pupils from a variety of backgrounds; the other units can thereafter be interwoven in a variety of different teaching sequences.

The *Students' Guides* are structured and written in short paragraphs with a liberal use of headings and diagrams. Each booklet contains a variety of teaching strategies. Their function is to guide the pupils through these various activities starting with an account of the prerequisite knowledge and a pre-test to assess the pupils' readiness to start. Each section lists the objectives to be achieved and this is followed by theoretical explanations, worked examples, revealing exercises, practical work, as well as the use of video and computer programmes. There is an emphasis on assessment (both teacher and self-assessment) with tests in each unit, as well as an abundance of problems and exercises, all of which have answers supplied at the back of the unit.

Finally, the *Teachers' and Technicians' Notes* outline strategy, suggest support materials, provide answers and a mark scheme for the teachers and give details of practical requirements for technicians.

The origins of the project can be looked at from two widely contrasting ideals. The preface at the start of the first booklet ILPAC S1: *The Mole* [7], states these two ideals:

> 'Although ILPAC was initially conceived as a way of overcoming some of the difficulties presented by uneconomically small sixth forms, it has frequently been adopted because its approach to learning has certain advantages over more traditional teaching methods. Students assume a greater responsibility for their own learning and can work, to some extent, at their own pace, while teachers can devote more time to guiding individual students and to managing resources.'

ILPAC [7]

The factors which prompted the ILEA to finance the ILPAC project can be categorized into two well-defined areas. One is purely educational; we might call this *virtue*. The other stems from administrative needs and pressures; we might call this *necessity*. It is rare in the world of education for *virtue* and *necessity* to join forces in such a potent and productive way.

Virtue

A recurring theme in the discussion of educational styles and methods is the role of 'autonomy'. It is a major aim in education. Waterhouse [8] amplifies it as:

> 'a sophisticated concept with connotations of responsibility, rationality and authenticity. The autonomous person is not guided by unbridled self-will; he or she is strong, independent, capable, but also responsible, rational and authentic.'

Waterhouse [8]

Shapiro [9] expresses anxiety that in some classes pupils are not being given the opportunity to develop fully. A question frequently raised was 'How are the learning processes made real to pupils unless they are allowed to become involved in such processes?' The charges of 'spoonfeeding' and 'overteaching' were frequently made by Her Majesty's Inspectorate (HMI). 'Learning how to learn' was becoming a major objective for secondary education. The published HMI reports, the discussion papers from the Department of Education and Science (DES), the TVEI curricula, the outlines of CPVE, and the local authorities' own curriculum guide-lines have given support to pupil autonomy by emphasizing some common themes. These use the language associated with the philosophy of autonomy in education:

- pupils taking more responsibility for their own learning;
- learning by doing rather than simply acquiring knowledge;
- aligning modes of teaching more closely with pupils' individual needs;
- negotiation of the curriculum to include diagnosis of learning needs and identification of appropriate learning activities;
- experiential learning centred on the young person;
- use of resource-based, participatory learning and teaching workshops.

'Negotiation', 'contract', 'experiential learning', 'continuous assessment', 'self-development' and 'participatory learning' have become the vogue words; and virtue is once again in fashion! This is all the more remarkable when set against the hard facts of falling school rolls and tight budgets.

Necessity

Schools have always wrestled with a galaxy of problems which originate from the problems of organization and the commitment of the schools to produce their educational offerings to meet the needs of the individual pupils. Some common examples are:

(i)   An option group falls below the size thought to be economical. Should the school discontinue it, or carry on with unfortunate consequences elsewhere in the timetable?

(ii) Failure to recruit a teacher for a specialist course puts a subject at risk, at least temporarily.

(iii) A school is forced into pupil groupings which are more heterogeneous than the teachers wish; upper school option sets contain pupils with different examination objectives as well as different abilities.

These examples are boundary problems and they are not new. Their presence was felt in the days of expansion during the '50s and '60s. What was new in the present situation was that contraction in the schools made the boundary problems assume greater proportions. In the late '70s anxiety was growing as to how schools could contain the balance and breadth of their curricula when the number of pupils began to decline. The local authorities found themselves facing in two different directions.

The uncertainty was foretold by the Briault Report [10]. Its main recommendation was that:

'Each LEA should establish the principles on which it intends to plan a system of good secondary schools for the 1980s.'

Then followed discussion of the possibilities of closure, amalgamation, new policy for staffing schools, and the problems of teacher redeployment. But in its last recommendation it changed tack abruptly:

'The DES should initiate or support studies of the possible enhancement of learning resources to meet the needs of individuals and small groups in schools; and of the cost implications of alternative courses of action to meet the fall in the secondary school roll.'

Briault and Smith [10]

For the most part LEAs sought solutions to their falling school roll problems through closure, amalgamations and the redeployment of teaching staff, rather than through the 'alternative course of action'. The ILEA's answer to help alleviate the problem was to sponsor three A-level science projects—ILPAC was one of these. However, it is not an exclusive solution to the problems.

EVALUATION OF ILPAC

ILPAC was set up at a time when the debate about falling school rolls and greater pupil autonomy was at the forefront of the educational debate [11, 12]. Some evaluation findings from Haines [13, 14] are presented here as a contribution towards informing the debate.

Inevitably the degree of confidence in the general outcomes of the scheme varies. Some can rightly be described as conclusions, others are more tentative; still more are accurate, but soon become outdated by the constantly changing pressure of events. Nevertheless, in my opinion, certain points are noteworthy.

(i)   Cost was a major factor in schools not buying the materials; only a few schools had purchased a large number of sets. However, even if no financial restrictions were in operation, over half the schools stated they would not wish to change fully to ILPAC.

(ii)   The implementation of curriculum materials does not rest simply on the provision of adequate equipment. Ultimately it depends on an acceptance by the teachers themselves that the materials can enhance their teaching. In the case of ILPAC most teachers saw the materials as a basis for updating their syllabuses, not as a model for restructuring their teaching method. Nevertheless, there was some evidence that ILPAC stimulated interest in independent learning and greater pupil autonomy in sixth-form chemistry courses.

(iii) Of the uses suggested by the teachers, the most popular was that of a resource to complement traditional teaching, although there were many other uses. Different activities in the materials served a wide variety of purposes.

(iv) Schools operating the full scheme suggested that the whole course was perhaps too structured. However, it could easily be adapted. Supported self-study was a method proposed to organize and manage the ILPAC materials and utilize it as a resource for pupil-centred learning.

(v)   A tentative finding was that teachers did not feel confident with pupil-centred learning and had experienced little training.

(vi) One feature of new curriculum materials is the impact they make upon teaching and learning. There was evidence to suggest that as a result of seeing and using ILPAC more teachers were now changing the emphasis in their teaching. The move was towards a more pupil-centred approach whereby the teacher gives individual attention to pupils instead of talking to the whole class—a move from a didactic approach to a more open-ended one. Pupils were being given more responsibility for their learning.

TOWARDS A SYSTEM FOR MANAGING LEARNING: SUPPORTED SELF-STUDY

Whilst the evaluation highlighted the variety of uses of ILPAC it is important to provide teachers with some guide-lines for the use of ILPAC. The concern over the scheme being too structured needs to be heeded. An overstructured course could have the effect of damping enthusiasm in the same way that traditional teaching sometimes does. Flexibility is important—for both pupil and teacher. The pupil–teacher relationship is the focal point of any system. Supported self-study was encountered in the evaluation of ILPAC and provides a system to utilize well written resources.

So what is supported self-study? Perhaps it is better to start by saying what it is not. It is *not* a do-it-yourself system with the teacher abdicating all responsibility; nor is it 'self-supported' study, whereby the pupil is left on his or her own with the responsibility for making an approach to the teacher if help is needed. Independence and isolation are not synonymous. A much more positive and involved approach is required; the learning resources must be rich and varied. It is not a stand alone system to be operated separately from other teaching.

Supported self-study is a system which helps teachers to train secondary school pupils to take more responsibility for their own learning. Its key features (illustrated in Figure 1) are:

(i)   learning materials and *resources*;

(ii)   support from regular *tutoring* organized in small groups;

(iii)   a *management* system for monitoring and control.

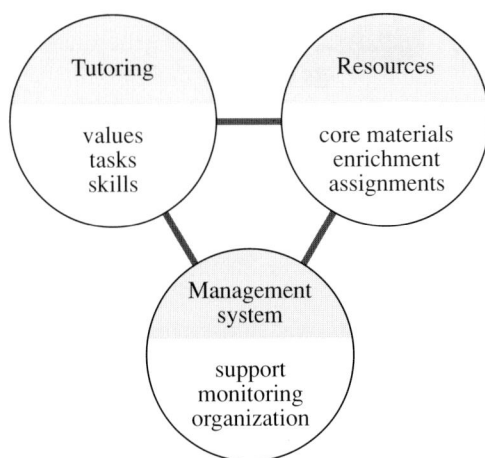

Figure 1   Key features of supported self-study (from Meed and Waterhouse [15]).

The aim is self-development, but two important points need to be emphasized. First the aim is a long term one. It is foolish to expect instant results and the job of the teacher is to provide supporting structures and procedures which will help the pupil gradually to develop a sense of responsibility and the skills which go with it.

Second, self-development is not an argument for isolating pupils and making them work on their own. Self-development is development 'of yourself' not 'by yourself'. Pupils need a wide variety of experiences if they are to be independent. These include both the opportunity to work intensively and privately in an efficient manner and the opportunity to share, cooperate and compete with others.

Organization of the system (illustrated in Figure 2) was of great importance as pupils need freedom, but this must be within a framework which offers support and guidance.

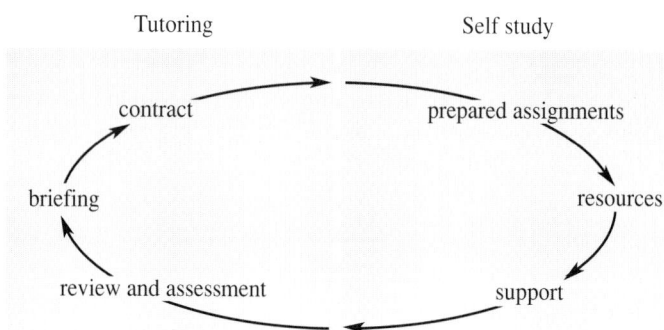

Figure 2   Organization of supported self-study (from Meed and Waterhouse [15]).

Waterhouse [8] likens the cycle to a 'two-stroke engine'. It comprises tutoring on the one hand and self study on the other. A group tutorial could begin with a strengthening of personal relationships which would be followed by pupil review and evaluation of the work already completed. After discussion and suggestions a briefing would be undertaken to stimulate interest in the new work which is about to be started. Help could be given to the pupil to make a plan of this work, adapting the guidance to the known abilities, interests and styles of the pupils. This would then be formalized in a contract (an example is shown in Figure 3). This would be a binding agreement between pupil and teacher and could be signed by both parties. It is something which is discussed, not imposed—it is a negotiation. A summary of the tutorial by the teacher and the pupil could complete the first stroke of the engine.

The self-study part would then follow using a range of activities and assignments using the resources available. These resources are those already available in the school. There is no need to buy in whole schemes of individualized learning. A good resource could be a textbook or a study guide. At all times the teacher is acting as a resource either by giving an introductory lecture, organizing a seminar, giving individual or small group help, or setting an assignment or practical. The role of the teacher, though, has changed. The flexibility *allows* for things to happen and for problems to be tackled as they arise.

Contract completed?   yes   no

If not why? ....

Was the plan suitable for you?   yes   no

If not why? ....

Evaluation of contract

	Could have been much better	$\rightarrow \rightarrow \rightarrow$		Was about as good as I'm capable of
My use of laboratory time				
My use of private study time				
My reading around the subject				
My follow up with difficult questions				

Any other comments? Anything you did particularly well, or felt very satisfied with on this contract?

Test score: ....   Tutor: ....

William de Ferrers School
Nuffield Advanced Science — Chemistry

STUDY CONTRACT

Name: ....   Completion date: ....

Missing work

Pupil signature: ....
Tutor signature: ....   Date: ....

Figure 3 Example of a pupil contract.

Between 1986 and 1989 I was Head of Science in a purpose-built community school in Essex where supported self-study made an impact in the teaching of chemistry. Our first group of sixth formers started their *Nuffield Chemistry A-level Course* [16] using a system of supported self-study. The ILPAC materials provided an excellent resource for the A-level course and was used as our starting point. Many of the features of the supported self-study system were later developed and integrated into the *Salters' GCSE Chemistry Course* [17]. Both ILPAC and *Salters'* courses provided resources which accommodated the principles of pupil-centred learning.

One early quote from a sixth-form pupil reflected pupil–teacher relationships:

> 'we as a group are continually supporting and helping each other ... our status is on a par with the teacher. He is used as a resource as well as a feeder of information. The tutorial gives us the opportunity to discuss the problems we are having as well as helping us to plan and organize how we use our time.'

The success of the system is shown by those pupils who have left school. They now deliver INSET and provide keynote addresses based around their experiences. They provide the evidence by talking about their experiences.

Tutoring

In the cycle described in Figure 2 there is an assumption that the style of the teacher–pupil relationship is different from that normally found. This is where the value of the tutorial and the teacher as tutor is essential. The idea of tutoring is still fairly new. Tutoring is the intensive support given to learners, usually in small groups to enhance the quality of their learning—however, it is more than small group teaching. It is the most significant difference in a pupil-centred approach.

Many observers reflect on pupil-centred approaches to teaching and learning and say 'we have been doing this already'. There is a danger of what Fullan [18] calls 'false clarity'. Good teaching and learning schemes do exist, especially in science, but we must be careful not to oversimplify what supported self-study offers.

The focal point of the supported self-study system is the group tutorial which aims to strengthen personal relationships, review and evaluate working methods, stimulate interest, plan future work, as well as providing a forum for discussion. These tutorials can be lively sessions whereby pupils gain confidence in a range of skills and also feel that they own part of the course they are following. Their ideas are discussed and taken into consideration when preparing future work. The tutor tries to improve the quality of teaching and learning based upon concrete evidence from the pupils—they are the ones learning. The system described was developed initially with A-level pupils using ILPAC as a resource. How does it fit into the 11–16 curriculum?

What about GCSE?

The influence of the GCSE has been significant in the development of pupil-centred learning in that coursework is now important and a stronger attachment has been given to the principle of criteria-referenced grading.

The vision of a small group tutorial is an inspiring one. But there are problems in the pre-16 curriculum. How can this be realized when:

- class sizes are large;
- pupils are not always well motivated;
- there is a shortage of resources;
- pupils lack the necessary skills of studying and organizing;
- teachers lack the confidence required for effective tutoring;
- teachers are not always clear about how they can shift from the traditional class teaching mode into a system involving the substantial use of small group tutorials.

These are real problems and there is no point in underestimating them. So it has to be accepted that the shift into the tutorial system usually needs to be made slowly and carefully. How are teachers to move pupils from their present situation onto the road to greater autonomy?

There are three aspects which teachers need to incorporate into their lessons if they are to create independent learners:

- they must put emphasis on engaging pupils in tasks that they *can* and want to complete;
- they must consider ways in which pupils receive a *variety* of tasks and assignments;
- they need to develop an understanding of what learning is by establishing a *dialogue* about learning between the pupil and the teacher.

These are the ingredients for teachers to address, but the pupils need to develop the appropriate skills:

- active learning processes;
- team work;
- independent learning.

These can all be introduced within class teaching. The basic idea is to shift the style gradually towards the small group tutorial. *Salters' GCSE Chemistry Course* [17] and *Salters' GCSE Science Course* [19] provide many of the active learning techniques, teaching styles and opportunities for independent learning assignments which provide the foundation resources necessary to shift towards more pupil-centred learning.

A useful technique to make the shift is the 'supervised study mode' as described by Waterhouse [20] in *Classroom Management* (illustrated in Figure 4).

The teacher starts by setting the whole class an assignment and prepares them for it by very thorough briefing. The teacher must ensure written instructions

```
┌─────────────────────┐                  ┌─────────────────────┐
│     whole class     │ ◄──────────────► │ small group tutorial│
└─────────────────────┘                  └─────────────────────┘
           │                                        │
           ▼                                        ▼
       assignment                               briefing
           │                                        │
           ▼                                        ▼
        briefing                                 clarify
           │                                        │
           ▼                                        ▼
          task                                     task
           │                                        │
           ▼                                        ▼
       monitoring                                 review
```

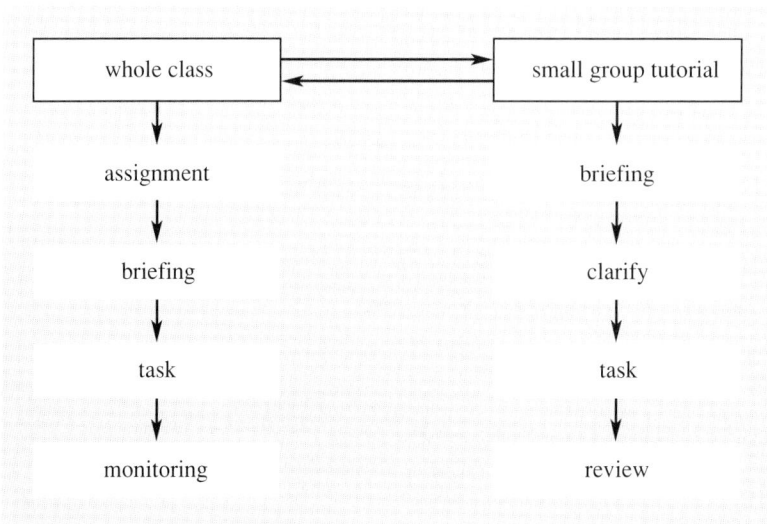

Figure 4   Supervised study mode. The pupils and teacher alternate between whole class and small group tutorials.

are clear and that resources are supportive and accessible, and that the topic chosen is likely to be interesting.

When the class has settled the teacher should start the first tutorial. The tutorial could be a simple briefing for a small assignment set in context. The teacher would work with a small group (ideally five) at their workplace. The tutorial would be rather prescriptive in its early stage with clarity the priority. The pursuit of clarity should be the main mission. The teacher should encourage pupils to take notes, set targets and ensure they come away knowing what they have to do and when. The tutorial would be very short, lasting 5 or 10 minutes.

The pupils are now ready to continue with their present task. However, they are fully briefed for the next task (as outlined in the tutorial). The next tutorial can then be undertaken and the process repeated, but not before the whole class, in supervised study mode, has been attended to.

When all the groups have had their briefing tutorial, the teacher can revert to a monitoring role, with the pupils trying to find solutions to their problems within their groups. When a group comes close to finishing the task, a review tutorial could be given. This allows for the pupils and teachers to react to the work. Recognition is important at this stage for each individual.

Naturally not all work in chemistry courses can be organized in groups and the transition to this way of working will bring problems such as differentiation and assessment. These are not new problems. They exist whatever system of teaching and learning is used. The tutorial system however does seem to bring them into the open.

In the long run the National Curriculum will help teachers with these problems by providing a firm and clear structure within which to work.

THE ROLE OF PUPIL-CENTRED LEARNING IN THE NATIONAL CURRICULUM

Teachers view the National Curriculum with a certain amount of anxiety. They have been concerned for the development of the whole pupil. Will some of the best methods and styles of teaching and learning have to be abandoned? Many teachers have been pleasantly reassured with what they have found. The National Curriculum is certainly demanding with regard to knowledge and understanding, but it addresses itself also to flexible methods of learning. In some cases it is actually demanding them [21], for example:

> Attainment Target 1: *Scientific investigation*
>
> Pupils should develop the intellectual and practical skills that allow them to explore the world of science and develop understanding of scientific phenomena, the nature and procedures of scientific exploration and investigation. This should take place through activities that require a progressively more systematic and quantified approach, which develops and draws upon an increasing knowledge and understanding of science. The activities should encourage the ability to plan and carry out investigations in which pupils:
>
> (i)   ask questions, predict and hypothesize;
>
> (ii) observe, measure and manipulate variables;
>
> (iii) interpret their results and evaluate scientific evidence.

These are general skills concerned with the process of learning. They imply intellectual and practical activities occur simultaneously and are mutually supportive. They paint a picture of communication, collaboration and cooperation. They also imply talk at a high intellectual level. These kind of targets simply cannot be reached through didactic teaching alone. They are the essence of pupil-centred learning. Further statements in the National Curriculum which encourage a pupil-centred approach come from the levels of attainment, for example:

> Level 8
>
> Pupils should carry out investigations in which they:
>
> (a) use scientific knowledge, understanding or theory to generate quantitative predictions and a strategy for the investigation.
>
> (c) justify each aspect of the investigation in terms of the contribution to the overall conclusion.
>
> Level 9
>
> (b) systematically use a range of investigatory techniques to judge the relative effect of the factors involved.
>
> (c) analyse and interpret the data obtained, in terms of complex functions where appropriate, in a way which demonstrates an appreciation of the uncertainty of evidence and the tentative nature of conclusions.

The implications from these statements are that pupils and teachers have to be involved in some formal negotiation and discussion about what they are trying to do, how they are progressing and how they can improve on what they are doing. Tutorials have a key role to play in this context.

An examination of the prescribed programmes of study is equally reassuring. In the general introduction to the Key Stage 4 programme of study the following note on communication is prominent:

> 'Pupils should be given opportunities to develop further their skills of reporting and recording. They should be encouraged to articulate their own ideas and work independently or contribute to group tasks. They should develop research skills through selecting and using reference materials and through gathering and organising information from a number of sources and perspectives. They should have opportunities to translate information from one form to another to suit audience and purpose and to use databases and spreadsheets in their work.'

Quite apart from the encouragement found in the attainment targets and programmes of study, the Order laid before Parliament is very encouraging. It makes no demands on how much time is to be allocated to science, on how it is to be timetabled, or how it is to be organized—separate subjects, integrated, combined or modular. It also allows flexibility for teaching outside the ranges of levels specified where it seems in the interests of an individual pupil. This is altogether reassuring and should, in the long run, strengthen the development of pupil-centred learning in science. Of course many teachers at the present stage are conscious of the burden of the proposals, as the amount of work involved in the change is considerable. The benefits will be seen when teachers are able to devote all their energies to the methods, styles and techniques of curriculum delivery.

MANAGEMENT AND ORGANIZATION

The National Curriculum together with other governmental initiatives have certainly not removed the need for the management of the curriculum at school level. However, the departmental structure is still used by the majority of schools for the delivery of the curriculum.

If the science department is the main vehicle for the delivery it must be strong enough, flexible and capable of development and improvement. Team-work is an important ingredient, although leadership must be of a high quality. Teachers need to be working towards common goals, but their work must be seen as part of their own professional development.

Courses should be broken up into modules or small units which greatly helps the organization and management. The planning of units or modules of work should be the responsibility of teams of teachers. Each unit should have a set of objectives, content summary and checklist presented in the form of a sheet and given to both pupils and teachers. It provides the pupils with a clear idea of where they are going and assists greatly in their planning and organization as well as being a focus within the tutorial. A tutors' planner lists all the references to the relevant resources for a particular unit. It is updated and amended as the course is evaluated, making efficient use of planning and preparation time. ILPAC and *Salters'* materials prove very valuable in the setting up of these tutors' planners, but perhaps the most significant effect of these materials is that the staff do not have to devise a whole range of learning materials and are able to concentrate on the management of the course.

A whole scheme can be organized so that a range of teaching and learning styles and features are experienced. These styles would include group work, small group teaching, problem solving, simulations, fieldtrips, investigations, surveys, individual projects, case studies and the use of audio, video and information technology. The range of styles provide stimulation especially when set in context. A science department can quickly develop these strategies if they share and centralize their experiences.

Resources

Resources are always near the top of the agenda in any discussion on teaching and learning styles. Resources alone, however, are unlikely to bring about real change in the classroom.

No resources will transform a teacher who is largely didactic into one whose teaching is pupil centred. No independent learning package, however well structured as ILPAC is, will turn a passive pupil into an autonomous learner overnight.

A pupil-centred approach involves a variety of approaches, tasks and resources to promote achievement. Not all resources have been prepared with the aims of this approach in mind. Teachers react in various ways. They reject them, they try to rewrite them, they use them as they are, or they blame them for their lack of success.

Resources need to be used wisely and pupils need guidance and support in how to use them. Powell [22] provides extensive coverage of how to choose, evaluate, adapt and manage existing resources for pupil-centred learning.

Monitoring

Pupil self-assessment plays an important role in a pupil-centred approach. Self-assessment sheets, which are part of the contract (illustrated in Figure 3), can provide an evaluation of previous work. Pupils can assess their use of time, resources, laboratory and library as well as making general comments, both positive and negative.

Another form of self-assessment are questions which are posed on workcards where pupils can check their own answers against model answers and only seek support when they get something wrong.

Assessment through written tests is becoming increasingly fashionable again, but regular end of unit tests, set in context, allow pupils to measure their level of understanding regularly. Both ILPAC and the *Salters' Course* provide excellent written tests so that they do not have to be created.

Accurate records of progress are vital and the contract sheet can give the pupil the opportunity to record work completed, missing work, comments and marks obtained: since these are open to others in the group the pupils are not only able to refer to their own progress, but also to measure it against their peers. Support is encouraged and it is interesting to note how pupils help each other when difficulties arise. The high level of cooperation and support that pupils give each other when studying in this way is gratifying.

Finally, there is a strong link with the developments in records of achievement and profiling, with pupils developing a portfolio of achievements and attainments.

Learning skills

Supported self-study supports and is supported by parallel developments which emphasize the active approach to learning and the move towards greater pupil responsibility including developments in study skills and information skills.

Active sessions on how to listen, take notes, skimming, scanning, self-organization, questioning, presenting, taking examinations as well as sharing useful revision techniques can be integrated into courses. These are all study skills and every teacher must be a teacher of these skills. The tutorial provides an excellent avenue to discuss them and for the pupils to share and support each others' ideas.

There is overlap between study skills and information skills. However, information skills concentrate on pupils finding, locating, selecting, recording and using information. Access to the information, either through the school library or in a departmental resource centre, is vital. An interest in learning skills can result in a whole school approach to learning as Lincoln [23] clearly describes.

By having a variety of teaching and learning styles throughout any course, pupils can acquire the learning skills in context. It is not a question of setting time aside to talk about learning skills. It is more a matter of introducing techniques and advice whenever the pupils seem ready for it and need it. Pupils in primary schools have developed a whole range of learning skills. These need to be progressed and built upon in the secondary phase.

WAYS FORWARD

As always, everything hinges on the quality of the performances of the teachers. Abandoning a total addiction to class teaching in favour of a more versatile repertoire which includes supported self-study is not easy. The management of pupil-centred learning and the tutoring styles that go with it are very different from class teaching. The teacher needs to make a conscious shift in both attitude and techniques, and this cannot be done without a sustained effort.

Like much development work there are trials and errors. Changes in styles and in direction have to be considered if things seem to be going astray. A universal recipe is to keep the personal relationships in a healthy state. Effective change is a learning process. Teachers need help and support when trying out ideas—it is an anxiety-ridden process and there is a fear of failure. We spend a lot of time creating a conducive climate for learning for our pupils, but seem to apply none of the lessons learned with our colleagues. Teachers as well as pupils need time for reflection on their current practice if they are to improve. Senior staff need to encourage and support risk-taking and experiment rather than frown upon it. They must build the self-confidence of the teacher—this can be done most effectively by emphasizing and building on strengths rather than highlighting weaknesses and failures. Teachers must not feel threatened.

For most schools a minimum commitment on a trial basis is the best way to start. There is no great threat to any teacher. A small segment of a course and a few pupils may be sufficient to give the desired experience. Growth can proceed with security and at a pace which suits all and gives plenty of opportunity to reflect, change and improve. However, for the committed, whole courses can be assigned.

The benefits could be substantial. In the current situation we have on the one side the aspirations of the profession, supported by new initiatives in curriculum and assessment. This, with its convictions about the importance of self-development in education, is the side of *virtue*. On the other side are the practical problems associated with falling school rolls and tight budgets. This is the side of *necessity*. Is it too much to hope that in exploring 'alternative course of action' the LEAs and schools together might discover a recipe of combining *virtue* and *necessity*? If they do, it will probably be a totally new experience!

Opportunities for all pupils to experience the benefits of being responsible for their own studies can exist, leading to true self-development, a vision which most teachers share, but which continues to be elusive.

REFERENCES

1   Bulman, L., *Teaching Language and Study Skills in Secondary Education*. (Heineman, 1985). pp. 54.

2   Green, E. L., 'Individualized Learning in Science', *School Science Review*, 1982, **63**(226), pp. 16–22.

3   *Independent Learning Project for Advanced Chemistry* (ILPAC). (John Murray, 1983).

4   *Flexible Learning: A Framework for Education and Training in the Skills Decade*, TVEI 4, Technical and Vocational Educational Initiative. (Employment Department, Moorfoot, Sheffield, 1991).

5   Eraut, M. and Nash, C., *Flexible Learning in Schools*. (Employment Department, Moorfoot, Sheffield, 1991).

6   Waterhouse, P., *Flexible Learning: An Outline*. (Network Educational Press, 1990).

7   *Independent Learning Project for Advanced Chemistry* (ILPAC) S1: *The Mole*. (John Murray, 1983).

8   Waterhouse, P., 'Supported Self Study in Secondary Schools', *Media in Education and Development*, 1985, March, pp. 29–32.

9   Shapiro, J. P., 'Back to Basics versus Freedom of Choice', *Forum*, 1981, **3**(23), pp. 81–83.

10   Briault, E. and Smith, F., *Falling Rolls in Secondary Schools*, Briault Report. (National Foundation for Educational Research, 1980).

11   Bulman, L., 'ILPAC in Hyderburn', *Education in Chemistry*, 1980, **5**(80), pp. 134.

12   Robertson, C. T. and Bulman, L., 'ILPAC: A New Approach to A-Level Chemistry', *Education in Chemistry*, 1980, **80**(5), pp. 133.

13   Haines, C. G., *An Evaluation of the Use of ILPAC Materials*, unpublished MSc Dissertation, University of East Anglia, 1987.

14   Haines, C. G., 'Experience with ILPAC: Individual Learning Via Supported Self Study?', *School Science Review*, 1989, **70**(253), pp. 103–107.

15   Meed, J. and Waterhouse, P., *Implementing Flexible Learning*, Resource Pack for Trainers, Managers and Tutors, National Council for Education Technology and National Extension College in Collaboration with the Training Agency. (HMSO, 1989).

16   *Nuffield Chemistry A-level Course*. (Longman, 1967).

17   *Salters' GCSE Chemistry Course*. (Science Education Group, University of York, 1988).

18   Fullan, M., *The New Meaning of Educational Change*. (Teacher Educational Press, 1991).

19   *Salters' GCSE Science Course*. (Science Education Group, University of York, 1988).

20   Waterhouse, P., *Classroom Management*. (Network Educational Press, 1990).

21   *Science in the National Curriculum*, Department of Education and Science. (HMSO, 1991).

22   Powell, R., *Resources for Flexible Learning*. (Network Educational Press, 1991).

23   Lincoln, P., *The Learning School*. (British Library, 1987).

CHAPTER 10

DEVELOPING PUPILS' SKILLS

Terry Hudson

INTRODUCTION

The word *skill* is often used but rarely defined. It is defined in the *Concise Oxford Dictionary* as 'expertness, practised ability, dexterity and the facility for doing something'. This definition highlights the dilemma—there are different types of skill, a footballer is described as having skill on the ball, a tightrope walker shows skill and daring, a person is said to be skilful debater and pouring a liquid is classed as a skill. All of these uses are correct, but the word skill is used differently in each case.

In answer to the question 'which skills concern the teacher of chemistry?' I have turned to three skills, (i) intellectual, (ii) motor and (iii) cognitive, listed and defined by White [1] as components of his seven elements of memory. White's seven elements (given in Table 1) can be interpreted as showing a progression of depth of learning, from simple recall to complex reasoning skills.

Table 1 Seven types of memory element (from White [1]).

Element	Brief definition	Example
String	A sequence of words or symbols recalled as a whole in an invariate form	'To every action there is equal and opposite reaction'
Proposition	A description of a property of a concept or of the relation between concepts	The yeast plant is unicellular
Image	A mental representation of a sensation	The shape of a thistle funnel: the smell of chlorine
Episode	Memory of an event one took part in or witnessed	An accident in the laboratory; setting up a microscope
Intellectual skill	The capacity to perform a whole class of mental tasks	Balancing chemical equations
Motor skill	The capacity to perform a whole class of physical tasks	Pouring a liquid to a mark
Cognitive skill	A general skill involved in controlling thinking	Perceiving alternative interpretations; determining goals; judging likelihood of success

One could argue that much formal, teacher-centred teaching has concentrated mainly, though not exclusively, on the development of memory elements presented higher in Table 1. Competence in the recall of strings (remembered laws) and propositions (information that may be paraphrased, but is still in the form of fragments of information) is expected more than in the other elements. Many test questions are designed to test these two skills, e.g.

Name the three common laboratory acids.

Write down the formula for water.

What is the ideal gas equation?

I would argue that no intellectual skill or cognitive skill is required to cope with these 'chunks' of knowledge, and that the ability to answer these questions is not a measure of understanding of chemical concepts. That is not to say that memorizing diverse pieces of information, the facts and figures associated with a subject or discipline, is a bad thing, but understanding could be said to occur only when this information is used for a wider purpose.

Images and episodes are also important elements in many chemistry lessons. Teacher demonstration and class practical work are common ways of placing these elements in the memory of the pupil. As with strings and propositions, however, recall of experiences of this type, if demanded in isolation, does not involve understanding.

The use of practical work and demonstration, possibly still amongst the most commonly used teaching and learning strategies in science teaching, bring in the elements of image, episodes and motor skills, but if the activity is passive—a sit and watch demonstration or a recipe practical—then little opportunity exists for intellectual and cognitive skill development.

Intellectual, motor and cognitive skills can be regarded as making higher order demands on the pupil, as other memory elements must be drawn on and used consciously. To engage these elements pupils must be involved actively in their learning, with learning becoming a personal challenge, rather than the task of taking on board parcels of information for recall later. Any information encountered is analysed and reflected on—a far cry from the rote learning of chemical or mathematical formulae in isolation. How many of the pupils we have taught in the past have 'learned' the symbols of the first 20 elements of the Periodic Table without having any understanding of atomic structure, physical and chemical trends, uses of the elements or even a clear understanding of what an element was?

If we are intending to teach chemistry so that the pupils have an opportunity to come to terms with the major concepts of the discipline, I would argue that teaching strategies should encourage the learner to use the 'higher order' elements of memory—intellectual skills, motor skills and cognitive strategy. These three elements are now discussed in more detail.

WHAT ARE INTELLECTUAL SKILLS?

White [1] subdivided intellectual skills into three main divisions; discrimination, classing, rules. This classification, though obviously artificial, is useful for looking at the types of intellectual demands made on pupils. Chemistry lessons contain numerous opportunities for allowing pupils to acquire and develop these skills. Some examples are given below.

Discrimination

Discrimination involves differentiating between different objects or substances. This is a very common occurrence in chemistry, for example, discriminating between solids, liquids and gases or between organic and inorganic compounds. Interestingly White [1] states that overestimation of pupils' discrimination skills can lead to learning difficulties, as what seems obviously different to teachers may not be so to pupils.

Classing

Classing, which draws on discrimination skills, involves placing objects into groups, for example, classing elements as metal or non-metal. Pupils must draw on previous experience of properties, or use observation and analysis in order to group the elements as metal or non-metal. Classing may be done instantly, as would be the case with very experienced chemists, or require the methodical analysis of a series of properties. The importance of classing in chemical studies should be readily apparent.

Rules

Rules are followed to carry out an operation. Examples would include rules for balancing chemical equations and carrying out chemical calculations. Usually rules are very specific and it would seem that anyone with certain basic skills can learn to follow rules. An example of this from chemistry teaching would be the pupil who is capable of calculating values of volume by placing numbers into gas equations, but who has no real understanding of kinetic theory. Rule following is an important skill, but unless the pupil is given the opportunity for using the skill in a wider context it is relegated to the level of a 'numbers trick'.

The difference between intellectual skills and simple recall is that intellectual skills can be adapted for use in new circumstances. For example, once a pupil can use the gas laws with one set of values, then any values for pressure, temperature or volume can be used, even if the values are previously unknown to the pupil.

WHAT ARE COGNITIVE SKILLS?

There are numerous cognitive skills, e.g. assessing, reflecting, goal setting, interpreting, generating ideas, evaluating, prioritizing, adapting, planning and deducing. It is important that these cognitive skills, which admittedly draw on other memory elements, are developed within chemistry teaching and learning. It could be argued that without showing competence in these skills, pupils cannot demonstrate an understanding of concepts, and without such an understanding there is no meaningful learning. Teaching strategies that are active and pupil-centred are more likely to develop these skills in young people than traditional teacher-led, didactic instruction, as the latter techniques make few intellectual and cognitive demands on pupils.

Referring specifically to the cognitive skills of planning and evaluation, a report from the Assessment of Performance Unit (APU [2]) states:

> 'Opportunities for students to design experiments, or comment critically on the design of others, are not often given in science lessons... If skills of experimental design are seen to be important, then opportunities need to be given to develop these skills explicitly.'

APU [2]

It could be argued that pupils are given too few opportunities to develop other cognitive skills. The pressure of time and external constraints, such as the examination system can direct much teaching towards the passing on of information (filling empty pots) but the emphasis on cognitive skills within Attainment Target 1 (*Scientific investigations*) of the National Curriculum for science should mean that greater emphasis is placed on such skills in the future.

WHAT CAN WE DO TO HELP PUPILS TO DEVELOP COGNITIVE SKILLS?

Skills are developed by careful instruction and relevant practice. As cognitive skills require the manipulation and control of other memory elements, such as recalled facts, remembered episodes, images and intellectual skills, it is important that account is taken of the previous experiences and levels of skill of the pupils at the earliest opportunity. In this respect cognitive skill development and learning can be regarded as synonymous and so the approach advocated by the Children's Learning in Science (CLIS) project described below is useful.

Researchers involved with CLIS have reported that there are a range of misconceptions about scientific ideas held by pupils. Many of these ideas are central to scientific education, such as the particulate nature of matter. The researchers concluded that only a minority of pupils use accepted scientific ideas with confidence [3–5].

The CLIS findings led to a model of learning that is now well known, and is increasingly accepted and adopted. The approach accepts that learners bring to the learning arena their own set of ideas and beliefs (schemes), and that the way that they assimilate new ideas will depend on this prior knowledge and belief.

In this sense each learner is unique. The CLIS model takes this into account and proposes that pupils will only learn new concepts if they are offered experiences that conflict with their own beliefs.

An example from chemistry (illustrated in Figure 1) would be to confront a learner, whose concept of matter is as one continuous substance, with practical examples of matter behaving in a manner supporting the concept of particles, e.g. evaporation, diffusion or dissolving.

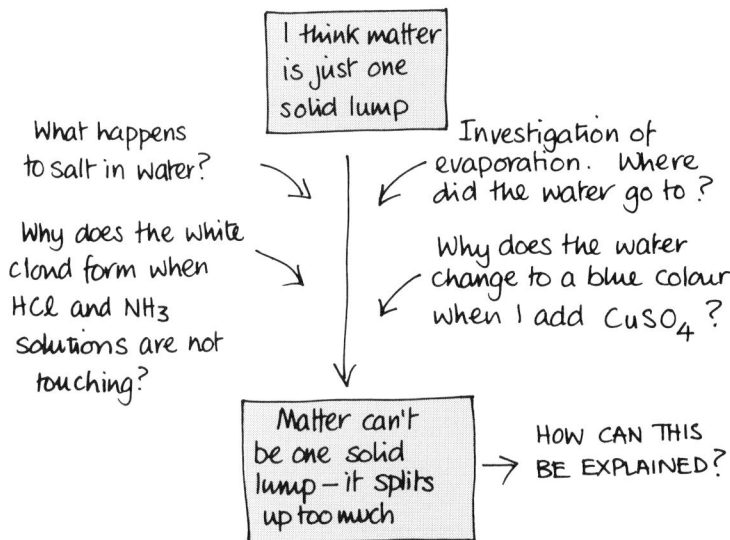

I think matter is just one solid lump

What happens to salt in water?

Investigation of evaporation. Where did the water go to?

Why does the white cloud form when HCl and NH₃ solutions are not touching?

Why does the water change to a blue colour when I add $CuSO_4$?

Matter can't be one solid lump – it splits up too much

HOW CAN THIS BE EXPLAINED?

Figure 1   Challenging a pupil's concept of matter.

These examples of the behaviour of matter cannot easily be explained by the pupil's continuous model of matter and, therefore, the possibility exists that new models will be searched for. It is important that the learner has been made overtly aware of his or her own ideas about matter, and has been given time to reflect on them.

The CLIS model is very important in the context of cognitive skill development as there are striking parallels between the development of understanding and the development of skills.

Classroom strategies for developing cognitive skills

Ten classroom strategies are briefly discussed below.

1   Encourage elaboration of work by allowing opportunities for pupils to paraphrase and make their own notes/diagrams. Place emphasis on pupil-designed summaries and conclusions as this creates the chance for pupils to consolidate their memory of work content and to develop vital cognitive skills such as *reviewing, evaluating and interpreting.*

2   Avoid questions, verbal and written, that exclusively demand simple recall, e.g. 'Is sucrose solution an electrolyte?'. *Group work responses* to more open-ended questions such as 'Plan and carry out an investigation—will sucrose solution conduct?' demand a variety of cognitive skills, such as reviewing, planning and critical analysis to be practised. Again, content is important, but an understanding of the concepts is paramount and is enhanced by engaging cognitive skills.

3   Attempt to produce *reading and writing tasks* that are active. There are many types of Directed Activities Related to Text (DARTs) but all involve the pupil in processing the text and having to adapt or use it in ways that demand greater understanding than simply reading. A simple example would be when presenting pupils with an experimental procedure. Rather than giving the procedure as a straightforward recipe, that could be followed or copied with little understanding, the order of instructions could be mixed up. The pupils, individually or in groups, then have the task of re-assembling the instructions in such a way as to allow the investigation to proceed in a scientifically valid and safe way. In order to do this the pupils must think carefully about the procedure and question each step. Diagrams and charts can also be presented in a form that requires processing, for example, cut up as a jigsaw or with sections deleted.

4   *Analogies or metaphors* can be very powerful ways of encouraging pupils to take a wider, more reflective view of a topic. White [1] gives the example of asking pupils about the similarities between a tree and a volcano. By comparing and contrasting these two items, pupils must recall many memory elements and engage in sorting and analysing each known detail of volcanoes and trees to deal with the analogy.

5   *Spider charts and networks* can be used to promote a range of processing skills, such as generalizing and reflection, as well as exercising the memory elements to do with factual recall. Pupils can be asked at the start, middle or end of a topic to draw a diagram containing as many aspects of the topic as they can think of. The items, words or phrases, are then linked together by arrows. Each arrow must be accompanied by an explanation of the link. This approach is a useful study technique and will be discussed later in the section on study skills.

6   *Concept mapping* is a technique similar to the one above, but in this case pupils are given a list of key words or phrases (Figure 2), possibly written on separate cards, and are told to order them on a table or poster in arrangements that make sense with arrows to link together words that are related. The relationships are then discussed. Pupils can be asked to write along the arrows so that a sentence is formed. For example, between elements and compounds in Figure 2, pupils could write 'combine to make'.

7   *Simulations* can be used to help develop cognitive skills. Not only do pupils get a 'feel' for what could be happening within a situation by actually being involved in representing part of a model, for example, representing atoms during a kinetic theory simulation, but by stopping the action and asking pupils for explanations and predictions there are opportunities for developing cognitive skills. Pupils can also be asked to design their own simulations, ensuring reflection and interpretation of chemical concepts.

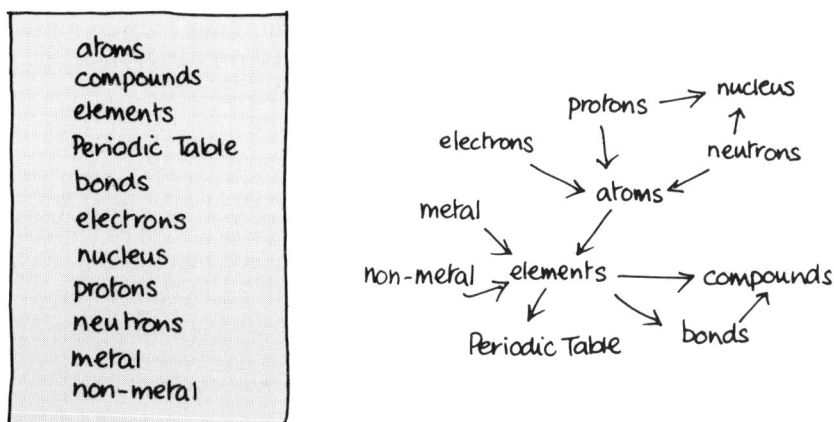

Figure 2   Concept mapping.

8   Allowing pupils to *design their own investigations* will offer opportunities for them to develop many cognitive skills. It is important that pupils unfamiliar with this approach are offered support and guidance. This can take many forms, for example, clue cards, prompt questions, investigation proformas such as the action plan illustrated in Figure 3, and teacher intervention. Pupils will draw on previous experience and knowledge to help them to carry out investigations and this aspect can be highlighted by considering an investigation involving acids. If asked to investigate which chemicals might be used to 'cure' indigestion, pupils would not progress far, even if practically competent, without an awareness of the acidic nature of indigestion, alkalinity, neutralization and ways of measuring acidity (pH). In addition to the value of previous experience, it is important that pupils are encouraged to take time to perform what are possibly the most neglected phases of designing investigations—planning in the beginning and evaluation throughout. Emphasis should be placed on these elements by the teacher, even to the point of formalizing the situation by asking to see plans and

activity	time	person	equipment	variables	measure
collect apparatus	2 min	Louise Stewart	beakers thermometer water Bunsen tripod	—	—
mix water	10 min	Bill		volume	temp + time

Figure 3   Investigation action plan.

stopping investigations to hear feedback about progress/opinions, etc. With potentially hazardous investigations teachers should always check plans to avoid danger to pupils, but with harmless investigations it is sometimes worth allowing pupils to learn from poorly formulated plans.

9　　　Problem solving can be regarded as an over-arching, composite skill that draws heavily on many intellectual and cognitive skills and is, therefore, an immensely important classroom strategy. Making pupils aware that they are involved in a process can be very useful, and it is possible to break down this process into stages for learning purposes. One model of problem solving developed by the *Problem Solving with Industry Project* (PSI) [6] has four stages (Figure 4) and it is possible to offer support at each stage.

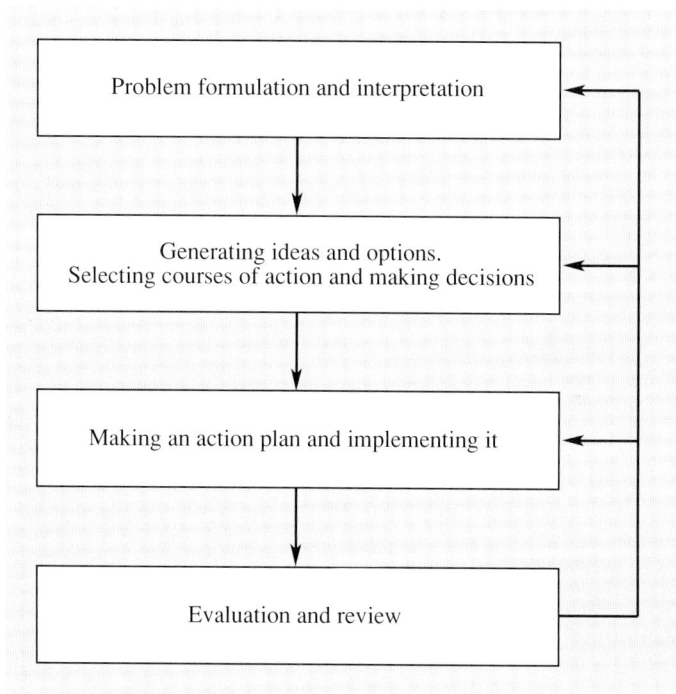

Figure 4　Stages of problem solving (PSI [6]).

Those pupils unable to progress from one stage to the next can be given support in the form of a written or verbal checklist of questions to act as prompt, e.g.

'What do the results tell you?'

'Does your solution match what you set out to do?'

In time this 'scaffolding' can be removed.

As with all effective learning the pupil must be clear about what the task is. Why are they doing it? What is the purpose?

10   Discovery learning, where pupils are given a lot of responsibility for finding out knowledge, requires a great deal of processing and analysis. In addition, participation and ownership of the learning experience can be very motivating. Pupils can very quickly become adept at carrying out research into topics and reporting back to their peers. There are some group work strategies that are designed to encourage this approach, for example, the jigsaw approach.

The jigsaw approach involves the formation of 'home groups', ideally of four or five pupils. Each home group is given the same communal task, but individual group members must move away to find out essential information. To do this they work with pupils from other home groups on 'expert tasks'. At a later stage the home group reforms, their information is shared, and the communal task is completed. The final stage is a whole-class briefing by the teacher to consolidate the main points of the investigation.

In attempting to develop intellectual and cognitive skills it is essential that the prior experiences of pupils are considered and that ample time is allowed for reflection and, hopefully, assimilation of new information. Teaching and learning strategies that are active, participative and give some responsibility to the learner make more cognitive demands than didactic methods. How many times have you heard chemistry teachers say that they didn't really understand a concept until they had to teach it? It could be argued that only when planning a lesson and really analysing and reflecting on the content, did learning take place with the teacher, so time for the pupil to undergo the same process should be allowed.

WHAT ARE MOTOR SKILLS?

Motor skills can be defined as the ability to carry out a whole range of physical tasks, e.g. pouring a liquid from one container to another. Motor skills involve memory of how the various muscles had to move to carry out a particular task. The task can then be duplicated. As with intellectual skills, motor skills are transferable—which is why those gifted in one ball sport are often very able in others. In addition, motor skills appear to be less easy to forget than other skills, but they do need to be practised to maintain good performance.

Knapp [7] states that motor skills cannot be divorced from what he calls mental skills, but that the overt part, the movement, forms the essential part in motor skills.

Motor skills are used extensively in chemistry and include those necessary for drawing apparatus and constructing charts, etc. as well as those needed for the safe manipulation of apparatus. In terms of chemistry learning, the objective must be to be able to perform repeated actions that accurately meet a predetermined standard. Obviously the standard can be altered to make realistic demands on pupils, for example, the difference between using a measuring cylinder to a tolerance of $0.1 \, cm^3$ or $1.0 \, cm^3$. Motor skills have predetermined goals and involve the development of sound technique.

HOW CAN MOTOR SKILLS BE DEVELOPED?

Motor skills must be learned by 'doing'—this may be why they are so unforgettable. Learning motor skills involves repetition, so that the muscle movements can be remembered, and this takes time. If this learning process is plotted on a graph then, despite differences between individuals and variations due to the type of activity, the resultant curve would resemble the one illustrated in Figure 5.

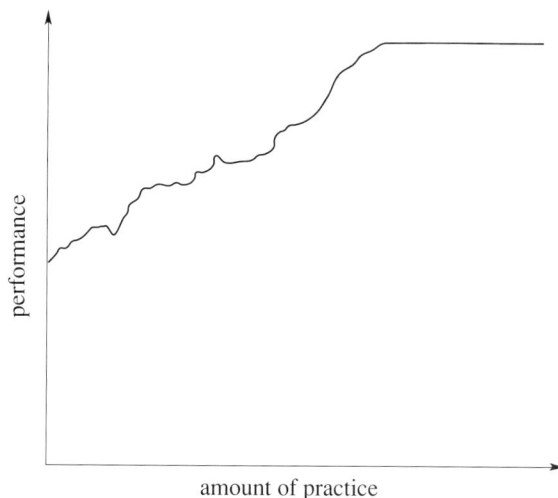

Figure 5   The learning process for motor skills.

There are some peaks and troughs in performance, brought about by fatigue, lack of interest, time of day, etc., but the general curve is upwards, until a plateau of performance is reached where vastly increasing the amount of practice will have very little effect on performance. It is important that this plateau does not lead to a loss of motivation. Once a pupil has mastered a skill and can carry out an operation accurately there is a danger that boredom will set in. This makes it very important to allow pupils to acquire and develop skills within an interesting and relevant context. Encouraging the practice of motor skills, even those that have been mastered, can take place within wider problem solving activities rather than as isolated tasks. Repeated actions that have already been mastered, such as fitting specific nuts and bolts in the motor industry before the use of robots, can be done with little or no intellectual or cognitive demand; factory workers carrying out complex motor actions can quite happily talk to each other about matters totally divorced from the task.

Complex manipulations can be split down into smaller elements whilst they are being learned. Good demonstration is a very powerful teaching tool as it is very important to give pupils a mental image of what the action is like. This must then be followed by 'hands-on' experience. A flow chart of a possible way of teaching motor skills is illustrated in Figure 6.

demonstration	Still involve pupils actively by questioning and allowing volunteers to try parts of the operation
practice	This allows pupils to start developing the muscle memory needed. Immediate feedback about performance is vital so that errors are not internalized. Keen golfers will know this syndrome well!
practice	Much tighter tolerances, increase level of accuracy
mastery	Skills, once mastered, should be used in ways that are demanding on the learner, e.g. within problem solving

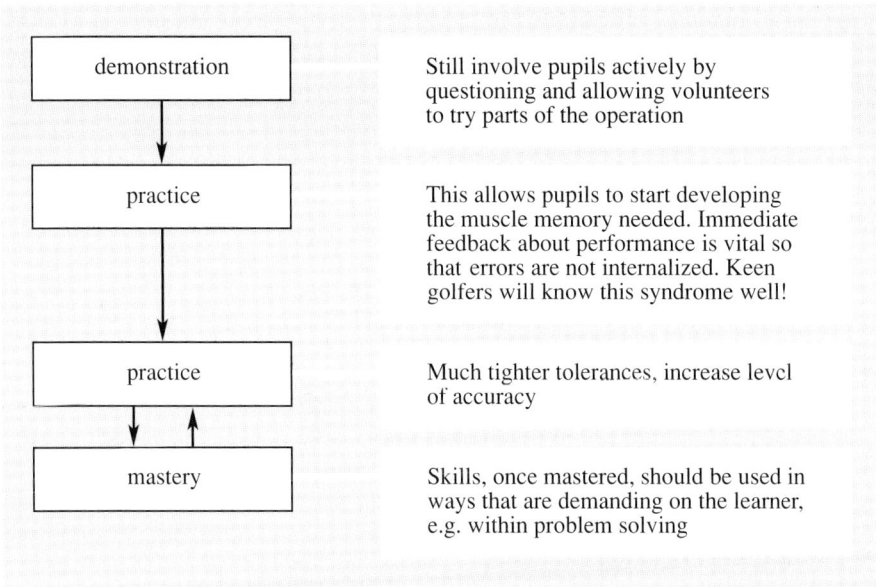

Figure 6   Teaching motor skills.

The key elements for teaching motor skills can be summarized as follows:

- take account of previous skills as motor skills are very transferable;
- break complex operations down into smaller elements;
- use good demonstrations;
- allow practice with wide tolerances initially;
- give immediate feedback about performance;
- allow skills development to take place within realistic situations when possible;
- decrease tolerances and increase the complexity of the activity as mastery improves.

It is possible for pupils to check the motor skill performance of their peers. Providing they have a clear idea of what the action(s) should be like, they will be able to judge colleagues on these criteria very accurately. This is very useful during practical lessons, particularly with large groups, when the individual time given by the teacher to each pupil is limited.

ASSESSING SKILLS

Skills can be assessed in two ways:

- judging the end product;
- judging performance.

The summative nature of the former makes it quick and efficient, but crude. For example, if a pupil has to measure out a specified volume of liquid and eventually does so, then summatively that pupil has the necessary motor skill.

They have matched the criteria for success. With this approach no idea of how the pupil performed the task is obtained. Issues such as safety and efficiency can only be assumed if the final 'answer' is obtained and there is not a great pool of liquid on the bench.

Judging cognitive skills is also problematic and involves the setting of tests or problems that can clearly demonstrate that these skills have been utilized. Traditional recall questions cannot do this and other strategies, for example, concept maps and spider charts, could be used for assessment. Even assessing skills such as planning can be difficult in isolation. Asking for written plans before an investigation can go some way to answer the problem, but no evidence of the thought processes involved can be gathered.

Judging the performance of skills must involve observations. These can be done by the teacher, another adult in the room or by peer observation. The performance is matched against predetermined criteria and a level of performance given. Making pupils aware of the criteria against which they will be judged is an important learning aid. Objectives are clarified and goals set. For example, the following criteria are given in the NEA *Science (Modular) Syllabus* for 1992–1993 [8]:

Skill 7 Devise and organize experiments

The candidate can:

2 marks   show rudimentary signs of achievement in the relevant skill

4 marks   with guidance and once given a simple idea that can be tested, plan a single-stage experiment and choose appropriate apparatus

6 marks   with help, formulate a simple idea that can be tested;

plan a single-stage experiment and choose appropriate apparatus;

show awareness of the need to control all but one dependent variable in order to achieve a fair test;

with prompting, recognize the more obvious weaknesses of an experimental design

8 marks   formulate an idea that can be tested;

take steps to control all but one dependent variable in order to achieve a fair test;

plan a sequence of stages for an investigation;

choose appropriate apparatus;

offer some ideas for the improvement of an investigation

10 marks   formulate clear ideas and predictions that can be tested;

suggest and collect information which might be relevant to an investigation;

describe how the dependent variables are to be controlled;

plan a sequence of stages for an investigation;

choose the most appropriate apparatus;

offer appropriate modifications to improve the investigation

NEA [8]

The cognitive skills that are used to meet the descriptions above become more demanding as progression from 2 marks to 10 marks takes place. How these skills are being used, for example, to gain insight or make decisions about solutions, is not revealed unless the process is observed.

Points to consider when assessing skills are:

- the pupil should understand how and why they are being assessed;
- the assessment should be seen as an integral part of the learning process;
- assessment should provide for all levels of achievement;
- assessment should concentrate on positive aspects of the pupils' abilities;
- pupils should be involved in their own assessment.

This shifts the role of 'evidence gathering' partly away from the teacher. How can 'evidence' be gathered? The various strategies for assessing skills are described below.

Pupil self-assessment

Pupil self-assessment will require a self-assessment checklist, possibly drawn up by or with the pupil, which should contain reference to the main aspects of the skill(s). This could be open-ended, or a detailed, structured checklist. An open-ended checklist could contain questions such as:

'What have you learned in the unit?'
'What skills do you think you have developed?'
'Which skill(s) do you think you need to work on?'

Peer assessment

One form of peer assessment is paired assessment. Pupils often work in pairs and this can be an ideal unit for assessment of skills. Again, some form of checklist or prompt sheet can support pupils during the assessment process. The checklist could contain questions such as:

'Did you partner's graph have the following:

the correct title,
labelled axes,
the correct units?'

Group assessment

Group assessment covers four main aspects:

- assessment of the group by group members;
- assessment of the group by other groups;
- assessment of an individual within a group by the teacher;
- assessment of the group by the teacher.

In collaborative work, where many skills such as discussion, planning, interpretation, evaluation and presentation take place, it can be difficult to monitor skill development. Possible approaches are:

- give each pupil a checklist or proforma as described above which can be completed during or after the activity;
- give one group member the role of monitoring group progress and reporting back to the teacher;

- monitor development by sitting with a group;
- use audio or video recorders to tape group work;
- use support teacher/colleagues during assessment.

For formal periods of assessment it may be necessary to split groups up by giving some active writing tasks or video, etc. whilst the teacher concentrates on assessing a small number of groups.

Teacher assessment

Teacher assessment covers assessing groups and individuals, and the basic principles hold for monitoring both motor and cognitive skills.

Two useful approaches are:

- interviewing;
- observation.

Interviewing is an ideal opportunity to probe pupils and ask questions that are designed to evaluate cognitive skills. Sitting one-to-one with a pupil allows the teacher to examine whether or not a pupil is able to deduce, predict, etc. and if this is linked to a written record of progress that the teacher and pupil complete, then this document can be used for record keeping and as a diagnostic tool.

When planning observations it is worth considering:

- why are you observing?
- what are you looking for?
- who are you going to assess and for how long?

It is very useful to draw up an observation checklist and to show it to the pupils before the assessment starts. A well designed checklist will remind you of the important points, provide a simple system of record keeping and still allow you to move between groups. The sort of questions that may be included in such a checklist are:

'Can the pupil:

plan an investigation with two variables?
select apparatus correctly?
manipulate apparatus?
evaluate results and suggest changes?'

DEVELOPING STUDY SKILLS

Improving the ways that pupils study involves the development of many intellectual and cognitive skills which are transferable rather than subject-specific. Pupils will benefit from help and guidance in this area. Aspects of study skills include understanding and memorizing concepts, organizing work, taking notes, coping with new vocabulary and using information sources.

Organizing work

The variety of approaches in chemistry teaching means that pupils can end up with a bewildering mixture of notebooks, files, handouts, homework sheets and practical sheets all containing vital information. It is all too easy for this collection of information to be so disorganized as to be of little value. It is important that pupils receive guidance in organizing their work. Some practical hints include:

- fix handouts into your notes immediately;
- separate sections with labelled (coloured) card;
- always have clear headings and dates;
- number pages and create an index.

Pupils often have difficulty in organizing their time. This is especially true of homework schedules, private study for project work and revision. Setting them tight deadlines will help, as will encouraging them to set themselves targets for completion. Revision timetables are simple to draw up and can be very motivating as each topic is crossed off the list! Interestingly, the act of designing and drawing up the timetable involves a great deal of review as pupils must consider which topics have been taught, how much 'information' is contained within each one and decide how much time to devote to each. They must also think about the sequence of revision, which involves consideration of links between the various topics.

A useful revision technique is to persuade pupils to write down or draw everything they know about a topic before they start to revise. This shows them the gaps in their knowledge. As with all revision techniques, as all teachers will know, the key is to start early, revise a little at a time and do it actively—not just reading. Twenty-minute bursts are better than three-hour marathons.

Taking notes

There are many situations in chemistry lessons when pupils will have to make their own notes. Note taking will be needed to record information from a variety of sources, e.g. teacher demonstration, teacher lecture, video, audio tape, practical work, literature research and class discussions. Pupils should be encouraged to:

- make their notes clear and easy to read;
- keep notes short and to the point;
- include headings and subheadings;
- highlight particularly important points;
- use their own words (especially true when using books!);
- build up a bank of new words (and meanings) and use them.

It is vital that pupils realize that notes will only be valuable if they understand them and they show up the main points. Highlighter pens or underlining may be useful for this.

Making summaries

This section could have been included in the section on note taking, but as it is such an important aid to understanding, encouraging cognitive skills, it is treated separately.

Making good summaries is a very useful way of sorting out the important aspects of a topic. The act of summarizing involves the pupil in making decisions about the topic covered and prioritizing information, sorting it, paraphrasing it and processing it into another form. Some hints to give pupils for drawing up summaries are:

*   make the summary stand out;
*   do not put too much in it;
*   include all the main ideas from a topic;
*   use your own words;
*   include drawings if it helps your understanding;
*   do not introduce new ideas;
*   try to draw links between the ideas.

An example of a summary drawn as a spider chart is given in Figure 7.

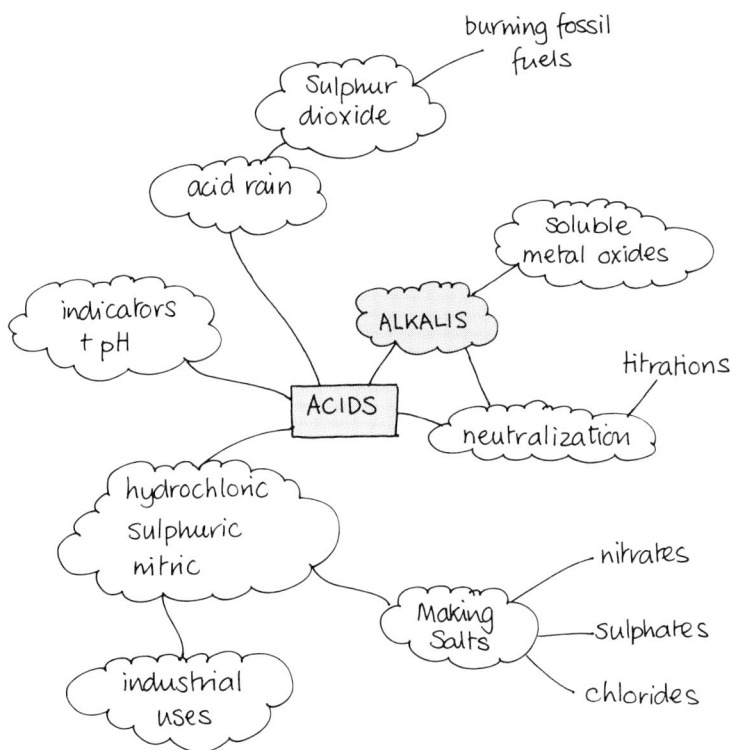

Figure 7   A spider chart used to summarize a topic.

Understanding and memorizing new concepts

As has been stressed earlier, learning about chemistry should not simply involve the memorizing of information but should encourage understanding by exercising intellectual, motor and cognitive skills. However, it is important that information about chemistry is remembered from week to week, otherwise little sense would be made of subsequent lessons and the memory elements drawn on in cognitive thought would be non-existent. Memory of ideas is linked to understanding in that recall is much easier if the facts and figures fit into an understandable framework.

Some suggestions you may wish to pass on to your classes are:

- never try to remember something you do not understand;
- try to link new ideas to ones you already understand;
- use your own words if possible, and if you have to memorize anything in a pre-set format, write your own interpretation underneath;
- use colour and underlining to highlight sections;
- try using diagrams or cartoons to explain a concept;
- keep referring back to the information—a little and often is a good rule for memorizing material;
- try to fill a blank piece of paper with the information, then check how well you have done.

Researching information

There are numerous sources of information that pupils can use for finding out information. These include television and radio, books, magazines, newspapers, teachers, adults other than the teachers, and computers. It is well worth investing time in helping pupils to develop the skills needed for effectively using these resources.

In my experience many GCSE and A-level pupils cannot use a library efficiently and a short course of instruction on catalogue systems and a simple index is beneficial. It may be possible to liaise with the English department in this. It is also useful to keep a check on school and local libraries to find out what they keep in stock.

There are many useful and interesting articles in scientific magazines such as *New Scientist* and *Scientific American*, as well as a great deal of information and data handling in *Which?* magazine. Even if the reading age is a little high for some pupils it is possible to use DART activities to make the text more understandable, for example, by giving pupils a list of headings to use for paraphrasing the article, or a simplified flow chart for them to complete if applicable.

Radio and television programmes can be excellent stimuli within classrooms, and can be used actively and imaginatively. Programmes do not have to be listened to or watched as a whole class activity, but can form very useful small group activities to promote discussion.

REFERENCES

1   White, R. T., *Learning Science*. (Basil Blackwell Ltd, 1988).

2   *Science at Age 15, Science Report for Teachers: 5*, Assessment of Performance Unit (APU). (HMSO, 1985).

3   Brook, A., Briggs, H. and Driver, R., *Aspects of Secondary Students Understanding of the Particulate Nature of Matter*. CLISP. (Centre for Studies in Science and Mathematics Education, The University of Leeds, 1984).

4   Driver, R., Guesne, E. and Tiberghen, A. (eds), *Children's Ideas in Science*. (Open University Press, 1985).

5   Nussbaum, J., 'The Particulate Nature of Science', in R. Driver, E. Guesne and A. Tiberghen (eds), *Children's Ideas in Science*. (Open University Press, 1985).

6   *Problem Solving with Industry Project* (PSI). (Centre for Science Education, Sheffield City Polytechnic, 1991).

7   Knapp, B., *Skill in Sport: The Attainment of Proficiency*. (Routledge and Kegan Paul, 1963).

8   NEA *Science (Modular) Syllabus* for the 1992 and 1993 Examinations, Northern Examining Association, p. 114.

CHAPTER 11

THE PRINCIPLES AND PRACTICE OF ASSESSMENT IN THE TEACHING AND LEARNING OF CHEMISTRY

Steve Dutch, Ralph Levinson and Dick West

PRACTICAL PURPOSES OF ASSESSMENT

Assessment can be used for different purposes, so it is important, therefore, to differentiate clearly between diagnostic, formative and summative assessment.

Diagnostic assessment

Diagnostic assessment uses questions or other tasks to enable teachers and pupils to identify gaps in the pupils' knowledge and understanding, and any particular difficulties they may have encountered in previous learning activities. A diagnostic test may take the form of a checklist of knowledge and skills needed before one can start a new topic. Diagnostic assessment should lead to a range of actions as some pupils will have demonstrated that they are ready to move to the next topic, whilst others may need a quick reminder of knowledge or skills they have not yet mastered. They may need to revisit a previous topic in a different way. A sound policy of diagnostic assessment can, and often will generate logistical and managerial problems. Ignoring these can lead to pupil frustration and consequent demotivation.

Formative assessment

Formative assessment is a mechanism for providing feedback to pupils as they move through a unit of teaching and learning. A typical question and answer session at the start of a lesson which reflects back to the previous lesson is a good way of providing formative feedback. A short pen and paper test or practical problem solving exercise at the end of a lesson will also provide good feedback. If the learning objectives and performance criteria are made open and explicit with pupils before a sequence of lessons, short tests, puzzles and other devices can make formative assessment fun as well as turning it into a powerful learning device. These strategies have been important in the development of schemes such as *Suffolk Science* [1] and various aspects of the Graded Assessment movement (see below). The key to effective formative assessment is that feedback is immediate and the need for any remedial action becomes obvious and acceptable to the pupil.

Summative assessment

Summative assessment has a different role and function in the teaching and learning process and is mainly used to make judgements on learning outcomes and teaching effectiveness. Summative assessment comes at the end of a module, a group of lessons, a project, a theme or an extended investigation. It seeks to measure in some way the sum total of what has been learnt and understood; or the level of skills gained; or the ability to apply knowledge and/or skills to new aspects of the subject. Public examinations, end of module tests, or the end of a continuous assessment scheme, are examples of summative assessment where some form of grade is determined to summarize the levels of performance achieved.

MODES OF ASSESSMENT

Assessment, in whatever form, provides a check for the pupils: Where am I? What have I learnt? Where do I go next? and, perhaps most importantly, Why am I doing this? It is important to appreciate from the outset that we take the basic view that assessment is a critical element in the teaching and learning process, and is not an adjunct to it. Assessment should be built into curriculum planning but it should serve, not drive, the curriculum.

Self-assessment

Self-assessment is a very powerful mode of assessment providing pupils are clear as to the *purpose* of learning tasks. Young people are very critically aware of what they can and cannot do, and what they do or do not understand. By encouraging self-assessment teachers can give their pupils ownership of learning and this tends to increase motivation and raise standards. It also enables pupils to *pace* their own assessment. End of lesson checklists which pupils fill in and then mark give immediate feedback—and also reduce the assessment burden on teachers, freeing them to concentrate on the effectiveness of their chosen teaching strategies.

Peer assessment

Peer assessment is a further variant which has similar educational advantages. It involves assessment of the pupil by friends or learning partners. Peer assessment should be of equal value to the assessor and the assessed by enabling the former to reflect on their own knowledge and skills attainment through critical analysis of a peer's work of a similar age and level of understanding. Ideally, the assessment should be mutual. Both self- and peer assessment have been used very successfully when linked to performance and learning targets in various schemes for graded assessment. It is essential however to allow pupils time to repeat elements of the learning scheme when they *demonstrate to themselves* that they have not mastered a concept, skill or process.

Teacher assessment

Teacher assessment, both formative and summative, is also a critical element in the overall assessment strategy. Teachers should continually monitor pupil progress which should reflect on the success, or otherwise, of their own performance and teaching strategies. Their assessment of pupils, which may or may not be moderated by an internal or external colleague, is central to the maintenance of progression in the subject.

METHODS OF ASSESSMENT

A teacher should have at her or his disposal a wide and varied range of tactics for assessing teaching and learning. These will range in formality from; oral tests, short pen and paper tests, formal examinations, the regular assessment of coursework, of homework, of practical skills, to the assessment of the outcomes of investigations, projects and assignments. The recent emphasis on the development of core and study skills suggests that pupils should also be assessed on their ability to present oral and written reports, use information technology and demonstrate their ability to work in groups. The decision as to which method of assessment to use has to be based on two fundamental criteria.

The first is related to the purpose of a particular learning task. For example, suppose the purpose of the task is to enable pupils to make accurate observations of chemical changes. This may best be done through allowing the pupils to describe their observations by oral means or in a simple table after a short practical or demonstration rather than in a formal written test.

The second is related to the purpose of the assessment. If the purpose of the assessment is formative then it is best mediated between pupil and teacher by oral questions and answers and discussion, through teacher observation of the pupils' development of skills over a period of time or through peer assessment. As stated before, summative assessment will be more formal.

Chemistry lends itself to a variety of assessment methods. Increasingly, schools, departments and subject groups are developing assessment policies which seek to standardize the form, regularity, nature, marking and reporting of pupil assessment. There is nothing more confusing for a pupil than finding that one teacher marks a short written report on a ten point numerical scale, whereas another uses a five point alphabetical scale and a third a series of red ticks and crosses summed up with a brief concluding comment such as 'This could have been better'. Clearly, with the introduction of the National Curriculum much standardization will arise from the mandatory aspects of assessment (see Chapter 6).

WHAT TO DO WITH THE OUTCOMES OF ASSESSMENT

The mandatory requirements in terms of Standard Assessment Tasks (SATs) and reporting to parents, governing bodies and LEAs are considered in detail in Chapter 6. Here we are concerned with good practice within a school and departmental assessment policy. Any form of assessment made by any method generates both positive and negative feedback to the person being assessed. The effect of this feedback is a function of the timing of feedback and of its quality. Immediate feedback is more effective than feedback that is given weeks or even months after the assessment was made. Poor quality feedback such as '2/10' or 'You are clearly trying' can have very negative effects indeed. In general, feedback should be as positive as possible but not uncritical as this aids and maintains motivation. It is also important that the outcomes of assessment are consistent and not arbitrary—a factor helped by having school assessment policies. It is also important not to use assessment as an *overt* negative feedback or control mechanism such as: 'You (often the class) have been naughty so instead of doing practical work next lesson I am going to give you a test'.

DEVELOPING A POLICY ON ASSESSMENT

The logical extension to an approach to teaching that takes account of the child's role in the learning process is an approach to assessment where the pupil is central to the process, leading us to the important notions of self-assessment and peer assessment. It can be argued that the skills of self-management and the ability to cope with peer evaluation will have longer lasting value than all the other outcomes of formal assessment. In addition, the motivating effects of involving pupils in the assessment of their performances are increased by giving pupils ownership of their learning. What then should be the main characteristics of a pupil-centred assessment scheme?

(i)   It should be planned as part of the course design and pupils should be introduced to the assessment criteria at the start of each unit or course.

(ii)   The pupils should be given the opportunity to test their progress at frequent intervals so as to use their self-assessments in a formative manner.

(iii) Adequate provision should be made for pupils to assess each other's work and to suggest suitable changes to assessment tasks and criteria—there should be joint ownership of assessment.

(iv)   Summative judgements should be reached and the results of all assessments should be incorporated in a Record of Achievement.

(v)   The whole process should place a high premium on recording positive achievements and successful performance, with Records of Achievement recording 'What I can do' 'How well I can perform' and the criteria used in making those judgements.

There is no reason why SATs, formal tests and suitably designed external examinations should not be incorporated into the approach outlined above and into the same cumulative records.

CASE STUDIES OF ASSESSMENT IN PRACTICE

The findings of the Assessment of Performance Unit

The first large scale study of assessment in England and Wales was initiated by the Assessment of Performance Unit (APU) in the 1970s and its purpose, findings and achievements are described by Watts in Chapter 15. Our aim here is to illustrate how some of the findings of the APU relate to assessment within the school curriculum.

Assessment is a process of measuring what a pupil has learned but the relationship between what has been learned and the techniques used to judge it are unclear. We now know through studies carried out by the APU and by the Children's Learning in Science (CLIS) project that pupils can produce acceptable answers to questions but still internalize their own conceptual models which contradict the accepted version. Conversely there are situations where a pupil may have understood a concept, but may have difficulty expressing it in terms of the question set. This certainly implies that there are faults in the questioning techniques. Many studies have shown that it is very difficult to devise a question or series of questions that can unambiguously determine the nature of a pupil's understanding of a particular concept. Through questioning, teachers can play more than a complementary role to the written examination because they can assess a pupil's understanding from a number of different vantage points and over a period of time. In addition the feedback is immediate and focused.

Table 1 Framework for the APU science assessment (adapted from [2]).

The categories of science performance	Skills	Assessment mode
1 Use of graphical and symbolic representation	reading information from graphs, tables and charts representing information as graphs, tables and charts	written test
2 Use of apparatus and measuring instruments	using measuring instruments estimating physical quantities following instructions for practical work	group practical test
3 Observation	making and interpreting observations	group practical test
4 Interpretation and application	(i) interpreting presented information (ii) applying: biology concepts physics concepts chemistry concepts	written test
5 Planning of investigations	planning parts of investigations planning entire investigations	written test
6 Performance of investigations	performing entire investigations	individual practical test

The depth of the APU survey in science is reflected in the way that it not only monitored written answers on content but investigated practical assessment, both in terms of process and manipulative skills. In summarizing some of the issues raised by the APU surveys it is important to realize that the APU's philosophy perceived science as an experimental subject concerned primarily with solving problems in everyday and scientific situations. Thus, science is an activity in which process skills and conceptual understanding are interlinked. In providing a framework for large scale assessment so that separate skills could be analysed it was necessary to separate process skills from conceptual understanding. Table 1 illustrates the categories of scientific performance that provided the framework for the APU's science assessment. Table 2 illustrates how these categories are broken down into process and conceptual skills. The object of category 6 is to reflect how conceptual and process skills are brought together in the context of a whole investigation.

Table 2 Process and conceptual skills in categories 1 to 6.

Categories	Process		Conceptual
	cognitive	manipulative	
1	✓		
2		✓	
3	✓		
4(i)	✓		
4(ii)			✓
5	✓		
6	✓	✓	✓

Issues arising from the APU survey

The APU's survey highlighted a number of problems connected with assessment. One problem is assessing measuring skills. Pupils who were capable of using measuring instruments correctly and accurately in category 2 did not use measuring techniques when they were appropriate in category 6 but gave qualitative responses. Thus, whilst pupils experienced little difficulty in demonstrating how to measure quantities, they needed more practice in deciding 'when' and 'what' to measure. For example, suppose the pupil were asked to find out the efficacy of different liquid soaps and detergents. They would need to use the same volume of each cleanser during each cleaning test. Therefore, when assessing a pupil's skill in measuring it is important that the teacher looks at how the pupil uses this skill in an investigation as well as under more rigorous controlled conditions.

Another problem that came to light was the way children perceived a problem. The teacher should try to ensure that the pupil formulates the question in the terms that they are going to pursue the investigation. Before assessment takes place the teacher should ask the pupil to either write out or explain orally what they think the question means. The next stage would be to clarify any misunderstandings that have arisen.

Several different issues emerged from the context in which an investigation was set. Preliminary conclusions from research over a range of investigations suggest that problems in a scientific context (in contrast to an everyday context) may affect the performance of some pupils because the topics or skills with which they may feel they have problems become more evident, e.g. a pupil who finds difficulty in measuring mass may feel inhibited by an activity which specifically asks them to weigh something in a laboratory but may approach the task more confidently when it is set in an everyday context. However, most pupils tended to use less quantitative techniques when the problem was set in an everyday context. It is possible that many pupils see 'science' as only being performed in school laboratories because, during the course of their everyday lives, they do not come across the instruments or concepts outside of the school laboratory. Care needs to be taken that pupils are introduced to, and recognize, the kinds of measurements they need to make when planning their first investigations [3].

Another influential factor is the form in which investigations are presented to pupils. Pupils who were asked only to plan and write about a 'find out' investigation without doing an experiment or testing their plans, tended to suggest less quantitative methods than those who performed the investigation through a practical method. This could be because in the latter case, pupils can do the investigation in a trial-and-error method and gradually arrive at a more refined approach. Pupils who wrote up their findings as a result of a practical investigation generally produced accurate versions of what they had done. This would support the 'hands-on' approach to learning [2].

Implications of the APU research

The APU research confirms that assessment is not a straightforward process. A number of factors have to be taken into consideration when assessing the type and quality of learning that takes place. These include the mode of questioning, the context of the investigation and the variety of responses that the assessment technique can deal with.

What is evident so far is that GCSE courses up to now do not meet all the criteria necessary to undertake a thorough assessment in terms of the points that have arisen as a result of APU research. Even the proposed SATs are likely to fall short in the same respect. To check whether a pupil has grasped a particular skill or concept often needs very sensitive tuning and needs a careful ear to help the pupil along. Teachers can assess a pupil's performance in a number of different contexts and over a range of time. They are able to clarify responses where pupils' perceptions of the question may differ from the intended meaning.

In terms of process skills it has become apparent that pupils need to be made aware of the skills they are using in the same way they are made aware of the content of the concepts they are learning. Pupils need practice in the use and function of variables, making observations, interpreting data and so on. Although these particular terms need not necessarily be used, the nature of these skills needs to be made explicit.

THE GRADED ASSESSMENTS IN SCIENCE PROJECT (GASP)

GASP is an assessment scheme [4] available for all science curricula and pupils of secondary school age. Its particular features are that it is a comprehensive scheme with significant teacher input. The project was initially funded by the Inner London Education Authority in association with King's College, London and is now validated, certificated and administered by London Education and Assessment Group. There are 15 levels of achievement in the scheme.

By taking on many of the recommendations which arose from the APU survey it provides pupils of all abilities with realistic goals and viable opportunities to experience success. Like the APU, GASP divides science into the content, process skills and exploration dimensions. It encourages motivation by setting pupils appropriate short-term objectives. Since the pupils know what the objectives are they can take part in the assessment process and discuss with the teacher to what extent they have attained the objectives. From this formative assessment, pupils are able to set for themselves the next stage of objectives. The objectives are designed to match the rate of pupil development ensuring they are assessed at the right time.

Pupils start at level 1 and then proceed at their own pace. Since the scheme is designed so that 95% of the pupils achieve level 5 by the end of Year 11 the majority of pupils should attain at least one level per year.

The mode of assessment is related to the dimension in which the pupil is being assessed. The content dimension encompasses facts, terminology, and the knowledge and understanding to make generalizations. This can be assessed by written answers to questions and a 75% correct response indicates achievement at that level. There is no fixed time level on answering all the questions and they should be read to pupils with reading problems and, if necessary, translated into a pupil's first language.

Each level of process skill is assessed twice and can be assessed either by the teacher watching the pupil at work, checking the outcome whether this be drawing a graph, compiling a set of results or writing a conclusion, and through peer assessment where small groups of pupils comment on each other's skills attainments supervised by the teacher: particularly useful if this is a practical skill.

Finally, there is the exploration dimension. This may involve a pupil or group of pupils working through an open-ended experiment which involves planning, implementing and drawing conclusions. Thus, planning might include the pupil's skill in drawing up a strategy which would enable him or her to carry out an experiment.

Successes and problems with GASP

Whilst record-keeping is an important and essential part of assessment it requires a great deal of administration and the number of levels and sub-units comprising each level in GASP could mean that the assessment degenerates into a tick sheet. Part of the importance of teacher assessment is that the teacher can pay attention to idiosyncratic remarks and judge whether a pupil is understanding a concept. This is often manifested in casual group discussions with peers, in play, and in general conversation. Thus, the teacher needs the time and the freedom to probe further. The problem with extensive record keeping is that the teacher may be forced to walk around with a tick sheet without having the time to encourage speculation and free-ranging discussion. Given the number of skills and explorations assessed the teacher may well have little time to do anything else.

It does appear that graded assessments have a motivating effect, that pupils prefer them to tests and by having clearly graded objectives they know what they have to achieve. The skills they are using are also made explicit (a point that was referred to in the APU survey). Furthermore, pupils can assess for themselves how far they have reached these objectives.

On the other hand, given the number of levels and the number of times pupils are assessed there is a danger that some pupils may feel that *all* they are doing is assessed explorations and might become bored with them. The perception becomes that assessment is done for assessment's sake and not as an integral part of learning.

It does seem that the able children who are passing through the levels very quickly are enjoying using GASP, but this may not be true of less able pupils who find they are on level 4, say, when their peers are on level 8 or 9. Though GASP is designed to test what pupils can achieve, the effect on pupil's perceptions of their abilities can be much the same for the less able pupil, as the effect produced by failure in old-style examinations.

GASP began trialling before the implementation of the National Curriculum so there is a well-tried assessment scheme in place which is designed to assess similar statements of achievement—knowledge and understanding of content, process skills and exploratory activities—to those prescribed by the National Curriculum.

A NOTE OF CAUTION

There is a very real fear in many minds that the SATs associated with the National Curriculum will constrain teaching methods and subject content, and lead again to teaching to the test. The introduction of the National Curriculum, which incorporates a close linkage between a specified curriculum, testing and reporting, could lead us back to a test-based model of assessment. This would seriously damage the progress which has been made by the introduction of curriculum-led assessment. Certainly in the USA, State prescriptions of the curriculum with centralized test procedures have led to a great deal of teaching to the test, and a related decline in curriculum development and 'ownership' of teaching and learning. Teachers 'teach' and pupils 'bubble' (fill in circles on score sheets as their system still relies heavily on multiple choice questions and optical scan marking). It is to be hoped that we will not go down this route. The work of the APU, the Secondary Science Curriculum Review and CLIS has, one hopes, immunized us against this particular form of educational plague. The report of the Task Group on Assessment and Testing [5] stated quite clearly that 'Assessment policy should follow decisions about the curriculum' and recommended that Records of Achievement should be used as a vehicle for recording progress and achievement within the national assessment system. But the doubt remains—to what extent will teachers teach to even the most ingenious and carefully constructed SAT and indulge in SAT spotting.

The more that we come to understand about the ways in which children learn, the more we begin to realize the complexity of thinking that is involved in a child's interpretation of questions intended to assess his or her knowledge and understanding. CLIS, APU and other research work has shown quite clearly that children can appear to regress in their ability to answer questions as they grow older, because their interpretation of the question becomes more complex. In addition their interpretation of the role of the question and the questioner changes. Assessment, at the end of the day, remains a very complex issue.

REFERENCES

1   *Suffolk Science*, Co-ordinated Science, The Suffolk Development. (Collins Educational, 1987).

2   *Assessing Investigations at ages 13 and 15. Science Report for Teachers: 9*, Assessment of Performance Unit (APU). (HMSO, 1987).

3   Black, P. J., 'APU Science—the past and the future'. *School Science Review*, 1990, **72**, p. 258.

4   Graded Assessment in Science Project (Science (GASP)). University of London Examination and Assessment Council. (1992).

5   *National Curriculum: Report of the Task Group on Assessment and Testing*. Department of Education and Science. (HMSO, 1988).

CHAPTER 12

EVALUATING TEACHING AND LEARNING

Di Bentley

'Let's keep hold of the idea that evaluation is mostly a matter of commonsense and learning from experience. That is not entirely true, but it keeps us from going technical or theological; and a little modest oversimplification is better than a lapse into jargon or pretentiousness.'

Lawrence Stenhouse [1]

INTRODUCTION

This Chapter broadly addresses the question 'How do we know that what we have planned for and taught pupils is working well?' Answering such a question of course involves a variety of other questions which can rarely be addressed just in chemistry, or indeed in science alone. Although the Chapter focuses on the chemistry teacher in her or his classroom, the ideas, qualities, assumptions and understanding of colleagues in the department, pupils and their parents and governors, are important facets of the questions. The broader context of the whole school curriculum also cannot be ignored, and in this time of the externally driven curriculum, the national requirements placed on teachers are a crucial part of the equation.

The products and rates of reaction of all these constituent compounds produces a heady brew, which this Chapter attempts to break down into its component parts, for more detailed analysis. It begins with an examination of the steps one would need to undertake in conducting an evaluation, discusses the pros and cons of some evaluation methods, and ends with a look at four issues in chemistry and how their evaluation might take place using the methods described.

WHAT IS EVALUATION?

We begin with a statement of what it means to evaluate. This is fraught with difficulties, because although as Ebbutt [2] points out, the definitions of evaluation have changed little over the past 20–30 years, there are some confusions over the use of the term. I start with some distinctions, between what evaluation is and what it is not, the framework for which appears in Ebbutt [3].

Distinction 1: Evaluation is not assessment

Evaluation describes aspects of the education service itself. Assessment describes aspects of pupils and their achievements. As Ebbutt states:

> 'Assessment is concerned with asking questions and informing decisions
> about... students. Which is the most appropriate set, course, curriculum
> provision for a group or an individual? Evaluation... is concerned to ask
> questions about the nature and form of the curriculum pupils have experienced,
> are experiencing, will experience.'

Ebbutt [2]

In other words, assessment tells us about pupils, evaluation tells us about the curriculum and more general aspects of education. This is important because although we may use assessment information to tell us about the outcomes of a particular curriculum, or the teaching and learning approaches used within that curriculum, assessment information can only tell us part of the story in evaluation terms.

Distinction 2: Evaluating process or outcomes?

This has been a long-running debate which has fuelled different styles, approaches and methodologies in evaluation over the years (see [1, 4–6]). It arises in trying to answer the question 'What am I trying to find out?' Evaluating outcomes presupposes that the outcomes can be observed, measured and specified in advance. It also makes the assumption that the achievements of pupils can be directly linked in a causal way to the curriculum they have experienced. The process evaluator makes no such assumptions—instead, the action in the classroom, rather than the achievement of the pupils, becomes the focus of the observations. Process evaluators use interviews, questionnaires, case studies as the tools for collecting information. In this Chapter I deal with the evaluation of the processes of teaching and learning in chemistry, as well as the evaluation of the outcomes of teaching and learning for both pupils and teachers.

Distinction 3: Evaluation for accountability or professional development?

There are some important issues here, particularly within the debates of the 1988 *Education Reform Act* [7] and the Parent's Charter. Increasingly the pressure on schools in general, and teachers in particular, has been one of accountability. Showing that resources are being used effectively and efficiently in the production of the required outcomes of the National Curriculum, that teaching staff are up to date, and producing results, is of crucial concern to governing bodies. Teachers themselves will want to look at the results of such evaluations for their own professional development. Those teachers used to a particular style of teaching and learning will want to be assured that if they make changes, this will benefit pupils, result in better learning outcomes, or certainly no worse ones, before they embark on a change. The audiences for these two types of evaluation are different, the first are (technically) outsiders—the governors, the finance holders. The second are the teachers themselves who should retain control over their own practice and its evaluation if professional development is the goal.

Distinction 4: Insider or outsider evaluation?

This definition follows on from the previous distinction. If the purpose of the evaluation is professional development, then the evaluator should be an insider. If the purpose is other than professional development, the evaluator may be someone outside the immediate situation. In this Chapter, the distinction does not really arise to any great extent, since the assumption is that the evaluator is *per se* an insider. For readers who want some insights into the complexities of the insider/outsider evaluator debate, there are some interesting accounts in [8, 9].

Distinction 5: Intended curriculum or curriculum in action

There are important differences between the curriculum as it appears in, for example, the National Curriculum Statutory Orders or teachers' schemes of work, and the curriculum as it eventually transpires in the classroom. The curriculum in action is subject to the forces and requirements of individuals, groups of pupils, the interactions of the class, the size of the laboratory, the fixed or non-fixed nature of the benches and the moods of pupils as they appear from another lesson. Which one of us has not had our best laid plans go awry because the timetable dictates that we get our only double period with Year 9 as the last two on Friday afternoon when they have just come from PE?

RESEARCH APPROACHES TO EVALUATION

There are a variety of different models or styles of evaluation. Hamilton's book *Curriculum Evaluation* [10] provides a detailed description of these. (For readers wanting a briefer account, Hopkins [11] is a good source.) In writing this Chapter, I have tried to be eclectic, since the purpose of the evaluation will in some measure dictate the methods used and thus (often) the model adopted. However, it behoves me to 'come clean' that in my evaluation of schools and education processes I try as far as possible to work within Stake's countenance model [12].

Stake's model is useful because he distinguishes between:

- *antecedents*: prior conditions which may relate to outcomes, e.g. one of the fourth year classes had a supply teacher who was not a chemist for two terms last year.

- *transactions*: what actually took place, e.g. the processes in the classroom, and teachers' and pupils' views of the value of the curriculum from their perspective.

- *outcomes*: the impact of the innovation on those involved, e.g. the change in teaching approaches and pupils' achievement.

Finally he contrasts the intentions at each phase with what actually took place, so that for example, teaching plans and schemes of work have a place in the evaluation, just as much as classroom observations. All of this represents the 'description matrix'. Once the data for this has been collected, the evaluator can then analyse the descriptions through the 'judgement matrix' applying criteria or performance indicators to the data collected so that the judgements can be made. Figure 1 shows the application of Stake's model to an evaluation of a new GCSE chemistry course in a school. Although Stake's model is very complex and extensive, it does allow all the possibilities to be taken into account and avoids the distinction between outcomes and product and insider/outsider evaluations mentioned above. The distinctions are important for professional researchers, but for teachers they are often false ones, in that the purpose of the evaluation may well dictate the type of evaluation and its methodologies.

Rationale

Examination of a switch from separate sciences to combined science and its effects on teaching approach and results

Intents	Observations		Criteria/standards	Judgements
Each teacher teaches one class all the sciences for 2 years, with one person 'floating'—available to help	Two staff leave after first year. Three supply teachers over the 2-year period—from content analysis	Antecedents	Pupils should show improvement due to greater continuity and progression	No improvement found
A range of teaching approaches, in units of equal length	A range of teaching and learning observed from content analysis of documents, staff interviewed	Transactions	Staff should feel happy about teaching combined sciences	Staff report some confidence
Pupil grades at least as good as last year, but preferably 5% improvement	Results analysed, comparisons made	Outcomes	School should have made a 5% improvement on the results	No improvement found

Description matrix   **Judgement matrix**

Figure 1   Application of Stake's countenance model to an evaluation of a new GCSE chemistry course.

STEPS IN EVALUATION

Getting started: some early decisions

Being an effective evaluator means being clear about what it is you want to know, who you are evaluating for and reporting to and what you will do with the judgements you make. Evaluation is not difficult but it does mean being careful about ideas, methods and people.

Generally the questions which give rise to evaluation are of two types, of 'why' and 'what'.

Step 1   Deciding on the purpose: the 'why' of evaluation

You need to make this the first decision. Four common purposes for evaluation are:

(i)   formative evaluation, e.g. to improve work as it is developing;

(ii)   summative evaluation, e.g. to give feedback about a course when it is finished;

(iii) evaluation for policy-making, e.g. to help gain support for changing from one GCSE course to another;

(iv)   evaluation for administration, e.g. to help choose between different lengths of lessons.

The need for the evaluation may arise through the demands of others—such as the governing body in drawing up a school development plan. It may also arise naturally through the work of the department in its own development plan. It may also arise through discussion in the department, between individual teachers or through self-questioning.

Step 2   Identifying the 'what' of evaluation

The *what* of evaluation varies too. Typical subjects of evaluation are:

•   courses, e.g. *Salters' Chemistry* as opposed to Midland Examination Group's chemistry course;

•   curricular provision, e.g. does the curriculum to GCSE give a good grounding for A-level in separate sciences, are the teaching and learning strategies we use effective?

•   the implementation of policies, e.g. is the equal opportunities policy being implemented consistently across the chemistry department?

•   managers' roles, e.g. has the re-organization of roles away from heads of subject departments to coordinators for a key phase fulfilled what was needed? Is the department effective as a team?

•   forms of administration, e.g. the ordering of apparatus from the technician for classes;

•   planning and its implementation, e.g. the targets in the departmental development plan; does the current scheme of work meet the programme of study?

These questions are just examples but at the start of the evaluation you need answers too. For example: Who wants the evaluation carried out? For what reasons? Who will see the information you provide? What actions are likely to be taken as a result? What constraints are there on your work?

Step 3   Preparing evaluation plans

Once the *what* has been decided, the *who* will do it, and *how* will they go about it are the next steps. Making decisions about the 'who' will be influenced by the purposes of the evaluation. To evaluate systematically means to gather evidence so that decisions and opinions can be presented openly and in a way that is supported by evidence. The methods you use to collect the evidence need to be congruent with the purposes of the evaluation. You will then be able to show how your evidence has been derived and how this leads you to the opinions and conclusions you make.

Who should evaluate?

If the purpose of the evaluation is simply for your own professional development or that of the department, then it can safely be an insider evaluation, where the evaluators are the persons who will be affected by the outcome and the only audience for the report. If you are required to report to a committee, or the governors, or the evaluation is part of the more formal system of school self-evaluation, you may need the added credibility that an outsider can provide. Outsiders do not just provide credibility, they can also provide a very useful function by raising what are called the naive questions. In a group which works together regularly, many things are understood. They have become part of accepted practice and no-one questions them any longer. The view of an outsider can be valuable in forcing the accepted practice to be re-examined rather than taken for granted. Outsiders could profitably be drawn from the ranks of deputy heads, the advisory/inspection service, governors, or industrialists. There can be a more subtle reason for including them in an evaluation too. If they are likely to be in a position of making a judgement about the department in another context, it may be important to help them be as well informed as possible. Being part of an evaluation assists them in having this information and access to your understanding and judgements too.

Drawing up the plans

Once the evaluation team has been decided upon, plans need to be drawn up with both the members of the evaluation team (if that is how you are working) and the people being evaluated. These plans should include:

*   discussions on the purpose of the evaluation;
*   methods of information gathering you want to use;
*   visits you want to make to schools and classes;
*   documents you want to read and analyse;
*   people (pupils, teachers, others) to whom you want to talk;
*   your timetable for collecting information, analysis and writing;
*   ways you will report your results and what feedback you want.

Be prepared to change plans even as you make them! Asking all evaluators to keep a diary of dated comments will help you to be systematic. This diary should include issues, impressions, feelings, early interpretations and ideas.

Planning for time

Allocate time to each part of the plan and leave plenty of time for the analysis and reporting stages. This is often much more time consuming than is imagined—too much information and not enough time to analyse and report it.

Planning for resources

The usual resources are time, skills, materials, strength of purpose, opportunity and access although it might help to mention image and PR too! Time, materials and access are issues to be negotiated in the context in which you are evaluating—they can sometimes lie outside your control. However, skill and image are your responsibility. It is important to practise your methods by piloting in advance if you can. If you choose to interview for example, use a 'critical friend' for a first attempt and then pilot your interview technique on close colleagues before you evaluate others.

Reporting the results

Who receives the report will depend on the reasons for the evaluation, and with whom you have negotiated release of the information. On the whole be very parsimonious with release unless you know that the documentation has been cleared for more open discussion.

Drawing up operational guide-lines: a code of conduct

The guide-lines are mostly commonsense ones, though they can involve some hard work. The most important ones are:

•   *be tactful*. Take care to ensure that you observe protocols with individuals and with organizations. So, ask permissions of people, teams, committees, departments, faculties in advance and in writing if necessary.

•   *be explicit*. Talk to people about what you want to do, your expected outcomes, the timetable for your work and report on progress from time to time. Allow people to make comments about the evaluation and understand that there are potential barriers to collecting evidence because of perceived status, power or privilege.

•   *be correct*. Do not examine files, documents, books or correspondence unless you have clear permission to do so. Don't make copies of papers or work unless you are authorized. You will need, too, to have permission to use verbatim quotations, comments or attributed observations.

•   *be confidential*. Control what you say and how, take responsibility for information in your possession and observe the wishes of others. Respect individuals' ownership of personal data so that they can add to or make changes in what has been recorded. You will need to be clear whether comments are made 'on' or 'off' the record and respect requests for confidentiality. Make sure people know what responsibilities you have for reporting and who will see the data you have collected.

Step 4   Deciding on the methods to be used in the evaluation

Collecting evidence

Wherever possible, information should be collected in several different ways. This helps to provide a variety of viewpoints, a process sometimes referred to as *triangulation*, and can act as a check against obvious bias. It is sometimes useful to use both *quantitative* and *qualitative* data as part of the same evaluation, where this is possible.

For example, if a department had recently changed to using *Salters' Chemistry* and wanted to evaluate the new teaching approaches which were part of the scheme but not part of their previous practice, they might collect pupils' opinions (perhaps by using a questionnaire), ask a colleague to join the group to observe progress (using an agreed observation schedule) and keep a diary or log.

It is important not to forget the value of documentation when evaluations take place. Statistics such as examination results, test scores, policy statements, staff qualifications may all have bearing on the information you collect by interviewing or observing teaching. Knowing that a class has 25% of the pupils within Warnock stages 1–3 (with special educational needs, but not having a statement) will affect the observations made of that class in a laboratory and thus the judgements which result from the observations. Such information is part of Stake's 'antecedents' [12]. There is often a great deal of information about courses and pupils documented within an institution which can also be used to help provide other viewpoints. So:

*   *do* check information from several sources;
*   *do* remember *all* the people involved;
*   *don't* rely on just one method.

What is acceptable evidence?

I mentioned above quantitative and qualitative data. Quantitative methods are based on counting and measuring what is taking place, e.g. option subject choices of boys and girls, examination results, truancy, pupil/teacher ratios, frequency of teaching approaches used. This is sometimes considered to be 'objective' data and more reliable than qualitative or 'subjective' data.

Qualitative methods are based on listening to reports of peoples' experiences. Thoughts, impressions, values, ideas, policy and principles are vital ingredients in judging the quality of teaching and learning.

Both kinds of data have their uses and neither is better or worse than the other—they simply tell different parts of the story. Some methods can combine both, so that a questionnaire, for instance, can be used to collect feedback from pupils on the quality of a course and provide statistics.

It is worth remembering that the evidence you collect is for a particular purpose. To show, for instance, that something is (or is not) the case. So, acceptable evidence:

- depends on the questions asked: if you want different information you must ask different questions;

- depends on the context: both *how* and *where* you ask the question. If an interview takes place in the Head's office the answers may be different than if it happens in the staffroom;

- depends on the methods used: different methods generate different information.

Clear evidence can be difficult to collect for some issues. For example, 'staff morale', 'learning readiness', can defy sharp definition and no one method alone can give acceptable evidence for (or against) such issues. One solution is to triangulate as described above. An additional difficulty is the quality of the link between data and decision making. Seldom can either quantitative or qualitative information give irrefutable evidence. Interpretation, re-interpretation, challenge and disagreement are inherent within the process.

Choosing methods of collecting evidence

There are five different methods of collecting evidence described here:

(i)   questionnaires and checklists;

(ii)   classroom observation;

(iii) structured interviews;

(iv)   personal documents and diaries;

(v)   content analysis (of policies or documents).

This is not an exhaustive list but represents some of the more common methods which are likely to be useful to chemistry teachers. The descriptions which follow are brief and focus primarily on the pros and cons of each method. For those who want a full analysis, McCormick and James [13] provides an excellent and detailed overview. However, knowing about the variety does not always assist in the choice. I present below some general criteria for choosing methods from a busy teacher's viewpoint. They should:

- be appropriate for the situation being investigated;
- be sensitive to the questions you want to ask;
- be quick to prepare;
- be simple to carry out;
- cost as little as possible in materials and time;
- give data which is straightforward to interpret;
- be able to capture complex processes;
- not require high levels of skill to use;
- be reliable;
- provide strong data, i.e. evidence which can be linked directly to what is being evaluated and can be seen by others to be valid.

However, a note of caution is important. There is no 'perfect' evaluation method—choosing methods which fit all these criteria could mean never getting started. Compromise plays a great part in making choices.

Some advantages and disadvantages of different methods

Questionnaires and checklists can provide very specific information though they are not usually able to deal with very sensitive issues. They can be difficult to design but easy to administer. They commonly have a poor rate of return, are time consuming to analyse and suffer from problems of constrained answers.

Classroom observations can provide very rich data, be simple and can detail action. They are very time consuming and can be difficult to construct to give meaningful categories. They can be both sensitive to complex interactions and yet threatening to the participants.

Structured interviews can be used throughout the system and can capture very in-depth and complex information. They are time consuming and can be awkward to analyse. They are good for specific, detailed information, impressions and opinions. They need skill to manage well.

Personal documents and diaries can be illuminative and provide novel and unusual perspectives. They are useful (and sometimes contentious) because they provide very subjective information. They are diagnostic of classroom issues and are very useful in triangulation.

Content analysis can provide a range of performance indicators against which a department or teacher can measure progress towards implementing the policy. The analysis of the policy is not sufficient on its own, it provides a framework of questions through which practices can be examined.

Step 5   Drawing up the process of evaluation and the ethics of operating

Evaluating education depends on personal interplay and involves the actions, intentions, meanings and feelings of a wide cross section of people. Evaluation means eventually making judgements about each of these. It can be a testy business and great care is needed not to damage relationships or create ill-feeling. The key words are *negotiate* and be *honest*, and where possible, achieve *agreement, cooperation* and *collaboration*.

The ideal is to be fully clear about the nature of the evaluation enterprise at the outset; who will do what and to whom, how data is to be collected, the timetable of events, what the outcomes are likely to be and how these are to be circulated and used. Briefings (before the event) and de-briefings (afterwards) are a must and, though time consuming, constitute a minimum level of courtesy. Drawing up a code of conduct, as described before, will help a great deal. Best of all, is the formulation of an evaluative framework, for example as described by Stake [12], which involves all in the enterprise to the same degree and so allows a free exchange of data and interpretations—a fully collaborative venture.

Step 6   Carrying out the evaluation

Once all the preparation has been done, the decisions made, the code of conduct agreed and the plan drawn up, the action needs to begin. In describing the action, I have chosen to take an issues approach. Examples of four major issues which a chemistry department or a teacher of chemistry might want to evaluate are given in the next section, and I described how such an evaluation might proceed. The methods of evaluation chosen are not described, but details are available in McCormick and James [13].

Step 7   Making judgements

Views, opinions and values are an important part of evaluation and reaching sound judgements underpins the purpose of evaluation. Agreeing criteria for those judgements in advance is an important part of the work. The criteria need to reflect the purpose of the evaluation, the audience for it and the participants in it. You will want to present a balanced view in your own evaluation. So, if you are evaluating, for example, a GCSE chemistry course, you will want to see how well it meets its own objectives, how well it is received by the participants, to judge value-for-money and the pupils' achievements.

In each of the four issues described in the next section, the power of making the judgements and the criteria against which those judgements can be made is left with the teachers. There are issues, though, where the judgements are not in the hands of the department. For example, when parents judge a department's performance on examination results, i.e. the pupil achievement outcomes. The criteria are set externally (nationally) and the judgements made outside the school. This seems less easily negotiable. However, even these can be used to reflect what the department values. The debates about 'value added' interpretations of results rather than the use of raw data are one example. In order to develop a criterion that states 'examination results will be judged in the light of the pupils' knowledge in chemistry when they entered the school', a chemistry department needs to collect and publish the input and outcome data so that judgements can be made by outsiders about the department's value to pupils—back to the 'what do we want to know' argument which was the start of our process.

ISSUES IN CHEMISTRY TEACHING

In the following section the evaluation of four major issues is described.

1   Evaluating approaches to teaching and learning

An individual chemistry teacher had recently been on an In-service course which had introduced new approaches to teaching. He felt that since his present methods enabled him to gain good results he would probably stick to them. However, he was aware that the advent of the National Curriculum would mean a change of curriculum units, a need to build on primary school work and perhaps their approaches and a greater development of continuity and progression in Attainment Target 1 (AT1). He decided to take a detailed look at what he was doing.

Evaluation plan

(i)   What I want to know:

  • What is the range of my approaches to teaching?

  • How effective do I feel they are?

  • How well will the present range match the needs of AT1 in particular and pupils' previous experience and knowledge?

  • Which ones do pupils enjoy most and which help them to learn most?

  • How often do I use particular approaches?

(ii) What methods will I use?

  • Keep a personal diary for a month—to tell me about effectiveness after I have used a particular method, how often I use it, and the range that I use.

  • Give pupils a questionnaire to find out what they like best and what they learn most from.

  • Analyse my scheme of work to find out how often I plan to use different methods, and what my intended range of methods is. (This will provide a cross check of my intentions against my actions in the diary.)

  • Analyse my scheme of work against the National Curriculum to check what methods will help me to deliver parts of AT1. (I shall need to draw up some criteria based on AT1 to be successful here.)

  • Invite a colleague to observe a particular approach to provide another view of effectiveness.

(iii) Who will I report it to?

  • The evaluation is intended for me. If I find out something interesting, it might be helpful to share some parts of it with other members of the department, although I will have to discuss some things with the colleague who observes in my classroom.

(iv) What will I do with my findings?

  • I'm not sure! If they indicate that change is needed I'll consider it, but I'm worried about the pupil's examination results being affected.

(v)   How long will it take?

  • If I carry out the diary for a month then I can analyse the results over half term. I need to give the pupils the questionnaire after the end of unit test, so that means I need to prepare it soon.

Some unanswered questions

Should I try out the questionnaire in advance? If so on whom?

2 Evaluating the health and safety policy in the department

A new head of chemistry had recently been appointed to a department. She examined the existing health and safety policy and saw that it was dated 1985. She felt that revision of the policy was necessary in the light of new guide-lines, but felt that she wanted to know how much of the existing policy was still valuable before she made sweeping changes. She discussed the issues with the department at a meeting and together they drew up a plan for the evaluation of the existing policy.

Evaluation plan

(i)   What we need to know:

- Are all staff aware of the present policy and its contents?
- How effectively do they implement the policy in their chemistry lessons?
- How well does the present policy match with the new legal requirements?
- What is the rate of accidents?
- Are technicians aware of risk factors of substances and is their behaviour in line with the policy?
- How will observed behaviour need to change to come in line with legal requirements?

(ii) What methods will we use?

- Head of chemistry will observe lessons to see if the present policy is being implemented. This will enable her to see what range of practices exist.
- All staff (teaching and technicians) will interview each other, using an agreed structured interview questionnaire to find out awareness of the present policy and see where staff feel it needs changing.
- The chief technician will observe the practice of other technicians in terms of safety against a set of criteria established through the policy and agreed by the department. The head of chemistry will look at the work of the chief technician.
- The department will devote a departmental meeting to producing a checklist of the new legal requirements against which the present policy can be checked.
- The school accident book will be analysed from 1985 (the date of the policy) to see what range of accidents come within the scope of the policy.

(iii) Who will we report it to?

- Initially this is a departmental exercise. However, it has important implications for the school in terms of health and safety. A synopsis of findings should be reported to the Health and Safety subcommittee of the governing body.

(iv) How long will it take?

- We need to take this steadily. There is a lot of extra work involved, and the time needs to be made available for lesson observation and interviews. The head of science will talk to the deputy head about this, but we should plan for at least a term. The next departmental meeting can be used to draw up the structured interview questionnaire.

Some unanswered questions

Should we involve a member of the governing body to help with analysing the present policy and looking at the accident book? Perhaps the governors will feel more involved and less 'got at' if our findings indicate that there are financial implications.

3 Evaluating the scheme of work

The advent of the National Curriculum has forced the school to re-examine schemes of work. The deputy head has requested that the science department should look at their existing schemes in order to answer the following questions:

- Does what is being delivered match with the requirements of the programmes of study for each key stage?
- Is the present format for presentation helpful?
- Is the scheme in line with what the National Curriculum Council (NCC) and the LEA considers to be 'good practice'?
- Is it 'parent friendly', since the requirements of circular 14/89 from the DES require that schemes of work should be available for parents to read at their request?

The teachers of the chemistry units agree to meet to draw up an evaluation plan.

Evaluation plan

(i)   What we need to know:

- This can be summarized by the four questions the deputy head has asked us.

(ii) We also want to ask:

- Should we keep an audit of teaching approaches in our scheme?
- Should the scheme include risk assessments as we write it?
- Would a technician's guide be helpful?
- What level of detail would staff find most helpful?

(iii) What methods will we use?

- The NCC non-statutory guidelines and LEA statements will be analysed to provide performance indicators for what constitutes a 'good' scheme of work. These will be used as a checklist that a group of us can apply to existing schemes of work.
- All staff (teaching and technicians) will complete a questionnaire about the present structure of the scheme of work. This will allow them scope to make suggestions for changes.
- A sample of staff will be interviewed as to their use of the present schemes and suggestions for level of detail encouraged in these interviews.

- The chief technician will hold informal discussions with colleagues about the proposals for a technicians' guide and see how this can be managed, if it is thought to be helpful.
- One or two parent governors will be given the existing schemes of work and asked to make suggestions for how they might be made more 'parent friendly'.

(iv) Who will we report it to?

- The deputy head requires a report on our evaluation by early next term. We then have to make changes in the light of the policy developed by the Senior Management Team (SMT) after their perusal of our evaluations.

(v) How long will it take?

- There is not a great deal of time. Our interviews and questionnaires need to be short and easy to analyse. We need to talk to parent governors about their involvement within a week.

Some unanswered questions

How will we act on the decisions of the SMT if we do not agree with them? What if the policy they develop is not flexible enough to meet the needs of the chemistry department? Should we involve the deputy head in the 'parent friendly' work so that at least he knows our views?

4 Evaluating the resources in the department

The school has just had an HMI one-day visit, which focused on equality of opportunity. One of the issues reported back to the headteacher was that the resources in the science department did not facilitate the school's equality of opportunity policy. The materials in particular were biased both racially and in gender terms. The headteacher asks that the department look at the issues and evaluate their existing resources and possible new ones.

Evaluation plan

(i) What we need to know:

- Are our resources racially and sexually biased?
- Can we make do with them, or do we need to plan a change, however gradually this may have to be done?
- What do the pupils think about the resources?
- What other resources could we use that would meet the needs?
- Can we continue to use our present resources but teach children to be critically aware of their shortcomings, i.e. use their weakness as a teaching point?

(ii) We also want to ask:

- Are we using our material resources effectively?
- How long are they in use?
- How long do they stay in the cupboard/on the shelf?

- Are our library books used sufficiently well?

(iii) What methods will we use?

- A frequency analysis of our apparatus ordering sheets will tell us how often certain pieces of equipment are used.
- A set of criteria for evaluating materials will be drawn up, or an already developed one employed, and a group will conduct an analysis of a sample of our materials and textbooks.
- A pupil questionnaire relating to the images and languages in our textbook will be drawn up for all pupils.
- The librarian will be asked to conduct a frequency audit of a sample of library books.
- The advisory teacher for science will be invited to apply our criteria to a range of new texts that he will bring along for our perusal.

(iv) Who will we report it to?

- The headteacher requires a report on our evaluation and suggestions for new texts before she will release any funds for new materials.

(v) How long will it take?

- It depends how long we want to wait before getting the new funding. It is probably not feasible in less than two terms if we are to be thorough.

Some unanswered questions

We haven't really addressed the issue of whether we can continue to use the texts and teach the children to be critical of them. This will have to wait for a second stage of evaluation.

CONCLUSION

The process of judgement is a difficult and complex one. It relies on drawing together of all the strands of information, and making sense for the evaluators out of all the possible conflicts contained therein.

REFERENCES

1   Stenhouse, L., *An Introduction to Curriculum Research and Development.* (Hienemann Educational, 1975).

2   Ebbutt, D., *Evaluation Position Paper 1: Ethical Principles and Practical Procedures*, Mimeograph. (Secondary Science Curriculum Review, 1983).

3   Ebbutt, D., *Evaluation Position Paper 2: A Strategy for the Evaluation of Aspects of the Work of the Secondary Science Curriculum Review*, Mimeograph. (Secondary Science Curriculum Review, 1983).

4   Tyler, R., *Basic Principles of Curriculum and Instruction.* (University of Chicago Press, 1949).

5   Partlett, M. and Hamilton, D., 'Evaluation as illumination: A new approach to the study of innovative programmes'. Occassional Paper No 9, Centre for Research in the Educational Sciences, University of Edinburgh (1972). Reprinted in D. Hamilton, D. Jenkins, C. King, B. McDonald and M. Partlett (eds). *Beyond the Numbers Game*. (Macmillan, 1977).

6   Hamilton, D., Jenkins, D., King, C., McDonald, B. and Partlett, M. (eds), *Beyond the Numbers Game*. (Macmillan, 1977).

7   *The Education Reform Act, 1988*. (HMSO, 1988).

8   *People in Science and Technology: An Evaluation of the Girls in Science Project*. (GIST). (Schools Council, 1983).

9   Ebbutt, D. and Bentley, D., 'Flags and Spears: a process evaluation of the Secondary science Curriculum Review as a model of change'. Unpublished paper: Schools Curriculum Development Council (1986).

10   Hamilton, D., *Curriculum Evaluation*. (Open Books, 1976).

11   Hopkins, D., *Evaluation for School Development*. (Open University Press, 1989). pp. 19–26.

12   Stake, R. 'The Contenance of educational evaluation', *Teachers College Record*, 1967, **68**, pp. 523–40.

13   McCormick, R. and James, M., *Curriculum Evaluation in Schools*, 3rd edition. (Croom Helm, 1990). Chapter 8.

FURTHER READING

Abbott, *et al.*, GRIDS Handbook, 2nd edition (Secondary school version). (Longmans for the SCDC, 1988).

McDonald, B. 'The experience of Innovation' Centre for Applied Research in Education, University of East Anglia. (1978).

Powney, J. and Watts, D. M., *Interviewing in Educational Research*. (Routledge and Kegan Paul, 1987).

PART 4
THE ROLE OF PRACTICAL WORK IN THE TEACHING OF CHEMISTRY

As indicated in the Introduction to *Open Chemistry* practical work has a key, and maybe multifarious role to play in the teaching of the subject. As in the teaching of biology, physics and earth science, chemistry makes quite specific demands in terms of regulations when it comes to the organization and delivery of practical work in schools. In Chapter 13 Linington explores the relationship between practical work and a range of other teaching and learning strategies that chemistry, and science, teachers can utilize in making the subject appealing and exciting to learners. She shows that the distinction between thinking about chemistry (theory) and doing chemistry (practical work) is a very artificial one. In the teaching and learning of chemistry ample opportunities exist for encouraging pupils to 'report' on their knowledge and experience of chemistry in a number of ways. For far too long reporting has been formalized via the traditional writing up of experiments. There has been too heavy an emphasis on formal transactional language—impersonal language—the language of scientific papers. Drama, role play, simulation, games and computer-aided instruction all have vital contributions to make to the teaching and learning of chemistry. Above all else, chemistry provides a myriad of ways whereby pupils can talk through their laboratory and classroom experiences.

In Chapter 14 Jenkins also discusses the functions and purposes of practical work in school chemistry and reflects on the broader implications of managing the school laboratory and resources—both human and material—in a way that enables teachers and pupils to explore chemistry in a safe and creative way. Throughout this Chapter Jenkins repeatedly questions many aspects of traditional practical work in a challenging and thought provoking way.

CHAPTER 13

INTEGRATING PRACTICAL WORK WITH OTHER TEACHING AND LEARNING STRATEGIES

Mary Linington

TEACHING AND LEARNING STRATEGIES

Teaching and learning strategies are those planned, and unplanned activities by which pupils interact with and come to understand the content, skills and concepts of chemistry. Many of these activities, such as talking and discussion, writing and reporting, reading and researching, games, drama (including role play), computer-aided learning (both simulations and data processing and capture) and practical experience, will also be used by teachers and learners in other subjects. Teaching requires learners to talk to the teacher and to each other. Such talk can be organized in several ways, for example, as a question and answer session, as a formal debate, or as an informal small-group discussion. If talking is to be used to teach a subject, then pupils need to be offered space and time to listen creatively and encouraged to practise this. The use of drama and role play can help.

Reading is a strategy often used by teachers as part of homework and so is not always as focused and as useful as it might be, and is often not integrated with other strategies, nor carefully followed up. Often the only reading given during a lesson is in the form of worksheets, and as such is undemanding. The use of DARTS (directed activities related to texts) enables pupils to interact with texts more meaningfully [1]. The development of study skills that include researching and using library books, for example, is important for learning chemistry.

The use of games and simulations can also play an important part in the teaching of chemistry; these can be quite realistic and may be computer-based. In the past, the use of computers for teaching chemistry has been underused by many teachers. This may have been because of a lack of knowledge of software and hardware, or because access to the hardware was difficult. However, there is now a wide range of software available for reinforcing chemical knowledge and understanding, this includes data capture, processing and analysis; simulation of experiments, e.g. reaction kinetics; programmed learning and games or exercises.

Practical work is often not properly integrated with other teaching strategies. As a specific teaching strategy, practical work requires detailed consideration of how it can be used to help pupils learn. Much practical work takes place in a laboratory, and so often the phrase practical work is used interchangeably with laboratory work, but fieldwork in chemistry can provide good examples of applied chemistry.

THE PURPOSE OF PRACTICAL WORK IN TEACHING CHEMISTRY

Before considering how practical work can or should be integrated with other teaching and learning strategies, it is important to consider the purpose(s) of practical work in chemistry teaching. Most teachers believe that science (and therefore chemistry) is a practical activity; as a discipline it is based on experiment and investigational work that involves hypothesis, observation, data collection and analysis. Since chemistry is a practical activity, practical work is seen as essential in the teaching of chemistry. Many teachers would argue that it is impossible to teach chemistry without doing practical work in a laboratory. However, research into the nature and purpose of practical work in school science teaching [2] pointed out that the 'overt consideration of the nature and purpose of practical work in science teaching was exceptional'.

Should laboratory work be used to teach and confirm the body of chemistry knowledge and/or enable pupils to become investigational chemists? Over recent years examination syllabuses have changed significantly (and will continue to do so!). There has been a steady decline in the testing of practical skills in public examinations; internal assessment has become the norm. Syllabuses have become investigation-loaded. Not only has there been an increase in the quantity of practical work in science teaching, but its character has changed. Whereas at one time syllabuses saw practical work as techniques to be learnt, pupils are now encouraged and enabled to follow scientific investigations in an effort to experience being a scientist. Teachers have been observed to have various views concerning the purpose of practical work [2], these include:

- the encouragement of accurate observation and careful recording;
- the promotion of simple scientific method and thought;
- the development of manipulative skills;
- training pupils in problem solving;
- fitting the requirements of practical examinations;
- elucidation of theory, aiding comprehension;
- verification of facts and principles already taught;
- establishing facts by investigation and arriving at principles;
- arousing and maintaining interest;
- making phenomena real.

These observed aims may, or may not be appropriate to individual lessons. Recent literature has explored the purposes of practical work in the teaching and learning of science. Woolnough and Allsop [3], through clear and detailed argument, suggested the rationale for a practical should be either that it elucidates, reinforces or supports the acquisition of knowledge and concepts, or it is part of the process of science itself, that is problem solving. The teaching approaches needed for these two aspects are not the same. Woolnough and Allsop argued that part of the knowledge of science is tacit knowledge, and therefore practical work which supports the development of this tacit knowledge is important in the education of young scientists. Hence one very important purpose of practical work is for 'getting a feel for phenomena'. They further argued that elucidation or comprehension of theory through experiment is difficult. Pupils often gain little understanding from their experiments because they fit their experimental results to the conceptual models which they bring to their lessons (see Chapter 15). The teacher has thus two tasks to make practical work successful; first to ascertain and disentangle the preconceptions which pupils bring with them to their work, and second to modify these preconceptions through activities such as discussion and demonstration. Quite rightly the acquisition of practical skills is frequently seen as a valid purpose for practical work. Head [4] suggested three reasons for the inclusion of practical work in science teaching: to motivate pupils, to acquire science skills and to enhance learning. The motivational role of practical work is rarely questioned, indeed the threat of its withdrawal is often used as a discipline strategy [5]. This may be counter productive, since although younger pupils respond well to practical work, older pupils often dislike practical work. Head warned that practical sessions are not always a good learning experience [4], and that as the most convincing case for practical work must be that it enhances learning, the quality of the learning experience is important.

ORGANIZING PRACTICAL WORK

It is important for you as the teacher, to analyse the reasons for your pupils doing practical work and to plan practical activities to match these. Planning any chemistry lesson must involve overt consideration of the type of practical work to be carried out, how the context for this work will be set, how it will be organized, what reporting strategies will be used and how pupils will be supported with the development of their practical skills and consolidation of their work.

It is for you as the teacher to decide what type of practical activities will complement your teaching style and how to organize these to achieve your planned purposes. Some of the pros and cons of various activities are discussed below.

Individual work

Individual work may be useful for learning and developing skills. It can enable pupils to work at their own pace and to organize their own learning. When all pupils are performing the same activity, but for example with different chemicals or concentrations of solution, class results can be collated, so giving an opportunity for discussion of a wider range of results. Individual work may need detailed support materials if there is to be meaningful learning without causing heavy demands on teacher time in the lesson. It frequently needs a change of teacher role to be successful; planning and preparation become more important than ever, otherwise the teacher cannot control the development of the lesson. Individual work makes heavier demands on apparatus and chemicals than whole-class or group work. It does not allow pupil–pupil interaction and discussion, although this can be planned as part of the consolidation and follow-up work. There are many examples of whole schemes of individualized learning for chemistry, such as *Independent Learning Project for Advanced Chemistry* (ILPAC) [6]. In such schemes practical work is also done on an individual basis.

Small-group work

Small-group work encourages collaborative working enabling pupils to explore their preconceptions and to discuss their results with their peers. Groups of pupils can tackle the same investigation differently, organize their own work, and learn at their own pace. There is some research evidence [7] to suggest that girls respond more positively to science when they are working in small groups. By controlling the formation of groups, pupils with different levels of experience can work together. This may have the advantage of encouraging pupils to learn from each other and if the group contains pupils for whom English is a second language, this can enable such pupils to work with peers as support for language acquisition. Potential difficulties may include the change in role of the teacher to tutor and organizer, and the many and various demands on the teacher from groups working at different paces.

Teacher demonstrations

Teacher demonstrations have in recent years become less popular. However, a good demonstration can startle or challenge pupils, provoke thought and discussion, whet pupils' appetites for further investigation and it can also be entertaining. Because it gives the teacher control of the lesson, there will always be an important reason for using a demonstration; that of safety. Sometimes a demonstration is used when there is a shortage of apparatus, but this is not a valid reason since such an activity could form part of a circus of practical work, where pupils each do the practical work by rotating round a series of activities over a period of time. However, a demonstration can be useful for introducing the use of new or difficult apparatus and procedures. Demonstration requires practice and a sense of theatre for the greatest effect, but it must not be overdone otherwise it can have the opposite effect to that intended, i.e. boring pupils. It is possible to enliven demonstrations (and to ensure all pupils are actively attending) by involving pupils, encouraging them to do the demonstration (either with or without previous practice!). How a teacher decides to organize practical work will be influenced by the amount of lesson structure needed to achieve the planned learning.

Unstructured practical work

Unstructured activities include problem solving and open-ended investigations. Genuine open-ended investigations are difficult to organize and introduce into lessons. Pupils are often set activities such as: 'What causes rusting?' or 'How can fibres be made fire resistant?'. For each investigation the teacher provides a limited range of information, apparatus or materials which constrain the pupils' work. Some investigations can be easily, or best, answered by reference to texts, whereas others may have a subjective result, for example, 'Which is the best detergent?'. In such cases it is important to establish definitions, for example, of what is 'best', or to agree that a compromise result will be acceptable. Unstructured activities require considerable time and equipment if pupils are to follow them to a successful outcome, and are best done in small groups. A problem-solving activity must be a real problem the pupils want to solve. These can be difficult to design in chemistry, although there have been examples such as the great chemical egg race [8]. It is unlikely that problem-solving activities can be used to 'discover' chemical facts or principles. However, like any other unstructured practical activity, problem solving can be used to help pupils gain some experience of what it is like to be a chemist, to help them appreciate that chemistry is not organized neatly but is a continuous process that cannot always be planned from the outset.

Structured practical work

Structured activities are planned by the teacher. Since there is a considerable range of skills and techniques that pupils need to acquire in order to become a chemist, these must be learnt through practical work. However, in a desire to teach skills it is easy for such lessons to become nothing more than a series of mundane activities, such as measuring the volume of liquid. Integrating the practice of skills into other practical work may be more appropriate, although there may well be good pedagogic reasons for the use of practical exercises.

REPORTING STRATEGIES

Before planning a complete lesson and considering how practical work might integrate with other teaching strategies it is necessary to consider possible reporting strategies. A clear distinction needs to be made between the careful recording of observations and notes taken during the practical activity, and the final reporting of the whole activity, perhaps for assessment purposes. Traditionally practical work has been reported under set headings, e.g. aim or hypothesis, apparatus, method, results and conclusion. If practical work is to help pupils' learning, so should the method of reporting it. Written reporting can take various forms, appropriate to the practical work, e.g. the use of brief notes, whether written by the pupil or as part of a gap-completion exercise, can ensure a quick, easy-to-read record is kept. More creative reporting techniques, such as poetry, newspaper reports and play writing may help consolidation. Pupils need not necessarily be constrained by one format. Written work is often done at a distance from the practical work and is not therefore an integral part of the activity. It is often done by individual pupils, giving them little opportunity to discuss their work, so individuals should give oral reports, both to the teacher and to the whole class. The organization of a whole-class debate can develop skills and attitudes not often thought of as part of chemistry, however the ability to offer a logical, well reasoned argument is crucial for practising chemists. Some curriculum areas have experimented with less traditional methods of reporting, such as audio-cassettes, photographs and video. It could be interesting to explore the use of this technology in reporting chemistry. Creating posters for display can be used as a reporting strategy, but it is also a powerful teaching and learning strategy that is often underused in the secondary laboratory or classroom.

INTEGRATING PRACTICAL WORK WITHIN A LESSON

The following examples of investigations illustrate how practical work may be integrated with other teaching and learning strategies. In the first example pupils were asked to investigate 'Which is the best stain remover?'.

To set the context, advertising literature was displayed in the laboratory, and the notion of testing manufacturers' claims was discussed. As homework pupils were asked to research what types of stain removers are available, their chemical contents and how the contents may be measured quantitatively. Initially small working groups discussed their research and how they would present it quickly to the class. During the class presentation and discussion a definition of what 'best' means was established. All groups tackled the same investigation, but on different stain removers, allocated such that each group had two removers for comparison. All groups estimated the strength of the bleaching agent used and did further tests against criteria which they chose. These tests were submitted to the teacher, in writing, for review before they were started. To enable comparison of class results for bleaching strength a proforma for recording results was used. Each pupil wrote up the quantitative investigation, as agreed by their group. Each group displayed their results before tackling further tests. The results of the group-designed tests were reported to the class in writing. Each group wrote no more than one A4 sheet, which was then photocopied and used for data analysis by individual pupils. During this analysis each pupil had to decide for themselves from the evidence collected by the class which was the best stain remover. The pupils then re-formed groups according to which stain remover they 'supported' and in a class debate each group argued their case. A consensus decision was then made, where possible.

The second investigation involves fieldwork, which can increase pupil motivation as well as provide a context for applied chemistry. An activity linked to pollution could provide links to the National Curriculum cross-curricular themes 'environmental education' and 'economic and industrial understanding'.

The analysis of water from a canal or stream flowing through an area that leaches heavy metals can help to locate the source of contamination. To set the context for the work, pupils were asked to research qualitative and quantitative tests for heavy metals. These were reported back to the whole group through a teacher-led discussion. Pupils were asked to decide which of the available tests provided a suitable method to test the water, bearing in mind the tests would have to be performed in the field. Through laboratory-based practical work the pupils worked in groups to investigate the reliability and sensitivity of the various tests. The results were reported back to the whole group, and through further teacher-led discussion one test was identified as suitable for further investigation. The next step was to pose the problem, how can the test be made portable? The use of standard reagents, graduated test-tubes and colour charts for quantitative estimation was explained to pupils. Each working group of pupils collected a testing kit, and was responsible for maintaining it. They discussed and planned how they would deploy themselves to ensure adequate results were collected, which sampling points were appropriate and how to record results in a consistent format. The collection of samples to confirm field results through laboratory testing was discussed and organized. Afterwards the fieldwork results were collected and displayed graphically to the whole group. The data collected was verified through laboratory testing of the samples brought back, so reinforcing the quantitative work done in the planning stage of the exercise. On completion of the data collection, pupils were posed the question, 'Can the source of the pollution be identified?' This lead to a whole new phase of research where pupils investigated economic and chemical solutions to the problem of the eradication of pollution. The whole project was reported back through a debate on the issue of jobs versus pollution.

Clearly this appears to be a lengthy activity, but it enables pupils to practise quantitative skills and to get a feel for being a chemist through research, testing, reporting and debating results. It is though, only one example of how practical work might integrate with written and oral work.

REFERENCES

1   Martin, S., Maskell, R. and Needlister, D., *Learning Strategies in Science Teaching*, Modular Secondary Science Resources. (John Murray, 1987) pp. 10.26–10.28.

2   Keer, J. F., Boulind, H., Scott, D., Rolls, M. and Stafford, E., *Practical Work in School Science*. (Leicester University Press, 1963).

3   Woolnough, B. and Allsop, T., *Practical Work in Science*. (Cambridge University Press, 1985).

4   Head, J., *The Personal Response to Science*. (Cambridge University Press, 1985).

5   Solomon, J., *Teaching Children in the Laboratory*. (Croom Helm, 1980).

6   *Independent Learning Project for Advanced Chemistry* (ILPAC). (John Murray, 1983).

7   Reay, D., 'Girls Groups as a Component of Anti-sexist Practice', *Gender and Education*, 1990, **2**(1).

8   Johnston, J. and Reed, N. (ed.), *In search of solutions: some ideas for chemical egg races and other problem-solving activities in chemistry*. (Royal Society of Chemistry, 1990).

CHAPTER 14

THE MANAGEMENT OF LABORATORY TEACHING

Edgar Jenkins

INTRODUCTION

Practical work in a laboratory is expensive in terms of equipment, apparatus and materials, and makes heavy demands on the time of pupils, technical staff and teachers. In addition, access to a laboratory imposes constraints, often severe, on a school timetable, and the work itself may present hazards and risks that demand knowledge and thorough preparation if chemistry is to be taught in ways that are safe but not dull or unimaginative. Nonetheless, practical work in a laboratory is widely accepted as an essential feature of school chemistry education and it is important to ask why this is so.

Fundamentally, the answer seems to be because chemistry is commonly perceived as a practical activity that requires a direct engagement with materials, apparatus and techniques in order to develop, probe and refine that body of imaginative ideas that constitutes chemical understanding. However, organizing pupils' learning in a chemistry lesson is not the same as undertaking research at the bench in a research laboratory and it is arguable that too great an emphasis on practical work encourages pupils to undervalue the creative, imaginative and intellectual aspects of the subject. In the school context, therefore, the teaching of practical chemistry is justified by educational and pedagogical concerns rather than by motives that stem from the development of the research skills essential to the generation of new scientific knowledge.

These concerns, of course, are informed by a number of perceptions, for example, of the broader purposes of chemical education, of the epistemology of chemical or scientific knowledge, of the relationship between 'theory' and 'practice', of the nature and status of 'observation' and of what it is actually like to undertake chemical research. Nonetheless, the distinction between, on the one hand, teaching and learning chemistry at school, and on the other, the advancement of the discipline itself, is important. Pupils at school are not research workers. Their motives, aspirations and expectations are different, and critically they lack the experience, craft and other skills acquired by a research worker only after a prolonged and demanding apprenticeship. Likewise, the chemistry teacher is not concerned with training research workers in a school laboratory. The notion of chemical education embraces much more than the acquisition of laboratory skills which are means not ends in themselves. Despite much of the rhetoric, the contemporary emphasis on pupils planning and conducting their own investigations derives essentially from educational motives rather than from a belief that pupils can, in any significant sense, actually behave as research scientists. Conducting a practical chemistry lesson, therefore, is an exercise in planning and organizing activities and experiences selected to foster particular learning outcomes.

The arguments that have been put forward for the laboratory teaching of chemistry are reviewed in Chapter 13, and it is important to recall that the relative emphasis given to these arguments has been markedly dependent upon time and social context [1]. Nonetheless, it is difficult to dissent from the broad assertion that the purpose of laboratory teaching is to help pupils develop their understanding of chemistry. Other objectives, such as the acquisition of manipulative skills (see Chapter 10), the enhancement of pupil motivation, the fostering of a 'feel for phenomena', or the accommodation of a variety of assessment requirements (see Chapters 10 and 11), are all subordinate to this overall aim.

Some notes of caution, however, are appropriate. It cannot be assumed that laboratory work conducted by pupils, or indeed by teachers, will necessarily enhance pupils' motivation or improve their understanding. Pupils whose laboratory exercises are not completed successfully, perhaps because of difficulty with the manipulation of apparatus, in following written or other instructions, or in making or interpreting observations, may be discouraged and/or find their understanding of a topic less, rather than more, secure.

Nor can it be assumed that winning knowledge from laboratory exercises is a straightforward task. When a piece of copper metal is heated in a clear Bunsen flame, agreement that the metal turns black at the surface can usually be reached relatively easily. What may not be so straightforward to secure is a common understanding of the cause. Indeed, it would be surprising if this were so, given the difficulties in understanding combustion that were only too evident in the 17th and 18th centuries. For the teacher, there is an 'obvious' and uniquely correct explanation. For pupils not yet familiar with Lavoisier's imaginative leap, the blackening of the surface of the copper may be dismissed as mere 'soot', or attributed to, for example, the burning gas of the Bunsen flame, to something escaping from the copper, or to some form of 'reaction' between the copper and the air, or between the copper and the Bunsen flame, or even between the copper, the Bunsen flame and the air. A priori, each of these hypotheses is worth serious consideration and testing each of them is a valuable, if time consuming, learning experience. But no hypothesis stands on its own. The conventional and currently accepted explanation of what happens when the copper blackens entails a substantial and interlocking set of concepts and assumptions that constitute the intellectual baggage of contemporary understanding of combustion [2]. Convincing pupils in an honest and, for them, satisfying way, that the blackening is not due to something from within the copper involves far more than, for example, establishing an increase in mass upon combustion. Such an increase is highly significant only for those who already subscribe to the role of oxygen in combustion. *Of itself*, the mass increase has little significance since another explanation can *always* be put forward to account for it.

In other cases, there may even be dispute about the observation itself, as any teacher who has ever asked pupils to judge whether or not some limewater has turned cloudy, will be only too well aware. The key point here is that while many observations seem unambiguous or straightforward, this is rarely the case. What is seen depends upon who is looking, i.e. upon the experience and skill of the observer.

There is the further difficulty that even when there is agreement about what is seen, no single observation or even set of observations is sufficient to refute a theory or explanation. Such refutation involves social and psychological, as well as cognitive, factors, a point too readily ignored by some so-called investigative/discovery approaches to laboratory teaching [3].

These comments about theory and observation are important in the present context because whenever a teacher engages a class in laboratory work, that class is presented with a set of assumptions about what is involved in 'doing chemistry' and in establishing chemical knowledge. Laboratory teaching inevitably sends messages about the relationship between observations and explanations, about the status of scientific explanations and about scientific methodology. In many instances, these messages are not easily reconciled with contemporary scholarship by historians, sociologists and philosophers of science. Ravetz [4], for example, has concluded that this scholarship has rendered antique 'the sort of ideology of science which, explicitly or implicitly, (has) provided coherence and security for generations of (science) teachers'.

More generally, pupils' laboratory experiences might reasonably lead them to form the impression that most chemists are engaged in finding out about the natural world in a disinterested pursuit of truth. In reality, most chemists work for industrial, military, pharmaceutical or other commercial or public organizations and their research is directed by the principal concerns of those organizations rather than by the 'pursuit of truth' in quite the way suggested by those chemists honoured in most chemistry textbooks, for example, Mendeléev and Dalton. Redner [5] has expressed this point with particular clarity.

> 'Science has changed its ends. It is no longer the old science of the last few centuries. That old science is coming to an end... Contemporary science is worldly in every sense of the word and quite different in its essential character from the European science of the recent past... these differences are apparent in all dimensions of scientific research, intellectual, instrumental and organizational.'

Redner [5]

Along with a number of others, the issues raised in the preceding paragraphs hint strongly at the need for a major reappraisal of the role of the laboratory in school science education. Hodson [6], for example, has referred to the need to draw a distinction between practical work and laboratory work and has argued for the replacement of the latter term by the wider notion of science learning activities.

The contemporary debate about the educational functions of laboratory teaching has a number of advantages in the present context. In particular, it exposes that such teaching may have a variety of rationales and highlights the importance of identifying the purpose of engaging pupils in a laboratory-based activity.

MANAGING LABORATORY TEACHING

The effective management of the laboratory learning environment requires:

(i)   a clear statement of purpose(s), translated into more specific objectives that include statements of intended learning outcomes;

(ii) the development of a teaching strategy consistent with those objectives;

(iii) the deployment of appropriate resources;

(iv) continuous and summative evaluation of the teaching strategy in bringing about the intended learning outcomes;

(v)   the revision of (i) to (iii) in the light of (iv).

The realization of these strategic aims requires knowledge of various kinds, for example:

• of the chemistry to be taught;

• of how pupils learn;

• of the manipulative or other skills that can be reasonably be expected of most pupils at a given age;

• of the various ways of securing and maintaining pupils' interest and motivation;

• of how best to deal with 'mixed ability' classes or with 'slow learners';

• of the means whereby learning can be monitored and progress determined;

• of the legislative and professional framework that establishes acceptable levels of risk in working with hazardous materials.

Some of these matters are discussed in some detail elsewhere in this book and others are considered below. However, it is important to note that although knowledge can be acquired from books, much can be given meaning only by experience of working with pupils. A critical and continuous reflection upon this experience, therefore, is an essential component of professional development as a teacher.

Also important is the ability to work with, and draw upon, the experience of others, including the technical staff. The latter have a wide range of responsibilities that includes personnel management and welfare, administration, stock control and ordering, safety and security, as well as servicing laboratory teaching and the maintenance, repair and construction of equipment. Schools differ considerably in the practice followed in ordering materials for practical lessons but whatever arrangement is made, it must be reliable and allow technical staff adequate time to provide the various resources. It is also important that any arrangement allows possible clashes of requirements to be identified in advance, particularly when longer-term projects or investigations are in progress. If the major part of the preparation has been done in good time, technical staff are in a better position to provide the support required to ensure that a lesson goes ahead as intended.

SOME SAFETY CONSIDERATIONS

Safety is a fundamental and *integral* component of lesson planning. It is *not* something to be considered after a lesson has been planned. In addition to the more general legal provisions relevant to the work of all teachers as employees, school science teaching is governed by a wide range of legislation governing matters as diverse as the making of explosives, the purchase of industrial methylated spirit, the storage and use of radioactive materials, the labelling of dangerous substances, the wearing of eye protection, and the disposal of waste. Of particular importance are *The Health and Safety at Work, etc. Act, 1974* [7] together with its associated Statutory Instruments and the Administrative Memoranda and Circulars issued from time to time by the DES, the Welsh Office, the Scottish Education Department and the Department of Education, Northern Ireland. *The Control of Substances Hazardous to Health Regulations, 1988* (COSHH) [8] require an employer (e.g. LEA, and school governors) to:

(i)   assess risks to health arising from the way a substance is used in a school or college, and

(ii) consider whether it is possible to avoid exposure to that substance.

Where (ii) is not possible steps must be taken to minimize and control the risk. Substantial advice on the operation of the COSHH Regulations is now available and these and other safety requirements are not considered here. (For further details, see [9–12].) Keeping up to date with relevant health and safety matters is an important aspect of a science teacher's work.

In accommodating safety within lesson planning, the COSHH Regulations must be complied with. However, good professional practice involves more than compliance. It presupposes an interrogative approach to safety which focuses attention on all aspects of a lesson undertaken with pupils. Thus, is there a safer way of:

(i)   distributing materials, in order to minimize possible confusion, improper mixing of reagents, congestion in the laboratory, potential problems of class control?

(ii) carrying out a reaction, e.g. by reducing the scale, using more readily controlled liquid–liquid, rather than solid–liquid, mixtures, or, in appropriate circumstances, using a tap funnel, rather than a thistle funnel?

(iii) illustrating a phenomenon, e.g. by reducing the scale, by using less-hazardous materials, by computer simulation, by using videotape or film, by conducting a teacher demonstration rather than pupil-based practical work?

It is also essential to address questions such as those raised in the following paragraphs.

(i)   Is the proposed activity commensurate with the age, experience and ability of the pupils? Judgements of this kind are, of course, central to the notion of risk assessment. What is appropriate for senior pupils may not be appropriate for younger pupils. In all cases, a pupil is a learner and what is obvious to the teacher may be far from obvious to someone less experienced and mature.

(ii)   What steps are to be taken to ensure that pupils know the hazards associated with a task they are to be asked to undertake, and understand the nature of the consequent safety measures? Can the methods of communicating instructions to pupils be improved? What steps are to be taken to ensure that pupils are conducting laboratory work in accordance with agreed procedures, for example, the wearing of eye protection?

(iii) Particular attention may need to be given to pupils who are disabled or have other special educational needs (see the relevant Chapters of Part 6). Note that the need to understand the nature of the hazards associated with a proposed activity is not confined to pupils. Non-teaching assistants working with disabled pupils and, in many cases technical staff, will be among those who also need to be appropriately informed.

(iv) Is the teacher thoroughly familiar with the procedures to be undertaken and aware of the associated hazards? This is important not just from the point of view of safety. It is a minimum condition of professional practice. In addition, there is evidence that when these conditions do not prevail, teachers resort to didactic methods of teaching or, if possible, avoid undertaking the practical activity.

(v)   Has the teacher identified the most likely accident associated with a given practical activity and how to deal with it? Although school science laboratories are remarkably safe places in which to teach and learn, inappropriate action can turn a minor accident into a major incident.

Safety in science teaching, therefore, depends upon effective and informed planning that embraces the action that would need to be taken when, for whatever reason, an accident occurs. If there is an accident, the teacher's duties are to:

(i)   assist any casualties;

(ii)   take appropriate steps to control the emergency;

(iii) avoid becoming a casualty him or herself;

(iv)   inform the appropriate authority, in accordance with established procedures, that an accident has occurred.

Note that the provision of first aid facilities for those *employed* in schools is governed by an *Approved Code of Practice* which came into force on 2 July 1990. Serious accidents such as a penetrating injury to any eye or an electric shock causing burns or loss of consciousness, must be reported in accordance with *The Reporting of Injuries, Diseases and Dangerous Occurrences Regulations, 1985* [13].

It should be recognized that class control is an important element in safety. Pupils engaged in practical work in a laboratory generate noise. Such noise must not be allowed to reach a level at which it constitutes a barrier to ready communication with a class. As always, class control is unlikely to be a significant problem if pupils' attention and interest are engaged by the tasks with which they are presented.

STRUCTURING PRACTICAL LESSONS

Most lessons do not stand in isolation. They relate directly to earlier work which thus sets the broad agenda for much of what follows. In addition, there will be few lessons that do not begin with one or more matters incidental to the main purpose in hand, for example, commenting on the quality of homework and dealing with missing work. At some point, however, it will be necessary to remind pupils of what has gone before and to gain their interest in the new ideas to be taught. This may be done in a number of ways, for example, a teacher may initiate a question and answer session relevant to the topic to be considered or may require pupils to observe what happens when they carry out a simple experiment in accordance with written or other instructions. Other strategies include showing part or all of a film or videotape, making use of cuttings from newspapers, magazines or journals, inviting a pupil or group of pupils to recount the essential features of a visit, for example, to a chemical plant, or to draw upon their own 'chemical experience', for example, the rusting of their bicycles, the ironing of synthetic fabrics, the use of detergents or shampoos.

The introduction of a laboratory lesson does more than bring into focus the topic to be addressed. It also determines in large measure the way in which that topic will be approached. If pupils are presented with one or more questions to be answered, the lesson that follows is likely to be more interrogative, investigative or 'open-ended' than if the introduction establishes an explanation that is then simply to be 'confirmed' by the practical. The following types of investigative tasks have been identified by Gott *et al.* [14].

(i)   *'Decide which' tasks*, e.g. investigating which of a small number of commercially available bleaches represents the best value for money, or which of a number of reagents is the best catalyst for a given chemical reaction. These provide excellent opportunities for pupils to devise and discuss their strategies for answering the question posed. At their simplest, these investigations have only one independent variable.

(ii)   *'Find the effect of' tasks*, e.g. an investigation of the effect of surface area or temperature on the rate of a chemical reaction, or of the effect of temperature on the rate of dissolution. Like the tasks in (i), this type of investigation is essentially procedural and requires competence at handling variables.

(iii)   *'Find a way to' tasks*, e.g. an investigation of how a chemical reaction may be used to lift a specified mass at a given rate or to a predetermined height. So-called 'chemical egg race' problems are of this type which requires the understanding and application of chemical concepts as well as manipulative and other skills.

Generally, an investigation becomes more difficult when the number and/or complexity of the variables to be controlled is increased, when the level of conceptual understanding is raised, or when the problem is presented in an unfamiliar form or context. As always, the wording of a problem is also important.

Note that an investigative approach, on the one hand, and a more expository approach on the other, must not be equated with laboratory work undertaken by pupils, and with teacher demonstration, respectively. Much so-called investigative work is highly didactic, and well-conducted teacher demonstrations offer an excellent opportunity to challenge pupils intellectually and enhance their understanding. The approach to be adopted should be determined always by fitness for purpose and safety constraints, with other considerations, notably cost and availability of apparatus being accommodated as appropriate.

Having determined the objectives of the practical lesson and established whether the practical work is to be conducted by the teacher or by pupils working individually, in pairs or in groups, identifying the apparatus and other requirements is a straightforward task. It is useful to remember, (i) that most chemical reagents are available in a variety of grades of purity and that the purest and, therefore, most expensive reagents, are needed for only a few chemical operations at school level, and (ii) that considerable savings, not least on the cost of breakages, can sometimes be made by using apparatus improvised from everyday items, rather than the laboratory glassware or equipment available from commercial suppliers. In addition, selecting and/or designing the apparatus to be used in an experimental investigation can be a valuable learning experience. For ideas on the improvisation of laboratory apparatus, see Lowe [15, 16].

A successful laboratory-based lesson will also require attention to the following.

(i)   Consider the need for variety in the tasks required of the pupils during a lesson that commonly lasts for 70–80 minutes. This is a particularly long time for younger pupils, the more so if the experimental work itself does not require their constant attention.

(ii)   Consider the methods to be used for recording pupils' results and, where appropriate, the treatment of these results on a class basis. Increasingly, quantitative outputs from an experiment are handled with the aid of a data logging device and this practice is likely to become commonplace. In planning a lesson, estimations of the time likely to be needed to complete the various activities will enable a judgement to be made whether or not it will be possible to discuss the results of experimental work within that same lesson. While this is desirable, it is not always possible.

(iii) Consider the range of pupil ability within the group being taught. When this is wide, it is often necessary to ensure additional activities for those pupils who are able to complete a task much more quickly than the others in the class.

(iv)   Consider the need for regular monitoring, not only of pupils' activities, but of the extent to which the intended learning outcomes are being achieved. This is often done informally by questioning pupils as they work at the bench, but from time to time (and commonly, at the end of a lesson) a more formal estimation will be needed. In most lessons, pupils' understandings can be developed and revealed by a variety of means, including dialogue and group discussion, pupil 'presentations', and writing or drawing diagrams on the blackboard or in exercise books [17].

ASSESSMENT

The introduction of a National Curriculum and the requirements of GCSE examinations have greatly enhanced the role of assessment, and of the assessment of practical competence in particular, in school chemistry teaching. Assessing this competence is important for a variety of reasons, not least because a lot of time is spent in laboratory work and it involves different abilities from those associated with the non-practical activities commonly assessed by paper and pencil tests. An estimation of practical competence, therefore, is an important element of a pupil's assessment profile.

The literature concerned with the assessment of practical work is substantial (e.g. [18–21]) and noteworthy for the variety and occasional ambiguity of terms used to describe the qualities teachers should seek to assess. Lock [22], drawing upon the work underlying the Oxford Certificate of Educational Achievement (OCEA), has referred to four processes (planning, performing, interpreting and communicating), each of which may be associated with a number of skills as illustrated in Table 1.

Table 1   Processes and skills (modified from OCEA [22]).

Process	Skill
Planning	Stating problems, designing investigations, reformulating problems
Performing	Manipulating, observing, data gathering
Interpreting	Data handling, predicting, explaining, inferring, evaluating
Communicating	Reporting, receiving information

Although any 'list' of this kind is open to substantial criticism, not least on philosophical grounds [23], something similar is likely to underpin the practical assessments undertaken by most science teachers. At Key Stage 4/GCSE level, teachers will be guided by the requirements of the examination boards, although these differ in a number of significant respects [24].

Equally problematic is the translation of a list of qualities to be assessed into the everyday world of teaching and learning. One response is to further subdivide the so-called skills into 'sub-skills' or 'task-specific processes', for example, the ability to read a measuring cylinder or a thermometer accurately. Whatever its merits as an assessment technique, this atomistic approach arguably over-emphasizes assessment at the expense of learning and threatens to reduce at least some science lessons to no more than a circus of measurement or other task-specific exercises. In contrast, a more holistic approach [25] seeks to assess broader areas of competence without isolating and, it might be argued, giving too much importance to mere technique. The differences between these two approaches are important, both technically and for their implications for the relationship between teaching and learning, on the one hand, and assessment on the other.

Important questions also arise about the mechanisms for carrying out practical assessments and the frequency with which such assessments should be made. In part, the answer to the latter question depends upon whether such an assessment is needed for diagnostic or summative purposes. At GCSE level, examination boards specify the number and nature of the assessments that must be made. The appropriate method of carrying out an assessment depends upon what is to be assessed. Thus, in addition to more familiar written exercises, the ability to communicate might be judged by pupils giving an oral account of what they are doing at the laboratory bench, or presenting a poster summarizing their findings. Detailed checklists of pupil 'behaviours' or lessons devoted to assessing sub-skills may have a place in an assessment programme but there is a real risk that the principal purpose of science teaching, which is learning, may be subverted. In all cases, reliability and validity are formidable problems, the more so when the assessment requirements are extended to the affective domain, e.g. 'the ability to work well with others in the laboratory'. It is doubtful whether any procedure that can be operated within the time available could ever overcome these formidable technical difficulties.

REFERENCES

1   Woolnough, B. E., *Practical Science. The Role and Reality of Practical Work in School Science*. (Open University Press, 1991).

2   Pumfrey, S., 'The Concept of Oxygen. Using History of Science in Science Teaching', in M. Shortland and A. Warwick (eds) *Teaching the History of Science*. (British Society for the History of Science/Blackwell, 1989).

3   Latour, B. and Woolgar, S., *Laboratory Life: The Social Construction of Scientific Facts*. (Sage, 1979).

4   Ravetz, J. R., 'New Ideas About Science Relevant to Education', in E. W. Jenkins (ed.) *Policy Issues and School Science Education*. (Centre for Studies in Science and Mathematics Education, The University of Leeds, 1990).

5   Redner, H., *The Ends of Science, an Essay in Scientific Authority*. (Westview Press, 1987).

6   Hodson, D., 'Experiments in Science and Science Teaching', *Educational Philosophy and Theory*, 1988, **20**(2), pp. 53–66.

7   *The Health and Safety at Work, etc. Act, 1974*. (HMSO, 1974).

8   *The Control of Substances Hazardous to Health Regulations, 1988* (COSHH). (HMSO, 1988).

9   *Topics in Safety*. Association for Science Education. (ASE, 1988).

10   *HAZCARDS*. Consortium of Local Education Authorities for the Provision of Science Services (CLEAPSS). (Brunel University, 1989).

11   Jenkins, E. W. and Everett, K., *A Safety Handbook for Science Teachers*, 4th edn. (John Murray Ltd, 1991).

12   *Preparing COSHH Assessments for Project Work in Schools*, The Scottish Schools Equipment Research Centre. (SSERC, 1991).

13 *The Reporting of Injuries, Diseases and Dangerous Occurrences Regulations, 1985*. (HMSO, 1985).

14 Gott, R., Welford, G. and Foulds, K., *The Assessment of Practical Work in Science*. (Blackwell, 1988).

15 Lowe, N. K., *Low cost equipment for science and technology education*. (Unesco, 1985).

16 Lowe, N. K., *Low cost equipment for science and technology education*, Vol. 2. (Unesco, 1986).

17 Hornsey, M. and Horsfield, J., 'Pupils' discussion in science. A stratagem to enhance quantity and quality', *School Science Review*, 1982, **63**(225), pp. 763–767.

18 Assessment of Performance Unit (APU), *Science Progress Report*, Department of Education and Science. (HMSO, 1978).

19 Bryce, T. G. K., McCall, J., MacGregor, J., Robertson, I. J. and Weston, R. A. J., *Techniques for the Assessment of Practical Skills in Foundation Science*. (Heinemann Educational Books Ltd, 1983).

20 Bryce, T. G. K., McCall, J., MacGregor, J., Robertson, I. J. and Weston, R. A. J., *How to Assess Open-ended Investigations in Biology, Chemistry and Physics*. (Oxford-Heinemann Educational Books Ltd, 1991).

21 Lock, R. J. and Ferriman, B., 'CCEA – The Development of a Graded Assessment Scheme in Science 1982–84', *School Science Review*, 1987, **68**(244), pp. 570–575.

22 Lock, R. J., 'Practical Work', in R. J. Lock and D. Foster (eds) *Teaching Science 11–13*. (Croom Helm Ltd, 1987).

23 Wellington, J. (ed.), *Skills and Processes in Science Education. A Critical Analysis*. (Routledge, 1989).

24 Buchan, S. A., 'Practical Assessment in GCSE Science: the diversity of the Examining Groups Practice', *School Science Review* (in press).

25 Woolnough, B. E., 'Towards a holistic view of processes in science education', in J. Wellington (ed.) *Skills and Processes in Science Education. A Critical Analysis*. (Routledge, 1989).

PART 5
TEACHING FOR UNDERSTANDING

John Paul Sartre in a famous passage in his existentialist essay *Nausea* (1938) describes vividly a schoolchild being so preoccupied with playing the role of the attentive pupil that he or she fails to learn anything. All of us with direct classroom experience know this problem first hand. It is far too easy to judge the outcomes of teaching by simple criteria such as the ability of pupils, in Rosen's words, to 'parrot the jargon' or present the outcomes in copybook handwriting on well structured worksheets. In Part 5 two authors question many of these assumptions and present a significant challenge to the orthodoxy of science teaching.

In Chapter 15 Watts reviews the research that has been undertaken to explore the nature of concepts that cause difficulty for pupils. He reviews a number of alternative models of learning and backs a constructivist model which has major ramifications for science teachers. One focus of this Chapter is a review of the main findings of the Children's Learning in Science project at the University of Leeds that has been so influential in developing constructivist frameworks for teaching and learning in science. Children, and many if not most adults, hold various, and often conflicting, views of reality. One of these is a scientific view which can all too easily conflict with their commonsense view. These are the issues Watts explores.

In Chapter 16 Sutton explores the finer details of the role language plays in the teaching and learning of science. There is a vast literature of research and thinking on the relationship between thought and language and Sutton presents a masterly synthesis of the implications of this to teachers of chemistry. At a purely functional level we can regard the problem as being one of moving between an everyday terminology and a technical one—the vernacular concept of an acid as something that burns—and the chemical concept of acid. If an acid burns why do we put vinegar on salads? To say to the layperson 'Vinegar is a weak acid' conveys little for he or she has probably little experience of a strong acid, such as sulphuric acid, even though it is in their 'easy care' car battery. At a higher level Sutton explores the deeper complexities of thought and language and the very rich pastures that linguists and scientists should collaboratively explore.

CHAPTER 15

CHILDREN'S LEARNING OF DIFFICULT CONCEPTS IN CHEMISTRY

Mike Watts

INTRODUCTION

One of my few regrets in life is that I never pursued philosophy as a formal academic subject, it has simply been a long-time hobby. Like many others, I once shunned courses on the philosophy of education—studies of White, Hirst and Peters failed, somehow, to satisfy my personal interests. This Chapter is not an attempt to redress the balance—there's precious little Plato, Kant or Sartre. I do, though, tackle some issues of philosophy. Principally the Chapter is about learning in chemistry through conceptual change.

Learning in all parts of science has been at the centre of some considerable discussion and debate for many years and I want here to look at this from two perspectives. Initially I deal with learning largely from the pupils' perspective, and talk about some of the difficulties they have in understanding chemistry concepts. They have difficulties, too with biology and physics but this is not for discussion here (see Driver *et al.* [1]). This section provides an opportunity to describe constructivism and one of the metaphors with which it is commonly associated. In a later section, I focus on teachers and teaching and consider some of the difficulties encountered. I explore also some lesser-known metaphors and their implications. The summary tries to tie the various perspectives together. Within all this discussion I want specifically to look at the work of the Children's Learning in Science (CLIS) project [2], based at the University of Leeds, and to explore the working assumptions it adopts and the philosophy which underlies its approach. Since I hold the view that all of us have individual 'philosophies of life' which form the basis of our opinions, principles, values and beliefs, I also want to examine some of the personal philosophies that bear upon the teaching and learning of science in classrooms.

The line between philosophy and psychology is very thin in places, and it is not clear at all how the two interrelate. There are philosophies of education and psychologies of learning which, sometimes, can seem both wholly separate and/or entirely the same thing. If words like 'integrity', 'coherence' or 'consistent' are to have any meaning then, presumably, we really should be looking for a fairly strong link between the principles on which education is based and the ways we think people learn and study. This link has been called 'congruence'—a clear matching which shows how actions and behaviour in the classroom are consistent with principles and beliefs about teaching and learning. While no one is perfect, the opposite extreme ('eclecticism') would seem to be an unprincipled, scatterbrained, 'opportunity knocks' approach, and I see no virtues there at all.

CONSTRUCTIVISM

Before we get going, let me start with the philosophical and psychological ideas within *constructivism* and examine how far they have influenced what happens in classrooms. There is a fair amount of literature dealing with constructivism both generally and in school science, and while there seem to be as many variations as there are constructivists (illustrated, for example, by the debates in Adey *et al.* [3]) there is also a clear trend towards a general constructivist view of learning in science education (e.g. [4–6]). Though it is possible to be purist about constructivism (as we explore in Watts and Bentley [7]) it can also be taken as a fairly broad church which encompasses writers like David Ausubel, the early Piaget, George Kelly and Lev Vygotsky (to note just a few).

Put briefly, within constructivism, learning is always an interpretative process involving individuals' *constructions of meaning* relating to specific occurrences and phenomena. New constructions are built through their relation to previously acquired knowledge. The challenge for science teachers is to focus on pupils' learning-with-understanding, rather than the more common (and straightforward) emphasis on 'covering content'. To learn science from a constructivist philosophy implies direct experience with science as a process of generating knowledge—in which previous understandings are elaborated and changed on the basis of fresh meanings negotiated with peers and teachers.

Constructivism is not the only 'ism' on the scene. Consumerism, for example, is the positive philosophy of the market which sports brisk, no-nonsense efficiency: wet 'nanny state' educational theorists should make way for hearty competition and 'useful', high-powered career-education in schools. This is not a debate I want to enter in any detail, except to note that there is in constructivism an emphasis on negotiation, cooperation, collaboration, and the personal and social construction of knowledge—an emphasis which is often at odds with a view of knowledge as a fixed, certain, consumer commodity to be 'got' or 'delivered' in value-for-money packages.

Well, I hope the tone makes clear some of my own philosophy at least.

DIFFICULTIES FOR PUPILS

One entry into the debate is the suggestion that youngsters' difficulties in chemistry arise from the technical, non-technical and general form of language used in lessons. That is, the words in chemistry get in the way: the very language of the subject is a barrier to understanding. Let's examine this, beginning with technical terms.

A technical term is one for which chemists reserve a fairly guarded definition and set of implications. Some common examples are reaction, bond, matter, solution, suspension and reduction. These may, at first glance, seem very non-technical—words like polymerization, endothermic or double decomposition are much more likely to be halting. The first list, though, contains words which have dual (at least) meanings in both chemistry and everyday life, e.g. people have 'reactions to a surprise', 'solutions to some problems' and 'things that don't much matter'. There is a wealth of research (see Chapter 16) which has explored the difficulties youngsters experience when trying to come to terms with such words (e.g. Kingdon and Critchley [8], Watts and Gilbert [9], Wellington [10]). On the whole, children seem to have a number of ways of dealing with technical terms: they may use the terms correctly and in context; they may simply transfer everyday uses inappropriately and incorrectly into a chemistry context, or they may develop a 'composite' understanding of these words which is their own interpretation and attempt to make sense of the language of chemistry. Using the terms correctly and in an appropriate context is, of course, the goal of much chemistry teaching—and clearly some pupils are successful at this. Some even continue with study in chemistry. We know, though, that correct usage at one point is no guarantee that correct usage will automatically follow in future. So, what is properly written at GCSE does not necessarily mean it will be so one year later, even in chemistry A-level classes. Children (and adults) forget, regress in their understanding, generate confusion and so on. One common confusion is mixing the everyday meaning with that of the specialist: 'dissolve' is a good example here. It can have the meaning to fade away or to annul (as in dissolve a partnership) and youngsters will use the terms dissolve and disappear (sometimes dissolve and melt) as synonymous [11].

Next we consider the non-technical terms. Marshall *et al.* [12] are some of the latest researchers to point out that although pupils may sometimes appear to understand the everyday words being used, it is often the case that their understanding is not the same as that of the teacher. Some of the many common examples which have been explored by Marshall *et al.* are: accumulate, agent, consistent, contribute, device, component, control, initial, source, crude, devise, estimate, diagnose, evacuate, exert, influence, limit and random. A similar list compiled by Cassels and Johnstone [13] is much longer.

Almost a decade earlier, in 1976, Cassels [14] noted that:

> 'the problem lay, not so much in the technical language of science, but in the vocabulary and usage of normal English in a science context. Pupils and teachers saw familiar words and phrases which both 'understood', but the assumption that both understandings were identical was just not tenable.'

Cassels [14]

Clearly, not much has changed since.

That said, teachers usually make strenuous efforts to define technical terms as soon as the class meets them. The problem, though, is that it is not just the words but also the 'register' of chemistry that confounds the teacher's good intentions. (A register in this sense is the form and structure of language being used in particular situations, so that everyday conversation is different in form and structure from, say, a legal debate or cricket commentary.) Richards' 1979 work [15] is still a cogent reminder of the complex language registers used in science education:

> 'Characteristically such language shows increased formality of style, makes use
> of a specialised vocabulary and contains certain repetitive patterns of syntactic
> structure which are often more complex than would occur in the language
> normally employed by the pupil...these features are most strongly represented
> in physics and chemistry.'

Richards [15]

One could ask 'so what?' We *know* that youngsters do not fully understand
chemistry—why else would we be teaching them? We know that only the most
able succeed—the ones that can get to grips with the language of science. We
know that language is a great discriminator—we only have time to get through
the syllabus/programmes of study without having to worry about teaching
English too.

Constructivism, however, provides a distinctive window onto the problems
children encounter with difficult concepts. It is a broader approach to children's
conceptual development than a focus solely on language and syntax: it rests on
the notion that how we look at the world depends on the concepts we know
and use in order to understand it. Constructivism implies that individuals
develop 'frameworks of understanding' through which they look at the world:
particular 'goggles' through which they construct reality. So, for instance,
when a youngster uses the word 'burn' he or she might well include in that not
just the obvious processes involved (heat, smoke, flames and ashes) but might
also consider the disappearance of material, and from this have some difficulties
with a principle of conservation of matter.

In Vygotsky's work [16] he describes two kinds of concepts, 'spontaneous' and
'scientific'. He suggests that children build spontaneous concepts long before
they are conscious enough of them to be able to define them in words. They do
this through their everyday interaction with people and objects in the world. In
contrast a scientific (non-spontaneous) concept is commonly formed through a
verbal definition and its use in non-spontaneous circumstances. That is, it starts
life in the child's thinking in a way which spontaneous concepts only reach
much later:

> 'In working its slow way upwards, an everyday concept clears a path for the
> scientific concept and its downward development. It creates a series of
> structures necessary for the evolution of a concept more primitive, elementary
> aspects, which give it body and vitality. Scientific concepts in turn supply
> structures for the upward development of the child's spontaneous concepts
> towards consciousness and use.'

Vygotsky [16]

Vygotsky's work, built upon a large body of empirical investigation, gives a
firm basis for the emphasis on the ability to express concepts (both spontaneous
and scientific) as a vital part of school life. In the complex relationship
between thought and language Vygotsky regards word meanings as a phenomena
of thinking, of dynamic formations which evolve and change as the child
develops. Words are not merely used to express thought, they are the means by
which thought comes into existence.

THE CHILDREN'S LEARNING IN SCIENCE PROJECT

At this point let me introduce the Children's Learning in Science (CLIS) project. The project began life in the '80s in the midst of a torrent of work in progress in science education. This torrent had three main tributaries:

(i)   The wealth of data being generated by the Assessment of Performance Unit (APU) [17], which provided an excellent basis for examining the kinds of answers pupils gave to a wide variety of questions in science.

(ii) A growing international body of research into pupils' understandings in science. This body of research began to take form in the late '70s and Ros Driver, the Director of CLIS, has been a major influence in its growth and development.

(iii) A period of review and renovation in school science curricula. This period is epitomized by the work of the Secondary Science Curriculum Review (SSCR), a project which spanned the '80s and the full gamut of issues in school science. The SSCR worked closely with CLIS throughout its second phase of activity.

The first of these is worth looking at a little closer (interested readers can explore the others in, for example [18–21]). The APU was set up in 1975 by the Department of Education and Science and the science surveys took place between 1980 and 1984. The aim was to produce a national picture of pupil performance, not to report on the performance of individual children, schools or Local Education Authorities. Assessing science performance at three ages (11, 13 and 15 years) using both written and practical tests developed against an overall framework of assessment of performance. In general terms the APU provided comprehensive information which was neither simple nor straightforward. For example, there is no evidence of changes in performance levels over the five years of the surveys:

> 'the picture is one of general stability, both in terms of the categories of
> performance and in terms of the relative performance of pupil subgroups such
> as boys and girls, and pupils in England, Wales or Northern Ireland.'
>
> *APU [17]*

It is not easy to answer why there should be stability during a period of curriculum growth. What the APU did so successfully was to establish a framework for considering the skills and conceptual bases of school science, and to leave an immense fund of questions (and answers from pupils) on a variety of science concepts. The framework drew on a particular view of science—as a body of skills, processes and concepts—which was then used as a basis for detailing school science. The early work of the CLIS project drew extensively on the APU data and re-interpreted the pupils' responses. The project was less interested in how many pupils got correct answers, as in the quality of the 'wrong' answers given.

This strand of their research work focuses on what have been called 'misconceptions', 'preconceptions', 'alternative conceptions' or 'children's science'. These various names are an attempt to describe the same phenomenon—

the kinds of ideas that youngsters have before and after they meet the 'proper' science concepts in school. In 1978 Ros Driver and Jack Easley were the first to coin the phrases 'alternative frameworks' [22]. Their article marked an important step in the research field: do not dismiss, deride or decry students' own ideas or their 'wrong answers', but see in them ways of exploring what understandings learners *do* have. Learners' frameworks of understanding are important because they help to shape new information and experiences. From a constructivist perspective, we come to understand things in terms of what we already understand—if we cannot lock new thoughts into the old ideas already generated, new experiences become somewhat meaningless.

The work of the CLIS project

To quote from their own literature, the aims of the CLIS project have been to investigate pupils' understanding of specific concepts in science and then to

> 'devise, implement and evaluate teaching strategies which promote better conceptual understanding in science'

CLIS [2]

The initial phase of investigating children's concepts, was implemented in two ways. The first entailed cataloguing research worldwide on children's understandings of a broad range of scientific concepts. The second was to explore in detail selected concepts, principally the concepts of energy, heat, plant nutrition and the particulate nature of matter. More recent work is focusing on sound, variety of life, and aspects of astronomy.

The pupils questionned were all in the secondary age range (11–16 years) and the questions were given during science lessons. The research drew heavily, too, on the involvement of classroom teachers—particularly in the subsequent stages of devising learning strategies for classroom use. In this later phase of classroom intervention, some 30 secondary science teachers have worked with the project to design and evaluate materials. Here the aim was for teachers to act as researchers in their own classes, as they were involved intimately in the process of curriculum development—constructing and refining materials for practical classroom use. The outline schemes are described later in this Chapter, and are generally adaptations of current good teaching practices: adaptations which are based squarely upon a constructivist approach. Briefly, the task was that of challenging children's existing ideas and encouraging conceptual change towards a more orthodox scientific view. Classroom strategies included small-group discussion work, the making of posters, pupils' personal logs and diaries, worksheets, structured writing, brainstorming in the classroom, card sort exercises, practical problem solving and pupils' own experimental designs, whole-class discussion, demonstrations and teacher talk. The teachers undertook trials of the schemes, reflecting on the progress of the class and so adding to the refinements of the process.

CHILD AS SCIENTIST

Before exploring the effects of schemes such as CLIS, I want to consider a metaphor: the 'child as scientist'.

This metaphor has been used by a number of authors (e.g. [23–25]) and it has become associated with a constructivist perspective. We are invited to suppose that, in the course of their everyday lives, pupils act like scientists. For instance, the essence of Kelly's ideas [23] is that each person builds a model of the world which enables him or her to chart a course of behaviour within it. This idea has been transposed to school life by, for example, Pope and Watts [25]. Like a scientist's model, this imagined model is then subject to change over time since constructions of reality are constantly being tested and modified to allow a better working model to be erected. 'Better' or 'worse' here means how well the model serves people in predicting and sorting out what is happening as they go about their daily business.

Neither constructivism in general, nor Kelly's theory of personal constructs in particular, is a suggestion that all people actually are scientists, simply that viewing people in their 'science-like aspects' can illuminate human behaviour. This approach is very similar in spirit to the proposals of National Curriculum Science Working Group [26] which adopted a very clear child-centred perspective as a broad rationale for their work. The child, they said, is the agent of his or her own learning in science. Children's learning in science is linked by analogy to scientists' advancement of ideas, hypotheses and principles when faced with new phenomena. Their prior knowledge and initial theorizing are therefore important as part of the process of reaching a scientific understanding of the world around them. This approach was used by the National Curriculum Council [27]:

> 'The ideas of young children are essentially scientific in so far as they fit the available evidence even though they will…fall a long way short of, or even be inconsistent with, formal theories.'
>
> *NCC [27]*

The next section considers some of the many implications for this way of thinking.

ALTERNATIVE CONCEPTIONS IN CHEMISTRY

Research into pupils' understanding of chemistry concepts is extensive and there is not too much point in reviewing it all here. Several bibliographies of research exist (for instance, Driver *et al.* [28] arising out of the CLIS archive and Pfundt and Duit [29]) and these list a wide range of chemistry concepts under review. My choice of exemplars here is intended largely to illustrate more of the CLIS research and to describe some of the general patterns to their work. Two members of the CLIS project (Briggs and Holding [30]) looked at children's understanding of 'element', 'mixture' and 'compound'. Their review of work in the field led them to four main frameworks:

(i)   A conception of the roles of individual elements in chemical reactions. In this case students thought that although a new substance with new properties is formed in a chemical reaction, the elements are really only loosely joined up together 'like pins to a magnet'. They also thought that the products of reaction, the new compounds, were really hiding there all along and would simply reveal themselves when conditions were right (based on Schollum [31]).

(ii) A 'magical' view whereby anything could happen once the chemicals set each other off.

(iii) A confirmed lack of conservation of matter in reactions so that 'substances are destroyed in chemical changes' (from Pfundt [32]). In this sense, burning alcohol, for instance, would be likened to 'evaporation' and in both cases the alcohol is thought to disappear or be destroyed.

Their own use of APU questions led them to the fourth notion:

(iv) Elements are solids, and can only be solid.

Other work within the CLIS team has focused generally on the particulate nature of matter where they note that the majority of students do not spontaneously use such ideas when describing the behaviour of matter in either physical or chemical situations.

Again, there is a sense of 'so what?' It is not a major discovery to most science teachers that pupils get chemistry wrong and are afflicted by a series of confused and *ad hoc* ideas. However, back to my main theme, such personal ideas are not just isolated flights of fancy, but can be seen to be imaginative attempts to explain how things work. Pupils have remembered parts of their science taught in class though it is highly unlikely that it is exactly what was said. Somewhere between hearing and understanding, between classroom and afterwards, they have re-interpreted issues, pieced together parts from previous lessons, added ideas and questions from their own experience and constructed a theory for themselves that makes sense and explains the situations.

While misunderstanding can contribute to an unorthodox view of the world, these theories or frameworks are not simply the result of misconstruing words, technical or otherwise. As a constructivist I regard such personal theories as a normal part of everyday life in their own right. They are the way we make sense of the world, how we go about learning and communicating ideas. They are not necessarily well thought out, and a person may well have several sets of conflicting ideas at the same time.

DIFFICULTIES FOR TEACHERS

Now comes the question 'so where from here?' Even if readers have bourne with me this far, I still need to indicate what practices are appropriate from here on in? As noted earlier, the CLIS response has been a programme of work with an extended series of working groups of science teachers, operating very much in an 'action research' mode. The project has taken a particular approach to constructivism and conceptual difficulties, and this is reflected in the development and evaluation of their teaching schemes.

The general features of constructivist schemes are shown in Figure 1 and the general structure to the schemes shown in Figure 2, both diagrams are taken from Driver [33].

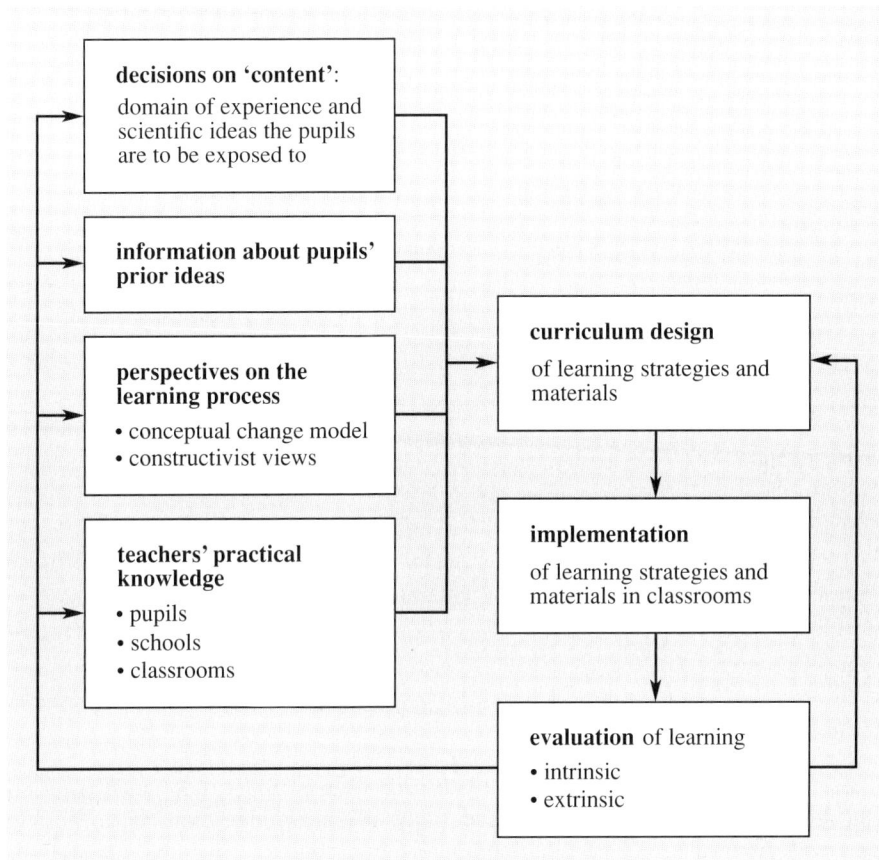

decisions on 'content':
domain of experience and scientific ideas the pupils are to be exposed to

information about pupils' prior ideas

perspectives on the learning process
• conceptual change model
• constructivist views

teachers' practical knowledge
• pupils
• schools
• classrooms

curriculum design
of learning strategies and materials

implementation
of learning strategies and materials in classrooms

evaluation of learning
• intrinsic
• extrinsic

Figure 1 Factors which were taken into account in the design of the teaching schemes.

The scheme outlined in Figure 1 is constructivism much in the shape I outlined above—conducted here through a system where the goals of learning are specified through the syllabus of work within the science department of the school; children's prior knowledge is of clear importance; teaching strategies are varied and wide-ranging; pupil organization alternates between individual, small-group and whole-class groupings; and teachers' professional knowledge is at a premium.

The core of the scheme is that through exposure and challenge, children's ideas will be restructured to come more easily in line with 'textbook' answers:

'since science knowledge cannot be transferred from teacher to learner, but must be individually constructed, the curriculum cannot be viewed as 'that which is to be taught' but rather as a set of experiences which enable and encourage children to make sense of scientific ideas.'

CLIS [2]

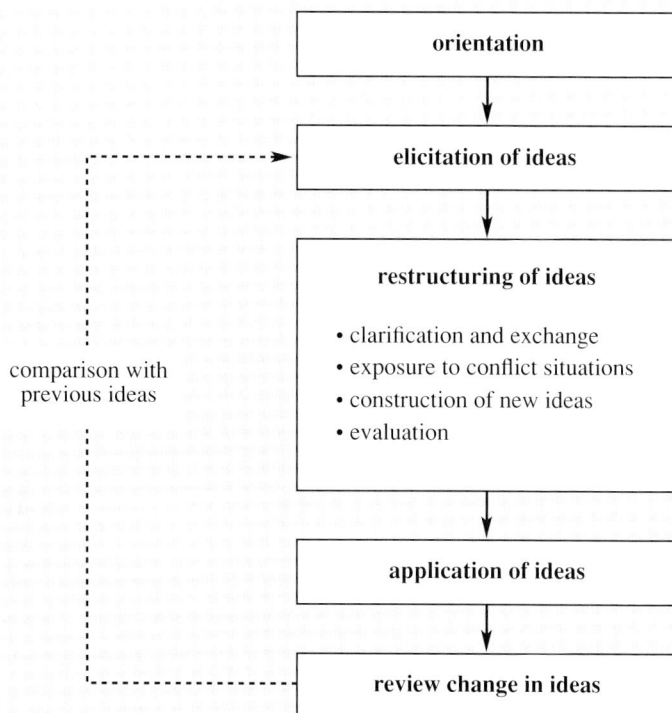

Figure 2   General structure to teaching sequence.

This view of the curriculum is allied to a relativistic view of science itself so that science is not seen as a 'fixed body of knowledge' but as a 'human enterprise involving imagination, communication and experiment'. This style of working is not without its critics and it is worth picking up a few opposing notions before continuing. However, leave aside here any discussions of the nature of curriculum and any objections to this view of science. Instead I focus on comments about the nature of conceptions and conceptual change.

Some opposing views of constructivism

Some problems are seen to arise with the 'restructuring of ideas' box in Figure 2. Some authors (e.g. Solomon [34]) suggest that the process of elicitation followed by clarification and exchange will serve to *confirm* children's misconceptions in chemistry. That is, when pupils are asked to make their own personal ideas explicit and to talk and swap these ideas with friends in small-group discussion, this process will give added strength to their incorrect ideas and help to shore them up against radical change. This will make the next stage (exposure to conflicting situations) all the more difficult and threatening—no one likes to have the personal thoughts they have just made public shot down in flames by the teacher. Solomon [34] parodies the process as:

- the pupils arrive with a range of incomplete prior notions;
- these are made explicit;
- they are then restructured to make them more robust *even though they are not scientifically correct*!
- cognitive *conflict* is then arranged;
- the children adopt new scientific ideas;
- they see how they have changed by reference to their previous ideas.

Solomon [34]

Any scheme which is based on cognitive conflict or challenge comes in for the same questions: How can you keep pupils' thinking fluid and flexible? How can you avoid the threat implicit in the process? How can the correct conceptions be assuredly built from the wreckage of the old? Another critique starts from the nature of the pupils' prior knowledge. How coherent and solid is it really? How resistant to change? CLIS found that children's frameworks are fairly substantial and, on the whole, difficult to change. They arise in response to phenomena in the world and are structured by the pupils trying to make sense of what is happening within their experiences. In their reports of the CLIS studies, Driver and Oldham [35] show a very mixed picture of success: where success is a measure of pupils changing to correct conceptions over time and repeated testing in response to traditional teaching. Their general conclusion is that forging conceptual change is not a trivial matter and it requires careful consideration of the pupils' prior knowledge and careful design of teaching sequences. Others though, like McClelland [36], argue that in many cases children simply do not have conceptions on certain topics: they have not been asked to think about the issue before and so, faced with impossible questions, reply as best they can in everyday terms. At other times ideas are just created by the pupil at the time of the question to avoid looking ignorant and embarrassed: as often as not the ideas are invented, fleeting and transparent. McClelland, then calls into doubt the stability and coherence of 'alternative frameworks' and calls instead for teachers to understand scientific concepts accurately themselves, to teach clearly and to then convince pupils that the effort of learning correct ideas is worth it.

It might help this discussion to take an example from the CLIS approach, by Wightman [37], who describes in some detail a series of six lessons dealing with 'particles'. The teacher in the study seems to echo some of these points. For example, he was not always comfortable with prolonged class discussion of pupils' own ideas, appearing at times to want to hurry things along almost as if this 'elicitation' was a 'necessary stage to get through before the real business (of teaching the right answers) could begin'. Towards the end he became disillusioned to find that there were 'still a lot of misconceptions around' and began to question the value of class discussion. The durability of frameworks here is open to question—are they long-lasting because they are tough, resilient ideas honed by use over time, or because transient fledgling ideas have been consolidated and hardened in the crucible of class and peer pressure. Small-group discussion work is a rich source of children's ideas but, as Wightman points out, how can any teacher take in all of this and make use of it positively. It asks a huge amount of teachers' skills:

'Although it may be possible for a teacher to be aware of some of the
alternative ideas which children are likely to have, some pretty fast reactions
are needed to cope with them satisfactorily when they occur in the classroom,
without being discouraging or dismissive. 'Are atoms alive, sir?' '

Wightman [37]

Teachers' roles

In my view the CLIS approach has been thoroughly and consistently developed
in the light of its own philosophy: it is a programme that is firmly congruent
in principle and practice. It uses a philosophy that once detailed, informs the
programme of research, the schemes of work, the classroom interactions and the
wider contribution of all participants.

Teachers, though, who are new to the kind of work involved in the CLIS
approach have a series of common responses. First they are incredulous that
children have such 'strange' ideas: but once they appreciate and become
accustomed to the kinds of consistent line in conceptions that children produce,
the temptation then is for them to argue that there 'just isn't time... we have
to cover the syllabus, we can't stop to tackle every misconcieved idea'. Those
who continue to explore a constructivist line of work become concerned by the
range and variety of teacher tasks involved: it is considerably more complex
than simply 'telling pupils the right answers'.

Most of us are all too familiar with the full range of complexities within
teachers' professional lives and it is too easy to understate the load carried in
attempting to meet all the demands being made. As was pointed out earlier, a
constructivist approach does ask of teachers far more than just quick wits, it
asks them to adopt a series of roles in the classroom which are difficult to
undertake [37]. Some of these teacher roles are listed below:

1   *Teacher as learner*: learning to think like a child. For some this may
come as second nature—which is not intended as an insult. It is not easy to
think in a child-like way, to predict the sorts of constructions they will make.
Some ideas seem so intuitively logical, but others create difficulties for
teachers in coming to terms with children's constructions in science.

2   *Teacher as psychologist*: making diagnoses and prognoses throughout
lessons. Of course there have always been psychologies of learning but
constructivism seems to sharpen issues. The tendency is to heighten teachers'
awareness of alternative conceptions and focus on the planning and preparation
of classroom techniques for how these might be used.

3   *Teacher as epistemologist*: exploring the nature of knowledge and
evidence. Here teachers need to be conscious of the status of knowledge, notions
of truth and 'correctness' and the stability, durability and applicability of
evidence. The lesson in Wightman's case study were premised on the notion that
direct evidence for the existence of atoms is very hard to find—and perhaps not
always convincing to the untutored eye.

4   *Teacher as practical philosopher*: testing the nature of meanings 'on the
go'. Any discussion of language, terms, labels and meanings entails a constant
revision of one's own concepts and understandings, and working for clearer

expressions. This kind of activity must extend teachers' awareness and children's use of expressions and foster a constant search for conceptual clarity.

5   *Teacher as author*: developing ideas and notions. Any forethought and creative plots saves some thinking on the spot. Some of the CLIS (and other) teaching strategies make constant use of teachers as facilitators of learning experiences. It is not a way of working that is instantly adoptable and a shift from 'director of learning' to 'neutral sounding board' and back again can be intense and demanding.

6   *Teacher as field researcher*: constantly monitoring data and effect. Each teacher in a classroom is awake to questions of the value of learning. This can be in terms of 'Why are we doing this, miss?' to 'But did they learn any *science* today, I wonder?'

7   *Teacher as natural philosopher*: we have to be scientists too. We always have to return to the central purpose, the learning objectives, of the activity— easing initiate chemists into the ways of thinking, talking and doing of chemists. Faced with questions about particles and matter, Wightman's class [37] wanted to reject 'strength' as a property of solids: it had not featured in their ideas of bonding and intermolecular forces. The teacher then accomplished the task of re-instating this property 'with tact and understanding without in any way devaluing the initial ideas of the pupils'.

FINAL THOUGHTS

To summarize the first part, I can say generally that school pupils have:

*   a number of individual and unorthodox ideas and understandings about a wide range of topics;

*   ideas that can remain intact in the face of normal everyday teaching;

*   understandings that shape how they make sense of new data and information, and which can even persist in the face of seemingly strong counter argument and evidence

The second part has been a discussion of one specific model and a scheme for tackling this in the classroom, the CLIS approach. The model is highly instructive but, necessarily, open to a series of both positive and negative comment. The CLIS approach is by no means the only one and others have focused on brainstorming in the classroom, the use of conceptual 'rafts', 'stepping stones' and 'bridges', while my own attempts have explored teaching strategies such as class discussion techniques [38], problem solving [39] and small-group activities [40]. In the latter cases youngsters worked either as a whole class or in pre-determined 'science teams' and the model was one of cooperation, learning and social collaboration. The emphasis during each session was that individuals were asked to cooperate and negotiate satisfactory solutions to a problem. In this sense, each child had the task of understanding what other members of the group were doing and the answers they had obtained. Where students disagreed, or failed to comprehend, they were to seek clarification and justification from the others and be willing to provide explanations of his or her own processes and solutions. Following teamwork, the groups then shared their solutions with the rest of the class—the emphasis here being on novel ways of reporting. An over-arching problem formed a *raison d'être* for the work: we were all 'scientists for the day', tackling an example of a real problem. It was understood that we might not reach a complete solution—but we would eventually reach feasible solutions for the problem.

The upshot of the two parts, then, is that while human beings are hugely individual, they are also highly social animals. No individual is isolated from group interaction and so living, and learning, takes place within a powerful social milieu. The central point here is that shaping new concepts, changing old ones, forming new links and connections or severing outdated ones, happens as we communicate with ourselves and when we share ideas (communicate) with others. It is the role of chemistry teachers to manage these processes in the classroom.

REFERENCES

1   Driver, R., Guesne, E. and Thiberghien, A. (eds) *Children's Ideas in Science*. (Open University Press, 1985).

2   *Children's Learning in Science*. 'CLIS in the Classroom: approaches to teaching'. Centre for Studies in Science and Maths Education, University of Leeds. (1985).

3   Adey, P., Bliss, J., Head, J. and Shayer, M., *Adolescent Development and School Science*. (Falmer Press, 1989).

4   Driver, R., 'A constructivist approach to curriculum development', in P. Fensham (ed.), *Developments and Dilemmas in Science Education*. (Falmer Press, 1988).

5   Bentley, D. and Watts, D. M., *Learning and Teaching in School Science Practical Alternatives*. (Open University Press, 1989).

6   Tobin, K., Butler-Kahle, J. and Fraser, B. J., *Windows into Science Classrooms*. (Falmer Press, 1990).

7   Watts, D. M. and Bentley, D., 'Constructivisn in the Curriculum: can we close the gap between the strong theoretical version and the weak version of theory-in-practice?' *The Curriculum Journal*, 1991, **2**(2), pp. 171–182.

8   Kingdon, J. M. and Critchley, W. E., 'The use of technical terms in CSE and O-level chemistry'. *School Science Review*, 1982, **64**(227), pp. 367–72.

9   Watts, D. M. and Gilbert, J. K., 'Enigmas in school science: students' conceptions for scientifically associated words'. *Research in Science and Technological Education*, (1983),1, (2) pp. 161–171.

10   Wellington, J., 'A taxonomy of scientific words'. *School Science Review*, 1983, **64**(229), pp. 767–773.

11   Driver, R., 'Beyond appearances: the conservation of matter under physical and chemical transformations', in R. Driver, E. Guesne and A. Thiberghien (eds), *Children's Ideas in Science*. (Open University Press, 1985).

12 Marshall, S., Gilmour, M. and Lewis, D., *Understanding and Misunderstanding in Science*. Research report 18, Department of Languages, University of Technology, Lae, Papua New Guinea. (1990).

13 Cassels, J. R. T. and Johnstone, A. H., *Words that Matter in Science. A report on a research exercise.* (The Royal Society of Chemistry, 1985).

14 Cassels, J. R. T., *Language in Chemistry—the effect of some aspects of language on 'O' Grade chemistry candidates.* Unpublished MSc thesis, University of Glasgow. (1976).

15 Richards, J., *Classroom Language: What sort?* (George, Allen and Unwin, 1979).

16 Vygotsky, L., *Thought and Language.* (MIT Press, 1986).

17 *Science at Age 13. A Review of APU Survey Findings, 1980–84.* Assessment of Performance Unit (HMSO, 1989).

18 Gilbert, J. K. and Watts, D. M., 'Concepts, misconceptions and alternative conceptions: changing perspectives in science education'. *Studies in Science Education*, 1983, **10**, pp. 61–98.

19 Watts, D. M. and Gilbert, J. K., 'The new learning: research, development and the reform of school science'. *Studies in Science Education*, 1989, **16**, pp. 75–121.

20 O'Connor, M. *Better Science: Making it happen*, Association for Science Education and Schools Curriculum Development Committee. (Heinemann Educational, 1987).

21 Eggleston, J. and Slade, J., *Some Outcomes of the Review. An Evaluation of the SSCR.* Evaluation in Focus; National Curriculum Council for the Secondary Science Curriculum Review and Association for Science Education. (ASE, 1990).

22 Driver, R. and Easley, J., 'Pupils and Paradigms: a review of literature related to concept development in adolescent science students'. *Studies in Science Education*, 1978, **5**, pp. 61–84.

23 Kelly, G. A., *The Psychology of Personal Constructs.* (W. W. Norton and Co, 1955).

24 Driver, R. *The pupil as Scientist?* (Open University Press, 1983).

25 Pope, M. L. and Watts, D. M., 'Constructivist goggles: implications for process in teaching and learning physics', *European Journal of Physics*, 1988, **9**, pp. 101–109.

26 *Report of the Science National Curriculum Working Group*. Department of Education and Science. (HMSO, 1988).

27 *Science Non-statutory Guidance*. National Curriculum Council. (HMSO, 1989).

28 Driver, R., Watts, D. M., Carmichael, C., Holding, B., Phillips, I. and Twigger, D., *Research on Students' Conceptions in Science: a bibliography.* Children's Learning in Science Project, Centre for Studies in Science and Maths Education, University of Leeds. (1990).

29 Pfundt, H. and Duit, R., *Bibliography. Students Alternative Frameworks and Science Education.* Institut für die Pädagogik der Naturwissenchaften Reports in Brief. Institute for Science Education. University of Kiel, Keil, Germany.

30 Briggs, H. and Holding, B. 'Aspects of Secondary Students' Understanding of Elementary Ideas in Chemistry'. *Children's Learning Science Project Report*, Centre for Studies in Science and Maths Education, University of Leeds. (1986).

31 Schollum, B., Chemical Change. *New Zealand Science Teacher*, 1982, **33**, pp. 5–9.

32 Pfundt, H., Pre-instructional conceptions about substances and transformations of substances, in *Proceedings of the International Workshop on Problems concerning the representation of Physics and Chemistry Knowledge.* Ludwigsburg, German. (1981).

33 Driver, R., 'Changing Conceptions', in P. Adey, J. Bliss, J. Head and M. Shayer (eds), *Adolescent Development and School Science.* (Falmer Press, 1989).

34 Solomon, J., Respondent (to Driver 1989), in Adey, P., Bliss, J., Head, J. and Shayer, M. (eds), *Adolescent Development and School Science.* (Falmer Press, 1989).

35 Driver, R. and Oldham, V., 'A constructivist approach to curriculum development in science'. *Studies in Science Education*, 1986, **13**, pp. 105–122.

36 McClelland, J. A. G., 'Alternative Frameworks: Interpretations of evidence'. *European Journal of Science Education*, 1984, **6**(1), pp. 1–6.

37 Wightman, T., *The construction of meaning and conceptual change in classroom settings: case studies on the particulate nature of matter.* Children's Learning in Science Project, Centre for Studies in Science and Maths Education, University of Leeds. (1986).

38 Watts, D. M., 'Discussing physics', in D. Bentley and D. M. Watts (eds), *Learning and Teaching in School Science: practical alternatives.* (Open University Press, 1989).

39 Watts, D. M., *Building a sound construction zone: problem solving in school science.* Paper presented to the British Educational Research Association Conference, Nottingham, August. (1991).

40 Bentley, D. and Watts, D. M., *Communicating in School Science: groups tasks and problem solving* 5–16. (Falmer Press, 1991).

CHAPTER 16

TEACHING SCIENCE WITH LANGUAGE IN MIND: CHEMISTRY AND ENGLISH

Clive Sutton

INTRODUCTION

Since the English variant of the language of chemistry has taken its alcohol from Arabic, its gas from Dutch and and its burettes and pipettes from French, the title of this Chapter might sound a trifle chauvinistic, lacking the multicultural awareness which should permeate our science teaching today. On the other hand, I am writing in English and you are reading it, so inevitably I must focus on English expression, even though it will be clear that many chemical ideas were first developed in other languages. One of the effects of attending to the language we use is an increased awareness of that fact; we come to see science more clearly as a cultural product which has involved human beings in many different cultural settings. I hope to show the benefits of seeing science in that way—a product of people, thinking and talking together, rather than as just a mountain of factual information.

As you grapple with new topics in chemistry, I recommend the cultivation of a personal habit—the habit of looking behind the information, to find the interpretive effort of the scientists and writers who created the ideas. What was their problem, and how did they express their solution? If you do that, and use language flexibly as you re-express the ideas for yourself, then you will be likely to set up classroom situations where pupils get similar experience and personal satisfaction. If my argument is valid they will gain a better understanding of the nature of science and greater confidence in their own ability to articulate scientific ideas.

There are several reasons why teachers and pupils should think about the people behind a scientific statement, as well as about the statement itself. One is the cultural aspect; it helps us to recover a human and personal dimension in science. Another is that if we work only with the products of scientific thought, and fail to show the *manner* of their production, pupils can pick up an altogether mistaken idea about how language works. In the extreme case scientific language gets degraded to a set of labels rather than a system of interpretation, and learners are left disadvantaged as learners because they have had too little experience of using language to process and work over ideas.

To explain what I mean by language 'as a system of interpretation', I will first have to make a few excursions into the history of the subject, to show how the development of chemistry has been intimately linked with the development of language.

CHEMISTRY AND THE DEVELOPMENT OF LANGUAGE

Whenever ideas change, the language we use changes too, and the new way of talking shifts our attention to different features of the topic under consideration. Lavoisier knew this well when he based his system of chemistry on reform of how substances were named [1]. He rejected, for example, all names which referred to their appearance, such as 'butter of arsenic', 'sugar of lead' and so on, believing that appearance was not the most important feature. What mattered to him was what he thought the substance was composed of, and he insisted that names like *oxyde d'argent* or *sulfure de fer* (oxide of silver, sulphide of iron) would be much better. Other people took up the new system of naming, and gradually it helped everyone to give more attention to what they thought the components of a substance were.

That is just one illustration of what I mean by 'using language interpretively'—steering one's own and other people's perceptions by one's choice of words. Scientists most obviously use language in this way at times of change in their subject, but teachers are always encountering the need to shift the way of looking at something and get pupils to re-interpret it in another light. To a teenager who is waving a metre-stick dangerously one might say 'Please put down that ruler', but it could make the point more effectively to say 'Please put down that weapon'. Of course we don't have to go into arguments about whether the stick is 'really' a ruler or 'really' a weapon; we are just altering the choice of word to draw attention to a particular aspect. I will return later to the importance of interpretive language in the classroom, but for the moment let me stay with its use at the point of development of new scientific ideas.

The switch to a 'better' or more useful way of talking about substances in Lavoisier's time was linked with a mental image or model of what happens in chemical changes, thinking of them more definitely as combining and decomposing. Once the new naming became widely used, it consolidated this preferred way of seeing things, and gave importance to a range of measuring techniques for tracing how much of each component was involved. Lavoisier put the matter very clearly in the Preface to his book *Traité Elementaire de Chimie* [1], and his translator in 1790 rendered his words as follows:

> 'we cannot improve the language of any science, without at the same time improving the science itself; neither can we improve the science without improving the language…which belongs to it.'

Several decades later Michael Faraday [2] made a similar point when he set out his new ways of talking about the effects of electricity on chemicals.

> '…I find the greatest difficulty in stating results, as I think, correctly, whilst limited to the use of terms which are current with a certain accepted meaning. Of this kind is the word pole, with its prefixes of positive and negative,…for the sake of greater precision than I can otherwise obtain, I have deliberately considered the subject with two friends, and with their assistance and concurrence in framing them, I propose henceforward using certain other terms,…The poles, as they are usually called, are only the doors or ways by which the electric current passes into and out of the decomposing body…'

He went on to justify calling them anode (way up) and cathode (way down), and collectively the electrodes (electrical ways). The same discussion with friends who were learned in the Greek language led to the formation of the words anion (that which goes up) and cation (that which goes down), and ions for both together, as well as electrolyse (he spelled it with a z) for the process of loosening and splitting by electrical means, and electrolyte for substance split. Words considered and rejected included eisode and exode, Voltode and Galvanode, 'electrostechions', 'electrobeids', and several others, but what emerged was a way of talking which was very successful as a guide to further thought and experiment, and communication about it. (The story of the reasoning behind the new words, and of Faraday's discussions with Dr Nicholl and correspondence with William Whewell is told by Partington in *A History of Chemistry* [3], and the letters exchanged with Whewell are available in L. Pearce Williams' collection [4].)

INTERPRETATIONS AND LABELS

At the point of innovation in science, then, the words chosen are the result of a conscious struggle to make sense of things, i.e. they are interpretations, and that is usually clear because of their novelty, and/or because of an explicit consideration of alternatives. After a time, however, these same words get taken for granted as 'obvious', with scarcely any calculation or choice of what to say. We pick up 'electrodes' in the laboratory and know immediately what to call them, or we find a flammable gas and know to call it 'hydrogen', forgetting the interpretive effort that went into the creation of that word (hydro-gen, water-maker). In effect our scientific words soon become labels for things, or processes or qualities, and as long as we all use the same label for the same thing, a reasonable communication is possible.

It is a natural process in language that expressions which were at first interpretations of experience gradually come to be used as arbitrary labels, and up to a point communication can be quite effective when we simply accept such words with a shared awareness of what they label. Everyday speech is full of expressions like 'Pull out the choke' in a motor car or 'Turn off the telly' at home; no one is in doubt about what choke or telly refer to, and you can live with them without entering into why anyone called them such names. It might seem that education is achieved if we get pupils to attach the right labels to the right things.

There are however, very good reasons why teachers should not leave it at that, and the main one is that when language is used interpretively it keeps the learners mentally active, making connections to other ideas, and ready to explore these connections as they sort out their own understanding. Here are some examples of how a teacher's language can be used to 'talk around' an idea, introducing the scientist's way of seeing it, but without imposing this as just a 'label' for a 'fact':

(i)   at the start of a lesson about possible arrangements of atoms in solids

   'Look at this raft of bubbles packing into lines, and how they squash into hexagons…Then look at the tray of marbles which aren't squashed at all, but you can still trace hexagons in the way they are arranged. So you get an idea of why this arrangement is called 'hexagonal close packing'

(ii)   looking at Brownian motion of particles with a projection microscope

'I wonder if Mr Brown really thought the particles were alive, when he saw these jiggety-jiggety movements under the microscope...'

(For a detailed account of Brown's ideas, see Chapter 1.)

(iii) in a lesson on what dissolves in water, and why oil doesn't

'Alan, your account of the oil clinging to oil and the water molecules clinging to other water molecules was very nicely put. Now how can we think about the effect of detergent?'

In each of these instances there is a strong suggestion of more than one acceptable way to express the idea, and an invitation to pupils to re-express it for themselves. Specialist and everyday expressions are intermingled, and there is no attempt to drag out specialist words and make them compulsory. To avoid misunderstanding, however, I should add that everyday expressions are not in my view a replacement for specialist terms in order to make the subject matter easier. Their value is in making bridges to other knowledge, and showing the flexibility of language, and for these purposes technical and non-technical expressions are needed together. Certainly the 'telling' role of a teacher in presenting the established public vocabulary, at the appropriate time, should not be neglected, and there is no need to protect pupils too much from difficult language; the teacher's job is not to avoid it, but to help the learners to make it a genuine part of their own competence.

Unfortunately, pressures of time and syllabus content sometimes make us leave out this exploratory work, and we use language in a more matter-of-fact way. Words then seem less for exploring ideas and more as if their only function were to describe facts and give information. For example:

'Air contains mainly two gases, nitrogen and oxygen, and there is also some carbon dioxide, some water vapour, and some other gases.'

This statement is almost entirely in the labelling style, and at one level it is acceptable teaching. Pupils can take such information, get it down in notes, and make use of it later. But it gives no suggestion of a problem in understanding air; rather the opposite—it implies that air just is, and we can describe it in a certain way and no other. There is no hint that coming to a conclusion about the nature of 'air' was a problem that absorbed the scientific community for the best part of a century. There is no acknowledgement that the word 'gas' was a triumph of theoretical insight, which eventually unified decades of talk about 'elastic aeriform vapours', and no mention that arguments raged about whether it was a good idea to use the new name 'oxygen'. The modern summary neglects to say that people wondered whether what we now label as nitrogen (nitre-maker) should be understood by calling it 'choking stuff' (*Stickstoff* in German) or 'lifeless' stuff (*azote* in French). The results of all these efforts of thought are taken for granted, and their products are presented as labels for materials about whose existence we now feel confident. Overall, such a statement about air appears like a description rather than an interpretation. Jan

Baptist van Helmont (1579–1644) chose the word *gas*, from the Greek *chaos*, for the essence or spirit of things, chaotic in its wild tendency to escape in all directions, e.g. on heating. The 'pneumatic chemists' of later decades became adept at trapping and collecting such things, and various 'airs' or 'elastic aeriform vapours' were described. Eventually van Helmont's word gained wide acceptance as a generic term for all of them, and it probably helped the kinetic interpretation of evaporation in terms of the chaotic movement of component bits. It is easy to slip into a habit of presenting the results (and only the results) of scientific thought in this way, and to treat words nearly all the time as labels for things, rather than instruments of interpretation. Many books give exactly that impression, with expressions such as:

> 'Atoms are made of protons, neutrons and electrons.'
>
> 'A chemical change is one in which …'

In this way some of the ideas of science get transformed into arbitrary information to be learned; they no longer retain the status of ideas at all, and scarcely seem to merit being puzzled over. If pupils are exposed to words in that way over and over again, they can get little sense of scientific language as an instrument of interpretation, and little incentive to use it themselves for sorting out the ideas. Many do pick up just that limited expectation, particularly in relation to their own writing. Writing to sort out your understanding is not what they expect to do—not in science that is! This is largely because any writing of that kind has been swamped by other kinds— factual description and standard records of practical work. (For a discussion of the assumed purposes of writing in school science, see [5, 6]). What do you have to write in science? You have to 'say what you did' and then 'say what happened'. I think this is a temporary aberration in school science, which became established in the 1870s and has persisted into the 1980s, but it may not last much longer, especially if we understand the influences which brought it about.

HOW THE INTERPRETIVE STATUS OF LANGUAGE CAME TO BE MISUNDERSTOOD

One influence is simply an effect of long familiarity with scientific terms. As products of scientific thought, they are always tentative at first, but they gain reality and become more thing-like with each new generation which accepts them. We speak now of 'a double bond between the carbon atoms' exactly as if we were pointing to and labelling an object, without any of the tentativeness and speculative tone which accompanied the first uses of the expression. Science has thousands of such expressions, and a conversation amongst scientific colleagues has to take most of them for granted. We who teach science have had five or six years of immersion in them during our own education and professionalization, and it is hard to stop taking them for granted.

Interestingly, the effect occurs not just with theoretical entities such as atoms, electrons and bond energies, but even with some of the technical tools of the laboratory. 'Herr Doktor Bunsen's burner' (a subtle and convenient heating device) becomes simply 'the Bunsen', a thing we have, rather than the product of careful design by a thinking and caring human being. So great is the impression that learning science is learning labels, that many important thoughts are not activated when this casual label is spoken. 'Will we need to heat this? If so, what with? Is Dr B's equipment right for the job? What about other possibilities—sun-bed lamp, oven, hotplate, burning glass, picnic stove, microwave oven, school radiator? In the absence of such thoughts, learning chemistry becomes learning that there are Bunsens, just as there are double bonds. It would not surprise me to find adult citizens who believe you can't do chemistry at all without Bunsens.

If this were the only influence it might have been overcome by the instinct of teachers to justify to outsiders what the insiders take for granted, but at least three other factors have combined to diminish the attention paid to the language in which ideas are expressed, and therefore to allow taken-for-grantedness to prevail. These are:

(i)   a desire to be precise in science;

(ii)   an image of science as 'discovering facts' in the real world rather than 'struggling to interpret it';

(iii)   the professionalization of science in the 19th century, and the resulting triumph of 'science for future scientists', with its emphasis on how to use the balance and burette, rather than on how to talk about scientific ideas in the context of quarries, mines, homes and streets.

The overall effect has been to make talking around an idea a feature of teachers' informal interactions with pupils, while the planned routines of the lesson give little scope for it. We organize practical work far more often than we organize discussion, and pupils write 'reports' far more often than they write to clarify ideas. Phrases like 'I think', 'It seems to me' even 'Please Miss I don't understand this at all' have often been excluded from the written page.

In this Chapter there is scarcely space to examine the three influences in detail, but in brief I trace their effects in the following way.

Precision

The tradition of defining one's terms has served science well, but language is constantly in flux and meanings change, both in the minds of scientists and in the mind of an individual pupil over time. Teachers need to be sensitive to these changes, and able to help pupils explore areas of vagueness at the edges of a word if those pupils are to build connections to everything else they know. A simplified answer to this dilemma is to keep back the definition of terms until some exploration of the meaning has occurred, but professional judgement will always be necessary in determining when precision should predominate.

'Discovery'

Practical work has a special importance for science teachers because of our belief that reliable knowledge must be based on learning by doing, and not just talking. That has slipped over into an ideology of science which suggests that 'the facts' are found by observation and experiment; drawing conclusions about them comes later. Such a 'Baconian' epistemology was dominant for most of the period of growth of school science, and it is seriously misleading. Prior ideas interact more subtly with what you 'find out' at the bench, and it is truer to say of the scientific community that reliable knowledge must be checked against experience in the real world and by discussion with other scientists. For science in school it means that practical work can never 'speak for itself' and if pupils are to make the most of their practical experience we should pay more attention to the language of the topic before, as well as after, the bench work.

Professionalization

When science was accepted into the curriculum of high-status secondary schools, in competition with classical and other studies, it got there with the encouragement and applause of a newly self-conscious community of professional scientists. School laboratories were built to give experience of procedures somewhat like those a scientist would use, and one of these procedures was the preparation of a defensible report of bench work. It is not always necessary in science for such reports to tell the whole story of the thought behind an investigation ('I thought that such and such might be happening and so I designed an experiment in which I expected to find such and such an effect, and after carrying it out my further thoughts were...'). Instead they carefully present what was done, and the outcomes, so the work is defensible if checked by other workers, the relatively small group who read it, and who are quite familiar with the thought patterns behind the design. To import this into education had a value in showing something of the discipline of how scientists work, and those who spent some years listing 'test/observation/inference' or tabulating weights, volumes and temperatures at least had a good drilling in an important part of the craft of science. Whether it counted as the best way of educating citizens about the importance of science was little questioned; the practical politics were that some science got into school by accepting this approach, and of those who learned it a reasonable proportion were in fact on track to become scientists.

An unintended side-effect was that suppression of statements about thought, especially preliminary thought ('I chose test A rather than test B because...') supported the view that knowledge arises directly from practical work. As well as giving an inadequate view of science, this nurtured a misunderstanding of language. Language seemed to be for reporting and describing rather than for wondering and puzzling and thinking and sorting out what you know, and relating with a reader to whom you want to communicate your thoughts. Undertones about 'objective reports' and the assumed undesirability of writing in the first person were further features of this phase. If they were ever true as a means of induction into the procedures of science itself they were not really appropriate to education in the sense of understanding the matrices of thought in which 'experiments' are embedded. It is not surprising that some pupils had to ask despairingly 'What shall we write as a conclusion?'.

From the 1960s onwards, bench practical work was emphasized yet more strongly, and although methods of writing were less stylized, the notion of reporting what you did and describing what happened remained influential. Meanwhile secondary education for all was gradually coming to be a reality, and from the mid-'80s the question of what is adequate as 'science for all' has been under more urgent consideration.

CURRENT CHANGES IN SCIENCE TEACHING

The biggest change is that science is now a foundation subject in the National Curriculum for all pupils aged 5 to 16. It cannot therefore be confined to drilling a few in the routines, or former routines, of professional science. Ideally it is supposed to give citizens competence to use the language of science to understand the world around them. With such a central place in the curriculum it must also contribute to their general growth of competence in speaking, writing, calculating and so on, and not just to the acquisition of vocationally specific arts. There is a tension here, because one of the objectives is still to recruit some people for future careers in science. Even for that end, however, it has begun to look as if direct pre-vocational training, with its Spartan approach to language, is not adequate, for while some are attracted by doing scientists' science in school, others are alienated by what they unjustly see as coldness and inhumanity.

With the recognition that science for all is not the same thing as science for future scientists, courses are becoming less obviously an introduction to the academic disciplines and more concerned with interpretation of the world around you. The starting point is less often the grammar of chemistry, and more usually something outside the school (the chemistry of a farm, or the chemistry of clothing fabrics). A typical publication is now *GCSE Questions on Everyday Chemistry* [7], or *Science and Technology in Society* (SATIS) [8]. Courses are being developed, e.g. *Salters' Science* [9], which move away from a sequential concept-led course (elements—the metals—the non-metals, etc.), where 'applications' are tacked on (uses of iron, uses of sulphur). Instead, the pupils' work is organized in themes or topics from the world outside the school (clothing, food, etc.). The authors try to make it clear which scientific concepts bear upon a modern understanding of these topics, and to show how some precise understanding can be firmed up. Designers of such courses still have some anxiety lest the result should be a fragmented understanding of the 'map' of chemistry, and it may be that a necessary auxiliary to this approach is some sort of study which provides that map. From a language point of view, I simply note that discussion of food or farm chemistry is unlikely to be as badly shorn of personal significance and intellectual content as one sometimes found with the description of three titrations.

Another change which is more crucial to the pupil's active use of language in his or her own learning is the fact that the range of activities considered normal in science lessons is being extended. This aspect of lesson planning is discussed in Chapter 13; here we can just say that the bench practical exercise is no longer as dominant as it was, and some teachers involve their pupils in activities of the following kinds (not all at once, you may be relieved to hear!):

- committee work by pupils around a table, to *plan*, or help to plan, an investigation, devising diagrams and charts to *communicate* the ideas and plans arrived at;

- presenting a *short talk* or a poster to explain ideas to other members of the class;

- putting ideas in *writing* for an *audience other than the teacher*;

- taking part in role-plays, simulations, or classroom drama;

- putting information *into* a computer, and planning how to process it;

- analysing case-studies of events (factory explosion, water-supply crisis, etc.);

- tackling a technological problem rather than a scientific one, where pupils try to *design* a solution, using scientific knowledge of materials;

- more desk work such as interpreting charts, tables and graphs, which again will often involve discussing ideas in a small group, and making a public presentation.

While many teachers are nervous of their abilities to manage this range of activity (and anyone unfamiliar with it is advised to seek help from colleagues), the notion of language-rich activities for the processing of ideas and developing personal competence and confidence can now be seen as a necessary part of science, and not something 'for the English department'. Consider these two examples from the SATIS collection given in Table 1.

Table 1   Examples of activities supported by SATIS materials [8].

Title of SATIS unit	Activities for the pupils
The limestone enquiry	Analysing technical data, identifying by discussion the relevant facts and issues for consideration at a Planning Enquiry about a quarry extension, writing notes for groups who will speak at the Enquiry, and then taking part in a role play of that meeting. Different groups have to put the case of the quarry company, its customers, the environmentalists, etc. adequately supported by clear knowledge of the science of limestone.
The label at the back	A survey at home of fabrics and their uses; collating the information and presenting a summary, with explanation.

To get best value from such activities one has to pluck up courage to 'sell' their value to the class, and be ready to use one's own expertise in the shifting context of discussion, rather than in presenting 'the facts'. It is also necessary to value interpretive language, and to enjoy waiting for youngsters to articulate thoughts, seldom perfectly first time round. SATIS activities won't automatically lead to the clarification of the full vocabulary and network of concepts in the related scientific topics, unless pupils and teacher approach them with that intention in mind. They are however a way of engaging the minds of the learners, placing them in positions of initiative, and giving them a different idea of the part played by their own use of language in their learning.

Don't underestimate what is involved in 'selling' such an activity to pupils who may not be used to it. The incipient question: 'Is it science?' must be addressed, because the pupils' attitudes about what counts as science, and those of their parents, have been formed over many months and years. Fortunately, there are phrases in the National Curriculum documents, stressing communication abilities and the need for pupils to be articulate and to use their scientific understanding. These can be quoted if the argument as presented in this Chapter is not sufficient on its own.

SCIENCE LESSONS AS APPRECIATION OF IDEAS

In considering how to get practical work into a better relationship with thinking and talking, I have suggested [10] that science lessons are too easily thought of as a direct study of nature ('Look at these two rocks; what do you see?'). It might be more helpful to think of them as a study of sets of ideas—what people have said about nature. ('This author says that some rocks solidified from something molten, but others are like hardened mud or sediment from a long vanished river delta. Talk about the passage in his book; pick out at least one difference which he was noticing; agree it in your group, then look at the samples and write a note about the idea of two kinds of rock.')

Such an approach would not only give a better idea of the relationship between theory and observation; it would also restore a personal dimension into the science. These people who told the 'story' of rocks in this way: who were they, what exactly did they have in mind, and how did they come to think that way? The general planning system for a science lesson then becomes something like the plan shown in Figure 1, with task A as the focus, and task B not allowed to dominate the whole time.

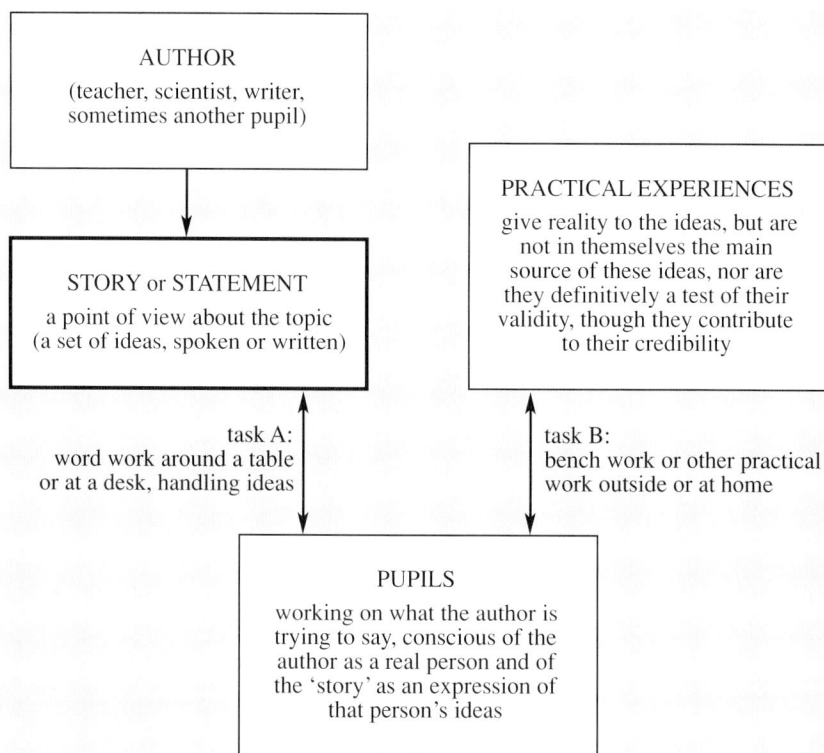

Figure 1   Planning system for a science lesson (adapted from [10]).

In the scheme represented in Figure 1, pupils are asked to focus on an expression of thought by a person who can be identified. Scientific language is therefore brought into the same realm as any other language, and is no longer privileged as a description of 'the facts' which have to be swallowed whole. There is a job to be done in deciding what we think the person meant. The focus is a human expression, with time to compare and weigh up interpretations of it. As science teachers we have the advantage of some tangible experience to give reality to the words, but if we let that hands-on experience dominate the time available, the interpretive effort may suffer. The actualization of such a plan therefore requires careful selection of short 'stories' or 'statements' at an appropriate level for the pupils, and short practicals that do leave time for the talking and writing.

A 'story' or 'statement' will need to take many different forms for pupils of different age and ability. Sometimes it could be the words of an actual scientist, e.g. Faraday's delight when he first made a 'Voltaic Pile', but it might often be another pupil's script, a food label, a short statement by the teacher, a snippet of film, a newspaper cutting, a page from a school book. The teacher needs to be able to say to the class 'What is the person saying here? What are the key ideas?' and to spread the notion of someone trying to communicate. This will make it worthwhile for more learners to say 'I think...'. Even if they fall back sometimes on 'Please tell us the 'right' answer', their own relationship with the public language of science will be changed.

Action points

What then are the main features of a policy to improve the learning environment when you are teaching a chemical topic with language in mind?

Your own preparation

Don't hesitate to use talking and writing to clarify your own ideas. Sort out distinctions; try out another way to express the same idea, and personalize your own understanding! If necessary, use Michael Faraday's method of writing letters to a friend. Don't take the language of any topic for granted, but look behind it and think: what was the problem, and why was the answer expressed in this way? Instead of taking new vocabulary as 'given', dwell on it and savour it. For example, even the the various ways in which some familiar blue crystals have been named can provide much enjoyment and illustrate the efforts of chemists to draw attention to the most salient features. Before Lavoisier, these crystals were called 'blue vitriol' and the corresponding iron compound was 'green vitriol'. Both had clear glassy (i.e. vitreous) crystals, and both were known to be related to 'oil of vitriol' (sulphuric acid). Nowadays, for young pupils it is sufficient to call them 'those blue crystals', and later 'the blue stuff from which we got copper', but the time comes to call them 'hydrated copper sulphate' or 'copper sulphate pentahydrate', or even 'copper(II) sulphate pentahydrate', with good reasons in each case (over and above the demands of an examination, I mean!). At some stage we might even want to show that there is another possible name within a systematic pattern of inorganic naming, i.e. 'copper(II) tetraoxosulphate(VI)'. This name has some value even though it has not yet acquired the status of 'preferred name' amongst chemists and teachers! [11]

What we call something depends on context, and even formulae are not really fixed. Without its water of crystallization, this material is usually written $CuSO_4$ but not so very long ago it was more commonly written $CuO.SO_3$ to emphasize its relationship to an acidic oxide on the one hand and a basic oxide on the other. When teaching what a salt is, such a formula may be resurrected to show the thought behind an important system of classification. A close inspection of some fertilizer sacks will show that this way of thinking about salts and writing their formulae is still widely used.

Thinking of science lessons as language-developing events

It is important to acknowledge that talking and writing for the purpose of sorting out ideas requires a proper place as a planned component of lessons and homework. To get it to work will require several important adjustments:

- in what happens to pupils' work after they have done it;
- in how time is shared out in a lesson;
- in the preparation for discussion and writing.

Reception of pupils' work

It is difficult to get an active language-for-learning system going without altering pupils' understanding of 'marking'. From the teacher's point of view this has to become 'responding to pupils' ideas' rather than 'correction of errors', except on those special occasions when it has been agreed in advance that error-correction is the order of that particular day [12]. Pupils must get to know by experience that giving in and getting back a script develops a kind of dialogue in which the teacher is able to take an interest in, and reply to, the individual's idea of what he or she has learned. Only then will it be safe to risk an expression of what they do or don't understand. It is a situation which parallels the one in talking; for the pupils to be free to talk well the teacher must be seen to be a genuinely interested listener. If discussion leads to a product such as a diagram or chart it should be acknowledged and used, or displayed and appreciated. Pupils will need opportunites to speak about such a product and be listened to by others, and it may take time to build up their confidence in such an unfamiliar activity. If they learn from experience that the teacher values even a partial expression of ideas, their fear of attempting it will diminish.

Pupils' preparation before they write

Pupils do have to be taught that their talking and writing is part of the means by which they learn, so it is necessary to put time into explaining why it is set, and what will happen afterwards. The quality of thought in writing can be very low if it is not preceded by discussion. It is not enough to say in the closing minutes of a lesson—'Oh, write it up for homework'. Successful writing for most pupils only comes if there has been some prior discussion of what points might be included, and they go away with some rough notes on which to build.

Most teachers who have adopted a policy of active language for learning recommend that there should be variety in what pupils write, and that they should be encouraged to write for different audiences. We can indeed set a variety of tasks to help them think through and explain a topic, but beware of over-use in the case of a 'let's pretend' audience. For example, in a topic on properties of metals, a teacher has posed the problem of what metals are appropriate for canning fruit, and asked pairs in the class to prepare a letter to the (fictitious) Leicester Cannning Corporation comparing the claims of aluminium and tinned steel. You might be able to get pupils to enter imaginatively into that game, but it would often be more honest and more real to say 'Let's prepare a plan of the kind of statement we would need if we had to report to a company'. (A few teachers manage to find real audiences—people who really want to know what the pupils think.) Again a caution is necessary about beginning any such work with a class accustomed to more formal and traditional writing. You need to be convinced yourself, to explain the purpose of the writing, and to negotiate it. Changes in the time devoted to preparing for writing and changes in the style of marking probably have a bigger effect than the work itself. Don't imagine you can do it overnight if pupils' expectations are quite different.

Planning the allocation of time

More time spent on talking and thinking must mean less time on something else. The only real point of give in the system is for practical work to be short and purposeful, rather than a lengthy routine which dominates lesson after lesson!

Reading policies

Reading for information should be supplemented by reading for human interest, and for the ideas and intentions behind the words on the page. The range of suitable material is gradually improving, but the key point is the spirit in which pupils are directed to the page, and how well the teacher can communicate the sense of a 'story' to be unravelled. Many pupils require support in getting used to such reading, and some of the activities known as DARTs (directed activities related to text) can be helpful in making it a positive experience rather than one which is too daunting. (See Chapter 10 for further information about such activities.)

SUMMARY

Teaching science with language in mind requires a constant awareness that scientific ideas and new areas of language have evolved together. To show it in action reveals science as a human activity. It increases the human interest of science and it also liberates pupils to have ideas of their own, and hence to become more active agents in their own learning. Once they grasp the language-base to science and to their own learning, they stand to gain a better comprehension of the science, a better command of language, and improved skill as active learners. For teachers, there is a motive here for organizing the classroom to help that process along.

This account is in marked contrast with some older assumptions about how language works, because it places language as part of our means of understanding, not as an independent commentary upon it. Language is an interpretive system in the first instance, not a labelling one. Consequently there is more to learning science than doing practical work, and perhaps we can bring a new generation of school pupils into contact with science by coaching them in their own abilities to talk and write about it! Science develops 'new ways of seeing' supported by 'new ways of talking' that have survived the critical checks demanded in science (experiment is one of those checks). We are therefore inevitably teachers of new talk-systems. To do it well, a wide range of classroom activities is needed, and some beliefs and routines will have to be left behind—relics of an earlier kind of science education. Chief amongst these is the supremacy of writing a defensible report. It will still have a place in science education, but not week in week out!

REFERENCES

1   Lavoisier, A., *Traité Elementaire de Chimie* (1789). English translation 1790 by Kerr, R. (republished by Dover Publications, 1965).

2   Faraday, M., On Electrochemical Decomposition, *Philosophical Transactions of the Royal Society* (1834).

3   Partington, J. R., *A History of Chemistry* (Macmillan, 1964). Vol. 4, pp. 116–118.

4   Williams, L. P., *The Selected Correspondence of Michael Faraday.* (Cambridge University Press, 1971).

5   Sheeran, Y. and Barnes, D., *School Writing.* (Open University Press, 1991). Chapter 2.

6   Sutton, C., 'Reading and Writing in Science: the hidden messages', in R. Millar (ed.), *Doing Science.* (Falmer Press, 1989).

7   Borrows, P., *GCSE Questions on Everyday Chemistry.* (Blackie, 1988).

8   *Science and Technology in Society* (SATIS). (Association for Science Education/Heinemann, 1986).

9   *Salters' Science.* (Science Education Group, University of York, 1987).

10   Sutton, C., *Words, Science and Learning.* (Open University Press, 1992). Chapter 9.

11   *Chemical Nomenclature, Symbols and Terminology for Use in School Science*, 3rd edn, Association for Science Education. (ASE, 1985).

12   Benton, P., 'Writing, how it is received', in C. Sutton (ed.), *Communicating in the Classroom.* (Hodder and Stoughton, 1981).

PART 6
CHEMISTRY AND EQUAL EDUCATIONAL OPPORTUNITIES

Open Chemistry, especially in the context of the National Curriculum and 'science for all' up to the age of 16 has major implications in terms of *open* opportunities. *The Education Reform Act* of 1988 requires all pupils to study chemistry as part of their broad and balanced science education or as a single science accompanied by a study of biology and physics. Either way a subject that many in the past 'dropped' at age 13 is now compulsory to age 16. Part 6 of *Open Chemistry* considers the implications of this change within a wider range of important equal opportunities issues.

In Chapter 17 Whitelegg explores a range of key issues relating to the teaching of chemistry to girls. She notes that historically chemistry has tended to recruit more or less equal numbers of boys and girls and has been less gender biased than biology and physics. But this should not be taken for granted and there is much still to be said about role models, instructional strategies, and teaching styles in order to make school chemistry even more gender inclusive. Whitelegg draws on a number of international studies as well as the important evidence drawn from the *Girls into Science and Technology* (GIST) project.

Chapters 18 and 19 are devoted to another dimension of equal opportunities policy, namely that of teaching chemistry in a multicultural context. In Chapter 18 Shaikh draws on his recent experience as Chair of the Multicultural Education Working Party of the Association for Science Education and presents a strong case for introducing both historical and cross-cultural references when teaching chemistry. He argues that a monocultural approach to the teaching of science disadvantages all pupils irrespective of their ethnic and cultural backgrounds and gives two examples, soap and salt, through which a broader cultural perspective may be presented. Farrar, in Chapter 19, addresses the more specific issue of the teaching of chemistry to pupils for whom English is not their first language. Through three distinctive case studies, of Asma, Tho and Yesim, Farrar explores the importance of developing speaking, reading and writing in English with young people who have different levels of fluency in their own first languages. Farrar gives a great deal of specific practical advice and also considers the role of support teachers in multilingual contexts.

Chapters 20 and 21 deal with two other important aspects of equal opportunities and present practical strategies for teaching chemistry to pupils who are visually impaired (Betts, Chapter 20) or who have other special educational needs (Rose, Chapter 21). Both authors welcome the National Curriculum as an opportunity to ensure that pupils who are disadvantaged should have access to science as part of their general education. As Rose states 'Faraday and Darwin, amongst others, emphasized the importance of a basic scientific education for all children'.

CHAPTER 17

GENDER AND CHEMISTRY

Elizabeth Whitelegg

INTRODUCTION

In 1987 Alison Kelly wrote 'By the time girls and boys reach examinations at 16+, chemistry is the science subject that shows the least sex differentiation in certification rates...' [1]. So, is there any problem with girls taking chemistry? Is it the model science subject where girls and boys have equal chances? Can it provide some lessons for more gendered subjects, such as physics?

Up to GCSE level, chemistry does appear to offer girls and boys a more gender-fair approach than is offered by physics. However, there are many other factors, that are external to the nature of chemistry itself, which affect girls' and boys' attitudes to science in general and which influence their view of chemistry in particular. In this Chapter I intend firstly to consider these broader science issues before focusing on the issues that relate specifically to chemistry and distinguish it from the other sciences.

Prior to the introduction of the National Curriculum that makes science compulsory for all up to age 16, many girls opted out of science, particularly physics and to a lesser extent chemistry, as soon as they could. It remains to be seen whether compulsory science up to 16 will lead to greater enjoyment and increased interest in science, or whether compulsion will lead to greater alienation from the subject. Without a change in the science and in the way it is taught, then the latter position may be the more likely one.

Much of the discussion about gender issues and science has focused on physics as this is the area that attracts the least number of girls, but most of these issues are also relevant to chemistry. The statistics for the take-up of chemistry by girls do not allow for complacency. In 1988 40% of the girls who were eligible took A-level chemistry compared to 58% who took biology and 21% who took physics. The implementation of balanced science will mean that much future discussion of secondary science is likely to be about science more broadly than the problems associated with one discipline. However, this thought should be tempered with the knowledge that the recent reworking of the new attainment targets in the National Curriculum [2] from 17 to 5 to 4, may in some way make a revision to the old subject divisions still quite possible! Furthermore, to support pupils' learning in science attention to potential gender differences *within the separate disciplines* will remain essential.

WHERE IT ALL BEGINS:
PRE-SCHOOL AND PRIMARY SCHOOLING

What is the image of a scientist and where do these images come from? In international studies to reveal what children think a scientist looks like and what he or she does, drawings have been collected, analysed and reported [3–5].

These studies found that the image of a scientist was overwhelmingly of a white, bespectacled male wearing a lab coat and carrying a test-tube. Even girls who had been taught by a female science teacher rarely drew a female figure and even after sustained intervention programmes designed to address the masculine stereotype of science and scientists, only 10% of boys and 28% of girls in the United States drew women scientists [6].

So the image of the scientist as male is a very powerful one and it carries direct and more subtle messages about scientific knowledge, processes and careers. For girls in particular, these messages may be damaging, especially when they are reinforced by a wide range of stereotyped images found in the media. However, the damaging image of scientific activity as a male domain is not a new one and over recent years there has been some positive action, especially by publishers, to counter it. A cursory examination of a few chemistry sets displayed in local toyshops found that they do now show pictures of girls as well as boys on the box *doing* the investigations, though the boxes still tend to be found with the boys' action toys rather than in the girls' sections. Textbooks have shown some improvement too although there is still quite a long way to go. An examination of six chemistry textbooks published between '84 and '89 showed female figures in 36% of the illustrations depicting people. I think it is also fair to say that in the more recent books women have been shown in more active roles in the illustrations rather than as passive observers. So there does seem to be an improvement and textbooks are gradually becoming more gender-fair, but these statistics still show more than two pictures of males to every female figure. Out of the six books I examined, however, only one showed a picture of a famous *female* scientist (compared to 26 famous male scientists) and predictably this was a photograph of Marie Curie (and husband!). There is obviously a need to re-discover some female chemists and send their photographs to publishers. I'm sure Lise Meitner, Ida Noddack, Rosalyn Franklin, Katherine Lonsdale, Dorothy Hodgkin *et al.* would approve! (Accounts of the lives and work of women chemists and physicists can be found in Walton [7].)

It is no surprise that during a child's early development through the pre-school and primary stage, a very powerful image of a scientist as a male human being is being created and although it does look as though more equitable images are now emerging, attitudes take a long time to change and subtle messages are still being conveyed. Counteracting this conditioning needs constant vigilance and much creative imagination to present alternative images which value different qualities to those currently in vogue and accepted as the norm.

Traditionally science in the primary classroom has not been divided up into its separate disciplines and given separate discipline labels as it used to be in secondary schools before the introduction of balanced science. In the National Curriculum, chemistry is now located mainly in Attainment Target 3 *Materials and their properties*. In the primary classroom chemistry is encountered in projects such as 'water', 'investigating foods', 'fuels' and so on. The treatment is purely qualitative and it is done without introducing chemical formulae, structures and so on. Some of the topics in these projects have been shown to appeal particularly to girls. They might be activities that appeal to the children's aesthetic qualities such as crystal growing, or areas that girls have traditionally been involved in such as cooking and investigating food colourings, or environmental issues such as air pollution, acid rain and the production of drinking water. Quite rightly, in the primary classroom, these topics are not labelled as 'chemistry' investigations. By not giving them this label, however, an opportunity is lost for allowing girls' interest to progress from the primary 'chemistry' activities to secondary chemistry topics. Pupils who may have acquired some confidence and enthusiasm in the primary phase, by doing some of the unrecognized chemistry referred to above, are not able to build on it at secondary school where they encounter a totally different environment for doing science—the laboratory with gas taps and Bunsen burners. In a chemistry lesson where some experiments may well be dangerous if safety procedures are not paid attention to, the hint of danger can make the experiment more attractive for the boys. It can be a discouraging factor for the girls and make them more willing to be passive observers of the experiments that the boys are actually performing. Boys also feel more comfortable wearing the white lab coat and carrying the test-tube—they fit into the image of a scientist pretty well.

The majority of primary school children are taught by female teachers. Most of these teachers have had very little science training themselves and so may not be very confident about their teaching in this area. Historically, biological topics have been ones that primary teachers have been used to delivering and probably feel more confident about. This may be another contributing factor that has reinforced girls' traditional option choices for biology at secondary school rather than the other sciences—it is something they know something about and know they can do it.

The introduction of the National Curriculum has demanded a massive training programme for primary teachers in order to enable them to deliver the programmes of study for science at Key Stages 1 and 2. It is hardly surprising therefore, that a female role model who is not confident about teaching science herself, does not have a strong positive effect in encouraging her female pupils to achieve in science.

AT THE SECONDARY SCHOOL

Girls entering secondary school already carry quite a lot of negative baggage with them which will influence their view of science and their engagement with science. Until about 10 years ago, intervention strategies to change girls' attitudes to science and increase the number opting for science subjects were all concentrated at the secondary level. The *Girls into Science and Technology* (GIST) project [8], which took place in several Manchester schools between '79 and '84, monitored the effectiveness of positive action programmes on girls' achievement in science. However, the strategies were not as effective as the researchers had hoped and it was found that by the time many girls came to make choices about science at 13 or 14 their image of science as inappropriate for them was firmly in place. Since then research has moved on to look at younger children's attitudes to science and also the nature of the science that is being taught—whether that could be changed to make it more appropriate for girls (and boys too) and whether differences in learning and teaching styles have anything to offer this debate.

Learning styles

Studies reveal that the difference between girls' and boys' achievement in science increases as pupils progress through school. Survey results from the Assessment of Performance Unit (APU) given in Table 1 show that at age 15 significant differences emerge between boys' and girls' performance in, (i) data manipulation and interpretation, (ii) use of apparatus and measuring instruments and (iii) tests of applications of chemistry concepts. On these particular measures these differences were noted at age 15—other differences, such as boys greater knowledge of physics concepts and girls better observational skills were already evident from APU surveys of 11+ and 13+ year-old pupils [9].

Table 1   Some international survey results (adapted from [9]).

APU test	Results from APU
use of graphs tables and charts	$B_{15} > G_{15}$
use of apparatus and measuring instruments	$B_{15} > G_{15}$
observation	$G > B$
interpretation	$B_{13, 15} > G_{13, 15}$
application of:	
biology concepts	$B = G$
physics concepts	$B > G$
chemistry concepts	$B_{15} > G_{15}$
planning investigations	$B = G$
performing investigations	$B = G$

B denotes boys' performance, G that of girls; B_x denotes the performance of boys aged x. The symbol '>' should read as 'better than'.

In a study by Kim Thomas [10] of students entering *higher* education, she found that physics and chemistry appear to demand different learning styles—physics is a subject which can be *understood*, it is fundamental and certain, and has the potential to provide answers, whereas chemistry (like French, history, etc.) has to be *learnt*. A female chemistry student interviewed in Thomas' study said:

> 'I find it difficult to remember so many different things about chemistry, where at least with physics I seem to remember what things are supposed to be about... With physics you see it and understand it and it's stored, with chemistry there are so many complicated formulae and whatever, you've got to look at it again before you can regurgitate it.'

According to another study that investigated understanding in chemistry undertaken in New Zealand by Burns and Bird [11], clear differences existed between Year 12 girls and boys in their perception of understanding in chemistry and in their corresponding study strategies. Girls appeared more likely to focus on the recognition of order among concepts and relationships between concepts—a pattern also associated with high achievement. A focus on relationships between ideas is characteristic of pupils with a 'deep' approach to learning who are more likely to be motivated by involvement with the learning activity itself. Girls therefore appeared to be more task-involved in their approach to understanding. This task involvement by girls is also evident in APU surveys of girls' use of measuring instruments. The APU results showed that girls do significantly less well than boys on the use of certain measuring instruments and that this is strongly related to those instruments which boys claim to have more experience of out of school.

> 'These different experiences of pupils affect not only the skills they develop but also their understanding of situations and problems where their skills can be used effectively. For girls to overcome this lack of experience they need to be faced with problems whose solutions, as they perceive them, require certain measurements to be taken. In this way girls will select instruments themselves and engage with them purposefully.'

Murphy [9]

Burns and Bird also found that lower achieving pupils and boys tended towards a learning style that relied heavily on the accumulation of knowledge. From the Thomas study cited above [10], accumulation of knowledge seems to be a learning style that is needed in chemistry and which boys find easier to develop. So, by the time they reach 16, when task involvement becomes more important to them, even those girls who have achieved success in science may not feel motivated to continue to A-level if the learning style required by chemistry is not one that girls find most appropriate for them. As chemistry becomes more abstract at the higher levels, then only those girls who can see through the abstractions, relate them to the applications of chemistry and see the patterns inherent in the subject, are likely to be motivated and succeed. This demands that girls see these patterns for themselves. Those that *do* are successful, as evidenced by the high percentage of girls (nearly equal to the percentage of boys) who, once entered for chemistry A-level, are successful. Over the period '84 to '89 an average of 74.6% of girls who entered for A-level chemistry passed compared to an average of 76.2% of boys.

Teaching styles

Many classroom observations have been undertaken to monitor the nature and frequency of teachers' interactions with male and female pupils. Despite both male and female teachers perceiving their interactions to be equal or even favouring the girls, the nature of this interaction has been found to be quite different for boys and girls. Girls have lower expectations than boys and tend to blame failure on a lack of ability unlike boys who are more likely to blame lack of effort or external circumstances (see Dweck and Licht [12]). This lack of self-confidence leads girls to adopt a strategy either of dependency on, or avoidance of, the teacher. Randall [13] also found that pupil–teacher interactions in science practical work were very different for girls and boys, and although the girls may have greater contact with the teacher, these interactions either took the form of many requests for help and encouragement of the 'what do I do next' type (dependency), or a reluctance to approach the teacher at all in case the teacher might notice their inadequacies!

It has also been shown that boys tend to be awarded higher marks just because they are boys! A marking exercise undertaken by Margaret Spear [14] found that identical work was awarded higher marks for scientific accuracy, richness, organization of ideas and conciseness if it carried a boy's name than if it carried a girl's. Additionally a 'boy' author was judged to display a greater interest and greater O-level suitability than a 'girl' author. The highest marks were awarded by female teachers marking work attributed to boys.

So the classroom climate created by teachers can have a major effect on how girls engage with science. In Kahle's study of the different teaching styles of a male and female teacher [15] she found that the male teacher displayed a style that reproduced sex-role stereotypes in his teaching behaviour. She also found that the examples he used to illustrate the topic he was teaching reinforced the gender differences that boys and girls brought to his classes. They continued to see science as masculine and they followed more stereotypical enrolment patterns on future option choices.

The woman teacher's style, however, provided a science classroom climate that was found to be particularly appealing to girls. Using the inquiring mode, the teacher ran small-group activities and avoided whole-class sessions. She lowered the risk level in her classroom and personalized both science and scientists. This study identified common positive behaviours and practices that were successfull in encouraging girls to continue to study science and seek non-traditional careers.

So the teaching styles adopted by science teachers do appear to have an effect on how well the pupils engage and relate to the subject. If we want more girls to be involved in chemistry, then developing teaching and learning styles that encourage this should be a priority. However, I do not wish to imply that all male teachers use the same method of teaching and that it is inappropriate for girls—this would be naive and unjust. I wish to argue that there are so many factors that discourage girls from engaging with and achieving in science and that they all reinforce one another, so even something that may have slight influence in isolation, when added to all the other factors, becomes significant.

INFLUENCE OF CULTURAL EXPECTATIONS

An international perspective

International surveys which have focused on gender differences in science achievement do note some cross-cultural conformity and Kelly [16] identified the 'masculine' image of science, common to all countries, as a contributory factor. In cultures where this masculine image is not as dominant we do see a reduction in the gender differences in achievement and even instances where girls' performance exceeds boys', even at age 15 and over.

In Thailand many of the issues that discourage girls from achieving in science considered in the previous sections do not apply. Chemistry, in particular, is perceived as a girls' subject and a study by Klanin et al. [17] showed that girls out perform boys in theoretical learning in chemistry and do equally well in physics. In single-sex schools girls are better than boys at practical skills in both chemistry and physics. Even those in coeducational schools performed better at practical chemistry and those in single-sex schools did better than boys in physics. Several factors are thought to account for this. In Thailand:

- there are a high proportion of women teachers in chemistry to act as positive role models;
- all three sciences are compulsory for those who enrol in the science stream;
- there are regular and substantial amounts of laboratory work;
- there are no differential expectations of pupils;
- women participate in all levels and fields of employment;
- chemistry tasks have a feminine image.

The last point is particularly interesting. Chemistry is recognized as involving similar tasks to cooking and other work done in the kitchen—stirring, heating, boiling, watching colour or temperature changes, that are all part of girls' and women's experience. Thai men do not get involved in any kitchen activities apart from the grinding of herbs and spices in the preparation of curry pastes. In the study the activity defined as 'Grinding solid chemicals in a mortar' was seen as men's work as it is similar to using a pestle and mortar for grinding herbs and spices.

In Thailand chemistry is seen by pupils to relate closely to an activity that is associated with girls' and women's role in society. When girls and boys are working together on a practical activity in chemistry, the girls predominantly do the investigations while the boys stand back. So the adoption of some activities in science lessons that reflect girls' everyday experiences can lead to their greater involvement with science tasks.

STRATEGIES

A study undertaken by Judith Ramsden [18] examined the attitudes of a class of 13-year-old girls who were studying physics, chemistry and biology for a double period each week, with a view to developing two new teaching units which would stimulate their interest more than previous teaching had done. Although her study focused on physics, the factors which influenced the success of the new material and the strategies which were found to be successful are equally applicable to chemistry particularly in these days of balanced science.

Effective strategies used by Ramsden include:

- the use of non-gender-biased illustrations showing girls and women performing less conventional tasks, e.g. women astronauts;
- role-play exercises;
- activities in which pupils could express personal opinions, e.g. a debate;
- writing instructions to someone on how to perform a task;
- proposing solutions to open-ended problems;
- designing games to bring a topic to life.

Experiments that pupils can relate to personally

As the Thai experience shows, relevance to everyday life and perceived usefulness to future life seems to be a major factor. Schemes of work such as the *Science and Technology in Society* (SATIS) project [19] and *Salters' Science Course* [20] already take this as a starting point for science investigations. However, teachers should be aware of a potential danger with this strategy and avoid creating a 'feminine' science that reinforces the stereotypes of girls' interest in cooking and other homemaking activities. A more appropriate strategy is to find contexts for teaching science that engage the interest of both girls and boys. Jones and Kirk [21] report that in general domestic contexts are not particularly interesting for girls or boys, but both are interested in the workings of microwave ovens, for example. Other items which girls and boys found interesting are given in Table 2.

Table 2   Differences in interests between boys and girls. (All significant at least at the 1% level using rank sum test applied to grouped data.) [21].

Boys	No significant differences	Girls
solar water heater	vacuum cleaner	apnoea mattress
kinetic energy of trolley	purity of water	what makes a rainbow appear
household burglar alarm	sugar content of kiwifruit	bicycle pump
transistor radio	microwave oven	foetal heartbeat monitor
how motor cars work	refrigerators	measurement of blood flow
nuclear powered ships	what gravity is	X-ray machine
microwave speed detectors	how light bends	muscles in the human body
communications satellites		bleeding in the brain (detection)

Cooperative learning

Girls seek out ways of working with others in the classroom. Commonly boys prefer to work on their own in the lab but very few girls do and it is common for girls to want to discuss the task with their friends and indeed make time for this. Girls are more willing than boys to ask the teacher for help, boys fear looking stupid whereas girls are less concerned about impressing the teacher (although this can sometimes backfire [13]). Asking for help from the teacher is another indication of a greater involvement with the task. If it is female pupils who are maintaining more cooperative and task-involved attitudes in their work by the time they reach secondary school, then this again points to a good basis for building more task-involvement in the classroom using strengths of the cooperative approach signalled by these young women. An increase in cooperative learning with pupils learning from their peers, as well as their teachers, decreases anxiety and makes the classroom a more comfortable and secure place in which to learn.

Open-ended assessment

There is considerable evidence from the APU [22] that girls engage with and perform better if they are set open-ended rather than closed assessment tasks.

Girls do not achieve as well as boys on multiple choice questions where there is only one correct answer. But given a question with many variables where real life factors have to be taken into account, then girls engage with the task more readily. This raises the issue of what sort of answers should be valid and who defines the curriculum. Do we value a single line or numerical answer over one that takes many factors into account and presents alternatives depending on different circumstances? Recent reports [23] on the outcome of the pilot Standard Assessment Tasks at Key Stage 3 have highlighted the danger for girls of switching to short written tests, as girls performed better than boys in science and maths on the longer answer pilot assessments.

It is too early to say what will be the effect on girls of all the new curriculum changes that science is still undergoing. Coursework and practical assessments in GCSE should improve things, provided open-ended questions and marking schemes that value contextualized answers are permitted. Science for all up to 16 and balanced science will prevent girls from dropping out at 13 or 14. Positive images of women scientists in textbooks and more mentoring by female teachers must help. Familiarity with science at primary school should build confidence. In order to achieve the aim of motivating girls to do well in science, all the factors must be considered and strategies developed to overcome all the discouragements to girls to engage with science. Simple, one-dimensional solutions that tinker around the edges of the issues, may be helpful and have some positive effects but will not lead to a sudden massive uptake of science amongst girls. It is very easy to become discouraged when positive action strategies are put into practice and appear to have little effect—these are complex issues and they carry a long history with them. Things are unlikely to change without a shift in the culture that predetermines separate roles for girls and boys in our society, and a curriculum that carries this through and values the different qualities, skills and attitudes that girls and boys bring to science.

REFERENCES

1   Kelly, A. (ed.), *Science for Girls?* (Open University Press, 1987).

2   *Science in the National Curriculum (1991)*, Department of Education and Science. (HMSO, 1991).

3   Mead, M. and Metraux, R., 'The image of the scientist among high school students: A pilot study', *Science*, 1957, **126**, pp. 385–90.

4   Chambers, D. W., 'Stereotypic images of the scientist: The draw-a-scientist test', *Science Education*, 1983, **67**, pp. 255–65.

5   Schibeci, R. A., 'Images of science and scientists and science education', *Science Education*, 1986, **76**(2), pp. 139–49.

6   Kahle, J. B., 'SCORES: A project for change?', *International Journal of Science Education*, 1987, **9**(3), pp. 325–333.

7   Walton, A., *It's a Woman's World Too*, Library and Learning Resources Services, City of London Polytechnic. (1984).

8   Kelly, A., Whyte, J. and Smail, B., *Girls into Science and Technology*. (Department of Sociology, University of Manchester, 1986).

9   Murphy, P., 'Gender differences in pupil's reactions to practical work', in B. Woolnough (ed.), *Practical Science*. (Open University Press, 1990).

10 Thomas, K., *Gender and Subject in Higher Education*, Constructing Science. (Open University Press, 1990).

11 Burns, J. and Bird, L., 'Girls co-operation and boys isolation in achieving understanding in chemistry' from Proceedings of Fourth GASAT Conference held at the University of Michigan, 1987.

12 Dweck, C. and Licht, B., 'Sex differences in achievement orientations: consequences for academic choices and attainments', in M. Marland (ed.), *Sex Differentiation and Schooling*. (Heinemann, 1983).

13 Randall, G. J., 'Gender differences in pupil–teacher interactions in workshops and laboratories', in G. Weiner and M. Arnot (eds), *Gender Under Scrutiny*. (Open University Press, 1987).

14 Spear, M. G., 'The biasing influence of pupil sex in a science marking exercise', in A. Kelly (ed.), *Science for Girls?* (Open University Press, 1987).

15 Tobin, K., Kahle, J. B. and Fraser, B., *Windows into Science Classrooms*. (Falmer Press, 1990).

16 Kelly, A., *The Missing Half*. (Manchester University Press, 1981).

17 Klanin, S., Fensham, P. and West, L. 'Some remarkable gender findings about learning the physical sciences in Thiland', from Proceedings of Fourth GASAT Conference held at the University of Michigan, 1987.

18 Ramsden, J., 'All quiet on the gender front?' *School Science Review*, 1990, **72**(259) (December), pp. 49–55.

19 *Science and Technology in Society* (SATIS) Project. (Association for Science Education/Heinemann, 1986).

20 *Salters' Science Course*. (Science Education Group, University of York, 1987).

21 Jones, A. T. and Kirk, C. M., 'Gender differences in students' interests in applications of school physics', *Physics Education*, 1990, **25**(6).

22 Johnson, S. and Murphy, P., *Girls and Physics Report*, Assessment of Performance Unit, Occasional Paper No. 4. Available from the Centre Educational Studies, King's College, University of London. (1986).

23 Hackett, G., 'Test change threatens girls', *Times Educational Supplement*, 29 November 1991.

CHAPTER 18

CHEMISTRY IN A MULTICULTURAL CONTEXT

Kabir Shaikh

INTRODUCTION

Chemistry was probably the first science to fascinate humans. The ability of fire and heat to change substances into products which bear little resemblance to the original material must have been noted very early on. This ability was not only recognized but respected by early civilizations, giving fire a prominent place in the religious hierarchy which still continues to the present day in many religions. Fire became one of the four or five basic Elements of Life; i.e. Earth, Water, Fire, Wind and Sky, to be recognized by these religions. It is certainly understandable how the idea of a 'soul' leaving a body and moving upwards towards 'heaven' might have been developed at the sight of a log of wood burning at night with all its products appearing to emerge as juices, steam, gas, odour, heat, smoke, colours, light, sound and the eventual left over, ash.

There was also another reason why humans were fascinated by chemistry, the zest to convert less valuable metals into more precious ones. Such efforts gave chemistry in its early days its somewhat secretive nature and made it a black art rather than a science.

Chemistry still remains an interesting subject but its accessibility to pupils is restricted because of the way it is presented and the various inherent difficulties in the study of chemistry such as its terminology, symbols, formulae, equations and the perceived lack of immediate relevance to everyday life.

CHEMISTRY AND EQUAL OPPORTUNITIES

Chemistry, like all other sciences has an important role to play in promoting equality of opportunity and accessibility to success and achievement. It, like all other sciences, also has a role in the overall education of children. It is more than just a subject area involved in the transfer of knowledge.

One important element with regard to equal opportunities in this process is the realization and acceptance that present-day society in Britain is composed of people who represent many different cultures, religions, ethnicities and backgrounds. This multiculturalism brings with it a richness, diversity and challenge, the positive impact of which can be easily lost if education fails to fully capitalize upon it. But there are many other dimensions which need to be given serious consideration in order that chemical education provides opportunities for pupils to succeed and to excel, irrespective of their background.

A second important factor in equal opportunities is the understanding of the growing interdependence of nations, the complexities of their relationships and the inequalities both between and within nations. This development makes specific demands on the education system and it would be a major disadvantage if pupils were to be educated in a system which accepts a monocultural, isolated and insular approach to the curriculum.

Efforts to promote and debate such ideas in education started in the '70s enhanced by factors such as the Swann Report [1], the anxiety felt in educational circles about the under achievement of black children in British schools and the recognition by the Home Office that a disproportionate number of black youth of school age were appearing to be involved in juvenile crime.

The science educationists' initial response to any efforts to address these issues was the reiteration of a belief that science was neutral and free from any cultural, ethnic or gender context. That view, thankfully, has changed over the years and in 1989 the Association for Science Education (ASE) established a working party to consider the issues related to race, equality and science teaching and to develop a policy statement for the ASE on these issues. During its deliberations the working party produced a detailed discussion document [2] which dealt with many of these issues in a comprehensive way. The work later resulted in a useful teaching manual for teachers and educators [3]. It is not the intention to cover the details of the discussion document here, but the following brief summary statements of the many issues raised emphasize the need for a multicultural approach to teaching and learning in science.

- Science teaching needs to prepare children for a society in which there is discrimination, inequalities and interdependence.

- In establishing equality of opportunity, racism and sexism will have a negative effect on children's learning, achievement and attitudes towards others, thus preventing them from a full National Curriculum entitlement.

- A monocultural science provision will disadvantage all children, some due to inequalities, others due to the loss of enrichment and challenge brought to science by the multicultural dimension.

- 'Race' is not a valid scientific concept.

- Science is a human activity: science and scientists are not 'neutral' and in that sense science is a multicultural activity.

- Reference to some nations as 'third-world' has a particular meaning which can for some children be demeaning.

- The effect of politics on science and the effect in turn of science on people is real and science education must, therefore, consider its human, social, cultural, environmental and political context.

- Science teaching and learning can be affected by racism and in schools and colleges it can be combated in a number of ways, e.g. presenting positive images from all cultures; challenging racist attitudes, assumptions and behaviour; developing a school or departmental policy; and appropriate choice of topics and materials.

The discussion paper [2] also addressed the issue of equality of access, as the quality of access affects achievement. The paper listed the following areas for action:

(i)   language;

(ii)   teaching and learning strategies in the classroom;

(iii) support in classrooms;

(iv)   assessment;

(v)   whole school issues.

The discussion document provided many thought provoking and challenging but practical ideas for action under the headings mentioned above. This article hopes to deal with a few of them, with a particular emphasis on chemistry and what can be done in the classroom.

The ASE discussion paper, as well as some other reports such as *Improving Secondary Schools* [4] and *Improving Primary Schools* [5], recognized commitment and motivation as the two most important aspects which affect pupils' achievement. In a subject like science, which is linked with the success, achievement and intellectual sophistication of a society, it is detrimental to the commitment and motivation of children from any culture to be given the impression that their particular society has made no contribution to the development of science. It is, therefore, important to look into the history of science and raise children's awareness of the contribution of non-European societies. It is not necessary to do this as an isolated curriculum exercise, nor is it right to overplay this aspect, but wherever an opportunity presents itself it can play an immensely helpful role as an integral part of the teaching and learning process. Teachers eager to implement such ideas nonetheless face the difficulty of finding appropriate material and the necessary background information to deliver it effectively in the classroom.

DEVELOPMENT OF CHEMISTRY: HISTORICAL ASPECTS

There are a number of societies which helped the advancement of science. These include the Indians, the Chinese, the Arabs and the Africans. One possible derivation of the word 'alchemy' is said to have been from the Egyptian 'kem-it' meaning 'the black'. This is not surprising given the mystery surrounding chemistry in the early days. The fundamental premises [6] of alchemy were that:

(i)   all matter consists of the same four elements in various mixtures;

(ii)   gold is the 'purest' and 'noblest' of all metals, with silver next to it;

(iii) transmutation of one metal into another is possible;

(iv)   transmutation of a 'base' metal into gold can be achieved by means of certain substances.

Jabir (*c*. 760–815) is regarded as the earliest alchemical writer in Arabic. His *Book of Properties* indicates his genuine chemical knowledge. He knew how to make ammonium chloride from organic matter and was the first Arab to describe the process.

Rhazes (865–925) was the greatest Arabic writing alchemist. He specialized in experimentation and described in amazing detail what a 'modern' laboratory should contain. He classified minerals into six categories including the 11 salts, one of which was 'kali' or 'al-kali', the source of both the word alkali and the symbol K for potassium. Both Jabir and Rhazes had a great influence on the West in the development of chemistry.

The Chinese showed the beginnings of alchemical literature [7] in the 2nd century. They, however, concentrated on what could be described as chemical technology. This included the discovery of gun powder and related pyrotechnics. The Chinese also made considerable advances in metallurgy, developing bronze and bronze casting further, and iron technology in making ploughs and forging swords. They mined tin and zinc, and also developed brass and some other alloys which remained unknown in the West until the 18th century. The Chinese also developed methods for refining sea-salt and invented deep drilling techniques for the exploitation of natural gas. The Chinese made numerous discoveries including the magnetic compass, silk technology, looms, paper making and block printing, dyeing and movable-type printing. They also contributed to other areas of science, such as biology, medicine, agriculture, pharmaceuticals, electrostatic phenomena, engineering and mechanical toys.

The Indian contribution to mathematics, medicine, chemistry and physics goes back to the days of Vedic sciences. The Dhanvantaries (3000–2000 BC) divided medicine into preventive, preservative and promotive under one section, with curative under another. Susruta (c. 1000 BC) is regarded as the father of Indian surgery. He devised surgical methods and instruments, and his work ranged from anaesthesia to plastic surgery. Caraka (800 BC) refined the techniques of diagnosis and the use of medicines from plants, animals and minerals. Indian sciences, however, developed as whole sciences rather than specific branches. In that sense, the medical scientists were as much chemists and technologists as practical surgeons.

The Africans were expert metallurgists. Some of the examples given in the following case studies show their practical understanding and knowledge of chemical processes.

CASE STUDIES IN MULTICULTURAL CHEMISTRY

By choosing a theme one can integrate issues more effectively. The following two examples demonstrate this in a small way. Ideas to extend these themes are mentioned at the end of these case studies.

The chemistry of ashes

Chemically ash is a product of the oxidation process achieved in many cases by burning or heating. However, in many societies it was significant enough to be included in their religion as well as in the day-to-day activities of their members. It is difficult to imagine that this significance came simply out of the fascination for fire or the burning process, or whatever inspiration it provided for the thoughtful or the philosophical occupation of the mind.

It is interesting to note that certain chemical properties of ash were known to people who put them to appropriate use. Ash was applied to the body by Indian holy men, many African tribes used ash as a protecting chemical to avoid attack from certain harmful species of ants, to clean utensils, and to rub the oil off the body before having a bath. All these uses indicate a more than simple understanding of ash and its caustic properties. It is also important to note the specific use of ash from particular plants for particular uses.

The ashes of banana peels were used to make soap in Ghana and a classroom experiment describing the process is included in the booklet *Soap* from the Third World Science Series [8]. It is important to note that the first product of burning banana peel is black ash which is of little use in the making of soap. However, the Ghanaian villagers used this black ash for cooking in much the same way as we use salt. The black ash needs to be burned further and more intensely in order to obtain calcium oxide—the white ash, which is necessary to make soap. The quality and efficiency of the final product depends upon the appropriate temperature and pH level. The villagers show considerable expertise in achieving the correct pH levels and temperature without the benefit of a thermometer or indeed pH paper.

Soaps have been around for many centuries and were originally produced mainly from sodium carbonate (soda ash). The soda ash was produced from a plant called 'barilla' or from a substance called 'natron'—the salt deposits in lakes found in Egypt. The Arabs became expert soap makers due to the abundance of soda in their region. The history of soap making and developments in Britain described in the booklet [8] makes interesting reading and provides valuable insights into the early 'cosmetic revolution'. Introduction of the manufacture of sodium hydroxide on an industrial basis led to a large scale production of soaps which eventually ended up with what we now recognize as the cosmetic industry. It is interesting to note that the local economies of some countries like Ghana make it difficult to produce soap at an acceptable price or profit level, and villagers have reverted to their centuries-old practice of producing soap from banana skins.

The soap from banana skins experiment can be done by a GCSE or lower-sixth group or can be demonstrated by a teacher. (However, it should be noted that this is an incredibly messy experiment!) It can lead to a number of individual or group projects, such as:

- group discussion or project on the history of soap;
- flame tests or other chemical tests to check the elements present in banana skin;
- understanding of economic issues related to the cosmetic industry;
- visiting any local industries related to cleaning products;
- preparing soap using laboratory chemicals and comparing the product with the 'banana' soap;
- working out the cost of 1001g of 'banana' soap;
- exploring other natural materials which might be used to obtain some modern necessities;
- discussing/exploring issues linked with 'recycling'.

When this particular topic was studied in a secondary school with a GCSE group, the pupils conducted the experiment in pairs with a degree of scepticism and disbelief. It was, therefore, a pleasant surprise for them to see the end product. The teacher chose to tell them about the history after the experiment rather than before which worked extremely well in that particular case. The discussion which followed the teacher's input and the experiment served to:

- inform the pupils about the socio-economic intricacies of nations and how they affect each other. (There is at present, considerable emphasis being placed upon pupils' understanding about how industries work and the income generation processes of a nation. The Training and Enterprise Councils are leading efforts in this direction. A topic like soap lends itself to this general aim.)

- raise their awareness of early scientific ventures of societies which they may have hitherto perceived to be less 'scientific';

- inform them that a banana skin has more to it than 'destabilizing' a pedestrian;

- illustrate that experimentation in chemistry can be interesting and has a human context.

The theme 'the chemistry of ashes' leads to the study of other oxidation products. It is of particular interest if in some cases, such as copper oxide, the reverse process can be studied, i.e. from 'ash' to the element. This theme can provide an interesting route into the study of chemistry.

The chemistry of table salt

Salt is taken for granted as an easily available compound in most parts of the world these days. There was however a time when salt was a very valuable commodity. Its necessity for human health was well understood and its effect on the taste and flavour of food was also well appreciated by most societies. Its antibacterial and preservative properties have been well used through such food products as pickles, salt beef and salt fish.

The Romans paid their soldiers in cubits of salt because of its scarcity during the Roman Empire—hence the term salary. Salt was available in the North of Africa and both the Romans and the people living south of the Sahara Desert (West Africa) had a great need for this salt. Around AD 600 the Ghanaian empire was prepared to exchange gold and ivory for the salt from North Africa. This led to the trans-Sahara trading routes between West and North Africa. By the 12th century this gold trade had extended to Southern Europe and by medieval times the gold coins struck in England were made from West African gold!

Salt played a curious role in the independence movement of India. Salt was taxed by the then British rulers of India. Mahatma Gandhi travelled many miles on foot to reach a place on the coast called Dandi and defied the British by declaring the salt 'free'. The movement gathered enormous momentum and became an important milestone in India's struggle for freedom.

Most early secondary pupils know that table salt comes from seawater or salt mines. (Only a few might think it comes from Sainsbury's!) If they are then shown a map of the world and their attention is drawn to places like parts of

Africa where there are no salt mines or easy access to the sea, an interesting problem-solving exercise can be created. The complexity can be increased by noting that centuries ago transport was difficult, expensive and far from safe. Asked how people in such places could have obtained their salt, pupils seldom think of plants as a likely source of salt. Tribes in many parts of Africa used various plants to meet their need for salt. It is also equally interesting to note that the methods they used involved several chemical processes, which can lead to a classroom experiment which is far more exciting than the often rather puzzling experiment of separating salt from sand. Amongst the plants used were the banana leaves and skins of bananas, certain grasses and Papyrus, which contains about 40% sodium chloride. Leaves were burnt on the ground and the resultant black ash was dissolved in water. The mixture was then filtered and the salt solution used for cooking.

The equipment still used by many tribes is illustrated in Figure 1. A porous clay pot, with tiny holes in the base, is lined with banana leaves with slits to act as a filter. The ash, dissolved in cold water, is then poured into the pot and the filtrate is collected in another clay pot at the bottom.

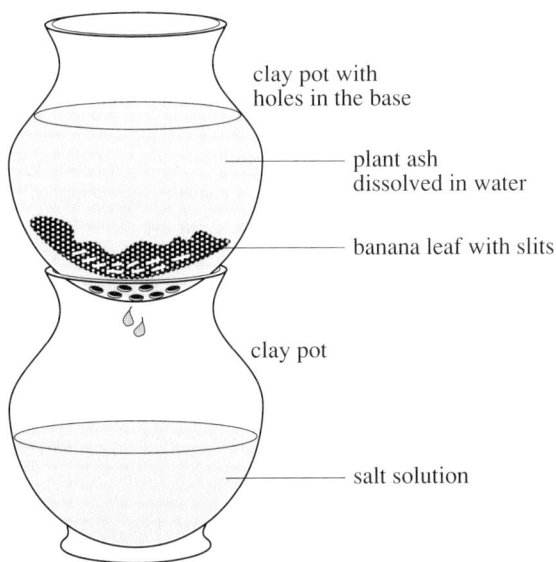

Figure 1   Equipment for filtering the salt solution.

For a classroom experiment leaves of a plant can be dried in an oven and burned directly or in a tin. The ash can be dissolved in a beaker, with heat provided if necessary, and the solution filtered in the usual way. After evaporation the pupils find it quite interesting to see the white salt crystals obtained from the black ash. Pupils might then wish to carry out further investigations such as flame tests to decide which particular salts are present. Usually a mixture of sodium and potassium salts is obtained. They might conduct studies to calculate the respective proportions of these. In any case they can do flame tests with pure sodium and potassium chlorides and compare their results with the product obtained by burning leaves. They might also try electrolysis of the salt solution.

The use of salt in the everyday context can then be discussed. Its properties in relation to raising the boiling temperature and lowering the freezing temperature of water, and the practical daily use made of these properties, will come as a surprise to most pupils. For example, the use of salt on roads during freezing conditions. Again this can lead to further experimentation if so desired. Current concerns about the health hazard due to over consumption of salt can also be discussed.

CULTURAL BACKGROUND AND LANGUAGE

As was mentioned earlier in this article, language remains a major barrier in the learning of science. This is even more true of chemistry because it communicates through symbols, formulae and equations. Teaching science with language in mind is discussed by Sutton in Chapter 16.

Most children from Asian and Far Eastern backgrounds are bilingual and English is their second language. (Some factors to be considered when teaching such pupils are discussed in detail in Chapter 19.) The effective use and mastery of any means of communication is vital for achievement and success, for language forms a medium for receiving knowledge as well as the means to indicate and express understanding. In the current educational system it is mostly through written language that knowledge and understanding is articulated and which forms the basis for judging the intellectual discipline and ability of pupils. The effect of language on pupil performance is well documented. The non-statutory guidance on the National Curriculum in English gives information on how linguistic skills affect learning. Thus language and assessment methods are closely linked with performance, which affects both commitment and motivation.

SUMMARY

Chemistry continues to fascinate scientists but its relevance and access to school children needs some attention. Experimentation in chemistry sparks interest in pupils but the theory often remains a barrier. A variety of teaching and learning strategies can help pupils understand and appreciate chemistry better. The lack of understanding about its relevance in everyday life is another barrier which can be easily overcome by the choice of relevant topics.

It is clear that equality of opportunity issues require a fundamental review of teaching and learning strategies. Effective teaching and learning strategies which address equality can be varied and stimulating. They value and build upon children's own experience. Ideas, assumptions and stereotypes are challenged through such strategies and children are enabled and encouraged to develop autonomy and responsibility for their own learning. Teaching and learning should be both shared and negotiated between pupils and teachers.

One extremely important, but often not fully appreciated, outcome of this approach to promote equality is its impact in raising the overall quality of teaching and learning experiences for all pupils. It is also equally important to understand that teaching for equality is not a soft and sloppy option to the rigours and demands of good science education. It is more difficult and often demands greater effort on the part of the teacher for it seeks to combine attitudes with understanding, knowledge with context, and diversity with enrichment.

REFERENCES

1   *Education for All*. The Swann Report. The Report of the Committee of Enquiry into the Education of Children from Ethnic Minority Groups. Chairman Lord Swann. (HMSO, 1985).

2   *Race, Equality and Science Teaching: A discussion document*, Association for Science Education, Multicultural Education Working Party. (ASE, 1991).

3   *Race, Equality and Science Teaching: An active INSET manual for teachers and educators*, Association for Science Education, Multicultural Education Working Party. (ASE, 1991).

4   *Improving Secondary Schools*, Report of the Committee on Secondary Education, Chaired by Hargreaves, D. (Inner London Education Authority, 1984).

5   *Improving Primary Schools*, Report of the Committee on Primary Education, Chaired by Thomas, N. (Inner London Education Authority, 1985).

6   Singer, C., *A Short History of Scientific Ideas to 1900*. (Oxford University Press, 1959).

7   Needham, J., 'Science and Civilisation in China', in *Chemistry and Industrial Chemistry*. (Cambridge University Press, 1954). Vol. 5.

8   *Third World Science: Soap*, Third World Science Project, School of Education, University College of North Wales, Bangor, Gwynedd. (1982).

CHAPTER 19

TEACHING CHEMISTRY TO PUPILS FOR WHOM ENGLISH IS A SECOND LANGUAGE

Maggie Farrar

INTRODUCTION

The science laboratory is a linguistically rich environment. Not only are pupils exposed to a wealth of vocabulary they are also engaged on a process of discovery which requires them to hypothesize, predict, observe, describe and draw conclusions. Much of what goes on in a chemistry lesson is observable and therefore concrete. The language used to describe chemical processes and the new vocabulary used by pupils in a chemistry laboratory means that science is in fact a second language to most pupils. Clive Sutton in his article 'Teaching science with language in mind: chemistry and English' (Chapter 16) demonstrates the 'new ways of talking' that science demands of our pupils and suggests a range of classroom activities to develop this.

This article will demonstrate how placing language at the forefront of your science teaching will lead to an enhanced learning experience for all pupils including those who are bilingual.

Let's begin by looking at the pupils. Who are our bilingual learners and what are their needs? A pupil who is a bilingual learner may or may not have studied science in another country. They may or may not be literate in their first language and their individual competence in speaking, reading and writing in English will probably be at dissimilar levels.

Before a bilingual pupil joins your class you need to find out:

- how long the pupil has been in England;
- what the pupil's previous educational experience is;
- if the pupil is literate in his or her mother tongue;
- what the pupil's level of English is.

I will use as examples three bilingual children who are at differing stages in their language development and look at how their needs might manifest themselves in the laboratory and how we as teachers can support them.

SUPPORTING THE PUPIL

Asma

Asma is a twelve-year-old pupil who has just arrived in this country from Bangladesh. She has completed two classes in primary school in Bangladesh. She speaks Sylheti, a dialect of Bengali, and is not literate in Bengali. She knows how to write her name, the name of her school, and she can count up to 20 in

English. She is beginning to become familiar with basic classroom vocabulary 'pen, pencil, bag, diary, etc.'. She will speak Bengali in a small group and has therefore been placed in a working group with another Bengali speaker. She is not confident about using English.

Many pupils go through a 'period of silence' when they first come to school in England. She should not be forced to speak until she is ready, but teachers need to be aware that the process of language acquisition has begun—she is already assimilating all the language patterns she is hearing around her.

Supporting Asma's learning in science

It's very easy as a teacher with a large demanding class to disengage from a pupil who does not speak to you or demand your attention. During the lesson ask her to give out paper, clean the blackboard and collect homework. Opportunities for a non-verbal response will enable her to communicate with you without speech. It will allow her to feel she belongs. When she begins to respond verbally she may do so with one- or two-word requests. Always give her the model of the language she is seeking. For example, if she comes up to you with a request, 'paper Miss' say to her 'You want another *piece of paper* Asma, here you are, here's another piece of paper'. *Every linguistic exchange is an opportunity to teach language.*

Similarly when she begins to answer questions give her the opportunity to respond by simple yes/no answers. Asking other pupils to think of and ask these questions is a useful learning exercise which involves the whole class.

Find ways of reinforcing new language. Put labelled pictures or photographs of apparatus on the wall. Give her five new words on cards to take home to learn for homework. Let her match the words with the apparatus when she comes to the next class. Let her build up this stock of cards and when she becomes a little more confident let her:

- turn over one card at a time and look at it for a few seconds;
- encourage her to look at the whole word and take a picture of it in her mind;
- then ask her to turn the card face down and to write the word from memory;
- she can then look at the card and check her attempt.

Reading

If the class are reading a complex text, give her five to ten vocabulary items (words) on cards and ask her to go through the text and see how many times she can see them. This is a useful exercise to help her to recognize the shapes of letters and words. If the text is disposable ask her to underline certain words in certain colours—a useful strategy for teaching and reinforcing colour. Talk to her about the text, using questions such as:

'Where is the title? Can you point to it?'

'How many words are in it? Write the number down.'

'How many paragraphs are there? Number them.'

'In which paragraph can you find this sentence...?'

It will be useful at this stage to build up your own store of texts on tape. Another pupil could tape a text for homework. This is a useful learning activity, especially if you ask them to tape their own summary at the end of the tape giving the gist of the text or the main learning points of the lesson. If Asma has a cassette player at home let her take tapes home. Even though not all the language will be comprehensible she will still be having exposure to language patterns and scientific terminology which she can listen to over and over again. It may be worth investing in a personal stereo for class use also. Let her listen to the tape when the rest of the class are involved in a silent individual activity.

Speaking

Use what she is doing to reinforce language. Take care to use consistent language and when you ask her questions initially you will need to supply both the question and the answer, e.g.

'What are you doing Asma? I'm boiling water.'

'What is this? It's a Bunsen burner.'

She may want to repeat this and speak with you. At this stage pupils can get very confused with the 'I'/'you' distinction and will repeat whatever you say. It's important that what they say is true *for them*, so as the teacher I usually stand behind the pupil and thus become *part of them* as I say, 'I'm boiling water'.

Remember, however, that the best models of language use she will have contact with will be her English speaking monolingual and bilingual peers. Make sure she is not isolated from them.

Writing

Give her plenty of chances to do some writing and therefore record what she's learning. At this early stage in language development simple copying will be most appropriate. You can check her level of scientific comprehension by giving her, for example, diagrams and labels to match and copy, or sentences to copy with gaps to fill in. This can be made more controlled by giving her the number of dashes to indicate the number of letters in the missing words, with the missing words given under the sentences, e.g.

Today I boiled _ _ _ _ _.

First I put on my safety _ _ _ _ _ _ _.

Then I put the _ _ _ _ _ _   _ _ _ _ _ _ on the mat.

water   Bunsen burner   goggles

She can be supported in making a record of the lesson or writing up an experiment by giving her the sequence of events jumbled up on paper. Then give her the ordered sequence on a tape. By using the sounds of the words on the tape and matching the sound to the word she can make a record of her learning.

It would be useful at this stage to ask Asma to begin her own personal dictionary of scientific terms (so helping her to learn the alphabet). Any words she has located in a text or used in writing can be added to it.

If a child (a little more advanced than Asma) is a beginner in English, but literate in their mother tongue, ask them to record what they've learned in the lesson in their own language. Ask another pupil to give you the gist of what has been written and to write this up in English for the next lesson. It gives a child who is a beginner in English great satisfaction to hear the results of their learning shared with their monolingual peers. This is a very salutary experience for others in the class also—little English does not equal low intelligence.

Teacher expectations

At this stage Asma should understand about safety in the laboratory. She should understand the geography of the laboratory and where to find things. This can be reinforced by always making sure she collects her own equipment and puts it away. She should be learning the names of basic apparatus and basic vocabulary associated with the area of the syllabus she is working on.

Tho

Tho is a Vietnamese speaker who has been at secondary school in England for 1 year. He is literate in Vietnamese and studied science at school in Vietnam before coming to England. He can communicate quite well orally, but he will discuss work more readily in a small group than in a class. He will need support to comprehend scientific texts and his writing if freely set, will contain many grammatical and spelling errors.

Supporting Tho's learning in science

When he listens to you presenting a new topic it will help him if key phrases are written on the blackboard to guide his listening. If you are introducing a topic on acids and alkalis the blackboard summary might look like Figure 1.

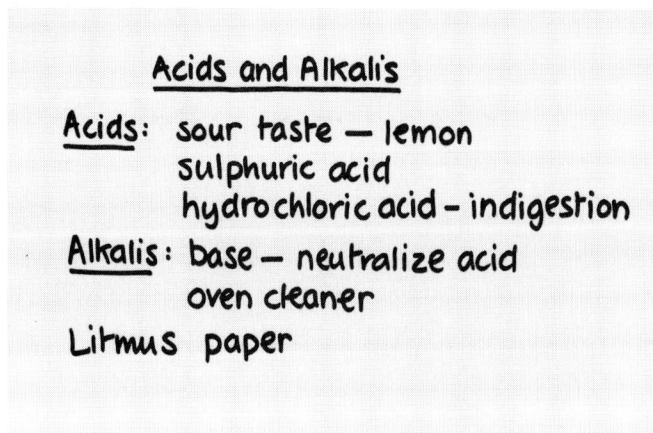

Figure 1   Introducing a topic on acids and alkalis.

Another day you might begin a new topic by asking pupils to brainstorm all the things they already know about a particular topic. It will also help Tho if your exposition is broken up into 3 to 5 minute slots. This will give the class a chance to articulate new information and put it in their own words.

After presenting or reinforcing new concepts, or summing up after a practical lesson, ask the class to 'retell' what you've been saying. Put keywords on the blackboard as the class reflects on what they've learned. One member of the class can then use all the keywords to give a summary, or pupils can have a go at doing this in a less exposed environment, e.g. a small group.

Repetition and retelling will help Tho to make new knowledge 'his own', so he will be more likely to internalize and remember it. This also helps him with new vocabulary items whose pronunciation may be problematic. The keywords and phrases could then be copied down by all the pupils and a summary written for homework.

Speaking

At this stage in language development, your observation of a pupil's practical work gives you the opportunity to stretch the pupil's manipulation of language structures. Ask basic questions such as:

'What do you think is going to happen?' (future tense)

'What's happening?' (present continuous)

'What's just happened?' (present perfect)

'Did the same thing happen last week?' (past)

The laboratory gives teachers the perfect context for practising some of the more difficult grammatical structures for a pupil such as Tho to grasp. When he responds, your role is to model and reinforce new language:

Teacher: 'What's going to happen?'

Tho: 'It change colour to blue.'

Teacher: 'That's right, it's going to change colour from white to blue isn't it. What's going to happen?'

Tho: 'It's going to change colour from white to blue.'

Reading

It will help Tho if the reading he has to do is about an activity he has just done so he can place it in a concrete framework in his mind. Tho should also be given strategies to help him to read the text with comprehension. Ask him to think about the title and to predict what the text might be about. Perhaps a group may like to brainstorm all the words they think might appear in the text. Then ask him to locate the words in the text. Give him the text cut up into paragraphs/phrases and stuck onto cards and ask him in his group to resequence the text. If the text is very complex, give each member of the group the piece of text and ask them to tell each other what their piece is about before sequencing it. This strategy is perfect for giving bilingual learners like Tho access to a whole text while only requiring them to read a small part of it.

This activity can be made more complex by writing keywords from the text on the back of each card (as illustrated in Figure 2) and asking pupils to share the information on their card using these keywords only.

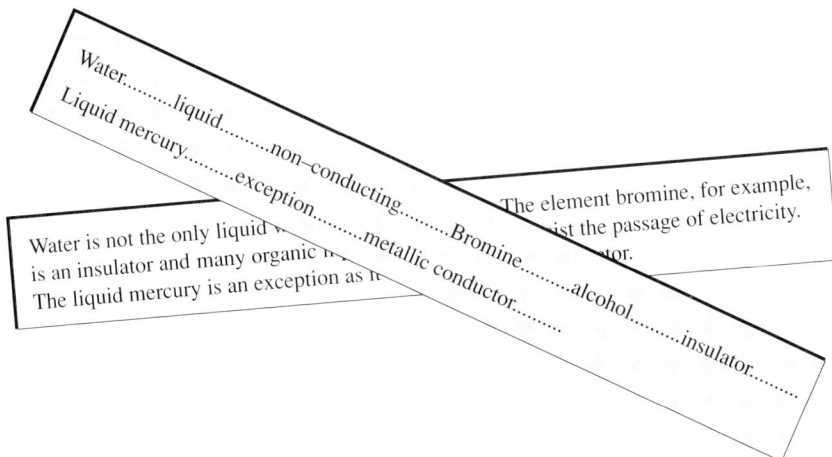

Figure 2   A piece of the text with keywords on the back.

Once the text has been reassembled, his understanding of it can be checked by the following strategy:

- Formulate a number of true and false sentences and ask him to mark them 'T' or 'F' according to his understanding of the text.

- Ask him to locate key sentences and vocabulary in the text which answer questions such as:

    'Which sentence tells you that… ?'

    'Which word means… ?'

    'Which is the most important sentence in the text?'

    'Which sentence do you find the most difficult?'

His scientific vocabulary can be increased by asking him to write down five new words from the text and to place them in order of how difficult he thinks they are to, (i) explain, (ii) spell, (iii) say, etc.

Writing

If Tho is expected to write freely his work will contain errors. His writing can be supported by the following:

(i)   Ask him to sequence sentences (or skeleton sentences) to form the basis of the write up of an experiment.

(ii)   Give him a substitution table (such as the one illustrated in Figure 3) to enable him to write scientifically and linguistically correct sentences. Substitution tables are useful as they give the pupil all the words they need to write sentences, but the correct choice of words depends on their understanding.

Sugar Orange juice	are	
Sand Glass	is	soluble in water.
Tea leaves Wood	isn't	
Coffee Chalk	aren't	

Figure 3   A substitution table.

(iii) Give him a model which he can then use as a basis for doing his own writing. In the following example a text which describes how to make salt from rock salt is used as a model for writing up the process of an experiment.

> 'In order to make salt from rock salt we used the following apparatus.
> A pestle and mortar, a measuring cylinder, a spatula, a Bunsen burner, a beaker,
> a filter funnel and filter paper. First of all we took a piece of rock salt and
> ground it to powder with the pestle and motar. Then we placed the ground
> rock salt in a beaker. Next we measured 100 cm^3 of water into a measuring
> cylinder and added this to the beaker. After that we...'

Pupils in a class, as well as Tho, can be asked to underline all the verbs in one colour and all the words that sequence events (first of all, then, next, after that, etc.) in another colour. They are then asked to use these words when they write up their own experiment. If the pupils are doing a different experiment they can be asked to underline all the words in the model text that they think they will use when writing up their own experiment. This is especially useful when pupils are beginning to use the passive voice when writing up experiments. When Tho writes freely, his writing (as illustrated in Figure 4) can be responded to positively in a number of ways.

> First I put water in to a beaker about 3/4. Then I burn
> the bunsen burner or on and put place the beaker on
> and leave it for to boil it. When it start to bubble, I
> turn the bunsen burner off and with a tweezers I clip
> the leaf into boiling water for a few secound to kill.

Figure 4   An example of Tho's writing.

As a science teacher you could comment on:

•   his degree of scientific understanding (tick and note correct descriptions of scientific processes and use of terminology);

•   his ability to sequence events in a logical order;

- how accurately he has copied language from the board, text or worksheet;

- his use of grammatical structures when writing up an experiment—how many can he manipulate?

Teacher expectations

In many ways a pupil like Tho is more vulnerable to underachievement than Asma. Because of the emphasis on practical work Tho will probably be exhibiting more understanding in science than in other areas of the curriculum. It's easy for teachers to presume that pupils such as Tho are competent because of their oral ability. They overlook the fact that support and help is still needed particularly in the areas of reading and writing. A lack of support at this stage in these areas can lead to progress in reading and writing reaching a 'plateau' and in particular for errors in writing to become internalized through habitual use.

Yesim

Yesim is a Turkish speaker who has been in England for 4 years. She is fluent in Turkish and her oral ability in English is approaching that of her English speaking peers.

Supporting Yesim's learning in science

All the strategies described previously for Asma and Tho will help Yesim. As a more fluent language user, she should be able to internalize and remember more complex new language and concepts but will need to have them reinforced and be reminded of them. Some strategies which are useful for developing the scientific vocabulary of all pupils in a class are as follows.

(i)   Write new vocabulary items on the blackboard and ask pupils to shut their eyes while you rub one off. When they open their eyes, ask them to guess which item is missing. This can be varied by asking the class to look at the blackboard for 15 seconds, and then covering it up. Then ask the pupils to work in groups to see how many items they can remember.

(ii) Write vocabulary from the previous lesson on the blackboard. As pupils come in, ask them to underline any word they have forgotten the meaning of. This helps you to see at a glance how much revision you need to do.

(iii) Some pupils benefit from words being broken up into syllables especially the names of elements which many pupils, not only bilingual pupils, find difficult to read. Syllables can be printed onto cards which are used by pupils to build up the names of elements, and then these are matched with their symbol, e.g.

mag	pot	alu	cop	ass	per	min	nes

ium	ium	ium	Mg	K	Al	Cu

Each of these activities can be used as a quick warm up at the beginning of a lesson, or to finish a lesson. Their value is that they ensure pupils are repeating vocabulary over and over again as they get caught up in the activity.

Reading

When Yesim is reading she will benefit from exposure to complex texts but with support available. She will be unable to 'read and make notes' without resorting to a degree of copying. The following strategies will support her note taking.

Give Yesim headings and keywords with which to make notes, for example ask her to read a text about reactivity. When she has finished, ask her to close the book and give her headings and keywords to use to make notes on what she has read. When she has finished ask her to read the text again to see if there's anything she's missed out.

Headings	Keywords
Reactivity—what is it?	metals / corrode / don't
	magnesium / reactive
	gold / unreactive / water pipes
Reactions with water	magnesium / steam
	oxygen / steam / hydrogen gas
Reactions with air	magnesium / zinc / layer / oxide
	damp air / iron
	magnesium / white magnesium oxide
	iron filings / sparklers

Another way to facilitate note taking is to ask her to read a section of the text and pick out the ten most important words. Take the text away and ask her to use the keywords she's chosen to make a summary. Alternatively, ask the class to pick out keywords for each other. This can lead to a lively debate about language and meaning as the pupils ask each other why particular keywords were chosen and not others.

Writing

It is sometimes assumed that pupils such as Yesim should be able to write without support. Teachers then spend a large amount of their time correcting errors in the writing. The writing support previously suggested will help Yesim, as will the following strategies which focus on spelling.

Ask Yesim to look at her own work and to:

- underline in blue all the sentences/words she is sure are correct;
- underline in red all the sentences/words she is not too sure of, but which she thinks are almost right;
- underline in green all the sentences/words she thinks she's got wrong.

When Yesim is given new vocabulary, e.g. the names of elements ask her to:

- underline the section of a word she thinks is going to 'trip her up', e.g. hydrogen;

- think of words with the same spelling pattern, e.g. sodium, potassium, magnesium;

- look for words inside words, e.g. sul<u>phide</u>/va<u>pour</u>.

CONCLUSION

Having looked at strategies for accessing scientific language let us now summarize what kind of chemistry lesson is most accessible to a bilingual learner and thus encourages the development of language.

As teachers we need to plan chemistry lessons that:

- are group orientated;

- encourage talk;

- encourage pupils to 'talk about' their learning throughout the practical activities;

- value the use of the mother tongue;

- give bilingual pupils access to monolingual peers' language;

- break up teacher presentation and allow pupils to 'make it their own';

- have a variety of reading and writing tasks which are accessible for all pupils;

- focus on language especially new vocabulary and actively teach and reinforce it;

- allow for language experimentation lessons where making errors is an acceptable part of learning.

Glancing down this list you will probably be saying to yourself—but surely this is just good teaching? Yes, it is. A good lesson, well delivered with the above elements in it *is a good language lesson*. It will deliver what all bilingual pupils need—the opportunity to develop their English language competence within the context of other learning.

SUPPORTING THE TEACHER

Teaching large groups with differing needs can sometimes seem like a daunting task. What other support is available to you and your pupils?

The learning environment

Are you making the most of your learning environment? Look round your laboratory and ask yourself:

(i)   Where is my blackboard? Can all the pupils see it? What does it look like at the end of the lesson? Is there an area of my blackboard specifically reserved for new language? After I've given oral instructions do I write them up on the blackboard as *visual reinforcement*?

(ii) How are the benches grouped? Where do I place myself in relation to them during the presentation stage/the practical stage. Where are the bilingual pupils sitting? What kind of language do they have access to in their groups?

(iii) What's on the walls?

keywords?

an aide memoire for the pupils of common errors?

models of good work?

visual reinforcement of new ideas?

language used regularly for hypothesizing and predicting, e.g. 'I think', 'perhaps', 'maybe', 'what if'?

(iv) What's on the benches besides equipment? Are there dictionaries or a thesaurus?

(v) Is there a common code of conduct that is visible to the pupils? For example, 'Always ask at least three other people in the room your question before you ask me'.

(vi) Is a marking scheme for both written and practical tasks displayed to allow pupils to comment on each other's work?

(vii) Is the lesson agenda on the wall? Do pupils know what the purpose of the lesson is? Is your lesson plan displayed? Do the pupils know what's going to happen in the lesson and how much time they have for particular activities?

Pupils internalize a lot of language as they gaze around the room. The more you can use this to reinforce the language you expect them to use in chemistry, the more beneficial it will be.

The department

Does your department have a policy on supporting bilingual pupils in chemistry lessons? As a member of a department you need to be able to draw on the support of your colleagues. A discussion about policy could centre on the following questions:

(i)   How do we identify the needs of bilingual pupils? How do we find out about their past learning experiences in science?

(ii) How do we ensure that beginner bilingual pupils understand enough basic scientific vocabulary and have the basic skills to operate safely in a laboratory? (A member of the department could be given specific responsibility for assessing bilingual pupils' basic scientific skills on entry, as well as devising and operating a short induction course to science.)

(iii) What is our grouping policy? Is it by ability, by language, by friendship/pupil choice? Are the groups mixed ability/multilingual?

(iv) What other support can we draw on in school and how do we wish to work in partnership with these staff, e.g. ESL teachers/teachers responsible for pupils with special needs?

Setting up partnership teaching with members of the learning support departments is a very rewarding experience for both departments if it is done effectively. For it to succeed, it is vital that discussion between the teachers involved, to clarify roles in the classroom, takes place before the work begins.

- Will you wish to work collaboratively with both teachers being equally responsible for presenting the lesson, setting and marking homework, discipline and classroom management, etc.?

- Do you want the support teacher to focus on a number of individuals in the classroom only and therefore to work in a support capacity making sure that the curriculum is accessible to these targeted pupils?

- Who are the pupils who will be targeted by the support teacher and what learning targets will be set for them?

- What is the aim in working together? Is it to develop a particular skill, e.g. writing up experiments, developing vocabulary or developing language skills to enable the pupils to take part in pupil-centred investigative work?

- How will the partnership be evaluated and at what stage—after half a term or a full term?

- How will the materials you have devised in partnership and the new insights gained in teaching and learning in science be fed back to your respective departments?

- What is the agreed procedure if either of you are dissatisfied with the partnership?

(v) What does it mean for us as science teachers to say that *all* pupils are our responsibility? What staff development needs emerge from this? How can we share ideas and strategies for supporting bilingual pupils in the laboratory?

How you teach and how you engage pupils in their own learning is central to how accessible the curriculum is for those pupils. A school and a department can either produce or reduce language and learning difficulties. Thinking about the above questions will give you a starting point.

CHAPTER 20

CHEMISTRY FOR PUPILS WITH VISUAL IMPAIRMENTS

Frances Betts

INTRODUCTION

This Chapter is included because many of you may face the prospect of having a pupil with a visual impairment in your laboratory. I was asked to write it because for the past two years I have been teaching chemistry up to A-Level in a Royal National Institute for the Blind (RNIB) residential secondary school and so have the daily challenge of coping with both the practical and theoretical aspects of the subject. In a sense my job is made easier by the fact that all my pupils are in the same boat, even if they do have widely ranging disabilities. A teacher of one visually-impaired pupil in a class of 25 to 30 has the added challenge of perhaps presenting the material to one pupil in a totally different way to the others. You may be faced with the attitude that a visually-impaired pupil, especially a totally blind one, is going to struggle with learning chemistry as much of the information received is visual. However, there are other channels through which information can be passed to such a pupil. Simply because a pupil is denied visual information, it does not follow that she or he cannot develop an understanding of the knowledge and concepts of chemistry and have access to the whole curriculum. In this Chapter, I will indicate some of the ways in which I seek to achieve this.

THE NATURE OF THE IMPAIRMENT AND HOW TO OVERCOME IT

First, try to understand your pupil's visual impairment. Put on a blindfold or wear spectacles which simulate the impairment and attempt to read the blackboard or perform an experiment. This will give you some idea of the problems faced by your pupil. However, you will still be working using your visual memory. You are familiar with the apparatus and know exactly how it should be set up and used, and will be able to anticipate likely problems. It will be much harder for your pupil. Second, spend some time discussing with your pupil how she or he would like the work presented. Many modern textbooks are full of visual stimulation such as photographs, newspaper cuttings, cartoons and flow charts. Much of this may be 'background noise' to your pupil and so their text may need to be modified and possibly enlarged and diagrams simplified. If your pupil works in braille, then brailled text or taped text and tactile diagrams will be needed. If all this is beginning to sound daunting, then don't despair! If your pupil has a severe visual impairment she or he will have the assistance of a support teacher from the local authority who will put the material into a suitable format. The support teacher may well accompany the pupil to lessons and take notes for them. Often some modified or special apparatus, or modified methods may help pupils. A partially sighted pupil might need:

- to get closer to the apparatus and chemicals;
- to view from an eccentric angle, e.g. to hold a test-tube close to the eye and to slide it up and down to get a better view;
- to use a low-vision aid, e.g. a magnifying lens for reading text or a telescope for distance vision;
- special lighting, e.g. an angle-poise lamp fixed to the bench;
- window blinds;
- the assistance of digital apparatus, LED or liquid crystal;
- 'talking' apparatus (discussed in a later section);
- luminous paint or tape to highlight apparatus, e.g. tripod legs, base of Bunsen burner and rims of test-tubes;
- a white background (or black!);
- black markings on scales;
- tactile markings on scales, e.g. Himark, an orange fluorescent paste which dries to give raised markings (see the RNIB catalogue [1]).

This list is not complete and all new suggestions are welcome!

A partially-sighted pupil may not be able to view all the apparatus in a set-up at once and so will need to be given time to understand the relationship between one item of apparatus and the next. A totally blind pupil will need tactile diagrams and 'talking' apparatus. Two useful publications for teachers which describe the more common visual impairments among school children are *The Visually Handicapped Child in your Classroom* [2] and *Sensory Handicaps in Children* [3].

LABORATORY ORGANIZATION AND SAFETY

Safety is important in every chemistry laboratory and I have assumed all the normal precautions and safety drill as taught to sighted pupils in science lessons. Certain additional procedures are recommended with a visually-impaired pupil. I might add here that I feel safer in my laboratory with six visually-impaired pupils than I did with a class of 30 fully sighted ones!

All practical activities in chemistry must be assessed in terms of risk to pupils and teacher. There will be a greater risk when a pupil has a visual impairment and this will obviously depend on the severity of the impairment. It is difficult to generalize in such an area. Judgement of any risks must be the responsibility of the teacher and support staff.

Your pupil must feel at home in the laboratory and it is important to spend some time with them and their support staff on their own so that they become familiar with the layout, the doors, emergency exit routine, the sinks and location of fixed furniture.

Apparatus and chemicals for experiments are best provided on a tray. Items of apparatus, when met for the first time, should be identified—what it is and how it is used. The support staff or other pupils in the group could be responsible for this. Chemicals should be labelled in clear black print or braille as appropriate. Any scales on measuring instruments should also be explained. Solids can be supplied in clearly labelled petri dishes or specimen bottles. Liquids can be in labelled beakers covered with cling film or by a watch-glass, or in dropping bottles. Hazardous liquids should be dispensed separately by the teacher when required. Eye or face protection is still necessary even though it might be an added visual impairment for some.

Visually-impaired pupils are unlikely to notice small spillages of solids and liquids and so an overall and close-fitting vinyl protective gloves are useful. These will not impair the sense of touch of a pupil with well developed tactile skills. The pupil should have easy access to a sink for washing in case there is skin contact with chemicals.

Such preparation is time consuming for both teacher and technician. It also takes time for the pupil to absorb all the information and work out how to set up any apparatus.

Ideally, your pupil should work on their own, to ensure 'hands on' experience of performing the experiment since this is often their only way of receiving information and of getting anything out of the practical. If this is not possible and they have to work as part of a group, make sure that they participate fully in the experiment. Sighted peers may need prompting by the teacher as to how they can best help their visually-impaired group member. They will need to learn to state what is obvious to them. The experience of doing this should prove mutually beneficial to all the group members.

The RNIB leaflet *Safety in Practical Lessons: Guide-lines for Working with Visually Impaired Pupils in Science and CDT* [4] gives more information about these matters (see also [5–7]).

SPECIAL APPARATUS

The practical work carried out by a visually-impaired pupil should be the same as that carried out by the other pupils in the class. However, the instructions and apparatus given to the pupil may need to be modified. The RNIB provides a leaflet [6] listing useful science equipment for visually-impaired pupils. The equipment need not be expensive and often the simpler it is, the more effective! The items in most use in my laboratory are disposable plastic syringes, used for measuring volumes of liquids. A notch is cut into the plunger which can be felt when the plunger is drawn out to the required volume. The pupil then only needs one decent finger nail to be able to measure volumes of 1, 2 ... $501 cm^3$ with a fair degree of accuracy. A set of these syringes giving a range of the more frequently needed volumes is money well spent. However, there can be a problem—the whole class will want them! Other useful items of apparatus are as follows:

- digital thermometers: inexpensive and a good range to choose from in most catalogues;

- talking thermometers: expensive but necessary for a totally blind pupil (see [1]);

- talking calculators: less than £30 for a basic one (see [1]);

- digital stopwatch/timer: widely available;

- talking balance: can be an expensive item if analytical quality is needed. Most electronic top-pan balances can interface with a BBC microcomputer for speech output. The RNIB offers advice on talking kitchen scales;

- level-arm balance: with braille markings is an alternative to the talking balance;

- light probe: helps blind pupils find the level of a liquid in a test-tube, burette or beaker. It is about the size of a fat pen and gives an audible signal, the pitch of which depends on the intensity of light falling on the end of the probe, so detecting the liquid/air interface. It can also be used to detect a significant colour change, e.g. the starch/iodine end-point (see [1]).

PRACTICAL WORK: SOME EXAMPLES AND USEFUL TECHNIQUES

Neutralization of an acid

Dilute acid ($251 cm^3$) is transferred to a beaker using a 25 cm^3 notched plastic syringe. A few drops of indicator are then added. The most appropriate indicator should be selected for the acid/alkali used, i.e. the one that gives a colour change which your pupil can spot. If your pupil is blind, phenolphthalein is useful as it has an end-point which a light probe can detect. Alkali is added using notched syringes of 10, 5, 2 and 1 cm^3 capacities, keeping a tally of total volume added until the end-point is reached. This corresponds to a 'rough' titration which is then repeated with smaller additions of alkali to improve the accuracy of the end-point determined.

Experiments using Bunsen burners

With practice, lighting a Bunsen burner is possible for all pupils, but careful supervision is needed until they are confident and competent. One method is for the pupil to locate the base of the Bunsen (air-hole closed) and to slowly raise a burning match to the top of the chimney, while turning on the gas with their other hand.

During use, always keep a tripod over the Bunsen to act as a 'fire guard'. A plain gauze folded over the top of the tripod will glow red over a hot flame, giving a visual warning of the heat.

If your pupil's eye/hand coordination is poor it is often better to clamp a test-tube in the correct position while it is heated. Alternatively, use a hot-water bath if this will supply enough heat.

Don't underestimate your pupil. They can feel the setting of the air-hole collar and they will be able to hear the flame when the air-hole is open. Very few people can see a hot Bunsen flame clearly in bright daylight.

Useful techniques

Reactions producing precipitates

A blind pupil will be able to detect the presence of a precipitate in a test-tube by stirring with a glass rod. Alternatively, using a light probe during the mixing of the two solutions should give the same information. It is often helpful to use control test-tubes of solutions to remind them of the 'before reaction' signal. The contents of the test-tube can always be filtered to discover the solid, but this is time consuming and adds unnecessary fuss.

Judging reactions by listening

Any reaction involving effervescence can be observed by listening. Reactions can also be timed in this way, e.g. the rate of reaction between magnesium and dilute hydrochloric acid can be followed (safety note: this produces hydrogen/spray which is 'choking'—a watch-glass over the top of the beaker helps reduce the risk). Similarly, the rate of reaction between marble chips and acid can be followed by placing the reaction vessel on a top-pan balance linked to a speech output. The noise made during the fountain experiment and the final sucking noise provide another good example.

Collecting gases

Collecting gases is easy if the gas can be collected over water, since the pupil will be able to feel and hear the overflow of bubbles (safety note: only non-hazardous gases should be collected in this way). Corking the tube and collecting a second tube simply needs practice.

Temperature changes

Exo- and endothermic reactions are an obvious clue that a chemical reaction has taken place and should be exploited wherever possible, e.g. the pupil can feel the outside of the test-tube (or use a thermometer) to detect the change.

Differences in texture

Whilst the feeling of metal surfaces before and after a chemical reaction would not normally be encouraged, a blind pupil with well developed tactile skills will notice a difference and this may be their only clue that a reaction has occurred. Make sure the surface is well rinsed with water first and that hands are washed afterwards.

Differences in smell

A blind pupil may be allowed to identify some chemicals by their smell, e.g. by wafting the vapour from a bottle of ethanol or dilute household bleach towards their nose.

Reactions involving colour

Reactions involving colour are perhaps the most difficult ones to tackle. For many people, school chemistry is associated with colourful things happening in test-tubes! Of the pupils I teach, very few were blind at birth and so they do have memories of colours. They have to learn by rote that copper sulphate solution is blue, etc. and have to ask their sighted peers to tell them of any colour changes in their test-tubes. The colour-blind pupils can often spot when there has been a colour change, even if they are not sure what the colours are. The item of apparatus most needed here is a 'talking' colorimeter which will accept test-tubes and boiling tubes giving the blind pupil independence in this area.

Demonstrations

Have your visually-impaired pupil as close to you at the demonstration bench as possible and allow them to handle the apparatus you are going to use. Give a running commentary, stating what will be obvious to the rest of the class.

ASSESSMENT OF PRACTICAL SKILLS AT GCSE AND UNDER THE NATIONAL CURRICULUM

This should not be a problem area provided the criteria set out in the syllabus are open-ended enough. If the syllabus states that pupils should be able to read the scale on a mercury thermometer, for example, then this is likely to be an impossible task for a visually-impaired pupil. Contact the Special Needs Officer for your examination board and discuss the matter with them well in advance of the examination date. They are quite likely to be flexible provided you offer acceptable alternatives and state if and when help is given to your pupil. In 1991, I entered two blind pupils for GCSE chemistry. They were allowed to use 'talking' apparatus and the disposable syringes as alternatives to measuring cylinders and the only help I gave them was to confirm colour changes in an ion analysis exercise.

I trust that similar arrangements will operate under the National Curriculum.

CONCLUDING REMARKS

Welcome your visually-impaired pupil into your chemistry lessons. I hope you will be agreeably surprised by what they can achieve. Be prepared to learn from them. They often have a way of expressing things that you have never thought of, to the advantage of all in your class.

REFERENCES

1   RNIB *Equipment and Games Catalogue*, Royal National Institute for the Blind, 224 Great Portland Street, London, W1N 6AA.

2   Chapman, E. K. and Stone, J. M., *The Visually Handicapped Child in your Classroom*. (Cassell, 1988).

3   Fitt, R. A. and Mason, H., *Sensory Handicaps in Children*. (National Council for Special Education, 1986).

4   *Safety in Practical Lessons: Guide-lines for Working with Visually Impaired Pupils in Science and CDT*, Royal National Institute for the Blind leaflet, RNIB Outreach Service, RNIB New College Worcester, Whittington Road, Worcester, WR5 2JX. (1991).

5   Minett, S., *Science for Visually Impaired Pupils*, Royal National Institute for the Blind leaflet, RNIB Outreach Service, RNIB New College Worcester, Whittington Road, Worcester, WR5 2JX.

6   Minett, S., *Science Equipment List*, Royal National Institute for the Blind leaflet, RNIB Outreach Service, RNIB New College Worcester, Whittington Road, Worcester, WR5 2JX. (1989).

7   Pill, B. J., (revised by Herring, F.), *Teaching Science to Visually Impaired Children*, Royal National Institute for the Blind leaflet, RNIB Outreach Service, RNIB New College Worcester, Whittington Road, Worcester, WR5 2JX. (1991).

CHAPTER 21

ENTITLEMENT AND ACCESS TO SCIENCE IN THE CURRICULUM FOR PUPILS WITH SPECIAL NEEDS

Richard Rose

INTRODUCTION

The introduction of the National Curriculum can be seen as one of the most significant changes in our education system in recent years. In particular, the identification of science as a core subject, thus elevating it to a pole position in the education of all pupils, has rekindled a debate whose origins can be traced back through history. (Faraday and Darwin, amongst others, both emphasized the importance of a basic scientific education for all children.) The current dialectic appears once again to have revived issues of definition. Indeed, the interpretation of the term science itself is of central concern. Schools are once again considering not only the content of their science curricula, but also the nature of the ways in which it is to be taught, and its relationships to other curriculum areas. There is a danger that a failure to clarify our terms at a time of such significant change could lead to a tokenistic approach to science teaching, especially for younger, or less able pupils. There is a further risk that in a system which places a renewed emphasis upon pen and paper testing, and which is concerned largely with measuring the success of schools through their published results, pupils with significant learning difficulties may become marginalized; identified through their failures rather than their achievements. For these reasons it is essential that now, more than at any other time in recent years, we must ensure that we address the needs of *all* pupils in science.

The term 'special needs' covers a vast spectrum of abilities, including those pupils in mainstream schools who have a moderate learning or sensory impairment, as well as those who exhibit more profound and multiple learning difficulties more often associated with special schools. Pupils with special needs, whether those needs take the form of long-term or permanent impairments such as severe learning difficulties, or deafness, or are of a more temporary nature such as may follow an emotional trauma or road accident, have a right to receive a well planned science education. In many instances the curriculum content for pupils with special needs will remain the same as that applied to their peers, though for pupils with more severe difficulties there may be a need to make considerable modifications. It is, however, our responsibility to reaffirm the entitlement of all pupils to a broad balanced, relevant, and well differentiated curriculum.

The National Curriculum [1] recognizes the need to build upon pupils' existing perceptions and experiences, plotting a course through science which demands that these should be questioned and examined in order to provide a new and greater understanding of the world in which they live. Such a course of action can be identified in much of today's most effective science teaching, and we must take care to preserve the finer traditions of science teaching which have been developed in our schools. Attainment Target 1 (AT1) in science with its emphasis upon observation, investigation, experimentation and recording of results, provides a platform on which to develop science for all pupils. The importance of AT1 which is intended to influence science teaching throughout the key stages, is of great significance for teachers who are concerned to be effective in meeting the special needs of pupils. The skills which it emphasizes provide a sound basis not only for science, but for all learning. Yet it is these very skills, of observation, investigation and interpretation which often cause the greatest difficulties for pupils with special needs.

Teaching pupils with special needs is often difficult precisely because of their lack of development in the areas demanded in the early stages of science. Here, however, we are presented with an opportunity. It is precisely these skills which have been identified in AT1 which pupils with special needs must acquire if they are to make significant strides in learning in any other curriculum area. Science can therefore be seen to provide a vehicle for learning for the pupil with special needs, and should not be viewed in isolation from other areas of the pupil's development. In order that progress can be made, however, the teacher will need to consider specific strategies which will enable pupils to overcome learning difficulties and will take full account of individual needs.

ACCESS

An initial concern for all teachers must be one of access to the curriculum and to those resources required for its delivery. As with all other aspects of meeting special needs this must begin with the assertion that all pupils can learn through science. For many, however, this will mean changes to the learning environment, and an acceptance that all pupils will learn at their own rates and levels. Problems of access can be divided into two categories, the technical, which for some pupils will involve such aspects as physical access for wheelchairs, or the use of a Perkins Brailler or a word processor, and the more difficult social access, which will assert the right of pupils with learning difficulties to be educated alongside their more able peers [2].

At first sight, the problems of technical access would appear to be easily overcome, and indeed many aspects of this provide only minor challenges to the teacher. The provision of lower worksurfaces for pupils in wheelchairs, low-vision aids (magnifiers which enlarge print), braille labels on bottles or apparatus, or large print for the visually impaired, or additional written materials and visual cues for pupils with hearing difficulties would seem to be obvious approaches to providing greater access. However, certain conditions need to be met in order that such approaches can prove effective. Initially, teachers preparing science lessons need to be aware of the diagnosis of learning difficulties or special needs, and to be provided with information regarding the implications of these needs for both the individual pupil, and the peers with whom he or she must work. Sadly, such information is all too often unavailable, or is not passed on to the teacher who is working directly with the pupil. Science teachers must demand access to such information if they are to ensure that pupils with special needs are to learn effectively in their classes. Once such information is available, the teacher must avoid making generalizations. There are still occasional assumptions that, for example, a pupil with a visual impairment will have major learning difficulties, whereas in fact the learning problems which many pupils have, result from the environment in which we expect them to work. (This issue has been covered by Betts in Chapter 20.) Attention to classroom management can often anticipate, and therefore minimize potential difficulties. For example, provision of an uncluttered work area when working with a clumsy child or one with limited physical control, will not just increase pupil confidence, but may also be a significant safety factor.

Methods of providing physical access to science have been well documented [3–8]. However, less consideration has been given to the question of social access. The reality of teaching today is that homogeneous classes of pupils who are of like ability, motivation and need are rare in most mainstream and all special schools. Science teachers are daily faced with classes of diverse ability and need. Inevitably, this means that one particular teaching style or approach is unlikely to suit every pupil in the class. Versatility and flexibility are key words here, but are not sufficient alone to ensure effective learning for all. Teachers need to give consideration to matters of classroom grouping and to differentiation. The assumption that pupils of like ability are more easily taught, or that pupils with special needs will have a detrimental effect upon group situations, is a false one. Research [9–13] suggests the contrary to be true, and indicates that heterogeneous grouping not only benefits the pupil with special needs through peer support, but also encourages the more able pupils to explain difficult concepts in a way which is more easily understood by all group members. This promotes clarity of thought, reduces peer pressure and encourages classroom interaction. This is not to suggest that grouping to include pupils with special needs is easy. Careful consideration of compatibility of characters, clear definition of the roles of pupils in a group ensuring that each member is fully involved, and that the pupil with special needs is not sidelined are all issues for the science teacher. McCall [14] has provided excellent guide-lines on classroom grouping, and has highlighted the need to ensure that all pupils in a group have a clear understanding of teacher expectations. This issue has been expanded by Johnson *et al.* [15] who have promoted techniques such as jigsawing, whereby a complete task is dependent upon the smaller tasks performed by each group member. This technique has been successfully used in teaching practical activities to pupils with severe learning difficulties (Rose [16]) and lends itself readily to use in science.

The nature of science is such that it demands the full involvement of the learner. Whilst the able pupil may in the past have gained scientific information and concepts through observation of an experiment demonstrated by a teacher at the front of the class, it is generally accepted that wherever possible pupils should have direct access to materials and apparatus which allow them to conduct experiments for themselves. This was never more true than for the pupil with learning difficulties. A pupil with a sensory impairment needs to make full use of all his or her senses in understanding and interpreting information. The importance of handling equipment for a pupil with a visual or hearing loss cannot be over emphasized. Similarly, a pupil with learning difficulties, moderate or severe, may have considerable trouble in perceiving the nature of materials used in an experiment. Direct access to the materials and apparatus must assist in overcoming such a problem. For example, a teacher conducting an experiment to examine the elasticity of materials should not assume that all of his or her pupils have a perception of the variations of the weights being used in the investigation, particularly where differences may be small. The pupil with learning difficulties needs opportunities to experience such differences at first hand, and even then may need to have these pointed out.

Many pupils with learning difficulties are alienated from science by the confusion which scientific language can cause. Assumptions made about seemingly simple concepts can cause major obstacles when teaching pupils with learning difficulties. For example, the difference between melting and dissolving, or between weight and mass may be concepts readily understood by some pupils whilst others will have greater difficulties of interpretation. The simplification of language, and time taken to explain the more difficult concepts is a vital element of increasing access for all pupils with special needs.

DIFFERENTIATION OF MATERIALS

Two areas where the presentation of materials can either enhance or deny access are in the use of worksheets and in the recording of results. Well differentiated materials can make a considerable difference and ensure the inclusion of pupils with special needs. The use of illustration or pictorial representation in place of words or, for some pupils with severe learning difficulties, symbols such as those used in the Makaton Vocabulary [17] or the Rebus Scheme [18] can help. (Two particularly helpful publications on the use of symbol systems are Peter and Barnes [19] and Van Oosterom and Devereux [20].) The use of chemical symbols has long proved confusing for some pupils, and here a little time ensuring that these are accompanied by written labels during the early stages of their introduction (e.g. writing carbon dioxide in full beneath CO_2) may reduce anxiety. Such supports can be gradually faded out as a pupil gains in confidence. The recording of worksheets on to audio tape which the pupil with limited literacy skills can then play back and repeat as necessary may also prove effective for some pupils. Shared worksheets, with careful pairing of pupils, or the appointment of one reader to a small group are also techniques which have been deployed with considerable success by some science teachers. One word of caution here—the sensitivities of the pupil with special needs must be considered. The presentation of a well differentiated worksheet which closely resembles that used by all other class members, can often save embarrassment and possible subsequent rejection of the subject. Being obviously different can on occasions add to the difficulties experienced by a pupil with special needs.

The promotion of different methods for the recording of results is an area in which science teachers have made considerable strides. Hopefully, the days when only one formally devised method of recording the outcomes of an investigation was permitted, are behind us. Science teachers have been resourceful in ensuring that non-written methods of recording results have become acceptable. Examples of different methods of recording results can be found in use in many schools. Possibly most notable of these has been the increased use of information technology and in particular the wealth of simple databases which are now available. The whole area of pupil self-recording, teacher recording and Records of Achievement for pupils with special needs has been well addressed by Lawson [21] whose discussion on the use of photographs, video recording and methods which make minimal demands on pupils' literacy skills provides a useful starting point for teachers.

TEACHING IN CONTEXT

This Chapter has highlighted those issues of access and differentiation which often present themselves when involving pupils with special needs in science. Most of these apply to such pupils in all situations, and not just in science lessons. One final area of concern which has been levelled specifically at science teaching must, however, be mentioned before I conclude. This concerns the matter of context. Pupils with learning difficulties invariably have problems with understanding abstract concepts. The teaching of science will from time to time of necessity require teachers to describe processes, or deal with matters which cannot be easily demonstrated. This is not, of course, a problem new to science teachers who have been effective in the use of models and diagrams for many years. The illustration of difficult concepts such as molecular patterns or cell structures through the use of models, is just one example of the way teachers have overcome this problem. Models can often be valuable in offering the pupil with special needs a chance to handle and identify parts of a structure, or the relationship of one part to another. There is, however, still a problem of understanding the relationship of some scientific procedures and experiments to the pupil's own understanding of the world. For example, investigating and recording a change which occurs when two chemicals are combined, may in itself be a useful part of a chemistry lesson. It encourages all of those skills which we have seen defined in AT1 of the National Curriculum. Yet for the pupil with learning difficulties, this may be a pointless exercise unless the experiment can be related to the world which he or she knows. When would such a chemical process be used in industry or commerce? Does it occur in the natural world? Does it have benefits or a detrimental effect upon the lives of people? Such questions need to provide a focus when teaching those aspects of science which may prove difficult for the pupil with special needs.

CONCLUSION

Science offers opportunities for all pupils, not least those with special needs. Well presented, science promotes enquiry and can stimulate the desire to discover more about the world in which we live. Teaching science to pupils with special needs presents many challenges to the teachers and it is vital that we all share our knowledge and approaches if we are to make progress in this area. The specialist teacher of pupils with special needs, just as the teacher in the special school, needs the expertise of the scientist. It is most encouraging that a book such as this, with its emphasis upon scientific content can find space to consider the special needs issue, for it is only through the sharing of our understanding that we will together advance the education of all pupils.

REFERENCES

1 *National Curriculum Council Consultation Report: Science*, National Curriculum Council. (HMSO, 1991).

2 Bogdan, R. and Kugelmass, J., 'Case Studies of Mainstreaming: A Symbolic Interactionist Approach to Special Schooling', in L. Barton and S. Tomlinson (eds), *Special Education and Social Interests*. (Croom Helm, 1984).

3 *Science for Children with Learning Difficulties*, Schools Council. (McDonald Education, 1983).

4 Jones, A., *Science for Handicapped Children*. (Souvenir Press, 1983).

5 Jones, A., Denley, P. and Butcher, C., 'Science: Access for All', *British Journal of Special Education*, 1988, **15**(4) (December), pp. 151–154.

6 Fagg, S., Skelton, S., Aherne, P. and Thornber, A., *Science for All*. (David Fulton, 1990).

7 *Access to Science for Pupils with Special Educational Needs at Key Stages 1 and 2*, Humberside County Council, Hull, Humberside LEA. (1990).

8 *Access to Science for Pupils with Special Educational Needs at Key Stages 3 and 4*, Humberside County Council, Hull, Humberside LEA. (1991).

9 Bennett, N., 'The Quality of Classroom Learning Experiences for Pupils with Special Educational Needs', in M. Ainscow (ed.), *Effective Schools for All*. (David Fulton, 1990).

10 Bennett, N. and Cass, A., 'The Effects of Group Composition on Group Interactive Processes and Pupil Understanding', *British Education Research Journal*, 1988, **15**(1), pp. 19–32.

11 Johnson, D. W. and Johnson, R. T., 'Mainstreaming and Cooperative Learning Strategies', *Exceptional Children*, 1986, **52**(1), pp. 533–561.

12 Salvin, R. E., Madden, N. A. and Leavey, M., 'Effects of Cooperation Learning and Individualised Instruction on Mainstreamed Students', *Exceptional Children*, 1984, **50**(5), pp. 434–443.

13 Swing, S. R. and Peterson, P. L., 'The Relationship of Student Ability and Small Group Interaction to Student Achievement', *American Education Research*, 1982, **19**(2), pp. 259–274.

14 McCall, C., *Classroom Grouping for Special Need*, National Council for Special Education, Coventry. (1983).

15 Johnson, D. W., Johnson, R. T. and Johnson-Holubec, E., *Circles of Learning*. (Minnesota Interaction Book Company, 1990).

16 Rose, R., 'A Jigsaw Approach to Group Work', *British Journal of Special Education*, 1991, **18**(2), pp. 54–58.

17 Makaton Vocabulary Development Project, *Symbols for Makaton*, Makaton, Camberley. (MVDP, 1985).

18   Woodcock, R. W., Clark, C. R. and Davies, C. D., *Teachers' Guide: The Peabody Rebus Reading Program*, Educational Evaluation Enterprises, Newham Gloucestershire. (1969).

19   Peter, M. and Barnes, R., *Signs, Symbols and Schools*, National Council for Special Education, Coventry. (1982).

20   Van Oosterom, J. and Devereux, K., *Learning with Rebuses*, National Council for Special Education, Coventry. (1985).

21   Lawson, H., *Practical Record Keeping for Special Schools.* (David Fulton, 1992).

INDEX